Practical MLOps
Operationalizing Machine Learning Models

Noah Gift and Alfredo Deza

Beijing · Boston · Farnham · Sebastopol · Tokyo

Practical MLOps

by Noah Gift and Alfredo Deza

Published by O'Reilly Media, Inc., 1005 Gravenstein Highway North, Sebastopol, CA 95472.

O'Reilly books may be purchased for educational, business, or sales promotional use. Online editions are also available for most titles (*http://oreilly.com*). For more information, contact our corporate/institutional sales department: 800-998-9938 or *corporate@oreilly.com*.

Acquisitions Editor: Rebecca Novack	**Indexer:** WordCo Indexing Services, Inc.
Development Editor: Melissa Potter	**Interior Designer:** David Futato
Production Editor: Daniel Elfanbaum	**Cover Designer:** Karen Montgomery
Copyeditor: Kim Cofer	**Illustrator:** Kate Dullea
Proofreader: Piper Editorial Consulting, LLC	

September 2021:   First Edition

Revision History for the First Edition

2021-09-14:   First Release

See *http://oreilly.com/catalog/errata.csp?isbn=9781098103019* for release details.

978-1-098-10301-9

[LSI]

Table of Contents

Preface. ix

1. Introduction to MLOps. 1
   Rise of the Machine Learning Engineer and MLOps   2
   What Is MLOps?   4
   DevOps and MLOps   5
   An MLOps Hierarchy of Needs   7
      Implementing DevOps   8
      Configuring Continuous Integration with GitHub Actions   13
      DataOps and Data Engineering   15
      Platform Automation   16
      MLOps   17
   Conclusion   20
   Exercises   21
   Critical Thinking Discussion Questions   22

2. MLOps Foundations. 23
   Bash and the Linux Command Line   23
   Cloud Shell Development Environments   24
   Bash Shell and Commands   26
      List Files   26
      Run Commands   26
      Files and Navigation   27
      Input/Output   27
      Configuration   28
      Writing a Script   28
   Cloud Computing Foundations and Building Blocks   29
   Getting Started with Cloud Computing   31

Python Crash Course   33
Minimalistic Python Tutorial   36
Math for Programmers Crash Course   37
   Descriptive Statistics and Normal Distributions   37
   Optimization   41
Machine Learning Key Concepts   50
Doing Data Science   54
Build an MLOps Pipeline from Zero   56
Conclusion   63
Exercises   64
Critical Thinking Discussion Questions   64

3. MLOps for Containers and Edge Devices. **67**
Containers   68
   Container Runtime   69
   Creating a Container   69
   Running a Container   72
   Best Practices   74
   Serving a Trained Model Over HTTP   76
Edge Devices   80
   Coral   81
   Azure Percept   84
   TFHub   85
   Porting Over Non-TPU Models   86
Containers for Managed ML Systems   89
   Containers in Monetizing MLOps   90
   Build Once, Run Many MLOps Workflow   91
Conclusion   91
Exercises   92
Critical Thinking Discussion Questions   92

4. Continuous Delivery for Machine Learning Models. **93**
Packaging for ML Models   95
Infrastructure as Code for Continuous Delivery of ML Models   99
Using Cloud Pipelines   107
   Controlled Rollout of Models   110
   Testing Techniques for Model Deployment   112
Conclusion   115
Exercises   116
Critical Thinking Discussion Questions   116

5. AutoML and KaizenML. **117**
  AutoML 118
    MLOps Industrial Revolution 123
    Kaizen Versus KaizenML 125
    Feature Stores 127
  Apple's Ecosystem 131
    Apple's AutoML: Create ML 132
    Apple's Core ML Tools 136
  Google's AutoML and Edge Computer Vision 139
  Azure's AutoML 144
  AWS AutoML 146
  Open Source AutoML Solutions 151
    Ludwig 151
    FLAML 153
  Model Explainability 154
  Conclusion 158
  Exercises 159
  Critical Thinking Discussion Questions 159

6. Monitoring and Logging. **161**
  Observability for Cloud MLOps 163
  Introduction to Logging 164
  Logging in Python 165
    Modifying Log Levels 169
    Logging Different Applications 170
  Monitoring and Observability 172
    Basics of Model Monitoring 174
    Monitoring Drift with AWS SageMaker 175
    Monitoring Drift with Azure ML 182
  Conclusion 184
  Exercises 185
  Critical Thinking Discussion Questions 185

7. MLOps for AWS. **187**
  Introduction to AWS 188
    Getting Started with AWS Services 189
    MLOps on AWS 206
  MLOps Cookbook on AWS 209
    CLI Tools 211
    Flask Microservice 218
  AWS Lambda Recipes 223
    AWS Lambda-SAM Local 223

     AWS Lambda-SAM Containerized Deploy   224
     Applying AWS Machine Learning to the Real World   229
     Conclusion   233
     Exercises   234
     Critical Thinking Discussion Questions   234

8. MLOps for Azure. **235**
     Azure CLI and Python SDK   236
     Authentication   238
       Service Principal   238
       Authenticating API Services   240
     Compute Instances   240
     Deploying   242
       Registering Models   243
       Versioning Datasets   245
     Deploying Models to a Compute Cluster   246
       Configuring a Cluster   246
       Deploying a Model   248
     Troubleshooting Deployment Issues   251
       Retrieving Logs   252
       Application Insights   253
       Debugging Locally   254
     Azure ML Pipelines   257
       Publishing Pipelines   259
       Azure Machine Learning Designer   260
     ML Lifecycle   262
     Conclusion   263
     Exercises   263
     Critical Thinking Discussion Questions   264

9. MLOps for GCP. **265**
     Google Cloud Platform Overview   265
       Continuous Integration and Continuous Delivery   270
       Kubernetes Hello World   272
       Cloud Native Database Choice and Design   280
     DataOps on GCP: Applied Data Engineering   282
     Operationalizing ML Models   287
     Conclusion   289
     Exercises   291
     Critical Thinking Discussion Questions   291

10. **Machine Learning Interoperability**................................... **293**
    Why Interoperability Is Critical   294
    ONNX: Open Neural Network Exchange   296
        ONNX Model Zoo   297
        Convert PyTorch into ONNX   299
        Create a Generic ONNX Checker   301
        Convert TensorFlow into ONNX   303
        Deploy ONNX to Azure   307
    Apple Core ML   310
    Edge Integration   314
    Conclusion   315
    Exercises   316
    Critical Thinking Discussion Questions   316

11. **Building MLOps Command Line Tools and Microservices**........................ **317**
    Python Packaging   319
    The Requirements File   320
    Command Line Tools   321
        Creating a Dataset Linter   321
        Modularizing a Command Line Tool   328
    Microservices   331
        Creating a Serverless Function   333
        Authenticating to Cloud Functions   338
        Building a Cloud-Based CLI   341
    Machine Learning CLI Workflows   342
    Conclusion   344
    Exercises   345
    Critical Thinking Discussion Questions   345

12. **Machine Learning Engineering and MLOps Case Studies**........................ **347**
    Unlikely Benefits of Ignorance in Building Machine Learning Models   348
    MLOps Projects at Sqor Sports Social Network   350
        Mechanical Turk Data Labeling   351
        Influencer Rank   352
        Athlete Intelligence (AI Product)   353
    The Perfect Technique Versus the Real World   355
    Critical Challenges in MLOps   357
        Ethical and Unintended Consequences   358
        Lack of Operational Excellence   358
        Focus on Prediction Accuracy Versus the Big Picture   359
    Final Recommendations to Implement MLOps   364
        Data Governance and Cybersecurity   365

MLOps Design Patterns   366
Conclusion   367
Exercises   367
Critical Thinking Discussion Questions   368

A. Key Terms. 369

B. Technology Certifications. 375

C. Remote Work. 393

D. Think Like a VC for Your Career. 399

E. Building a Technical Portfolio for MLOps. 403

F. Data Science Case Study: Intermittent Fasting. 409

G. Additional Educational Resources. 415

H. Technical Project Management. 427

Index. 431

Preface

Why We Wrote This Book

We've both spent most of our careers automating things. When we first met and Alfredo didn't know Python, Noah suggested automating one task per week. Automation is a core pillar for MLOps, DevOps, and this book throughout. You should take all the examples and opinions in this book in the context of future automation.

If Noah could summarize how he spent 2000–2020, it was automating just about anything he could, from film pipelines to software installation to machine learning pipelines. As an engineering manager and CTO at startups in the Bay Area, he built many data science teams from scratch. As a result, he saw many of the core problems in getting machine learning to production in the early stages of the AI/ML revolution.

Noah has been an adjunct professor at Duke, Northwestern, and UC Davis in the last several years, teaching topics that primarily focus on cloud computing, data science, and machine learning engineering. This teaching and work experience gives him a unique perspective about the issues involved in the real-world deployment of machine learning solutions.

Alfredo has a heavy ops background from his Systems Administrator days, with a similar passion for automation. It is not possible to build resilient infrastructure without push-button automation. There is nothing more gratifying when disaster situations happen than rerunning a script or a pipeline to re-create what crashed.

When COVID-19 hit, it accelerated a question we both had, which was, "why aren't we putting more models into production?" Noah touched on some of these issues in an article he wrote for Forbes (*https://oreil.ly/Qj8ut*). The summarized premise of the article is that something is wrong with data science because organizations are not seeing returns on their investments.

Later at O'Reilly's "Foo Camp" (*https://oreil.ly/ODJvG*), Noah led a session on "Why can we not be 10X faster at ML in production?" where we had a great discussion with many people, including Tim O'Reilly, Mike Loukides, Roger Magoulas, and others. The result of that discussion was: "Yes, we can go 10X faster." So thanks to Tim and Mike for stirring such a fascinating discussion and getting this book on its way.

Machine learning feels a lot like many other technologies that have appeared in the past several decades. At first, it takes years to get results. Steve Jobs talked about how NeXT wanted to make it 10X faster to build software (and he did). You can watch the interview on YouTube (*https://oreil.ly/mWRoO*). What are some of the problems with machine learning currently?

- Focus on the "code" and technical details versus the business problem
- Lack of automation
- HiPPO (Highest Paid Person's Opinions)
- Not cloud native
- Lack of urgency to solve solvable problems

Quoting one of the things Noah brought up in the discussion: "I'm anti-elitism across the board. Programming is a human right. The idea that there is some priesthood that is only allowed to do it is just wrong." Similar to machine learning, it is too crucial for technology to lie only in the hands of a select group of people. With MLOps and AutoML, these technologies can go into the public's hands. We can do better with machine learning and artificial intelligence by democratizing this technology. "Real" AI/ML practitioners ship models to production, and in the "real" future, people such as doctors, lawyers, mechanics, and teachers will use AI/ML to help them do their jobs.

How This Book Is Organized

We designed this book so that you can consume each chapter as a standalone section designed to give you immediate help. At the end of each chapter are discussion questions that are intended to spur critical thinking and technical exercises to improve your understanding of the material.

These discussion questions and exercises are also well suited for use in the classroom in a Data Science, Computer Science, or MBA program and for the motivated self-learner. The final chapter contains several case studies helpful in building a work portfolio as an expert in MLOps.

The book is divided into 12 chapters, which we'll break down a little more in the following section. At the end of the book, there is an appendix with a collection of valuable resources for implementing MLOps.

Chapters

The first few chapters cover the theory and practice of both DevOps and MLOps. One of the items covered is how to set up continuous integration and continuous delivery. Another critical topic is Kaizen, i.e., the idea of continuous improvement in everything.

There are three chapters on cloud computing that cover AWS, Azure, and GCP. Alfredo, a developer advocate for Microsoft, is an ideal source of knowledge for MLOps on the Azure platform. Likewise, Noah has spent years getting students trained on cloud computing and working with the education arms of Google, AWS, and Azure. These chapters are an excellent way to get familiar with cloud-based MLOps.

Other chapters cover critical technical areas of MLOps, including AutoML, containers, edge computing, and model portability. These topics encompass many cutting-edge emerging technologies with active traction.

Finally, in the last chapter, Noah covers a real-world case study of his time at a social media startup and the challenges they faced doing MLOps.

Appendixes

The appendixes are a collection of essays, ideas, and valuable items that cropped up in years between finishing *Python for DevOps* (O'Reilly) and this book. The primary way to use them is to help you make decisions about the future.

Exercise Questions

In this book's exercises, a helpful heuristic considers how you can leverage them into a portfolio using GitHub and a YouTube walkthrough of what you did. In keeping with the expression "a picture is worth a thousand words," a YouTube link to a walk-through of a reproducible GitHub project on a resume may be worth 10,000 words and puts the resume in a new category of qualification for a job.

As you go through the book and exercises, consider the following critical thinking framework.

Discussion Questions

According to Jonathan Haber in *Critical Thinking* (MIT Press Essential Knowledge series) and the nonprofit Foundation for Critical Thinking (*https://oreil.ly/FXoTU*), discussion questions are essential critical thinking components. The world is in dire need of critical thinking due to the proliferation of misinformation and shallow content in social media. A mastery of the following skills sets an individual apart from the pack:

Intellectual humility
 Recognition of the limits of your knowledge.

Intellectual courage
 The ability to argue for your beliefs even in the face of social pressure.

Intellectual empathy
 The ability to put yourself in the minds of others to understand their position.

Intellectual autonomy
 The ability to think for yourself independently of others.

Intellectual integrity
 The ability to think and argue with the same intellectual standards you expect others to apply to you.

Intellectual perseverance
 The ability to provide evidence that supports your position.

Confidence in reason
 The belief that there are indisputable facts and that reason is the best solution to gain knowledge.

Fairmindedness
 The ability to put in the good-faith effort to treat all viewpoints fairly.

Using these criteria, evaluate the discussion questions in each chapter.

Origin of Chapter Quotes

By Noah

I graduated college in late 1998 and spent a year training to play professional basketball in the minor leagues in the United States or Europe while working as a personal trainer. My backup plan was to get a job in IT. I applied to be a Systems Administrator at Caltech in Pasadena and got a Mac IT expert position on a fluke. I decided the risk/reward ratio of being a low-paid professional athlete wasn't worth it and accepted the job offer.

To say Caltech changed my life is an understatement. At lunch, I played ultimate frisbee and heard about the Python programming language, which I learned so I would "fit in" with my ultimate frisbee friends, who were staff or students at Caltech. Later, I worked directly for Caltech's administration and was the personal Mac expert at Caltech for Dr. David Baltimore, who got the Nobel Prize in his 30s. I interacted with many famous people in many unexpected ways, which boosted my self-confidence and grew my network.

I also had many Forrest Gump–style random encounters with people who would later do incredible things in AI/ML. Once, I had dinner with Dr. Fei-Fei Li, head of AI at Stanford, and her boyfriend; I remember being impressed that her boyfriend spent the summer writing a video game with his dad. I was highly impressed and thought, "Who does that kind of thing?" Later, I set up a mail server under the famous physicist Dr. David Goodstein's desk because he kept getting grief from IT about hitting his mailbox storage limits. These experiences are where I acquired a taste for building "shadow infrastructure." Because I worked directly for the administration, I got to flaunt the rules if there was a good reason for it.

One of the people I randomly met was Dr. Joseph Bogen, a neurosurgeon and visiting professor at Caltech. Of all the people I met at Caltech, he had the most profound impact on my life. One day I responded to a help desk call to come to his house to fix his computer, and later this turned into a weekly dinner at his home with him and his wife, Glenda. From around 2000 until the day he died, he was a friend and mentor.

At the time, I was very interested in artificial intelligence, and I remember a Caltech Computer Science professor telling me it was a dead field and I shouldn't focus on it. Despite that advice, I came up with a plan to be fluent in many software programming languages by 40 years old and writing artificial intelligence programs by then. Lo and behold, my plan worked out.

I can clearly say I wouldn't be doing what I am doing today if I didn't meet Joe Bogen. He blew my mind when he told me he did the first hemispherectomy, removing half of a brain, to help a patient with severe epilepsy. We would talk for hours about the origins of consciousness, the use of neural networks in the 1970s to figure out who would be an Air Force pilot, and whether your brain contained "two of you," one in each hemisphere. Above all, what Bogen gave me was a sense of confidence in my intellect. I had severe doubts up until that point about what I could do, but our conversations were like a master's degree in higher-level thinking. As a professor myself, I think about how big of an impact he had on my life, and I hope to pay it forward to other students I interact with, both as a formal teacher or someone they meet. You can read these quotes yourself from an archive of Dr. Bogen's Caltech home page (*https://oreil.ly/QPIIi*) and his biography (*https://oreil.ly/EgZQO*).

Conventions Used in This Book

The following typographical conventions are used in this book:

Italic
> Indicates new terms, URLs, email addresses, filenames, and file extensions.

`Constant width`
> Used for program listings, as well as within paragraphs to refer to program elements such as variable or function names, databases, data types, environment variables, statements, and keywords.

`Constant width bold`
> Shows commands or other text that should be typed literally by the user.

`Constant width italic`
> Shows text that should be replaced with user-supplied values or by values determined by context.

 This element signifies a tip or suggestion.

 This element signifies a general note.

 This element indicates a warning or caution.

Using Code Examples

Supplemental material (code examples, exercises, etc.) is available for download at *https://github.com/paiml/practical-mlops-book*.

If you have a technical question or a problem using the code examples, please send email to *bookquestions@oreilly.com*.

This book is here to help you get your job done. In general, if example code is offered with this book, you may use it in your programs and documentation. You do not need to contact us for permission unless you're reproducing a significant portion of the code. For example, writing a program that uses several chunks of code from this book does not require permission. Selling or distributing examples from O'Reilly books does require permission. Answering a question by citing this book and quoting example code does not require permission. Incorporating a significant amount of example code from this book into your product's documentation does require permission.

We appreciate, but generally do not require, attribution. An attribution usually includes the title, author, publisher, and ISBN. For example: "*Practical MLOps* by Noah Gift and Alfredo Deza (O'Reilly). Copyright 2021 Noah Gift and Alfredo Deza, 978-1-098-10301-9."

If you feel your use of code examples falls outside fair use or the permission given above, feel free to contact us at *permissions@oreilly.com*.

O'Reilly Online Learning

 For more than 40 years, *O'Reilly Media* has provided technology and business training, knowledge, and insight to help companies succeed.

Our unique network of experts and innovators share their knowledge and expertise through books, articles, and our online learning platform. O'Reilly's online learning platform gives you on-demand access to live training courses, in-depth learning paths, interactive coding environments, and a vast collection of text and video from O'Reilly and 200+ other publishers. For more information, visit *http://oreilly.com*.

How to Contact Us

Please address comments and questions concerning this book to the publisher:

O'Reilly Media, Inc.
1005 Gravenstein Highway North
Sebastopol, CA 95472
800-998-9938 (in the United States or Canada)
707-829-0515 (international or local)
707-829-0104 (fax)

We have a web page for this book, where we list errata, examples, and any additional information. You can access this page at *https://oreil.ly/practical-mlops*.

Email *bookquestions@oreilly.com* to comment or ask technical questions about this book.

For news and information about our books and courses, visit *http://oreilly.com*.

Find us on Facebook: *http://facebook.com/oreilly*.

Follow us on Twitter: *http://twitter.com/oreillymedia*.

Watch us on YouTube: *http://www.youtube.com/oreillymedia*.

Acknowledgments

From Noah

As mentioned earlier, without Mike Loukides inviting me to Foo Camp and having a great discussion with Tim O'Reilly and me, this book wouldn't be here. Next, I would like to acknowledge Alfredo, my coauthor. I have had the pleasure of writing five books, two for O'Reilly and three self-published, in a little over two years with Alfredo, and this is primarily due to his ability to embrace work and get things done. An appetite for hard work is perhaps the best talent, and Alfredo has this skill in abundance.

Our editor, Melissa Potter, did tremendous work getting things into shape, and the book before she edited and afterward are almost two different books. I feel lucky to have worked with such a talented editor.

Our technical editors, including Steve Depp, Nivas Durairaj, and Shubham Saboo, played a crucial role in giving us great feedback about where to zig and when to zag. Many enhancements are particularly due to Steve's thorough feedback. Also, I wanted to thank Julien Simon and Piero Molino for enhancing our book with real-world thoughts on MLOps.

I want to thank my family, Liam, Leah, and Theodore, for giving me the space to finish this book on a tight deadline in the middle of a pandemic. I am also looking forward to reading some of the books they write in the future. Another big group of thanks goes out to all the former students I taught at Northwestern, Duke, UC Davis, and other schools. Many of their questions and feedback made it into this book.

My final thanks go out to Dr. Joseph Bogen, an early pioneer in AI/ML and Neuroscience. If we didn't bump into each other at Caltech, there is zero chance I would be a professor or that this book would exist. His impact was that big on my life.

From Alfredo

I'm absolutely thankful for my family's support while writing this book: Claudia, Efrain, Ignacio, and Alana—your support and patience were essential to get to the finish line. Thanks again for all the opportunities to work with you, Noah; this was another incredible ride. I value your friendship and our professional relationship.

Thanks to Melissa Potter (without a doubt the best editor I've worked with) for her fantastic work. Our technical editors did great by finding problems and highlighting places that needed refinement, always a hard thing to do well.

Also extremely grateful for Lee Stott's help with Azure. The Azure content wouldn't be as good without it. And thanks to Francesca Lazzeri, Mike McCoy, and everyone else I contacted at Microsoft about the book. You were all very helpful.

## CHAPTER 1

Introduction to MLOps

By Noah Gift

> Since 1986, I have had a few more deaths, several from insufficient attention but mainly from deliberately pushing the limits in various directions—taking a chance in bonsai is a bit like taking a chance with love; the best outcome requires risky exposure to being hurt and no guarantee of success.
>
> —Dr. Joseph Bogen

One of the powerful aspects of science fiction is its ability to imagine a future without constraints. One of the most influential science fiction shows of all time is the TV show *Star Trek*, which first aired in the mid-1960s, approximately 60 years ago. The cultural impact inspired designers of technology like the Palm Pilot and hand-held cellular phones. In addition, *Star Trek* influenced the cofounder of Apple computer, Steve Wozniak, to create Apple computers.

In this age of innovation in machine learning, there are many essential ideas from the original series relevant to the coming MLOps (or Machine Learning Operations) industrial revolution. For example, *Star Trek* hand-held tricorders can instantly classify objects using pretrained multiclass classification models. But, ultimately, in this futuristic science-fiction world, domain experts like the science officers, medical officers, or captain of the ship, don't spend months training machine learning models. Likewise, the crew of their science vessel, the *Enterprise*, are not called data scientists. Instead, they have jobs where they often use data science.

Many of the machine learning aspects of this *Star Trek* science fiction future are no longer science fiction in the 2020s. This chapter guides the reader into the foundational theory of how to make this possible. Let's get started.

Rise of the Machine Learning Engineer and MLOps

Machine learning (ML), with its widespread adoption globally, has created a need for a systematic and efficient approach toward building ML systems, leading to a sudden rise in demand for ML engineers. These ML engineers, in turn, are applying established DevOps best practices to the emerging machine learning technologies. The major cloud vendors all have certifications targeting these practitioners. I have experience working directly with AWS, Azure, and GCP as a subject matter expert on machine learning. In some cases, this includes helping create machine learning certifications themselves and official training material. In addition, I teach machine learning engineering and cloud computing at some of the top data science programs with Duke and Northwestern. Firsthand, I have seen the rise in machine learning engineering as many former students have become machine learning engineers.

Google has a Professional Machine Learning Engineer certification (*https://oreil.ly/83skz*). It describes an ML engineer as someone who "designs, builds, and productionizes ML models to solve business challenges…" Azure has a Microsoft Certified: Azure Data Scientist Associate (*https://oreil.ly/mtczl*). It describes this type of practitioner as someone who "applies their knowledge of data science and machine learning to implement and run machine learning workloads…" Finally, AWS describes an AWS Certified Machine Learning specialist (*https://oreil.ly/O0cLK*) as someone with "the ability to design, implement, deploy, and maintain machine learning solutions for given business problems."

One way to look at data science versus machine learning engineering is to consider science versus engineering itself. Science gears toward research, and engineering gears toward production. As machine learning moves beyond just the research side, companies are eager for a return on investment in hiring around AI and ML. According to payscale.com and glassdoor.com, the results show that at the end of 2020, the median salary for a data scientist, data engineer, and machine learning engineer was similar. According to LinkedIn in Q4 of 2020, 191K jobs mentioned cloud, there were 70K data engineering job listings, 55k machine learning engineering job listings, and 20k data science job listings, as shown in Figure 1-1.

Another way to look at these job trends is that they are a natural part of the hype cycle of technology. Organizations realize that to generate a return on investment (ROI), they need employees with hard skills: cloud computing, data engineering, and machine learning. They also need them in a much larger quantity than data scientists. As a result, the decade of the 2020s may show an acceleration in treating data science as a behavior, rather than a job title. DevOps is behavior, just like data science. Think about the principles of both DevOps and data science. In both cases, DevOps and data science are methodologies for evaluating the world, not necessarily unique job titles.

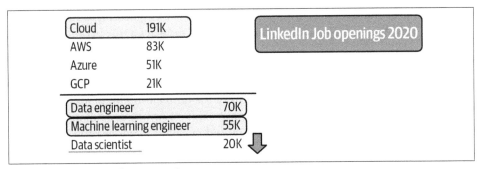

Figure 1-1. *Machine learning jobs*

Let's look at the options for measuring the success of a machine learning engineering initiative at an organization. First, you could count the machine learning models that go into production. Second, you could measure the impact of the ML models on business ROI. These metrics culminate in a model's operational efficiency. The cost, uptime, and staff needed to maintain it are signals that predict a machine learning engineering project's success or failure.

Advanced technology organizations know they need to leverage methodologies and tools that decrease the risk of machine learning projects failing. So what are these tools and processes used in machine learning engineering? Here is a partial list:

Cloud native ML platforms
> AWS SageMaker, Azure ML Studio, and GCP AI Platform

Containerized workflows
> Docker format containers, Kubernetes, and private and public container registries

Serverless technology
> AWS Lambda, AWS Athena, Google Cloud Functions, Azure Functions

Specialized hardware for machine learning
> GPUs, Google TPU (TensorFlow Processing Unit), Apple A14, AWS Inferentia Elastic inference

Big data platforms and tools
> Databricks, Hadoop/Spark, Snowflake, Amazon EMR (Elastic Map Reduce), Google Big Query

One clear pattern about machine learning is how deeply tied it is to cloud computing. This is because the raw ingredients of machine learning happen to require massive compute, extensive data, and specialized hardware. Thus, there is a natural synergy with deep integration with cloud platforms and machine learning engineering. Further supporting this is that the cloud platforms are building specialized platforms to enhance ML's operationalization. So, if you are doing ML engineering, you are probably doing it in the cloud. Next, let's discuss how DevOps plays a role in doing this.

What Is MLOps?

Why isn't machine learning 10X faster? Most of the problem-building machine learning systems involve everything surrounding machine learning modeling: data engineering, data processing, problem feasibility, and business alignment. One issue with this is a focus on the "code" and technical details versus solving the business problem with machine learning. There is also a lack of automation and the issue of HiPPO (Highest Paid Person's Opinions) culture. Finally, much of machine learning is not cloud native and uses academic datasets and academic software packages that don't scale for large-scale problems.

The quicker the feedback loop (see Kaizen), the more time to focus on business problems like the recent issues of rapid detection of Covid, detecting mask versus non-mask computer vision solutions deployed in the real world, and faster drug discovery. The technology exists to solve these problems, yet these solutions aren't available in the real world? Why is this?

What is Kaizen? In Japanese, it means improvement. Using Kaizen as a software management philosophy originated in the Japanese automobile industry after World War II. It underlies many other techniques: Kanban, root cause analysis & five why's, and Six Sigma. To practice Kaizen, an accurate and realistic assessment of the world's state is necessary and pursues daily, incremental improvements in the pursuit of excellence.

The reason models are not moving into production is the impetus for the emergence of MLOps as a critical industry standard. MLOps shares a lineage with DevOps in that DevOps philosophically demands automation. A common expression is *if it is not automated, it's broken.* Similarly, with MLOps, there must not be components of the system that have humans as the levers of the machine. The history of automation shows that humans are the least valuable doing repetitive tasks but are the most valuable using technology as the architects and practitioners. Likewise, coordination between developers, models, and operations must coordinate through transparent teamwork and healthy collaboration. Think of MLOps as the process of automating machine learning using DevOps methodologies.

What is DevOps? It combines best practices, including microservices, continuous integration, and continuous delivery, removing the barriers between Operations and Development and Teamwork. You can read more about DevOps in our book *Python for DevOps* (O'Reilly). Python is the predominant language of scripting, DevOps, and machine learning. As a result of this, this MLOps book focuses on Python, just as the DevOps book focused on Python.

With MLOps, not only do the software engineering processes need full automation, but so do the data and modeling. The model training and deployment is a new wrinkle added to the traditional DevOps lifecycle. Finally, additional monitoring and instrumentation must account for new things that can break, like data drift—the delta between changes in the data from the last time the model training occurred.

A fundamental problem in getting machine learning models into production is the immaturity of the data science industry. The software industry has embraced DevOps to solve similar issues; now, the machine learning community embraces MLOps. Let's dive into how to do this.

DevOps and MLOps

DevOps is a set of technical and management practices that aim to increase an organization's velocity in releasing high-quality software. Some of the benefits of DevOps include speed, reliability, scale, and security. These benefits occur through adherence to the following best practices:

Continuous integration (CI)
CI is the process of continuously testing a software project and improving the quality based on these tests' results. It is automated testing using open source and SaaS build servers such as GitHub Actions, Jenkins, Gitlab, CircleCI, or cloud native build systems like AWS Code Build.

Continuous delivery (CD)
This method delivers code to a new environment without human intervention. CD is the process of deploying code automatically, often through the use of IaC.

Microservices
A microservice is a software service with a distinct function that had little to no dependencies. One of the most popular Python-based microservice frameworks is Flask. For example, a machine learning prediction endpoint is an excellent fit for a microservice. These microservices can use a wide variety of technologies, including FaaS (function as a service). A perfect example of a cloud function is AWS Lambda. A microservice could be container-ready and use CaaS (container

as a service) to deploy a Flask application with a Dockerfile to a service like AWS Fargate, Google Cloud Run, or Azure App Services.

Infrastructure as Code

Infrastructure as Code (IaC) is the process of checking the infrastructure into a source code repository and "deploying" it to push changes to that repository. IaC allows for idempotent behavior and ensures the infrastructure doesn't require humans to build it out. A cloud environment defined purely in code and checked into a source control repository is a good example use case. Popular technologies include cloud-specific IaC like AWS Cloud Formation or AWS SAM (Serverless Application Model) (*https://oreil.ly/4Q3XE*). Multicloud options include Pulumi (*https://pulumi.com*) and Terraform (*https://terraform.io*).

Monitoring and instrumentation

Monitoring and instrumentation are the processes and techniques used that allow an organization to make decisions about a software system's performance and reliability. Through logging and other tools like application performance monitoring tools such as New Relic, Data Dog, or Stackdriver, monitoring and instrumentation are essentially collecting data about the behavior of an application in production or data science for deployed software systems. This process is where Kaizen comes into play; the data-driven organization uses this instrumentation to make things better daily or weekly.

Effective technical communication

This skill involves the ability to create effective, repeatable, and efficient communication methods. An excellent example of effective technical communication could be adopting AutoML for the initial prototyping of a system. Of course, ultimately, the AutoML model may be kept or discarded. Nevertheless, automation can serve as an informational tool to prevent work on an intractable problem.

Effective technical project management

This process can efficiently use human and technology solutions, like ticket systems and spreadsheets, to manage projects. Also, appropriate technical project management requires breaking down problems into small, discreet chunks of work, so incremental progress occurs. An antipattern in machine learning is often when a team works on one production machine model that solves a problem "perfectly." Instead, smaller wins delivered daily or weekly is a more scalable and prudent approach to model building.

Continuous integration and continuous delivery are two of the most critical pillars of DevOps. Continuous integration involves merging code into a source control repository that automatically checks the code's quality through testing. Continuous delivery is when code changes are automatically tested and deployed, either to a staging environment or production. Both of these techniques are a form of automation in the spirit of Kaizen or continuous improvement.

A good question to ask is who on the team should implement CI/CD? This question would be similar to asking who contributes to taxes in a democracy. In a democracy, taxes pay for roads, bridges, law enforcement, emergency services, schools, and other infrastructure, so all must contribute to building a better society. Likewise, all MLOps team members should help develop and maintain the CI/CD system. A well-maintained CI/CD system is a form of investment in the future of the team and company.

An ML system is also a software system, but it contains a unique component: a machine learning model. The same benefits of DevOps can and do apply to ML systems. The embrace of automation is why new approaches like Data Versioning and AutoML hold many promises in capturing the DevOps mindset.

An MLOps Hierarchy of Needs

One way to think about machine learning systems is to consider Maslow's hierarchy of needs, as shown in Figure 1-2. Lower levels of a pyramid reflect "survival," and true human potential occurs after basic survival and emotional needs are met.

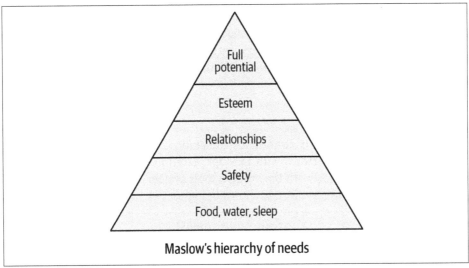

Figure 1-2. Maslow's hierarchy of needs theory

The same concept applies to machine learning. An ML system is a software system, and software systems work efficiently and reliably when DevOps and data engineering best practices are in place. So how could it be possible to deliver the true potential of machine learning to an organization if DevOps' basic foundational rules don't exist or data engineering is not fully automated? The ML hierarchy of needs shown in Figure 1-3 is not a definitive guide but is an excellent place to start a discussion.

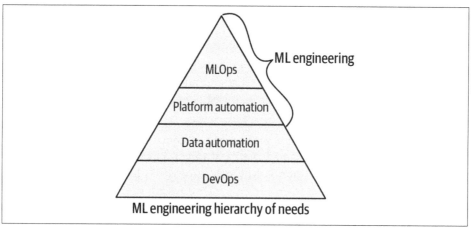

Figure 1-3. ML engineering hierarchy of needs

One of the major things holding back machine learning projects is this necessary foundation of DevOps. After this foundation is complete, next is data automation, then platform automation, and then finally true ML automation, or MLOps, occurs. The culmination of MLOps is a machine learning system that works. The people that work on operationalizing and building machine learning applications are machine learning engineers and/or data engineers. Let's dive into each step of the ML hierarchy and make sure you have a firm grasp of implementing them, starting with DevOps.

Implementing DevOps

The foundation of DevOps is continuous integration. Without automated testing, there is no way to move forward with DevOps. Continuous integration is relatively painless for a Python project with the modern tools available. The first step is to build a "scaffolding" for a Python project, as shown in Figure 1-4.

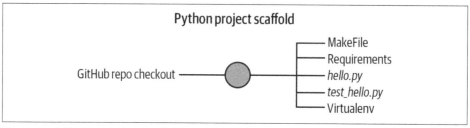

Figure 1-4. Python project scaffold

The runtime for a Python machine learning project is almost guaranteed to be on a Linux operating system. As a result, the following Python project structure is straightforward to implement for ML projects. You can access the source code for this example on GitHub (*https://oreil.ly/4dei0*) for reference as you read this section. The components are as follows:

Makefile

A *Makefile* runs "recipes" via the make system, which comes with Unix-based operating systems. Therefore, a Makefile is an ideal choice to simplify the steps involved in continuous integration, such as the following. Note that a Makefile is a good starting point for a project and will often evolve as new pieces need automation.

 If your project uses a Python virtual environment, you source it before you work with a Makefile, since all a Makefile does is run commands. It is a common mistake for a newcomer to Python to confuse Makefile with a virtual environment. Similarly, suppose you use an editor like Microsoft Visual Studio Code. In that case, you will need to tell the editor about your Python virtual environment so it can accurately give you syntax highlighting, linting, and other available libraries.

Make install

This step installs software via the make install command

Make lint

This step checks for syntax errors via the make lint command

Make test

This step runs tests via the make test command:

```
install:
        pip install --upgrade pip &&\
                pip install -r requirements.txt
lint:
        pylint --disable=R,C hello.py

test:
        python -m pytest -vv --cov=hello test_hello.py
```

Why a Makefile?

A common reaction to hearing about a Makefile from an absolute beginner to Python is "Why do I need this?" Generally, it is healthy to have skepticism about things that appear to add work. In the case of a Makefile, though, they are actually less work because they keep track of complicated build steps that are very difficult to remember and type out correctly.

A great example is a lint step with the `pylint` tool. With a Makefile, you only need to run `make lint`, and the same command can run inside a continuous integration server. The alternative approach is to type out the complete directive each time you need it, such as the following:

```
pylint --disable=R,C *.py
```

This sequence is very prone to errors and quite tedious to repeatedly type over your project's life. Instead, it is much simpler to type the following:

```
make lint
```

When you embrace the Makefile approach, it simplifies your workflow and makes it easier to integrate your project into a continuous integration system. There is less code to type, and this is always a good thing for automation. Further, Makefile commands are recognized by shell auto-completion, making it easy to "tab-complete" the steps.

requirements.txt

A *requirements.txt* file is a convention used by the `pip` installation tool, the default installation tool for Python. A project can contain one or more of these files if different packages need installation for different environments.

Source code and tests

The Python scaffolding's final portion is to add a source code file and a test file, as shown here. This script exists in a file called *hello.py*:

```
def add(x, y):
    """This is an add function"""

    return x + y


print(add(1, 1))
```

Next, the test file is very trivial to create by using the `pytest` framework. This script would be in a file *test_hello.py* contained in the same folder as *hello.py* so that the `from hello import add` works:

```
from hello import add


def test_add():
    assert 2 == add(1, 1)
```

These four files: *Makefile*, *requirements.txt*, *hello.py*, and *test_hello.py* are all that is needed to start the continuous integration journey except for creating a local Python virtual environment. To do that, first, create it:

```
python3 -m venv ~/.your-repo-name
```

Also, be aware that there are generally two ways to create a virtual environment. First, many Linux distributions will include the command-line tool `virtualenv`, which does the same thing as `python3 -m venv`.

Next, you source it to "activate" it:

```
source ~/.your-repo-name/bin/activate
```

 Why create and use a Python virtual environment? This question is ubiquitous for newcomers to Python, and there is a straightforward answer. Because Python is an interpreted language, it can "grab" libraries from anywhere on the operating system. A Python virtual environment isolates third-party packages to a specific directory. There are other solutions to this problem and many developing tools. They effectively solve the same problem: the Python library and interpreter are isolated to a particular project.

Once you have this scaffolding set up, you can do the following local continuous integration steps:

1. Use `make install` to install the libraries for your project.
   The output will look similar to Figure 1-5 (this example shows a run in GitHub Codespaces (*https://oreil.ly/xmqlm*)):

   ```
   $ make install
   pip install --upgrade pip &&\
           pip install -r requirements.txt
   Collecting pip
     Using cached pip-20.2.4-py2.py3-none-any.whl (1.5 MB)
   [.....more output suppressed here......]
   ```

Figure 1-5. GitHub Codespaces

2. Run make `lint` to lint your project:

```
$ make lint
pylint --disable=R,C hello.py

------------------------------------
Your code has been rated at 10.00/10
```

3. Run make `test` to test your project:

```
$ make test
python -m pytest -vv --cov=hello test_hello.py
===== test session starts ====
platform linux -- Python 3.8.3, pytest-6.1.2,\
/home/codespace/.venv/bin/python
cachedir: .pytest_cache
rootdir: /home/codespace/workspace/github-actions-demo
plugins: cov-2.10.1
collected 1 item

test_hello.py::test_add PASSED

----------- coverage: platform linux, python 3.8.3-final-0 -----------
Name        Stmts    Miss  Cover
```

```
----------------------------
hello.py      3      0    100%
```

Once this is working locally, it is straightforward to integrate this same process with a remote SaaS build server. Options include GitHub Actions, a Cloud native build server like AWS Code Build, GCP CloudBuild, Azure DevOps Pipelines, or an open source, self-hosted build server like Jenkins.

Configuring Continuous Integration with GitHub Actions

One of the most straightforward ways to implement continuous integration for this Python scaffolding project is with GitHub Actions. To do this, you can either select "Actions" in the GitHub UI and create a new one or create a file inside of these directories you make as shown here:

```
.github/workflows/<yourfilename>.yml
```

The GitHub Actions file itself is straightforward to create, and the following is an example of one. Note that the exact version of Python sets to whatever interpretation the project requires. In this example, I want to check a specific version of Python that runs on Azure. The continuous integration steps are trivial to implement due to the hard work earlier in creating a Makefile:

```
name: Azure Python 3.5
on: [push]
jobs:
  build:
    runs-on: ubuntu-latest
    steps:
    - uses: actions/checkout@v2
    - name: Set up Python 3.5.10
      uses: actions/setup-python@v1
      with:
        python-version: 3.5.10
    - name: Install dependencies
      run: |
        make install
    - name: Lint
      run: |
        make lint
    - name: Test
      run: |
        make test
```

An overview of what GitHub Actions looks like when run on "push" events from a GitHub repository is shown in Figure 1-6.

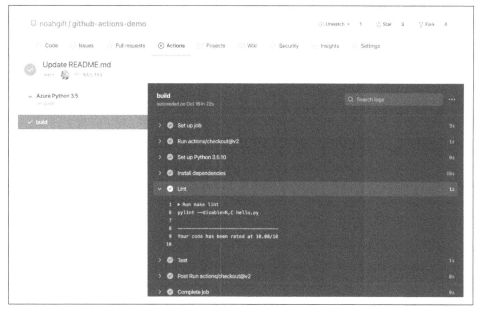

Figure 1-6. GitHub Actions

This step completes the final portion of setting up continuous integration. A continuous deployment—i.e., automatically pushing the machine learning project into production—would be the next logical step. This step would involve deploying the code to a specific location using a continuous delivery process and IaC (Infrastructure as Code). This process is shown in Figure 1-7.

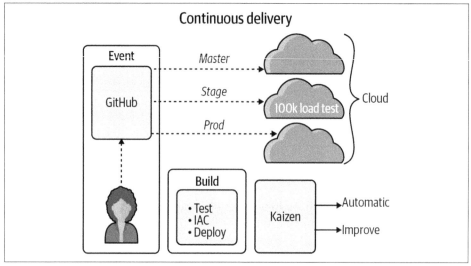

Figure 1-7. Continuous delivery

DataOps and Data Engineering

Next up on the ML hierarchy of needs is a way to automate the flow of data. For example, imagine a town with a well as the only water source. Daily life is complicated because of the need to arrange trips for water, and things we take for granted may not work, like on-demand hot showers, on-demand dishwashing, or automated irrigation. Similarly, an organization without an automated flow of data cannot reliably do MLOps.

Many commercial tools are evolving to do DataOps. One example includes Apache Airflow (*https://oreil.ly/p55kD*), designed by Airbnb, then later open sourced, to schedule and monitor its data processing jobs. AWS tools include AWS Data Pipeline and AWS Glue. AWS Glue is a serverless ETL (Extract, Load, Transform) tool that detects a data source's schema and then stores the data source's metadata. Other tools like AWS Athena and AWS QuickSight can query and visualize the data.

Some items to consider here are the data's size, the frequency at which the information is changed, and how clean the data is. Many organizations use a centralized data lake as the hub of all activity around data engineering. The reason a data lake is helpful to build automation around, including machine learning, is the "near infinite" scale it provides in terms of I/O coupled with its high durability and availability.

A data lake is often synonymous with a cloud-based object storage system such as Amazon S3. A data lake allows data processing "in place" without needing to move it around. A data lake accomplishes this through near-infinite capacity and computing characteristics.

When I worked in the film industry on movies like *Avatar* (*https://oreil.ly/MSh29*), the data was immense; it did need to be moved by an excessively complicated system. Now with the cloud, this problem goes away.

Figure 1-8 shows a cloud data lake–based workflow. Note the ability to do many tasks, all in the exact location, without moving the data.

Dedicated job titles, like data engineer, can spend all of their time building systems that handle these diverse use cases:

- Periodic collection of data and running of jobs
- Processing streaming data
- Serverless and event-driven data
- Big data jobs
- Data and model versioning for ML engineering tasks

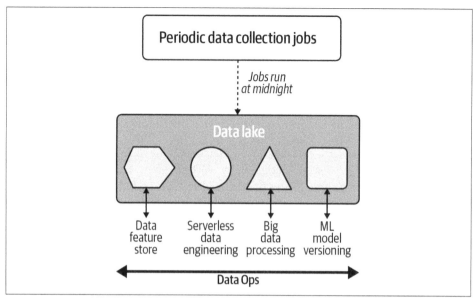

Figure 1-8. Data engineering with a cloud data lake

Much like a village without running water cannot use an automated dishwashing machine, an organization without data automation cannot use advanced methods for machine learning. Therefore, data processing needs automation and operationalization. This step enables ML tasks further down the chain to operationalize and automate.

Platform Automation

Once there is an automated flow of data, the next item on the list to evaluate is how an organization can use high-level platforms to build machine learning solutions. For example, if an organization is already collecting data into a cloud platform's data lake, such as Amazon S3, it is natural to tie machine learning workflows into Amazon Sagemaker. Likewise, if an organization uses Google, it could use Google AI Platform or Azure to use Azure Machine Learning Studio. Similarly, Kubeflow (*https://kube flow.org*) would be appropriate for an organization using Kubernetes versus a public cloud.

An excellent example of a platform that solves these problems appears in Figure 1-9. Notice that AWS SageMaker orchestrates a complex MLOps sequence for a real-world machine learning problem, including spinning up virtual machines, reading and writing to S3, and provisioning production endpoints. Performing these infrastructure steps without automation would be foolhardy at best in a production scenario.

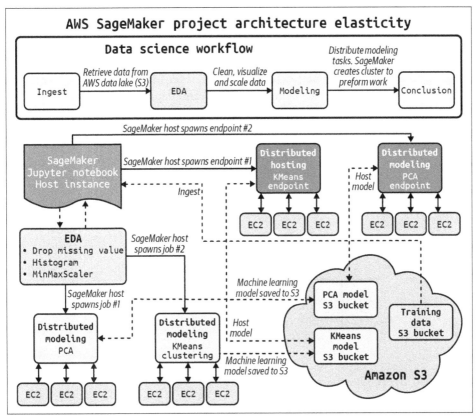

Figure 1-9. Sagemaker MLOps pipeline

An ML platform solves real-world repeatability, scale, and operationalization problems.

MLOps

Assuming all of these other layers are complete (DevOps, Data Automation, and Platform Automation) MLOps is possible. Remember from earlier that the process of automating machine learning using DevOps methodologies is MLOps. The method of building machine learning is machine learning engineering.

As a result, MLOps is a behavior, just as DevOps is a behavior. While some people work as DevOps engineers, a software engineer will more frequently perform tasks using DevOps best practices. Similarly, a machine learning engineer should use MLOps best practices to create machine learning systems.

DevOps and MLOps combined best practices?

Remember the DevOps practices described earlier in the chapter? MLOps builds on those practices and extends specific items to target machine learning systems directly.

One way to articulate these best practices is to consider that they create reproducible models with robust model packaging, validation, and deployment. In addition, these enhance the ability to explain and observe model performance. Figure 1-10 shows this in more detail.

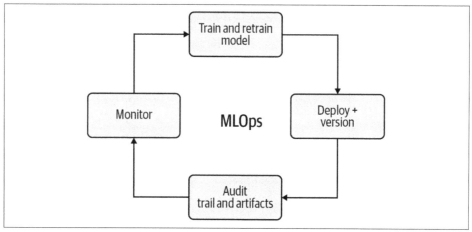

Figure 1-10. MLOps Feedback Loop

The feedback loop includes the following:

Create and retrain models with reusable ML Pipelines
  Creating a model just once isn't enough. The data can change, the customers can change, and the people making the models can change. The solution is to have reusable ML pipelines that are versioned.

Continuous Delivery of ML Models
  Continuous delivery of ML Models is similar to continuous delivery of software. When all of the steps are automated, including the infrastructure, using IaC, the model is deployable at any time to a new environment, including production.

Audit trail for MLOps pipeline
  It is critical to have auditing for machine learning models. There is no shortage of problems in machine learning, including security, bias, and accuracy. Therefore, having a helpful audit trail is invaluable, just as having adequate logging is critical in production software engineering projects. In addition, the audit trail is part of the feedback loop where you continuously improve your approach to the problem and the actual problem.

Observe model data drift use to improve future models

One of the unique aspects of machine learning is that the data can literally "shift" beneath the model. Thus, the model that worked for customers two years ago most likely won't work the same today. By monitoring data drift, i.e., the delta of changes from the last time a model training occurred, it is possible to prevent accuracy problems before causing production issues.

Where Can You Deploy?

A key aspect of MLOps is creating a cloud native platform model and then deploying it to many different targets, as shown in Figure 1-11. This ability to build once and deploy many times is a critical feature in modern machine learning operations. On the one hand, deploying a model to an HTTP endpoint that can elastically scale is a typical pattern but not the only way. A new paradigm of edge machine learning uses dedicated, specialized processers called ASICS. Examples of this include Google's TPU and Apple's A14.

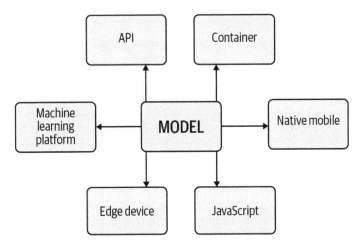

Figure 1-11. Machine learning model targets

In Figure 1-12, the cloud platform could use AutoML, as in Google AutoML vision, which deploys TensorFlow to TF Lite, TensorFlow.js, Core ML (an ML framework from Apple), a Container, or Coral (edge hardware that uses a TPU).

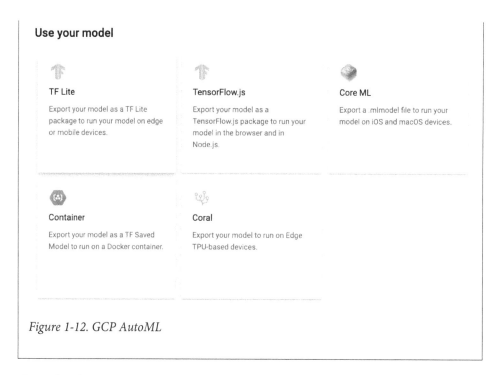

Use your model

TF Lite

Export your model as a TF Lite package to run your model on edge or mobile devices.

TensorFlow.js

Export your model as a TensorFlow.js package to run your model in the browser and in Node.js.

Core ML

Export a .mlmodel file to run your model on iOS and macOS devices.

Container

Export your model as a TF Saved Model to run on a Docker container.

Coral

Export your model to run on Edge TPU-based devices.

Figure 1-12. GCP AutoML

Conclusion

This chapter discussed the importance of using DevOps principles in the context of machine learning. Beyond just software, machine learning adds the new complexities of managing both the data and the model. The solution to this complexity is to embrace automation the way the software engineering community has done with DevOps.

Building a bookshelf is different from growing a tree. A bookshelf requires an initial design then a one-time build. Complex software systems involving machine learning are more like growing a tree. A tree that grows successfully requires multiple dynamic inputs, including soil, water, wind, and sun.

Likewise, one way to think about MLOps is the rule of 25%. In Figure 1-13, software engineering, data engineering, modeling, and the business problem are equally important. The multidisciplinary aspect of MLOps is what makes it tough to do. However, there are many good examples of companies doing MLOps following this rule of 25%.

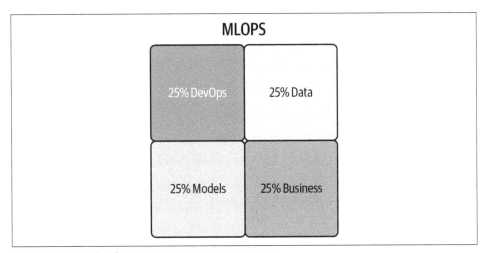

Figure 1-13. Rule of 25%

Tesla cars are one good example; they provide customers with what they want in the form of semi-autonomous vehicles. They also have excellent software engineering practices in that they do constant updates. Simultaneously, the car's system continuously trains the model to improve based on new data it receives. Another example of a product following the rule of 25% is the Amazon Alexa device.

Foundational skills necessary for MLOps are discussed in the next chapter. These include math for programmers, examples of data science projects, and a complete end-to-end MLOps process. By doing the recommended exercises at the end of this chapter, you put yourself in a great position to absorb the following content.

Exercises

- Create a new GitHub repository with necessary Python scaffolding using a `Make file`, linting, and testing. Then, perform additional steps such as code formatting in your Makefile.
- Using GitHub Actions (*https://oreil.ly/csmNI*), test a GitHub project with two or more Python versions.
- Using a cloud native build server (AWS Code Build, GCP CloudBuild, or Azure DevOps Pipelines), perform continuous integration for your project.
- Containerize a GitHub project by integrating a Dockerfile and automatically registering new containers to a Container Registry.
- Create a simple load test for your application using a load test framework such as locust (*https://locust.io*) or loader io (*https://loader.io*) and automatically run this test when you push changes to a staging branch.

Critical Thinking Discussion Questions

- What problems does a continuous integration (CI) system solve?
- Why is a CI system an essential part of both a SaaS software product and an ML system?
- Why are cloud platforms the ideal target for analytics applications? How do data engineering and DataOps assist in building cloud-based analytics applications?
- How does deep learning benefit from the cloud? Is deep learning feasible without cloud computing?
- Explain what MLOps is and how it can enhance a machine learning engineering project.

## CHAPTER 2

MLOps Foundations

By Noah Gift

Medical school was a woeful experience, an endless litany of fact, whose origins were rarely explained and whose usefulness was infrequently justified. My distaste for rote learning and my questioning attitude were not shared by most of the class of 96 students. This was particularly evident on one occasion when a biochemistry lecturer claimed to be deriving the Nernst equation. The class was faithfully copying what he wrote on the board. Having only a year before taken the Pchem course for chemistry majors at UCLA, I thought he was bluffing.

"Where did you get that value for k?" I asked.

The class shouted me down: "Let him finish! Just copy it."

> —Dr. Joseph Bogen

Having a solid foundation to build on is critical to any technical endeavor. In this chapter, several key building blocks set the foundation for the rest of the book. When dealing with students new to data science and machine learning, I have commonly encountered misconceptions about the items covered in this chapter. This chapter aims to build a strong foundation for using MLOps methodologies.

Bash and the Linux Command Line

Most machine learning happens in the cloud, and most cloud platforms assume you will interact with it to some degree with the terminal. As such, it is critical to know the basics of the Linux command line to do MLOps. This section aims to bootstrap you with just enough knowledge to ensure you have success doing MLOps.

There is often a look of both shock and horror when I expose a student to the terminal. The initial reaction is reasonable in most modern computing areas due to the power of GUI interfaces like the MacOS operating system or Windows. However, a better way to think about the terminal is the "advanced settings" of the environment you are working on: the cloud, machine learning, or programming. If you need to do advanced tasks, it is the way to perform them. As a result, competence in the Linux terminal can enormously enhance any skill set. Further, it is a better idea to develop in a cloud shell environment, in most cases, which assumes familiarity with Bash and Linux.

Most servers now run Linux; many new deployment options are using containers that also run Linux. The MacOS operating system terminal is close enough to Linux that most commands are similar, especially if you install third-party tools like Homebrew (*https://brew.sh*). You should know the Bash terminal, and this section will give you enough knowledge to be competent with it.

What are the critical and minimalistic components of the terminal to learn? These components include using a cloud-based shell development environment, Bash shell and commands, files and navigation, input/output, configuration, and writing a script. So let's dive into each one of these topics.

Cloud Shell Development Environments

Whether you are new to cloud computing or have decades of experience, it is worth shifting gears from a personal workstation to a web-based cloud shell development environment. A good analogy is a surfer who wants to surf each day at the beach. In theory, they could drive 50 miles each way to the beach each day, but it would be widely inconvenient, inefficient, and expensive. The better strategy, if you could afford it, would be to live at the beach, wake up each morning, walk to the beach, and surf.

Similarly, there are multiple problems a cloud development environment solves: it is more secure since you don't need to pass around developer keys. Many problems are intractable using a local machine since you may not transfer extensive data back and forth from the cloud. The tools available in cloud-based development include deep integration, which makes work more efficient. Unlike moving to the beach, a cloud development environment is free. All major clouds make their cloud development environments available on free tiers. If you are new to these environments, I would recommend starting with the AWS Cloud platform. There are two options to get started on AWS. The first option is the AWS CloudShell shown in Figure 2-1.

The AWS CloudShell is a Bash shell with unique AWS command completion built in the shell. If you regularly use the AWS CloudShell, it is a good idea to edit the ~/.bashrc to customize your experience. To do that, you can use the built-in vim editor. Many people put off learning vim, but they must be proficient in the cloud shell era. You can refer to the official vim FAQ (*https://oreil.ly/wNXdm*) for how to get things done.

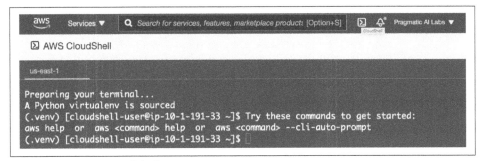

Figure 2-1. AWS CloudShell

A second option on AWS is the AWS Cloud9 development environment. A critical difference between AWS CloudShell and the AWS Cloud9 environment is that it is a more comprehensive way to develop software solutions. For example, you can see a shell and a GUI editor in Figure 2-2 to do syntax highlighting for multiple languages, including Python, Go, and Node.

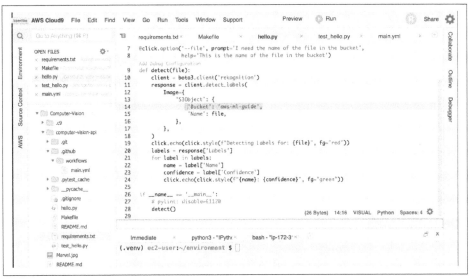

Figure 2-2. AWS Cloud9 development environment

In particular, when developing machine learning microservices, the Cloud9 environment is ideal since it allows you to make web requests from the console to deployed services and has deep integration with AWS Lambda. On the other hand, suppose you are on another platform, like Microsoft Azure or Google Cloud. In that case, the same concepts apply in that the cloud-based development environments are the ideal location to build machine learning services.

There is an optional video resource I created called "Bash Essentials for Cloud Computing" that walks you through the basics. You can view it on the O'Reilly platform (*https://oreil.ly/jEWr2*) or the Pragmatic AI Labs YouTube Channel (*https://oreil.ly/shtb9*).

Bash Shell and Commands

The shell is an interactive environment that contains a prompt and the ability to run commands. Most shells today run either Bash or ZSH.

A couple of immediately valuable things to do in an environment you commonly use for development are installing ZSH and vim configurations. For vim, one recommended setting is awesome vim (*https://oreil.ly/HChFQ*), and for ZSH, there is ohmyzsh (*https://ohmyz.sh*).

What is "the shell"? Ultimately it is a user interface that controls a computer, just like the MacOS Finder. As MLOps practitioners, it is worth knowing how to use the most robust user interface, the command line, for people who work with data. Here are a few things you can do.

List Files

With the shell, you can list files through the ls command. The flag -l adds additional listing information:

```
bash-3.2$ ls -l
total 11
drwxrwxr-x 130 root admin 4160 Jan 20 22:00 Applications
drwxr-xr-x  75 root wheel 2400 Dec 14 23:13 Library
drwxr-xr-x@  9 root wheel  288 Jan 1 2020 System
drwxr-xr-x   6 root admin  192 Jan 1 2020 Users
```

Run Commands

In a GUI, you click a button or open an application to do work. In the shell, you run a command. There are many helpful built-in commands in the shell, and they often work well together. For example, an excellent way to figure out the location of shell executables is to use which. Here is an example:

```
bash-3.2$ which ls
/bin/ls
```

Notice that the ls command is in the */bin* directory. This "hint" shows that I can find other executables in this directory. Here is a count of the executables in */bin/* (the pipe operator | will be explained in just a bit, but, in short, it accepts the input from another command):

```
bash-3.2$ ls -l /bin/ | wc -l
37
```

Files and Navigation

In a GUI, you open a folder or a file; you use commands to accomplish the same thing in a shell.

pwd shows the full path to where you are:

```
bash-3.2$ pwd
/Users/noahgift
```

cd changes into a new directory:

```
bash-3.2$ cd /tmp
```

Input/Output

In a previous example, the output of ls redirects to another command. Piping is an example of input and output operations working to accomplish a more sophisticated task. It is common to use the shell to pipe one command into another.

Here is an example that shows a workflow with both a redirect and a pipe. Notice that first, the words "foo bar baz" direct to a file called *out.txt*. Next, the contents of this file print out via cat, and then they pipe into the command wc, which can count either the number of words via -w or characters via -c:

```
bash-3.2$ cd /tmp
bash-3.2$ echo "foo bar baz" > out.txt
bash-3.2$ cat out.txt | wc -c
      12
bash-3.2$ cat out.txt | wc -w
       3
```

Here is another example that directs the output of the shuf command to a new file. You can download that file from my GitHub repository (*https://oreil.ly/CDudc*). The shuf executable "shuffles" a file while limiting it to the rows specified. In this case, it takes an almost 1 GB file and takes the first 100,000 rows, and outputs a new file using the > operator:

```
bash-3.2$ time shuf -n 100000 en.openfoodfacts.org.products.tsv >\
10k.sample.en.openfoodfacts.org.products.tsv
1.89s user 0.80s system 97% cpu 2.748 total
```

Using a shell technique like this can save the day when working on a CSV file too large to process data science libraries on a laptop.

Configuration

The ZSH and Bash shell configuration files store settings that invoke each new time a terminal opens. As I mentioned earlier, customizing your Bash environment is recommended in a cloud-based development environment. For ZSH, an excellent place to start is *.zshrc*, and for Bash, it is *.bashrc*. Here is an example of something I store in my *.zshrc* configuration on my MacOS laptop. The first item is an alias that allows me to type the command flask-azure-ml, cd into a directory, and source a Python virtual environment in one fell swoop. The second section is where I export the AWS command line tool variables so I can make API calls:

```
## Flask ML Azure
alias flask-azure-ml="/Users/noahgift/src/flask-ml-azure-serverless &&\
source ~/.flask-ml-azure/bin/activate"

## AWS CLI
export AWS_SECRET_ACCESS_KEY="<key>"
export AWS_ACCESS_KEY_ID="<key>"
export AWS_DEFAULT_REGION="us-east-1"
```

In summary, my recommendation is to customize your shell configuration file for both your laptop and for cloud-based development environments. This small investment pays big dividends as you build in automation to your regular workflows.

Writing a Script

It can be a bit daunting to think about writing your first shell script. The syntax is much scarier than Python with weird characters. Fortunately, in many ways, it is easier to get started. The best way to write a shell script is to put a command into a file, then run it. Here is an excellent example of a "hello world" script.

The first line is called the "shebang" line and tells the script to use Bash. The second line is a Bash command, echo. The nice thing about a Bash script is that you can paste any commands you want in it. This fact makes the automation of small tasks straightforward even with little to no knowledge of programming:

```
#!/usr/bin/env bash

echo "hello world"
```

Next, you use the chmod command to set the executable flag to make this script executable. Finally, you run it by appending ./:

```
bash-3.2$ chmod +x hello.sh
bash-3.2$ ./hello.sh
Hello World
```

The main takeaway of the shell is that you must have at least some basic skills to do MLOps. However, it is easy to get started, and before you know it, you can dramatically improve things you do daily via the automation of shell scripts and the use of the Linux command line. Next, let's talk get started with an overview of the essential parts of cloud computing.

Cloud Computing Foundations and Building Blocks

It is safe to say that almost all forms of machine learning require cloud computing in some form. A key concept in cloud computing is the idea of near-infinite resources, as described in "Above the Clouds: A Berkeley View of Cloud Computing" (*https://oreil.ly/Ug8kx*). Without the cloud, it simply isn't feasible to do many machine learning models. For example, Stephen Strogatz, the author of *Infinite Powers: How Calculus Reveals the Secrets of the Universe* (Mariner Books), makes the case that "By wielding infinity in just the right way, calculus can unlock the secrets of the universe." For centuries specific problems like finding the shape of a circle were impossible without calculus to deal with infinite numbers. It is the same with cloud computing; many issues in machine learning, especially the operationalizing of models, are not feasible without the cloud. As shown in Figure 2-3, the cloud provides near-infinite compute and storage and works on the data without moving it.

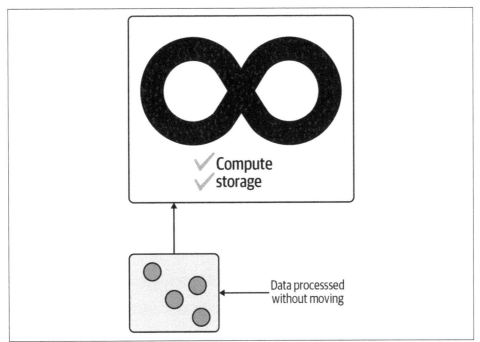

Figure 2-3. Cloud computing harnesses near-infinite compute and data

It turns out that the ability to harness computing power on data without moving it, using near-infinite resources via machine learning platforms like AWS SageMaker or Azure ML Studio, is the killer feature of the cloud not replicable without cloud computing. Coupled with this killer feature is something I call the "Automator's law." Once the general public starts talking about automation of a vertical—self-driving cars, IT, factories, machine learning—it eventually happens.

This concept doesn't mean that some magic unicorn appears that sprinkles fairy dust on projects, and they get more manageable; it is that humans are good at spotting trends as a collective group. For example, when I worked in the television industry as a teenager, there was only the concept of "linear" editing. This workflow meant you needed three different tapes to dissolve to a black screen—the source tape, the edit master tape, and a third tape that contained the black footage.

I remember people talking about how much work it was to keep swapping out new tapes and how it would be fantastic if this workflow became automated. Later it did become fully automated through the introduction of nonlinear editing. This technology allows you to store digital copies of the material and perform digital manipulation of footage versus inserting new material in a linear tape. These nonlinear editing systems cost hundreds of thousands of dollars in the early 1990s. Now I do more complicated editing on my thousand-dollar laptop with enough storage capacity to store thousands of such tapes.

The same scenario occurred with cloud computing in the early 2000s. Many companies I worked at used their own data centers staffed by teams of people that maintained them. When initial components of cloud computing cropped up, many people said, "I bet companies in the future can control an entire data center on their laptop." Many expert data center technicians scoffed at the idea of their job falling victim to automation, yet, the Automator's law struck again. A majority of companies in 2020 and beyond have some form of cloud computing, and newer jobs involve harnessing that power.

Similarly, the automation of machine learning via AutoML is a nontrivial advancement that enables the creation of models more quickly, with higher accuracy and better explainability. As a result, jobs in the data science industry will change, just like editors and data center operator jobs changed.

AutoML is the automation of the modeling aspect of machine learning. A crude and straightforward example of AutoML is an Excel spreadsheet that performs linear regression. You tell Excel which column is the target to predict and then which column is the feature.

More sophisticated AutoML systems work similarly. You select what value you want to predict—for example, image classification, a numerical trend, categorical text classification, or perhaps clustering. Then the AutoML software system performs many of the same techniques that a data scientist would perform, including hyperparameter tuning, algorithm selection, and model explainability.

All major cloud platforms have AutoML tools embedded into MLOps platforms. As a result, AutoML is an option for all cloud-based machine learning projects and is increasingly becoming another productivity enhancement for them.

Tyler Cowen is an economist, author, and columnist for Bloomberg and grew up playing competitive chess. In his book *Average is Over* (Plume), Cowen mentions that chess software eventually beat humans, also proving the Automator's law in action. Surprisingly, though, at the end of Cowen's book, expert humans and chess software won versus chess software alone. Ultimately, this story may occur with machine learning and data science. Automation may replace simple machine learning tasks and make the domain expert humans controlling the ML automation orders of magnitude more effective.

Getting Started with Cloud Computing

A recommended approach to getting started with cloud computing is setting up a multicloud development environment, as shown in the O'Reilly Video Course: Cloud Computing with Python (*https://oreil.ly/MGZfz*). This video is an excellent companion to this section but isn't required to follow along. The basic structure of a multicloud environment shows that a cloud shell is something all these clouds have in common, as shown in Figure 2-4.

A source control repository using GitHub, or a similar service, is the central location where all three cloud environments initially communicate. Each of the three clouds—AWS, Azure, and GCP—has cloud-based development environments via a cloud shell. In Chapter 1, a necessary Python scaffolding showed the advantages of developing a repeatable and testable structure. A CI/CD (continuous integration/continuous delivery) process via GitHub Actions ensures the Python code is working and of high quality.

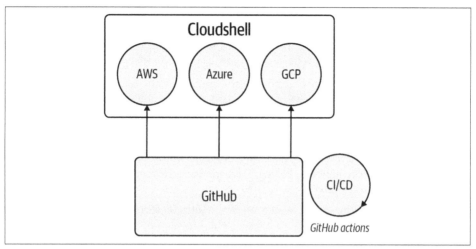

Figure 2-4. Starting cloud computing

Testing and linting Python code is a process that validates the quality of a software project. A developer will run testing and linting locally to assist with keeping software quality high. This process is similar to having a robotic vacuum machine (robovac) you turn on when you want to clean a room in your house. The robovac is a helpful assistant that keeps your room in a known good state, and running lints and testing your code keeps your code in a known good state.

A CI/CD pipeline runs these quality-control checks in an external environment to ensure the application is working before its release into another production. This pipeline allows software deployment to be repeatable and reliable and is a modern software engineering best practice—another word for these software engineering best practices is DevOps.

Using all three major clouds is a great way to familiarize yourself with cloud computing if you are learning the cloud. This cross-cloud workflow helps because it solidifies knowledge. After all, the names of things are different, but the concepts are identical. If you need help with some of the terminologies, refer to Appendix A.

Let's dive into Python next, which is the de facto language of DevOps, cloud computing, data science, and machine learning.

Python Crash Course

A key reason for Python's dominance is that the language is optimized for the developer and not for the computer. Languages like C or C++ have excellent performance because they are "lower-level," meaning the developer must work much harder in solving a problem. For example, a C programmer must allocate memory, declare types, and compile a program. On the other hand, a Python programmer can put in some commands and run them, and there is often significantly less code in Python.

For that convenience, though, Python's performance is much slower than C, C#, Java, and Go. Further, Python has limitations inherent to the language itself, including lack of true threads, lack of a JIT (Just in Time) compiler, and lack of type inference found in languages like C# or F#. With cloud computing, though, language performance does not bind to many problems. So it would be fair to say that Python's performance got accidentally lucky because of two things: cloud computing and containers. With Cloud computing, the design is fully distributed, building on top of it using technologies like AWS Lambda and AWS SQS (Simple Queuing Service). Similarly, containerized technology like Kubernetes does the heavy lifting of building distributed systems, so Python threads become suddenly irrelevant.

AWS Lambda is a function as a service (FaaS) technology that runs on the AWS platform. It has the name FaaS because an AWS Lambda function can be just a few lines of code—literally a function. These functions can then attach to events like a cloud queuing system, Amazon SQS, or an image uploaded to Amazon S3 object storage.

One way to think about a cloud is that it is an operating system. In the mid-1980s, Sun Computer used the marketing phrase, "The Network is the Computer." This slogan may have been premature in 1980, but in 2021 it is very accurate. For example, instead of spawning threads on a single machine, you could spawn AWS Lambda functions in the cloud, which behaves like an operating system with infinitely scalable resources.

In a talk I attended at Google, Dr. Patterson, a retired Berkeley Computer Science Professor and co-creator of the TPU (TensorFlow Processing Unit), mentioned that Python is 64,000 times slower than equivalent matrix operations in C shown in Figure 2-5. This fact is in addition to not having true threads.

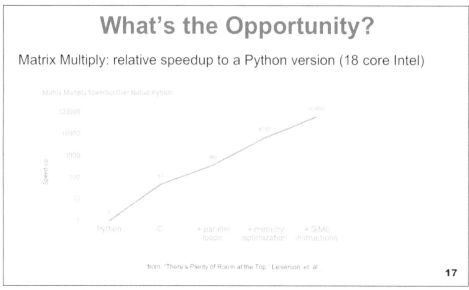

Figure 2-5. Python performance is 64,000 times worse than matrix operations in C

Simultaneously, a research paper, "Energy Efficiency across programming languages" (*https://oreil.ly/4g5u2*), shows that many operations in Python require 50 times more energy than equivalent operations in C. This research into energy efficiency also pegs Python as one of the worst-performing languages regarding how much power it requires to perform tasks compared to other languages, as shown in Figure 2-6. As Python has surged in popularity as one of the most popular languages on the planet, it does raise concerns on whether it is more like a coal powerplant than a green energy solar system. Ultimately, Python could need rescuing again for energy consumption. One solution could be for a major cloud vendor to actively build a new runtime for Python that takes advantage of modern computer science techniques like a JIT compiler.

One final technical hurdle I have seen with newcomers to data science programming is their adoption of the traditional computer science approach to learning to code. For example, cloud computing and machine learning are very different from conventional software engineering projects like developing user-facing applications via a GUI (graphical user interface). Instead, much of the cloud and ML world involves writing small functions. Most of the time, these other Python parts are not needed, i.e., object-oriented code, and discourage a newcomer from speaking the language.

	binary-trees			
	Energy	Time	Ratio	Mb
(c) C	39.80	1125	0.035	131
(c) C++	41.23	1129	0.037	132
(c) Rust ⇓$_2$	49.07	1263	0.039	180
(c) Fortran ⇑$_1$	69.82	2112	0.033	133
(c) Ada ⇓$_1$	95.02	2822	0.034	197
(c) Ocaml ↓$_1$ ⇑$_2$	100.74	3525	0.029	148
(v) Java ↑$_1$ ⇓$_{16}$	111.84	3306	0.034	1120
(v) Lisp ↓$_3$ ⇓$_3$	149.55	10570	0.014	373
(v) Racket ↓$_4$ ⇓$_6$	155.81	11261	0.014	467
(i) Hack ↑$_2$ ⇓$_9$	156.71	4497	0.035	502
(v) C# ↓$_1$ ⇓$_1$	189.74	10797	0.018	427
(v) F# ↓$_3$ ⇓$_1$	207.13	15637	0.013	432
(c) Pascal ↓$_3$ ⇑$_5$	214.64	16079	0.013	256
(c) Chapel ↑$_5$ ⇑$_4$	237.29	7265	0.033	335
(v) Erlang ↑$_5$ ⇑$_1$	266.14	7327	0.036	433
(c) Haskell ↑$_2$ ⇓$_2$	270.15	11582	0.023	494
(i) Dart ↓$_1$ ⇑$_1$	290.27	17197	0.017	475
(i) JavaScript ↓$_2$ ⇓$_4$	312.14	21349	0.015	916
(i) TypeScript ↓$_2$ ⇓$_2$	315.10	21686	0.015	915
(c) Go ↑$_3$ ⇑$_{13}$	636.71	16292	0.039	228
(i) Jruby ↑$_2$ ⇓$_3$	720.53	19276	0.037	1671
(i) Ruby ⇑$_5$	855.12	26634	0.032	482
(i) PHP ⇑$_3$	1,397.51	42316	0.033	786
(i) Python ⇑$_{15}$	1,793.46	45003	0.040	275
(i) Lua ↓$_1$	2,452.04	209217	0.012	1961
(i) Perl ↑$_1$	3,542.20	96097	0.037	2148
(c) Swift		n.e.		

Figure 2-6. The Python language is among the worst offenders in energy consumption

Computer science topics include concurrency, object-oriented programming, meta-programming, and algorithm theory. Unfortunately, studying these topics is orthogonal to the programming style necessary for most programming in cloud computing and data science. It isn't that these topics are not valuable; they are beneficial to the creators of platforms, libraries, and tools. If you are not initially "creating" libraries and frameworks but "using" libraries and frameworks, then you can safely ignore these advanced topics and stick to functions.

This crash-course approach temporarily ignores the creator of code used by others in favor of the consumer of code and libraries, i.e., the data scientist or MLOps practitioner. This brief crash course is for the consumer, where most people spend their career in data science. After these topics, if you are curious, you will have a solid foundation to move onto more complex computer science–focused topics. These advanced topics are not necessary to be productive immediately in MLOps.

Minimalistic Python Tutorial

If you wanted to learn the smallest amount of Python necessary to get started, what would you need to know? The two most essential components of Python are statements and functions. So let's start with Python statements. A Python statement is an instruction to a computer; i.e., similar to telling a person "hello," you can say to a computer to "print hello." The following example is the Python interpreter. Notice, the "statement" in the example is the phrase `print("Hello World")`:

```
Python 3.9.0 (default, Nov 14 2020, 16:06:43)
[Clang 12.0.0 (clang-1200.0.32.27)] on darwin
Type "help", "copyright", "credits" or "license" for more information.
>>> print("Hello World")
Hello World
```

With Python, you can also chain together two statements with a semicolon. For example, I import the `os` module, which has a function I want to use, `os.listdir`, then I call it to list the contents of a directory I am inside:

```
>>> import os;os.listdir(".")
['chapter11', 'README.md', 'chapter2', '.git', 'chapter3']
```

This pattern is pervasive in data science notebooks, and this is all you need to know to get started with Python. I would recommend trying things out in Python or IPython, or Jupyter REPL as the first way to get familiar with Python.

The second item to know is how to write and use functions in Python. Let's do that in the following example. This example is a two-line function that adds two numbers together, x and y. The entire point of a Python function is to serve as a "unit of work." For example, a toaster in the kitchen works as a unit of work. It takes bread as input, warms the bread, then returns toast. Similarly, once I write the `add` function, I can use it as many times as possible with new inputs:

```
>>> def add(x,y):
...     return x+y
...
>>> add(1,1)
2
>>> add(3,4)
7
>>>
```

Let's assemble our knowledge and build a Python script. At the beginning of a Python script, there is a shebang line, just like in Bash. Next, the `choices` library is imported. This module is later used in a "loop" to send random numbers to the `add` function:

```
#!/usr/bin/env python
from random import choices

def add(x,y):
```

```
    print(f"inside a function and adding {x}, {y}")
    return x+y

#Send random numbers from 1-10, ten times to the add function
numbers = range(1,10)
for num in numbers:
    xx = choices(numbers)[0]
    yy = choices(numbers)[0]
    print(add(xx,yy))
```

The script needs to be made executable by running chmod +x add.py, just like a Bash script:

```
bash-3.2$ ./add.py
inside a function and adding 7, 5
12
inside a function and adding 9, 5
14
inside a function and adding 3, 1
4
inside a function and adding 7, 2
9
inside a function and adding 5, 8
13
inside a function and adding 6, 1
7
inside a function and adding 5, 5
10
inside a function and adding 8, 6
14
inside a function and adding 3, 3
6
```

You can learn about Python a lot more, but "toying" around with examples like the one shown here is perhaps the quickest way to go from "zero to one." So let's move on to another topic, math for programmers, and tackle it in a minimalistic fashion as well.

Math for Programmers Crash Course

Math can be both daunting and irritating, but understanding the basics is essential for working with machine learning. So let's tackle a few useful and essential ideas.

Descriptive Statistics and Normal Distributions

Many things in the world are "normally" distributed. A good example is height and weight. If you plot the height of every person in the world, you will get a "bell-shaped" distribution. This distribution is intuitive in that most people you encounter are of average height, and it is unusual to see a seven-foot-tall basketball player. Let's walk through a Jupyter notebook (*https://oreil.ly/i5NF3*) containing 25,000 records of human heights and weights of 19-year-old children:

```
In [0]:
import pandas as pd

In [7]:
df = pd.read_csv("https://raw.githubusercontent.com/noahgift/\
regression-concepts/master/height-weight-25k.csv")

Out[7]:
IndexHeight-InchesWeight-Pounds
01        65.78331        112.9925
12        71.51521        136.4873
23        69.39874        153.0269
34        68.21660        142.3354
45        67.78781        144.2971
```

Next, a plot, shown in Figure 2-7, shows a linear relationship between height and weight, which most of us intuitively know. The taller you are, the more you weigh:

```
In [0]:
import seaborn as sns
import numpy as np

In [9]:
sns.lmplot("Height-Inches", "Weight-Pounds", data=df)
```

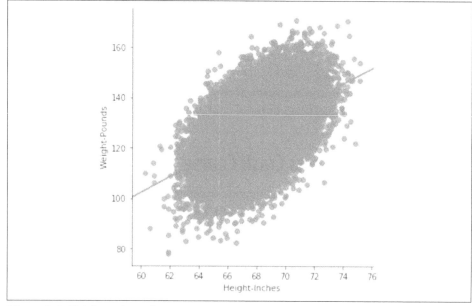

Figure 2-7. Height and weight

The step of visualizing the data in a dataset is called "Exploratory Data Analysis." The general idea is to "look around" using a combination of math and visualization. The next step is to look at the descriptive statistics of this "normal distribution."

In Pandas, you get these descriptive statistics through the use of `df.describe()`. One way to consider descriptive statistics is to view them as a way of "seeing" numerically what the eye sees visually. For example, the 50th percentile, or median, shows the number that represents the exact middle height. This value is about 68 inches. The max statistic in this dataset is 75 inches. Max represents the most extreme observation or the tallest person measured for this dataset. The max observation in a normally distributed dataset is rare, just as the minimum is. You can see this trend in Figure 2-8. The `DataFrame` in Pandas comes with a describe method that when called gives a full range of descriptive statistics :

```
In [10]: df.describe()
```

	Index	Height-Inches	Weight-Pounds
count	25000.000000	25000.000000	25000.000000
mean	12500.500000	67.993114	127.079421
std	7217.022701	1.901679	11.660898
min	1.000000	60.278360	78.014760
25%	6250.750000	66.704397	119.308675
50%	12500.500000	67.995700	127.157750
75%	18750.250000	69.272958	134.892850
max	25000.000000	75.152800	170.924000

Figure 2-8. Height/weight descriptive statistics

One of the best ways to visualize height and weight's normal bell-shaped distribution is to use a Kernel Density plot:

```
In [11]:
sns.jointplot("Height-Inches", "Weight-Pounds", data=df, kind="kde");
```

Both the weight and the height show a "bell distribution." The extreme values are rare, and most of the values are in the middle, as shown in Figure 2-9.

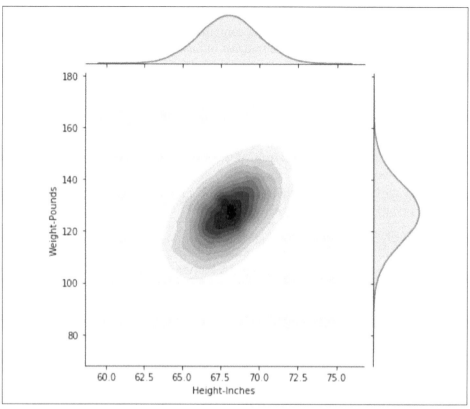

Figure 2-9. Kernel Density plot of weight and height

Machine learning heavily builds on the idea of a normal distribution, and having this intuition goes a long way to building and maintaining machine learning models. However, it is essential to note that other distributions are beyond the normal distribution, making the world much harder to model. An excellent example of this is what the author Nassim Taleb calls "fat tails," i.e., hard-to-predict and rare events that significantly affect the world.

Another example of the danger of being too confident in modeling the world can be found in Dr. Steven Koonin's book, *Unsettled* (BenBella Books). I worked with Dr. Koonin when he was in the administration of Caltech and found him to be an enthusiastic scientist and fun person to have a random conversation with. Here is a quote about modeling from his book:

> Since we have a very solid understanding of the physical laws that govern matter and energy, it's easy to be seduced by the notion that we can just feed the present state of the atmosphere and oceans into a computer, make some assumptions about future human and natural influences, and so accurately predict the climate decades into the future. Unfortunately, that's just a fantasy, as you might infer from weather forecasts, which can be accurate only out to two weeks or so.

Optimization

A fundamental problem in machine learning is the concept of optimization. Optimization is the ability to find the best, or good enough, solution to a problem. Gradient descent is an optimization algorithm at the heart of deep learning. The goal of gradient descent is to convert to the global minimum, i.e., the optimal solution, versus getting stuck in a local minimum. The intuition behind the algorithm is relatively straightforward if you imagine walking down a mountain in the dark. The global minimum solution means you get off the mountain alive at the bottom. The local minimum means you walked accidentally into a lake on the side of the mountain 1,000 feet from the bottom.

Let's walk through an example of optimization problems. An excellent place to start is by observing the types of notation involved with optimization. When creating a model, you need to understand the Python method of notating algebraic expressions. The quick summary in Figure 2-10 compares terms between a spreadsheet, algebra, and Python. A key takeaway is you can do the same thing on a whiteboard, in Excel, or with a bit of code.

Assume $A_1, ..., A_{10}$ are **parameters** and $X_1, ..., X_{10}$ are **decision variables:**		
Spreadsheet	**Algebra**	**Python**
sum(X1:X6)	$\sum_{i=1}^{6} X_i$	sum(range(1,6))
sum(A3:A7)	$\sum_{j=3}^{7} A_j$	sum(range(3,7))
sumproduct(A1:A5,X1:X5)	$\sum_{i=1}^{5} A_i X_i$	sum(reduce(operator.mul,data)
sumproduct(A3:A10,X3:X10)	$\sum_{j=3}^{10} A_j X_j$	sum(reduce(operator.mul,data)

Figure 2-10. Notation is relative

Now, let's look at a solution to making the correct change. You can find the code to this solution on GitHub (*https://oreil.ly/eIR26*). The general idea with this code example is to pick a *greedy* solution to make the change. Greedy algorithms work by always taking the best option first. They also work well if you don't care about the perfect solution, or it is impossible to find the perfect solution, but you are OK with a "good enough" solution. In this case, it would be the highest value coins and making the change with those, then moving onto the next highest:

```
python change.py --full 1.34

Quarters 5: , Remainder: 9
Dimes 0: , Remainder: 0
Nickles 1: , Remainder: 4
Pennies 4:
```

The following is the core section of the code that does a greedy match. Note that a recursive function solves each iteration of the problem since the large coins eventually run out. The algorithm next finds medium coins that run out; finally, it moves to the smallest coins:

```python
def recursive_change(self, rem):
    """Greedy Coin Match with Recursion
    >>> c = Change(.71)
    >>> c.recursive_change(c.convert)
    2 quarters
    2 dimes
    1 pennies
    [1, 0, 2, 2]

    """
    if len(self.coins) == 0:
        return []
    coin = self.coins.pop()
    num, new_rem = divmod(rem, coin)
    self.printer(num,coin)
    return self.recursive_change(new_rem) + [num]
```

While there are many different ways to express the concept algorithmically, the idea is the same. Without knowing how to find the "perfect" solution, the appropriate answer is always picking the best choice when presented. Intuitively, this is like walking to a city's diagonal destination and going straight or turning right each time the light ahead of you turns red.

Here is a series of tests for this algorithm. They show how the algorithm performs, which is often a good idea when testing a solution involving optimization:

```python
#!/usr/bin/env python2.5
#Noah Gift
#Greedy Coin Match Python

import unittest
```

```
import change

class TestChange(unittest.TestCase):
    def test_get_quarter(self):
        c = change.Change(.25)
        quarter, qrem, dime, drem, nickel, nrem, penny =\
            c.make_change_conditional()
        self.assertEqual(quarter,1)   #quarters
        self.assertEqual(qrem, 0)    #quarter remainder
    def test_get_dime(self):
        c = change.Change(.20)
        quarter, qrem, dime, drem, nickel, nrem, penny =\
            c.make_change_conditional()
        self.assertEqual(quarter,0)   #quarters
        self.assertEqual(qrem, 20)    #quarter remainder
        self.assertEqual(dime, 2)     #dime
        self.assertEqual(drem, 0)     #dime remainder
    def test_get_nickel(self):
        c = change.Change(.05)
        quarter, qrem, dime, drem, nickel, nrem, penny =\
            c.make_change_conditional()
        self.assertEqual(dime, 0)     #dime
        self.assertEqual(drem, 0)     #dime remainder
        self.assertEqual(nickel, 1)   #nickel
        self.assertEqual(nrem, 0)     #nickel remainder
    def test_get_penny(self):
        c = change.Change(.04)
        quarter, qrem, dime, drem, nickel, nrem, penny =\
            c.make_change_conditional()
        self.assertEqual(penny, 4)   #nickel
    def test_small_number(self):
        c = change.Change(.0001)
        quarter, qrem, dime, drem, nickel, nrem, penny =\
            c.make_change_conditional()
        self.assertEqual(quarter,0)   #quarters
        self.assertEqual(qrem, 0)     #quarter remainder
        self.assertEqual(dime, 0)     #dime
        self.assertEqual(drem, 0)     #dime remainder
        self.assertEqual(nickel, 0)   #nickel
        self.assertEqual(nrem, 0)     #nickel remainder
        self.assertEqual(penny, 0)    #penny
    def test_large_number(self):
        c = change.Change(2.20)
        quarter, qrem, dime, drem, nickel, nrem, penny =\
            c.make_change_conditional()
        self.assertEqual(quarter, 8)  #nickel
        self.assertEqual(qrem, 20)    #nickel
        self.assertEqual(dime, 2)     #nickel
        self.assertEqual(drem, 0)     #nickel
    def test_get_quarter_dime_penny(self):
        c = change.Change(.86)
        quarter, qrem, dime, drem, nickel, nrem, penny =\
```

```
            c.make_change_conditional()
        self.assertEqual(quarter,3)   #quarters
        self.assertEqual(qrem, 11)    #quarter remainder
        self.assertEqual(dime, 1)     #dime
        self.assertEqual(drem, 1)     #dime remainder
        self.assertEqual(penny, 1)    #penny
    def test_get_quarter_dime_nickel_penny(self):
        c = change.Change(.91)
        quarter, qrem, dime, drem, nickel, nrem, penny =\
            c.make_change_conditional()
        self.assertEqual(quarter,3)   #quarters
        self.assertEqual(qrem, 16)    #quarter remainder
        self.assertEqual(dime, 1)     #dime
        self.assertEqual(drem, 6)     #dime remainder
        self.assertEqual(nickel, 1)   #nickel
        self.assertEqual(nrem, 1)     #nickel remainder
        self.assertEqual(penny, 1)     #penny

if __name__ == "__main__":
    unittest.main()
```

Next, let's build on greedy algorithms in the following problem. One of the most studied problems in optimization is the traveling salesman problem. You can find the source code on GitHub (*https://oreil.ly/3u5Hd*). This example is a list of routes that are in a *routes.py* file. It shows the distance between different companies in the Bay Area.

It is an excellent example of a perfect solution that doesn't exist, but a good enough one does. The general problem asks the question, "How can you travel to a list of cities and minimize the distance?"

One way to do this is to use a "greedy" algorithm. It will pick the right solution at every choice. Often this can lead to a good enough answer. In this particular example, a "random" city is chosen each time as the starting point. This example adds the ability for simulations to pick the lowest distance. A user of the simulations could simulate as many times as they have time. The smallest total length is the best answer. The following is a sample of what the input looks like before processing into the TSP algorithm:

```
values = [
("AAPL", "CSCO", 14),
("AAPL", "CVX", 44),
("AAPL", "EBAY", 14),
("AAPL", "GOOG", 14),
("AAPL", "GPS", 59),
("AAPL", "HPQ", 14),
("AAPL", "INTC", 8),
("AAPL", "MCK", 60),
("AAPL", "ORCL", 26),
("AAPL", "PCG", 59),
```

```
("AAPL", "SFO", 46),
("AAPL", "SWY", 37),
("AAPL", "URS", 60),
("AAPL", "WFC", 60),
```

Let's run the script. First, note that it takes as an input of the complete simulations to run:

```python
#!/usr/bin/env python
"""

Traveling salesman solution with random start and greedy path selection
You can select how many iterations to run by doing the following:

python greedy_random_start.py 20 #runs 20 times


"""


import sys
from random import choice
import numpy as np
from routes import values

dt = np.dtype([("city_start", "S10"), ("city_end", "S10"), ("distance", int)])
data_set = np.array(values, dtype=dt)


def all_cities():
    """Finds unique cities

    array([["A", "A"],
    ["A", "B"]])

    """
    cities = {}
    city_set = set(data_set["city_end"])
    for city in city_set:
        cities[city] = ""
    return cities


def randomize_city_start(cities):
    """Returns a randomized city to start trip"""

    return choice(cities)


def get_shortest_route(routes):
    """Sort the list by distance and return shortest distance route"""

    route = sorted(routes, key=lambda dist: dist[2]).pop(0)
    return route
```

```
def greedy_path():
    """Select the next path to travel based on the shortest, nearest path"""

    itinerary = []
    cities = all_cities()
    starting_city = randomize_city_start(list(cities.keys()))
    # print "starting_city: %s" % starting_city
    cities_visited = {}
    # we want to iterate through all cities once
    count = 1
    while True:
        possible_routes = []
        # print "starting city: %s" % starting_city
        for path in data_set:
            if starting_city in path["city_start"]:
                # we can't go to cities we have already visited
                if path["city_end"] in cities_visited:
                    continue
                else:
                    # print "path: ", path
                    possible_routes.append(path)

        if not possible_routes:
            break
        # append this to itinerary
        route = get_shortest_route(possible_routes)
        # print "Route(%s): %s " % (count, route)
        count += 1
        itinerary.append(route)
        # add this city to the visited city list
        cities_visited[route[0]] = count
        # print "cities_visited: %s " % cities_visited
        # reset the starting_city to the next city
        starting_city = route[1]
        # print "itinerary: %s" % itinerary

    return itinerary


def get_total_distance(complete_itinerary):

    distance = sum(z for x, y, z in complete_itinerary)
    return distance


def lowest_simulation(num):

    routes = {}
    for _ in range(num):
        itinerary = greedy_path()
        distance = get_total_distance(itinerary)
```

```
        routes[distance] = itinerary
    shortest_distance = min(routes.keys())
    route = routes[shortest_distance]
    return shortest_distance, route


def main():
    """runs everything"""

    if len(sys.argv) == 2:
        iterations = int(sys.argv[1])
        print("Running simulation %s times" % iterations)
        distance, route = lowest_simulation(iterations)
        print("Shortest Distance: %s" % distance)
        print("Optimal Route: %s" % route)
    else:
        # print "All Routes: %s" % data_set
        itinerary = greedy_path()
        print("itinerary: %s" % itinerary)
        print("Distance: %s" % get_total_distance(itinerary))


if __name__ == "__main__":
    main()
```

Let's run this "greedy" algorithm 25 times. Notice that it finds a "good" solution of 129. This version may or may not be the optimal solution in a more extensive set of coordinates, but it is good enough to start a road trip for our purposes:

```
> ./greedy-random-tsp.py 25
Running simulation 25 times
Shortest Distance: 129
Optimal Route: [(b'WFC', b'URS', 0), (b'URS', b'GPS', 1),\
(b'GPS', b'PCG', 1), (b'PCG', b'MCK', 3), (b'MCK', b'SFO', 16),\
(b'SFO', b'ORCL', 20), (b'ORCL', b'HPQ', 12), (b'HPQ', b'GOOG', 6),\
(b'GOOG', b'AAPL', 11), (b'AAPL', b'INTC', 8), (b'INTC', b'CSCO', 6),\
(b'CSCO', b'EBAY', 0), (b'EBAY', b'SWY', 32), (b'SWY', b'CVX', 13)]
```

Notice that if I run the simulation just once, it randomly selects a worse distance of 143:

```
> ./greedy-random-tsp.py 1
Running simulation 1 times
Shortest Distance: 143
Optimal Route: [(b'CSCO', b'EBAY', 0), (b'EBAY', b'INTC', 6),\
(b'INTC', b'AAPL', 8), (b'AAPL', b'GOOG', 14), (b'GOOG', b'HPQ', 6),\
(b'HPQ', b'ORCL', 12), (b'ORCL', b'SFO', 20), (b'SFO', b'MCK', 16),\
 (b'MCK', b'WFC', 2), (b'WFC', b'URS', 0), (b'URS', b'GPS', 1),\
 (b'GPS', b'PCG', 1), (b'PCG', b'CVX', 44), (b'CVX', b'SWY', 13)]
```

Notice in Figure 2-11 how I would run multiple iterations of the code in a real-world scenario to "try out ideas." If the dataset was enormous and I was in a hurry, I may do only a few simulations, but if I was leaving for the day, I might let it run 1,000 times and finish by the time I come back in the morning the next day. There could be many local minima in a geographic coordinates dataset—that is, solutions to the problem that don't quite reach the global minima, or the optimal solution.

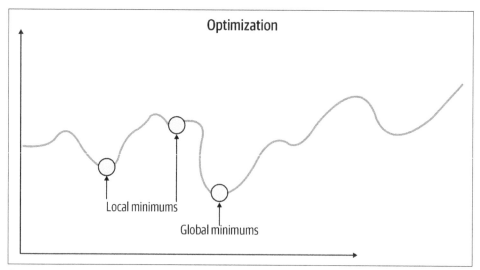

```
(.or) → or git:(master) ✗ ./greedy-random-tsp.py 25
Running simulation 25 times
Shortest Distance: 129
Optimal Route: [(b'WFC', b'URS', 0), (b'URS', b'GPS', 1), (b'GPS', b'PCG', 1), (b'PCG', b'MCK', 3), (b'MCK', b'SFO',
16), (b'SFO', b'ORCL', 20), (b'ORCL', b'HPQ', 12), (b'HPQ', b'GOOG', 6), (b'GOOG', b'AAPL', 11), (b'AAPL', b'INTC', 8
), (b'INTC', b'CSCO', 6), (b'CSCO', b'EBAY', 0), (b'EBAY', b'SWY', 32), (b'SWY', b'CVX', 13)]
(.or) → or git:(master) ✗ ./greedy-random-tsp.py 1
Running simulation 1 times
Shortest Distance: 143
Optimal Route: [(b'CSCO', b'EBAY', 0), (b'EBAY', b'INTC', 6), (b'INTC', b'AAPL', 8), (b'AAPL', b'GOOG', 14), (b'GOOG'
, b'HPQ', 6), (b'HPQ', b'ORCL', 12), (b'ORCL', b'SFO', 20), (b'SFO', b'MCK', 16), (b'MCK', b'WFC', 2), (b'WFC', b'URS
', 0), (b'URS', b'GPS', 1), (b'GPS', b'PCG', 1), (b'PCG', b'CVX', 44), (b'CVX', b'SWY', 13)]
(.or) → or git:(master) ✗
```

Figure 2-11. TSP simulation

Optimization is part of our lives, and we use greedy algorithms to solve everyday problems because they are intuitive. Optimization is also at the core of how machine learning works using gradient descent. A machine learning problem iteratively walks toward a local or global minimum using the gradient descent algorithm, as shown in Figure 2-12.

Figure 2-12. Optimization

Notes on Deep Learning Intuition

For MLOps, convergence, i.e., creating a model that finds a solution that won't be improved by adding more data, is an essential operational issue. For example, would a GPU-based training cluster allow faster convergence? Would a CPU-based training cluster offer lower costs? Operating costs could break a company or a project in the real world, and it is essential to both have an intuition for how optimization works and test it out in practice.

A valuable tool to enhance intuition about gradient descent is the TensorFlow Playground (*https://oreil.ly/2N9DI*). In particular, experimenting with the learning rate shows how too high a rate can lead to oscillation, as shown in Figure 2-13. Notice how the Test loss sticks at 0.984 because the learning rate is too high to use the gradient descent algorithm effectively. Likewise, if you set the learning rate too low, it may not reach the global minimum or will take too long to converge on the right solution.

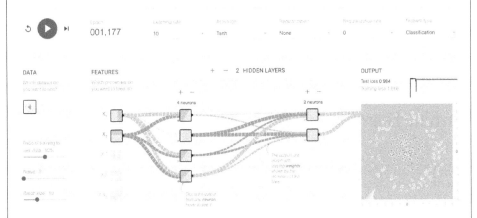

Figure 2-13. Learning rate too high

Mathematically this set of trade-offs shows up in Figure 2-14. The optimal learning rate converges on the global minimum, but too high leads to thrashing, as shown in the TensorFlow Playground example. Alternatively, too low can lead to getting stuck in a local minimum or taking too long to converge.

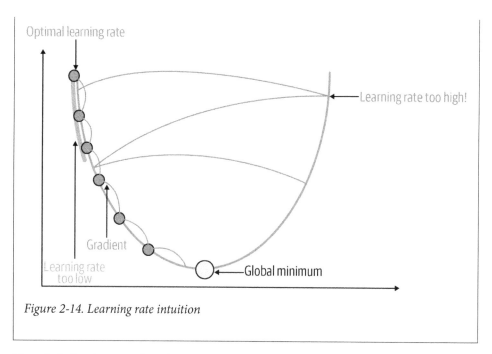

Figure 2-14. Learning rate intuition

Next, let's dive into machine learning core concepts.

Machine Learning Key Concepts

Machine learning is the ability for computers to perform tasks without explicit programming. They do this by "learning" from data. As discussed earlier, a good intuition would be a machine learning model that could predict weight based on height. It could "learn" from 25,000 observations and then give a prediction.

Machine learning involves three categories: supervised, unsupervised, and reinforcement learning. Supervised machine learning is when the "labels" are known, and the model learns from historical data. In the previous example, height and weight are labels. Additionally, the 25,000 observations are an example of historical data. Note that all machine learning requires data to be in a numerical form and requires scaling. Imagine if a friend bragged about running 50. What did they mean? Was it 50 miles or 50 feet? Magnitude is the reason for scaling data before processing a prediction.

Unsupervised machine learning works to "discover" labels. A good intuition of how this works is to consider an NBA season. In the visualization shown in Figure 2-15 from the 2015–2016 NBA season, the computer "learned" how to group the different NBA players. It is up to the domain expert, in this case, me, to select the appropriate labels. The algorithm was able to cluster groups, one of which I labeled the "best" players.

As a domain expert in basketball, I then added a label called "best." Another domain expert may disagree, though, and call these players "elite well-rounded" or some other label. Clustering is both an art and a science. Having a domain expert who understands the trade-offs for what to label a clustered dataset could make or break the usefulness of the unsupervised machine learning prediction.

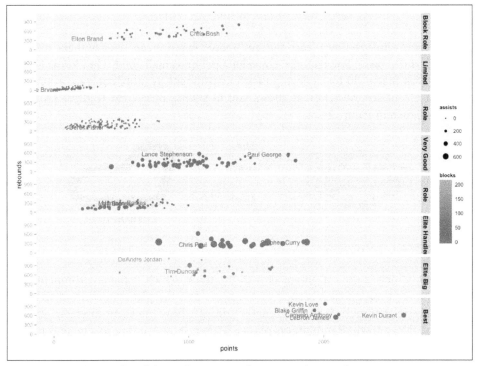

Figure 2-15. Clustered and faceted K-means clustering of NBA players

The computer grouped the data based on a comparison of four attributes: points, rebounds, blocks, and assists. Then, in multidimensional space, players with the lowest total distance from each other were grouped to form a label. This clustering algorithm is why LeBron James and Kevin Durant group together; they have similar metrics. Additionally, Steph Curry and Chris Paul are alike since they score many points and give out many assists.

A common dilemma with K-means clustering is how to select the correct number of clusters. This part of the problem is also an art and science problem as there isn't necessarily a perfect answer. One solution is to use a framework to create elbow plots for you, like Yellowbrick (*https://oreil.ly/wwu35*) for sklearn.

Another MLOps-style solution is to let the MLOps platform, say AWS Sagemaker, do the K-means cluster assignment through automated hyperparameter tuning (*https://oreil.ly/XKJc2*).

Finally, with reinforcement learning, an "agent" explores an environment to learn how to perform tasks. For example, consider a pet or a small child. They know how to interact with the world by exploring their environment. A more concrete example is the AWS DeepRacer system that allows you to train a model car to drive around a track, as shown in Figure 2-16.

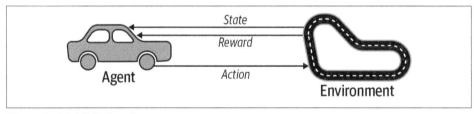

Figure 2-16. AWS DeepRacer

The agent, which is the car, interacts with the track, which is the environment. The vehicle moves through each section of the track, and the platform stores data about where it is on the track. A reward function decides how the agent interacts on each run through the track. Randomness plays a huge role in training this type of model, so different reward function strategies could yield different results.

The following is an example of a reward function in Python for AWS DeepRacer that rewards following the centerline:

```
def reward_function(params):
    '''
    Example of rewarding the agent for following the centerline
    '''

    # Read input parameters
    track_width = params['track_width']
    distance_from_center = params['distance_from_center']

    # Calculate 3 markers that are at varying distances away from the centerline
    marker_1 = 0.1 * track_width
    marker_2 = 0.25 * track_width
    marker_3 = 0.5 * track_width

    # Give higher reward if the car is closer to centerline and vice versa
```

```
    if distance_from_center <= marker_1:
        reward = 1.0
    elif distance_from_center <= marker_2:
        reward = 0.5
    elif distance_from_center <= marker_3:
        reward = 0.1
    else:
        reward = 1e-3  # likely crashed/ close to off track

    return float(reward)
```

Here is a different reward function that rewards the agent for staying inside the two borders of the track. This approach is similar to the previous reward function, yet it could yield dramatically different results:

```
def reward_function(params):
    '''
    Example of rewarding the agent for staying inside the two borders of the
    track
    '''

    # Read input parameters
    all_wheels_on_track = params['all_wheels_on_track']
    distance_from_center = params['distance_from_center']
    track_width = params['track_width']

    # Give a very low reward by default
    reward = 1e-3

    # Give a high reward if no wheels go off the track and
    # the agent is somewhere in between the track borders
    if all_wheels_on_track and (0.5*track_width - distance_from_center) >= 0.05:
        reward = 1.0

    # Always return a float value
    return float(reward)
```

Doing machine learning in production requires the foundational knowledge covered in this chapter, i.e., knowing which approach to use. For example, discovering labels through unsupervised machine learning can be invaluable to determining who are the best paying customers. Similarly, predicting the number of units that will sell next quarter can be accomplished through a supervised machine learning approach that takes the historical data and creates a prediction. So next, let's dive into the basics of data science.

Doing Data Science

Another foundational skill to master is "the data science way." I recommend creating the following formulaic structure in a notebook in classes I teach: *Ingest*, *EDA*, and *Modeling* and *Conclusion*. This structure allows anyone in a team to quickly toggle through different project sections to get a feel for it. In addition, for a model deployed to production, it is beneficial to have a notebook checked in alongside the code that deploys the model to serve as a *README* for thinking behind the project. You can see an example of this in Figure 2-17.

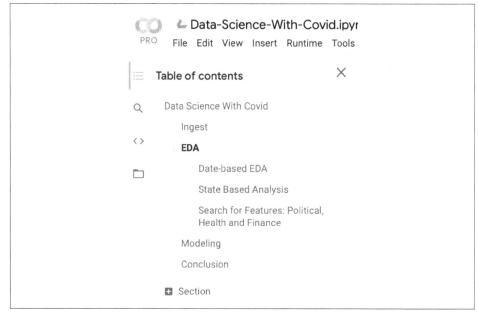

Figure 2-17. Colab notebook

You can see an example of this structure in the Colab notebook Data Science with Covid (*https://oreil.ly/1iQps*).

This clean breakdown of parts of the notebook means that each section can be a "chapter" in writing a data science book. The Ingest section benefits from data sources that load via a web request, i.e., feed directly to Pandas. The notebook data sources can be replicated by others using this approach, as shown in Figure 2-18.

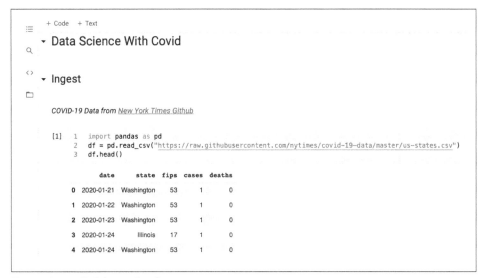

Figure 2-18. Colab notebook structure

The EDA section is for the exploration of ideas. What is going on with the data? This is the opportunity to find out, as the top Covid states show in the following chart using Plotly in Figure 2-19.

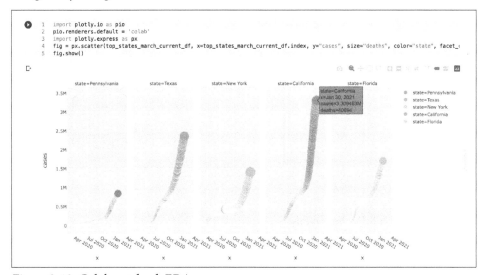

Figure 2-19. Colab notebook EDA

The Modeling section is where the model lives. Later, this repeatability can be critical since the MLOps pipeline may need to reference how the model creation occurred. For example, you can see an excellent example of a serialized sklearn model in this

Boston Housing Pickle Colab notebook (*https://oreil.ly/9XhWC*). Note that I test out how this model will eventually work in an API or cloud-based system, like this Flask ML deployment project. (*https://oreil.ly/6glox*)

The Conclusion section should be a summary for a business leader making the decision. Finally, check your project into GitHub to build your MLOps portfolio. The rigor in adding this additional documentation pays off as an ML project matures. Operations teams, in particular, may find it very valuable to understand the original thinking for why a model is in production and decide to remove the model from production since it no longer makes sense.

Next, let's discuss building an MLOps pipeline step by step.

Build an MLOps Pipeline from Zero

Let's put everything in this chapter together, and let's dive into Deploy Flask Machine Learning Application on Azure App Services. Notice in Figure 2-20 that GitHub events trigger a build from the Azure Pipelines build process, which then deploys the changes to a serverless platform. The names are different on other cloud platforms, but conceptionally things are very similar in both AWS and GCP.

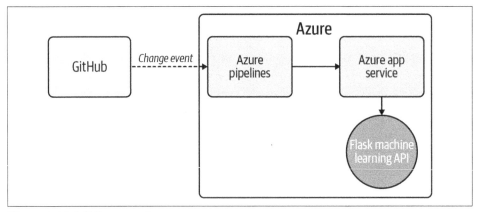

Figure 2-20. MLOps overview

To run it locally, follow these steps:

1. Create virtual environment and source:

```
python3 -m venv ~/.flask-ml-azure
source ~/.flask-ml-azure/bin/activate
```

2. Run make install.

3. Run `python app.py`.

4. In a separate shell, run `./make_prediction.sh`.

To run it in Azure Pipelines (refer to Azure Official Documentation guide (*https://oreil.ly/OLM8d*) throughout):

1. Launch Azure Shell as shown in Figure 2-21.

Figure 2-21. Launch Azure Cloud Shell

2. Create a GitHub repo with Azure Pipelines enabled (which could be a fork of this repo) as shown in Figure 2-22.

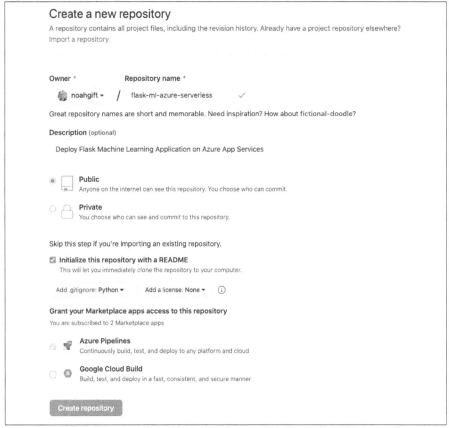

Figure 2-22. Create GitHub repo with Azure Pipelines

3. Clone the repo into Azure Cloud Shell.

 If you need more information on how to setup SSH keys, you can follow this YouTube video guide on how to setup SSH keys and configure cloud shell environment (*https://oreil.ly/ RJaWz*).

4. Create virtual environment and source:

```
python3 -m venv ~/.flask-ml-azure
source ~/.flask-ml-azure/bin/activate
```

5. Run `make install`.

6. Create an app service and initially deploy your app in Cloud Shell, as shown in Figure 2-23.

```
az webapp up -n <your-appservice>
```

Figure 2-23. Flask ML service

7. Verify the deployed application works by browsing to the deployed url: `https:// <your-appservice>.azurewebsites.net/`.

You will see the output as shown in Figure 2-24.

Sklearn Prediction Home

Figure 2-24. Flask deployed app

8. Verify machine learning predictions work, as shown in Figure 2-25.

Change the line in `make_predict_azure_app.sh` to match the deployed prediction `-X POST https://<yourappname>.azurewebsites.net:$PORT/predict`.

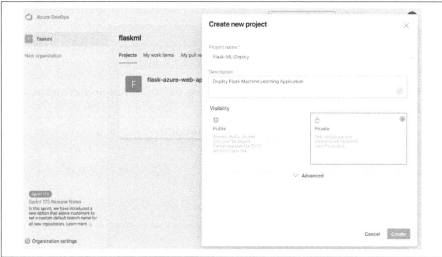

```
Bash        v   @  ?   @  []  []  {}  []                                              —  □  ×
{
    "URL": "http://flask-ml-service.azurewebsites.net",
    "appserviceplan": "noah_asp_Linux_centralus_0",
    "location": "centralus",
    "name": "flask-ml-service",
    "os": "Linux",
    "resourcegroup": "noah_rg_Linux_centralus",
    "runtime_version": "python|3.7",
    "runtime_version_detected": "-",
    "sku": "PREMIUMV2",
    "src_path": "//home//noah//flask-ml-azure-serverless"
}
(.flask-ml-azure) noah@Azure:~/flask-ml-azure-serverless$ ls
app.py  boston_housing_prediction.joblib  Makefile  make_predict_azure_app.sh  make_predict.sh  README.md  requirements.txt
(.flask-ml-azure) noah@Azure:~/flask-ml-azure-serverless$ vim make_predict_azure_app.sh
(.flask-ml-azure) noah@Azure:~/flask-ml-azure-serverless$ ./make_predict_azure_app.sh
Port: 443
{"prediction":[20.35373177134412]}
(.flask-ml-azure) noah@Azure:~/flask-ml-azure-serverless$
```

Figure 2-25. Successful prediction

9. Create an Azure DevOps project and connect to Azure (as official documentation describes (*https://oreil.ly/YmpSY*)), as shown in Figure 2-26.

Figure 2-26. Azure DevOps connection

10. Connect to Azure Resource Manager as shown in Figure 2-27.

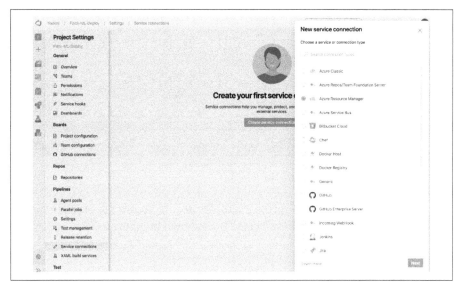

Figure 2-27. Service connector

11. Configure the connection to the previously deployed resource group as shown in Figure 2-28.

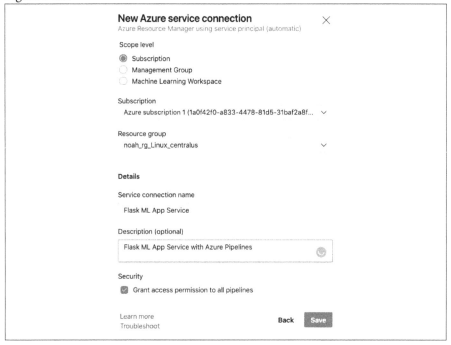

Figure 2-28. New service connection

12. Create a new Python pipeline with GitHub integration, as shown in Figure 2-29.

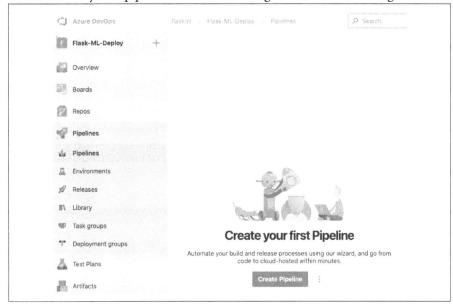

Figure 2-29. New Pipeline

Finally, set up the GitHub integration as shown in Figure 2-30.

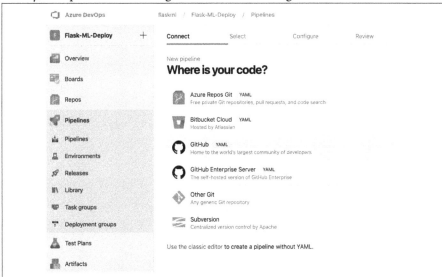

Figure 2-30. GitHub integration

This process will create a YAML file that looks roughly like the YAML output shown in the following code. Refer to the official Azure Pipeline YAML documentation (*https://oreil.ly/mU5rS*) for more information about it. This is the first part of the machine generated file:

```
# Python to Linux Web App on Azure
# Build your Python project and deploy it to Azure as a Linux Web App.
# Change python version to one thats appropriate for your application.
# https://docs.microsoft.com/azure/devops/pipelines/languages/python

trigger:
- master

variables:
  # Azure Resource Manager connection created during pipeline creation
  azureServiceConnectionId: 'df9170e4-12ed-498f-93e9-79c1e9b9bd59'

  # Web app name
  webAppName: 'flask-ml-service'

  # Agent VM image name
  vmImageName: 'ubuntu-latest'

  # Environment name
  environmentName: 'flask-ml-service'

  # Project root folder. Point to the folder containing manage.py file.
  projectRoot: $(System.DefaultWorkingDirectory)

  # Python version: 3.7
  pythonVersion: '3.7'

stages:
- stage: Build
  displayName: Build stage
  jobs:
  - job: BuildJob
    pool:
      vmImage: $(vmImageName)
    steps:
    - task: UsePythonVersion@0
      inputs:
        versionSpec: '$(pythonVersion)'
      displayName: 'Use Python $(pythonVersion)'

    - script: |
        python -m venv antenv
        source antenv/bin/activate
        python -m pip install --upgrade pip
        pip install setup
```

```
pip install -r requirements.txt
    workingDirectory: $(projectRoot)
```

13. Verify continuous delivery of Azure Pipelines by changing *app.py*.

    You can watch this YouTube Walkthrough of this process (*https://oreil.ly/3Qczi*).

14. Add a lint step (this gates your code against syntax failure):

```
- script: |
    python -m venv antenv
    source antenv/bin/activate
    make install
    make lint
  workingDirectory: $(projectRoot)
  displayName: 'Run lint tests'
```

 For a complete walkthrough of the code, you can watch the follow-ing YouTube walkthrough of this MLOps deployment process (*https://oreil.ly/I3si7*).

Conclusion

This chapter aimed to give you the foundational knowledge necessary to deploy machine learning into production, i.e., MLOps. One of the challenges of MLOps is how multidisciplinary the field is. When dealing with something inherently complex, a good approach starts small and gets the most basic solution working, then iterates from there.

It is also essential to be aware of foundational skills for an organization wishing to do MLOps. In particular, this means a team must know the basics of cloud computing, including the Linux terminal and how to navigate it. Likewise, a firm understanding of DevOps—i.e., how to set up and use CI/CD—is a required component to do MLOps. This final exercise is an excellent test of your skills before diving into more nuanced topics later in the book and pulls together all of these foundational compo-nents into a minimalist MLOps-style project.

In the next chapter, we'll dive into containers and edge devices. These are essential components of most MLOps platforms like AWS SageMaker or Azure ML Studio and build on the knowledge covered in this chapter.

Exercises

- Run a hello world Python GitHub project and check it out and run your tests on all three clouds: AWS, Azure, and GCP.

- Make a new Flask application that serves out a "hello world" type route using AWS Elastic Beanstalk you think other people would find helpful and put the code into a GitHub repo along with a screenshot of it serving out a request in the GitHub *README.md*. Then, create a continuous delivery process to deploy the Flask application using AWS CodeBuild.

- Fork this repository (*https://oreil.ly/IItEr*) that contains a Flask machine learning application and deploy it with continuous delivery on AWS using Elastic Beanstalk and Code Pipeline.

- Fork this repository (*https://oreil.ly/JSsEQ*) that contains a Flask machine learning application and deploy it with continuous delivery on GCP using Google App Engine and Cloud Build or Cloud Run and Cloud Build.

- Fork this repository (*https://oreil.ly/F2uBk*) that contains a Flask machine learning application and deploy it with continuous delivery on Azure using Azure App Services and Azure DevOps Pipelines.

- Use the Traveling Salesman code example and port it to work with coordinates you grab from an API, say all of the best restaurants in a city you want to visit. You will never think about vacation the same again.

- Using the TensorFlow Playground (*https://oreil.ly/ojebX*), experiment with changing the hyperparameters across different datasets as well as problem types. Can you identify optimal configurations of hidden layers, learning rate, and regularization rate for different datasets?

Critical Thinking Discussion Questions

- A company specializing in GPU databases has a key technical member advocating they *stop* using the cloud because it would be much more practical to buy their GPU hardware since they run it 24/7. This step would also allow them to get access to specialized GPUs much more quickly than they are available. On the other hand, another critical technical member who has *all* of the AWS certifications has promised to get him fired if he dares to try. He claims that they have already invested too much into AWS. Argue for or against this proposal.

- A "Red Hat Certified Engineer" has built one of the most successful data centers in the Southeast for a company with only 100 employees. Even though the company is an e-commerce company and not a cloud company, he claims this gives the company a huge advantage.

On the other hand, a "Google Certified Architect" and "Duke Data Science Masters" graduate claims the company is in a risky position by using a data center they own. They point out that the company keeps losing data center engineers for Google and has no disaster recovery plan or fault tolerance. Argue for or against this proposal.

- What are the key technical differences between AWS Lambda and AWS Elastic Beanstalk including the pros and cons of each solution?

- Why would a managed file service like EFS on AWS or Google Filestore be helpful in a real-world MLOps workflow in corporate America?

- Kaizen starts with a simple question: can we do better? If so, what should we do to get better this week or today? Finally, how can we apply Kaizen to our machine learning projects?

## CHAPTER 3

MLOps for Containers and Edge Devices

By Alfredo Deza

Split-brain experiments started with the problem of interocular transfer. That is, if one learns with one eye how to solve a problem, then with that eye covered and using the other eye, one readily solves the problem without further learning. This is called "interocular transfer of learning." Of course, the learning is not in the eye and then transferred to the other eye, but that is the way it is usually described. The fact that transfer occurs may seem obvious, but it is in the questioning of the obvious that discoveries are often produced. In this case, the question was: How can the learning with one eye appear with use of the other? Put in experimentally testable terms, where are the two eyes connected? Experiments showed that the transfer actually occurs between the hemispheres by way of the corpus callosum.

—Dr. Joseph Bogen

When I started in technology, virtual machines (virtualized servers hosted in a physical machine), were well positioned and pervasive—it was easy to find them everywhere, from hosting providers to regular companies with big servers in the IT room. A lot of online software providers were offering virtualized hosting. At work, I honed my skills, trying to learn as much as possible about virtualization. The ability to run virtual machines within some other host offered a lot of (welcomed) flexibility.

Whenever a new technology solves a problem (or any number of issues really), a trail of other problems tags along to be resolved. With virtual machines, one of these problems was to deal with moving them around. If host server *A* needed to have a new operating system installed, a system administrator would need to move the virtual machines over to host server *B*. Virtual machines were as large as the data when initially configured: a 50 GB *virtual drive* meant a file representing the virtual drive existed at 50 gigabytes. Moving around 50 gigabytes from one server to the other would take time. If you are moving around a critical service running a virtual machine, how can you minimize downtime?

Most of these issues had their strategies to minimize downtime and increase robustness: snapshots, recovery, backups. Software projects like the *Xen Project* and *VMWare* specialized in making these issues relatively easy to solve, and cloud providers practically eliminated them.

These days, virtual machines still have an important place in cloud offerings. Google Cloud calls them *Compute Engine*, for example, and other providers have a similar reference. A lot of these virtual machines offer enhanced GPUs to provide better performance targeted at machine learning operations.

Although virtual machines are here to stay, it is increasingly important to grasp two types of technologies for model deployments: containers and edge devices. It is unreasonable to think that a virtual machine would be well suited to run on an edge device (like a cellphone) or quickly iterate during development with a reproducible set of files. You will not always face a decision of using one or the other, but possessing a clear understanding of these options (and how they operate) will make you a better machine learning engineer.

Containers

With all the power and robustness of virtual machines, it is critical to grasp containers and containerization technology in general. I remember being in the audience at PyCon in Santa Clara in 2013, when Docker was announced. It felt incredible! The *lean virtualization* demoed was not new for Linux. What was new and sort of revolutionary was the tooling. Linux has had *LXC* (or *Linux containers*), which provided a lot of the functionality we take for granted with containers today. But the tooling for LXC is dismal, and Docker brought one key factor to successfully become a leader: easy collaboration and sharing through a registry.

Registries allow any developer to *push* their changes to a central location where others can then *pull* those changes and run them locally. Registry support with the same tooling that deals with containers (and all seamlessly) propelled the technology forward at an incredible pace.

 For this section, make sure you have a container runtime installed. For the examples in this section, it might be easier to use Docker (*https://oreil.ly/iEX4x*). After installation, ensure that the docker command will show the help output to verify a successful install.

One of the most significant descriptions (*https://oreil.ly/SQUjS*) I've seen about containers in comparison to virtual machines comes from Red Hat. In short, containers are all about the application itself, and only what the application is (like the source code and other supporting files) versus what it needs to run (like databases).

Traditionally, engineers often use virtual machines like an all-in-one service where the database, the web server, and any other system service are installed, configured, and run. These types of applications are *monolithic*, with tied interdependencies in an all-in-one machine.

A *microservice*, on the other hand, is an application that is fully decoupled from system requirements like databases and can run independently. Although you can use virtual machines as microservices, it is more common to find containers fitting better in that concept.

If you are already familiar with creating and running containers, in "Infrastructure as Code for Continuous Delivery of ML Models" on page 99 I cover how to build them programmatically with pretrained models, which takes these concepts and enhances them with automation.

Container Runtime

You might've noticed that I've mentioned containers, Docker, and container runtime. These terms might get confusing, primarily when people use them interchangeably. Since Docker (the company) initially developed the tooling to create, manage, and run containers, it became common to say "Docker container." The runtime—that is, the required software to run a container in a system—was also created by Docker. A few years after the new container technology's initial release, Red Hat (the company behind the RHEL operating system) contributed to making a different way to run containers, with a new (alternative) runtime environment. This new environment also brought a new set of tools to operate containers, with some compatibility with those provided by Docker. If you ever hear about container runtime, you have to be aware that there is more than one.

Some benefits of these new tools and runtime mean that you are no longer required to use a superuser account with extensive privileges, which makes sense for many different use cases. Although Red Hat and many other open source contributors have done an excellent job with these tools, it is still somewhat complicated to run them in operating systems that aren't Linux. On the other hand, Docker makes the work a seamless experience regardless of whether you are using Windows, MacOS, or Linux. Let's get started by going through all the steps needed to create a container.

Creating a Container

The *Dockerfile* is at the heart of creating containers. Anytime you are creating a container, you must have the Dockerfile present in the current directory. This special file can have several sections and commands that allow creating a container image. Open a new file and name it *Dockerfile* and add the following contents to it:

```
FROM centos:8

RUN dnf install -y python38
```

The file has two sections; a unique keyword delimits each one. These keywords are known as *instructions*. The beginning of the file uses the `FROM` instruction, which determines what the base for the container is. The *base* (also referred to as *base image*) is the CentOS distribution at version 8. The version, in this case, is a tag. Tags in containers define a point in time. When there are no tags defined, the default is the *latest* tag. It is common to see versions used as tags, as is the case in this example.

One of the many useful aspects of containers is that they can be composed of many layers, and these layers can be used or reused in other containers. This layering workflow prevents a base layer of 10 megabytes from getting downloaded every time for each container that uses it. In practice, you will download the 10 megabyte layer once and reuse it many times. This is *very* different from virtual machines, where it doesn't matter if these virtual machines all have the same files: you are still required to download them all as a whole.

Next, the `RUN` instruction runs a system command. This system command installs Python 3, which isn't included in the base CentOS 8 image. Note how the `dnf` command uses the `-y` flag, which prevents a prompt for confirmation by the installer, triggered when building the container. It is crucial to avoid any prompts from running commands as it would halt the build.

Now build the container from the same directory where the *Dockerfile* is:

```
$ docker build .
[+] Building 11.2s (6/6) FINISHED
 => => transferring context: 2B
 => => transferring dockerfile: 83B
 => CACHED [1/2] FROM docker.io/library/centos:8
 => [2/2] RUN dnf install -y python38
 => exporting to image
 => => exporting layers
 => => writing
image sha256:3ca470de8dbd5cb865da679ff805a3bf17de9b34ac6a7236dbf0c367e1fb4610
```

The output reports that I already have the initial layer for CentOS 8, so there is no need to pull it again. Then, it installs Python 3.8 to complete image creation. Make sure you start a build pointing to where the *Dockerfile* is present. In this case, I'm in the same directory, so I use a dot to let the build know that the current directory is the one to build from.

This way of building images is not very robust and has a few problems. First, it is challenging to identify this image later. All we have is the sha256 digest to reference it and nothing else. To see some information about the image just built, rerun `docker`:

```
$ docker images
docker images
REPOSITORY     TAG       IMAGE ID        CREATED          SIZE
<none>         <none>    3ca470de8dbd    15 minutes ago   294MB
```

There is no repository or tag associated with it. The image ID is the digest, which gets reduced to only 12 characters. This image is going to be challenging to deal with if it doesn't have additional metadata. It is a good practice to tag it when building the image. This is how you create the same image and tag it:

```
$ docker build -t localbuild:removeme .
[+] Building 0.3s (6/6) FINISHED
[...]
 => => writing
image sha256:4c5d79f448647e0ff234923d8f542eea6938e0199440dfc75b8d7d0d10d5ca9a
 => => naming to docker.io/library/localbuild:removeme
```

The critical difference is that now localbuild has a tag of removeme and it will show up when listing the images:

```
$ docker images localbuild
REPOSITORY      TAG          IMAGE ID        CREATED          SIZE
localbuild      removeme     3ca470de8dbd    22 minutes ago   294MB
```

Since the image didn't change at all, the build process was speedy, and internally, the build system tagged the already built image. The naming and tagging of images helps when pushing the image to a registry. I would need to own the *localbuild* repository to push to it. Since I don't, the push will get denied:

```
$ docker push localbuild:removeme
The push refers to repository [docker.io/library/localbuild]
denied: requested access to the resource is denied
```

However, if I re-tag the container to my repository in the registry, pushing will work. To re-tag, I first need to reference the original tag (localbuild:removeme) and then use my registry account and destination (alfredodeza/removeme):

```
$ docker tag localbuild:removeme alfredodeza/removeme
$ docker push alfredodeza/removeme
The push refers to repository [docker.io/alfredodeza/removeme]
958488a3c11e: Pushed
291f6e44771a: Pushed
latest: digest: sha256:a022eea71ca955cafb4d38b12c28b9de59dbb3d9fcb54b size: 741
```

Going to the registry (*https://hub.docker.com*) (in this case, Docker Hub) now shows that the recently pushed image is available (Figure 3-1).

Since my account is open and the registry is not restricting access, anyone can "pull" the container image by running: docker pull alfredodeza/removeme. If you've not been exposed to containers or registries before, this should feel revolutionary. Like I mentioned at the beginning of this chapter, it is the foundation of why containers went viral in the developer community. The answer to *"How do I install your software?"* can now be *"just pull the container"* for almost anything.

Figure 3-1. Docker Hub image

Running a Container

Now that the container builds with the *Dockerfile*, we can run it. When running virtual machines, it was common practice to enable the SSH (also known as the Secure Shell) daemon and expose a port for remote access, and perhaps even add default SSH keys to prevent getting password prompts. People who aren't used to running a container will probably ask for SSH access to a running container instance. SSH access is not needed; even though you can enable it and make it work, it is not how to access a running container.

Make sure that a container is running. In this example, I run CentOS 8:

```
$ docker run -ti -d --name centos-test --rm centos:8 /bin/bash
1bb9cc3112ed661511663517249898bfc9524fc02dedc3ce40b5c4cb982d7bcd
```

There are several new flags in this command. It uses `-ti` to allocate a TTY (emulates a terminal) and attaches `stdin` to it to interact with it in the terminal later. Next, the `-d` flag makes the container run in the background to prevent taking control of the current terminal. I assign a name (`centos-test`) and then use `--rm` so that Docker removes this container after stopping it. After issuing the command, a digest returns, indicating that the container has started. Now, verify it is running:

```
$ docker ps
CONTAINER ID      IMAGE         COMMAND          NAMES
1bb9cc3112ed      centos:8      "/bin/bash"      centos-test
```

Some containers get created with an `ENTRYPOINT` (and optionally a `CMD`) instruction. These instructions are meant to get the container up and running for a specific task. In the example container we just built for CentOS, the `/bin/bash` executable had to be specified because otherwise the container would not stay running. These instructions mean that if you want a long-running container, you should create it with at least an ENTRYPOINT that executes a program. Update the *Dockerfile* so that it looks like this:

```
FROM centos:8

RUN dnf install -y python38

ENTRYPOINT ["/bin/bash"]
```

Now it is possible to run the container in the background without the need to specify the /bin/bash command:

```
$ docker build -t localbuild:removeme .
$ docker run --rm -it -d localbuild:removeme
023c8e67d91f3bb3998e7ac1b9b335fe20ca13f140b6728644fd45fb6ccb9132
$ docker ps
CONTAINER ID      IMAGE         COMMAND          NAMES
023c8e67d91f      removeme      "/bin/bash"      romantic_khayyam
```

I mentioned before how it is common to use SSH to gain access to a virtual machine and that gaining access to a container is somewhat different. Although you could enable SSH for a container (in theory), I don't recommend it. This is how you can get access to a running container using the container ID and the exec subcommand:

```
$ docker exec -it 023c8e67d91f bash

[root@023c8e67d91f /]# whoami
root
```

In that case, I have to use the command I want to run. Since I want to interactively manipulate the container (as I would with a virtual machine), I call out the executable for the Bash (a ubiquitous Unix shell and command language) program.

Alternatively, you may not want to gain access using an interactive shell environment, and all you want to do is run some command. The command must change to achieve this. Replace the shell executable used in the previous example with that of the command to use:

```
$ docker exec 023c8e67d91f tail /var/log/dnf.log

    python38-setuptools-wheel-41.6.0-4.module_el8.2.0+317+61fa6e7d.noarch

2020-12-02T13:00:04Z INFO Complete!
2020-12-02T13:00:04Z DDEBUG Cleaning up.
```

Since there is no interactive need (I'm not sending any input via a shell), I can omit the -it flag.

One common aspect of container development is to keep its size as small as possible. That is why a CentOS container will have a lot fewer packages than that of a newly installed CentOS virtual machine. This leads to surprising experiences when you expect a package to be present (e.g., a text editor like Vim) and it isn't.

Best Practices

The first thing I do (and highly recommend) when trying a new language or tool is to find a linter that can help navigate conventions and common usage that I may not be familiar with. There are a few linters for creating containers with a Dockerfile. One of these linters is hadolint. It is conveniently packaged as a container. Modify the last *Dockerfile* example, so it looks like this:

```
FROM centos:8

RUN dnf install -y python38

RUN pip install pytest

ENTRYPOINT ["/bin/bash"]
```

Now run the linter to see if there are any good suggestions:

```
$ docker run --rm -i hadolint/hadolint < Dockerfile
DL3013 Pin versions in pip.
    Instead of `pip install <package>` use `pip install <package>==<version>`
```

This is a good suggestion. Pinning packages is always a great idea because you are safe from an update in a dependency being incompatible with the code your application needs. Be aware that pinning dependencies and never going through the chore of updating them isn't a great idea. Make sure you come back to pinned dependencies and see if it would be useful to update.

Since one of the goals of containerizing tools is to keep them as small as possible, you can accomplish a couple of things when creating a Dockerfile. Every time there is a RUN instruction, a new layer gets created with that execution. Containers consist of individual layers, so the fewer the number of layers, the smaller the container's size. This means that it is preferable to use a single line to install many dependencies instead of one:

```
RUN apk add --no-cache python3 && python3 -m ensurepip && pip3 install pytest
```

The use of && at the end of each command chains everything together, creating a single layer. If the previous example had a separate RUN instruction for each install command, the container would end up being larger. Perhaps for this particular example, the size wouldn't make that much of a difference; however, it would be significant in containers that require lots of dependencies.

There is a useful option that linting can offer: the opportunity to automate the linting. Be on the lookout for chances to automate processes, removing any manual step and letting you concentrate on the essential pieces of the process of shipping models into production (writing a good Dockerfile in this case).

Another critical piece of building containers is making sure there aren't vulnerabilities associated with the software installed. It is not uncommon to find engineers who think that the application is unlikely to have vulnerabilities because they write high-quality code. The problem is that a container comes with preinstalled libraries. It is a full operating system that, at build time, will pull extra dependencies to satisfy the application you are trying to deliver. If you are going to serve a trained model from the container using a web framework like Flask, you have to be well aware that there might be Common Vulnerabilities and Exposures (CVEs) associated with either Flask or one of its dependencies.

These are the dependencies that Flask (at version `1.1.2`) brings:

```
click==7.1.2
itsdangerous==1.1.0
Jinja2==2.11.2
MarkupSafe==1.1.1
Werkzeug==1.0.1
```

CVEs can get reported at any given time, and software systems used to alert on vulnerabilities ensure they are updated several times during the day to report accurately when that happens. A critical piece of your application like Flask may not be vulnerable today for version 1.1.2, but it can undoubtedly be tomorrow morning when a new CVE is discovered and reported. Many different solutions specialize in scanning and reporting vulnerabilities in containers to mitigate these vulnerabilities. These security tools scan a library that your application installs and the operating system's packages, providing a detailed and accurate vulnerability report.

One solution that is very fast and easy to install is Anchore's `grype` command line tool. To install it on a Macintosh computer:

```
$ brew tap anchore/grype
$ brew install grype
```

Or on any Linux machine:

```
$ curl -sSfL \
  https://raw.githubusercontent.com/anchore/grype/main/install.sh | sh -s
```

Using `curl` in this way allows deploying `grype` into most any continuous integration system to scan for vulnerabilities. The `curl` installation method will place the executable in the current working path under a *bin/* directory. After installation is complete, run it against a container:

```
$ grype python:3.8
✓ Vulnerability DB      [no update available]
.: Loading image        ────────────────────── [requesting image from docker]
✓ Loaded image
✓ Parsed image
✓ Cataloged image       [433 packages]
✓ Scanned image         [1540 vulnerabilities]
```

Over a thousand vulnerabilities look somewhat surprising. The output is too long to capture here, so filter the result to check for vulnerabilities with a severity of *High*:

```
$ grype python:3.8 | grep High
[...]
python2.7     2.7.16-2+deb10u1     CVE-2020-8492     High
```

There were a few vulnerabilities reported, so I reduced the output to just one. The CVE (*https://oreil.ly/6Q1O2*) is worrisome because it can potentially allow the system to crash if an attacker exploits the vulnerability. Since I know the application uses Python 3.8, then this container is not vulnerable because Python 2.7 is unused. Although this is a Python 3.8 container, the image contains an older version for convenience. The critical difference is that now you know what is vulnerable and can make an executive decision for the eventual deployment of the service to production.

A useful automation enhancement is to fail on a specific vulnerability level, such as high:

```
$ grype --fail-on=high centos:8
[...]
discovered vulnerabilities at or above the severity threshold!
```

This is another check that you can automate along with linting for robust container building. A well-written *Dockerfile* with constant reporting on vulnerabilities is an excellent way to enhance containerized models' production delivery.

Serving a Trained Model Over HTTP

Now that a few of the core concepts of creating a container are clear, let's create a container that will serve a trained model over an HTTP API using the Flask web framework. As you already know, everything starts with the Dockerfile, so create one, assuming for now that a *requirements.txt* file is present in the current working directory:

```
FROM python:3.7

ARG VERSION

LABEL org.label-schema.version=$VERSION

COPY ./requirements.txt /webapp/requirements.txt
```

```
WORKDIR /webapp

RUN pip install -r requirements.txt

COPY webapp/* /webapp

ENTRYPOINT [ "python" ]

CMD [ "app.py" ]
```

There are a few new things in this file that I have not covered before. First, we define
an argument called VERSION that gets used as a variable for a LABEL. I'm using a label
schema convention (*https://oreil.ly/PtOSK*) that is useful to normalize how these
labels are named. Using a version is a helpful way of adding informational metadata
about the container itself. I will use this label later when I want to identify the version
of the trained model. Imagine a situation where a container is not producing
expected accuracy from a model; adding a label helps identify the problematic model's version. Although this file uses one label, you can imagine that the more labels
with descriptive data, the better.

There is a slight difference in the container image used. This build
uses Python 3.7 because at the time of writing, some of the dependencies do not work yet with Python 3.8. Feel free to swap 3.7 for
3.8 and check if it now works.

Next, a *requirements.txt* file gets copied into the container. Create the requirements
file with the following dependencies:

```
Flask==1.1.2
pandas==0.24.2
scikit-learn==0.20.3
```

Now, create a new directory called *webapp* so that the web files are contained in one
place, and add the *app.py* file so that it looks like this:

```
from flask import Flask, request, jsonify

import pandas as pd
from sklearn.externals import joblib
from sklearn.preprocessing import StandardScaler

app = Flask(__name__)

def scale(payload):
    scaler = StandardScaler().fit(payload)
    return scaler.transform(payload)

@app.route("/")
def home():
```

```
        return "<h3>Sklearn Prediction Container</h3>"

@app.route("/predict", methods=['POST'])
def predict():
    """
    Input sample:

        {
            "CHAS": { "0": 0 }, "RM": { "0": 6.575 },
            "TAX": { "0": 296 }, "PTRATIO": { "0": 15.3 },
            "B": { "0": 396.9 }, "LSTAT": { "0": 4.98 }
        }

    Output sample:

        { "prediction": [ 20.35373177134412 ] }
    """

    clf = joblib.load("boston_housing_prediction.joblib")
    inference_payload = pd.DataFrame(request.json)
    scaled_payload = scale(inference_payload)
    prediction = list(clf.predict(scaled_payload))
    return jsonify({'prediction': prediction})

if __name__ == "__main__":
    app.run(host='0.0.0.0', port=5000, debug=True)
```

The last file needed is the trained model. If you are training the Boston Housing pre‐
diction dataset, make sure to place it within the *webapp* directory along with the
app.py file and name it *boston_housing_prediction.joblib*. You can also find a trained
version of the model in this GitHub repository (*https://oreil.ly/ibjG0*).

The final structure of the project should look like this:

```
.
├── Dockerfile
└── webapp
    ├── app.py
    └── boston_housing_prediction.joblib

1 directory, 3 files
```

Now build the container. In the example, I will use the run ID that Azure gave me
when I trained the model as the version to make it easier to identify where the model
came from. Feel free to use a different version (or no version at all if you don't need
one):

```
$ docker build --build-arg VERSION=AutoML_287f444c -t flask-predict .
[+] Building 27.1s (10/10) FINISHED
 => => transferring dockerfile: 284B
 => [1/5] FROM docker.io/library/python:3.7
 => => resolve docker.io/library/python:3.7
```

```
=> [internal] load build context
=> => transferring context: 635B
=> [2/5] COPY ./requirements.txt /webapp/requirements.txt
=> [3/5] WORKDIR /webapp
=> [4/5] RUN pip install -r requirements.txt
=> [5/5] COPY webapp/* /webapp
=> exporting to image
=> => writing image sha256:5487a63442aae56d9ea30fa79b0c7eed1195824aad7ff4ab42b
=> => naming to docker.io/library/flask-predict
```

Double-check that the image is now available after building:

```
$ docker images flask-predict
REPOSITORY       TAG       IMAGE ID       CREATED         SIZE
flask-predict    latest    5487a63442aa   6 minutes ago   1.15GB
```

Now run the container in the background, exposing port 5000, and verify it is running:

```
$ docker run -p 5000:5000 -d --name flask-predict flask-predict
d95ab6581429ea79495150bea507f009203f7bb117906b25ffd9489319219281
$docker ps
CONTAINER ID IMAGE          COMMAND         STATUS         PORTS
d95ab6581429 flask-predict "python app.py" Up 2 seconds 0.0.0.0:5000->5000/tcp
```

On your browser, open *http://localhost:5000* and the HTML from the home() function should welcome you to the Sklearn Prediction application. Another way to verify this is wired up correctly is using curl:

```
$ curl 192.168.0.200:5000
<h3>Sklearn Prediction Container</h3>
```

You can use any tool that can send information over HTTP and process a response back. This example uses a few lines of Python with the requests library (make sure you install it before running it) to send a POST request with the sample JSON data:

```
import requests
import json

url = "http://localhost:5000/predict"

data = {
    "CHAS": {"0": 0},
    "RM": {"0": 6.575},
    "TAX": {"0": 296.0},
    "PTRATIO": {"0": 15.3},
    "B": {"0": 396.9},
    "LSTAT": {"0": 4.98},
}

# Convert to JSON string
input_data = json.dumps(data)
```

```
# Set the content type
headers = {"Content-Type": "application/json"}

# Make the request and display the response
resp = requests.post(url, input_data, headers=headers)
print(resp.text)
```

Write the Python code to a file and call it *predict.py*. Execute the script to get some predictions back on the terminal:

```
$ python predict.py
{
  "prediction": [
    20.35373177134412
  ]
}
```

Containerizing deployments is an excellent way to create portable data that can be tried by others. By sharing a container, the friction of setting up the environment is greatly reduced while ensuring a repeatable system to interact with. Now that you know how to create, run, debug, and deploy containers for ML, you can leverage this to start automating noncontainerized environments to speed up production deployments and enhance the whole process's robustness. Aside from containers, there is a push to get services closer to the user, and that is what I will get into next with edge devices and deployments.

Edge Devices

The computational cost of (fast) inferencing was astronomical a few years ago. Some of the more advanced capabilities of machine learning that are available today were cost-prohibitive not long ago. Not only have costs gone down, but more powerful chips are getting produced. Some of these chips are explicitly tailored for ML tasks. The right combination of needed features for these chips allows inferencing in devices like mobile phones: fast, small, and made for ML tasks. When "deploying to the edge" is mentioned in technology, it refers to compute devices that are not within a data center along with thousands of other servers. Mobile phones, Raspberry PI, and smart home devices are some examples that fit the description of an "edge device." In the last few years, large telecommunication companies have been pushing toward edge computing. Most of these edge deployments want to get faster feedback to users instead of routing expensive compute requests to a remote data center.

The general idea is that the closer the computational resources are to the user, the faster the user experience will be. There is a fine line that divides what may land at the edge versus what should go all the way to the data center and back. But, as I've mentioned, specialized chips are getting smaller, faster, and more effective; it makes sense to predict that the future means more ML at the edge. And the edge, in this case, will mean more and more devices that we previously didn't think could handle ML tasks.

Most people living in countries with plenty of data centers hosting application data do not experience much lag at all. For those countries that do not, the problem is exacerbated. For example, Peru has several submarine cables that connect it to other countries in South America but no direct connectivity to the US. This means that if you are uploading a picture from Peru to a service that hosts its application in a data center in the US, it will take exponentially longer than a country like Panama with multiple cables going back to North America. This example of uploading a picture is trivial but gets even worse when computational operations like ML predictions are done on the sent data. This section explores a few different ways on how edge devices can help by performing fast inferencing done as close to the user as possible. If long distances are a problem, imagine what happens when there is no (or very limited) connectivity like a remote farm. If you need fast inferencing done in a remote location, the options are limited, and this is where the *deploying to the edge* has an advantage over any data center.

Remember, users don't care that much about the spoon: they are interested in having a seamless way to try the delicious soup.

Coral

The Coral Project (*https://coral.ai*) is a platform that helps build local (on-device) inferencing that captures the essence of edge deployments: fast, close to the user, and offline. In this section, I'll cover the USB Accelerator (*https://oreil.ly/id47e*), which is an edge device that supports all major operating systems and works well with Tensor-Flow Lite models. You can compile most TensorFlow Lite models to run on this edge TPU (Tensor Processing Unit). Some aspects of operationalization of ML mean being aware of device support, installation methods, and compatibility. Those three aspects are true about the Coral Edge TPU: it works on most operating systems, with Tensor-Flow Lite models as long as they can get compiled to run on the TPU.

If you are tasked to deploy a fast inferencing solution at the edge on a remote location, you must ensure that all the pieces necessary for such a deployment will work correctly. This core concept of DevOps is covered throughout this book: repeatable deployment methods that create reproducible environments are critical. To ensure that is the case, you must be aware of compatibility.

First, start by installing the TPU runtime. For my machine, this means downloading and unzipping a file to run the installer script:

```
$ curl -O https://dl.google.com/coral/edgetpu_api/edgetpu_runtime_20201204.zip
[...]
$ unzip edgetpu_runtime_20201204.zip
Archive:  edgetpu_runtime_20201204.zip
   creating: edgetpu_runtime/
  inflating: edgetpu_runtime/install.sh
[...]
```

```
$ cd edgetpu_runtime
$ sudo bash install.sh
Password:
[...]
Installing Edge TPU runtime library [/usr/local/lib]...
Installing Edge TPU runtime library symlink [/usr/local/lib]...
```

 These setup examples use a Macintosh computer, so some of the installation methods and dependencies will vary from other operating systems. Check the getting started guide (*https://oreil.ly/B16Za*) if you need support for a different computer.

Now that the runtime dependencies are installed in the system, we are ready to try the edge TPU. The Coral team has a useful repository with Python3 code that helps run image classification with a single command. Create a directory to clone the contents of the repository to set up the workspace for image classification:

```
$ mkdir google-coral && cd google-coral
$ git clone https://github.com/google-coral/tflite --depth 1
[...]
Resolving deltas: 100% (4/4), done.
$ cd tflite/python/examples/classification
```

 The `git` command uses a `--depth 1` flag, which performs a shallow clone. A shallow clone is desirable when the complete contents of the repository are not needed. Since this example is using the latest changes of the repository, there is no need to perform a full clone that contains a complete repository history.

For this example, do not run the *install_requirements.sh* script. First, make sure you have Python3 available and installed in your system and use it to create a new virtual environment; make sure that after activation, the Python interpreter points to the virtual environment and not the system Python:

```
$ python3 -m venv venv
$ source venv/bin/activate
$ which python
~/google-coral/tflite/python/examples/classification/venv/bin/python
```

Now that the *virtualenv* is active, install the two library dependencies and the TensorFlow Lite runtime support:

```
$ pip install numpy Pillow
$ pip install https://github.com/google-coral/pycoral/releases/download/\
release-frogfish/tflite_runtime-2.5.0-cp38-cp38-macosx_10_15_x86_64.whl
```

Both *numpy* and *Pillow* are straightforward to get installed in most systems. The outlier is the very long link that follows. This link is crucial to have, and it has to match your platform and architecture. Without that library, it is not possible to interact with the Coral device. The Python installation guide for TensorFlow Lite (*https://oreil.ly/ VjFoS*) is the right source to double-check what link you need to use for your platform.

Now that you have everything installed and ready to perform the image classification, run the *classify_image.py* script to get the help menu. Bringing back the help menu, in this case, is an excellent way to verify all dependencies were installed and that the script works correctly:

```
usage:
   classify_image.py [-h] -m MODEL -i INPUT [-l LABELS] [-k TOP_K] [-c COUNT]
classify_image.py:
   error: the following arguments are required: -m/--model, -i/--input
```

Since I didn't define any flags when I called the script, an error returned, mentioning that I do need to pass some flags. Before we start using the other flags, we need to retrieve a TensorFlow model to work with an image to test it.

The Coral AI site (*https://oreil.ly/VZAun*) has a models section where you can browse some of the specialized pretrained models it has for doing some image classification. Find the *iNat insects* one that recognizes over a thousand different types of insects. Download both the *tflite* model and the labels.

For this example, download a sample image of a common fly. The original source of the image is on Pixabay (*https://oreil.ly/UFfxq*), but it is also conveniently accessible in the GitHub repository for this book (*https://oreil.ly/NHNIN*).

Create directories for the model, labels, and image. Place the required files respectively in their directories. Having this order is not required, but it is useful to start adding more classification models, labels, and images later to play around more with the TPU device.

This is how the directory structure should look now:

```
.
├── README.md
├── classify.py
├── classify_image.py
├── images
│   └── macro-1802322_640.jpg
├── install_requirements.sh
├── labels
│   └── inat_insect_labels.txt
└── models
    └── mobilenet_v2_1.0_224_inat_insect_quant_edgetpu.tflite

3 directories, 7 files
```

Finally, we can try classification operations using the Coral device. Make sure that the device is plugged in with the USB cable, otherwise you will get a long traceback (which unfortunately doesn't really explain what the problem is):

```
Traceback (most recent call last):
  File "classify_image.py", line 122, in <module>
    main()
  File "classify_image.py", line 99, in main
    interpreter = make_interpreter(args.model)
  File "classify_image.py", line 72, in make_interpreter
    tflite.load_delegate(EDGETPU_SHARED_LIB,
  File "~/lib/python3.8/site-packages/tflite_runtime/interpreter.py",
    line 154, in load_delegate
      raise ValueError('Failed to load delegate from {}\n{}'.format(
ValueError: Failed to load delegate from libedgetpu.1.dylib
```

That error means that the device is unplugged. Plug it in and run the classification command:

```
$ python3 classify_image.py \
  --model models/mobilenet_v2_1.0_224_inat_insect_quant_edgetpu.tflite \
  --labels labels/inat_insect_labels.txt \
  --input images/macro-1802322_640.jpg
----INFERENCE TIME----
Note: The first inference on Edge TPU is slow because it includes loading
the model into Edge TPU memory.
11.9ms
2.6ms
2.5ms
2.5ms
2.4ms
-------RESULTS--------
Lucilia sericata (Common Green Bottle Fly): 0.43359
```

The image was classified correctly, and the common fly was detected! Find some other insect pictures and rerun the command to check how the model performs with different inputs.

Azure Percept

When this book was being written, Microsoft announced the release of a platform and hardware called Azure Percept. Although I didn't have enough time to get hands-on practical examples on how to take advantage of its features, I feel it is worth mentioning some of its functionality.

The same concepts that apply to the Coral device in the previous section and to the edge, in general, apply to the devices for Percept: they allow seamless machine learning operations at the edge.

First, it is important to emphasize that although the Percept products are mostly advertised as pieces of hardware, Azure Percept is a whole platform for doing edge computing, from the devices themselves all the way to deployment, training, and management in Azure. There is also support for the major AI platforms like ONNX and TensorFlow, making it easier to try out with prebuilt models.

One downside of the Azure Percept hardware compared to the Coral devices is that it is much more expensive, making it harder to buy one of its bundles to try the new technology. As always, Microsoft has done a stellar job in documenting and adding a good amount of context and examples (*https://oreil.ly/MFIKf*) that are worth exploring if you are interested.

TFHub

A great resource to find TensorFlow models is the TensorFlow Hub (*https://tfhub.dev*). The hub is a repository of thousands of pretrained models ready to be used. For the Coral Edge TPU, not all models will work, though. Since the TPU has separate instructions specific to the device, a model needs to be explicitly compiled for it.

Now that you can run classifications with the Coral USB device, you can use TFHub to find other pretrained models to work with. At the hub, a Coral model format is available; click on it to get to the models ready to use for the TPU (*https://oreil.ly/mJv9N*) as shown in Figure 3-2.

Figure 3-2. TFHub Coral models

Select the *MobileNet Quantized V2* model for download. This model can detect over a thousand objects from images. The previous examples using Coral require the labels and the model, so make sure you download that as well.

 When these models are presented in the TFHub website, multiple different formats are available. Ensure you double-check which model format you are getting, and that (in this case) it is compatible with the Coral device.

Porting Over Non-TPU Models

You might find that the model you need is available in some situations but not compiled for the TPU device you have. The Coral Edge TPU does have a compiler available, but it isn't installable in every platform as the runtime dependencies are. When such situations come up, you have to get creative on the solutions and always attempt to find the automation within any workarounds possible. The compiler documentation requires a Debian or Ubuntu Linux distribution, and the instructions on how to get everything set up for the compiler are tied to that particular distro.

In my case, I'm working from an Apple computer, and I don't have other computers running Linux. What I *do have* is a container runtime installed locally in which I can run any image from any distro with a few commands. We've already covered how to get started with containers, how to run them, and how to create them. And this is the perfect use case for creating a new Debian-based container with everything installed for the compiler to solve this problem.

Now that we understand the problem and have a solution in mind with containers, create a new *Dockerfile* to build a container image for the compiler:

```
FROM debian:stable

RUN apt-get update && apt install -yq curl build-essential gnupg

RUN curl https://packages.cloud.google.com/apt/doc/apt-key.gpg | \
    apt-key add -

RUN \
  echo "deb https://packages.cloud.google.com/apt coral-edgetpu-stable main" | \
  tee /etc/apt/sources.list.d/coral-edgetpu.list

RUN apt-get update && apt-get install -yq edgetpu-compiler

CMD ["/bin/bash"]
```

With the newly created *Dockerfile*, create a new image to run the compiler:

```
$ docker build -t tpu-compiler .
[+] Building 15.5s (10/10) FINISHED
```

```
=> => transferring dockerfile: 408B
[...]
=> [5/5] RUN apt update && apt install -yq edgetpu-compiler
=> exporting to image
=> => exporting layers
=> => writing image
   sha256:08078f8d7f7dd9002bd5a1377f24ad0d9dbf8f7b45c961232cf2cbf8f9f946e4
=> => naming to docker.io/library/tpu-compiler
```

I've identified a model (*https://oreil.ly/b7o64*) that I want to use with the TPU compiler but doesn't come compiled for it.

 Only models that are precompiled for TensorFlow Lite and are quantized will work with the compiler. Ensure that models are both *tflite* and *quantized* before downloading them to convert them with the compiler.

Download the model locally. In this case, I use the command line to save it in the current working directory:

```
$ wget -O mobilenet_v1_50_160_quantized.tflite \
  https://tfhub.dev/tensorflow/lite-model/\
  mobilenet_v1_0.50_160_quantized/1/default/1?lite-format=tflite

Resolving tfhub.dev (tfhub.dev)... 108.177.122.101, 108.177.122.113, ...
Connecting to tfhub.dev (tfhub.dev)|108.177.122.101|:443... connected.
HTTP request sent, awaiting response... 200 OK
Length: 1364512 (1.3M) [application/octet-stream]
Saving to: 'mobilenet_v1_50_160_quantized.tflite'

(31.8 MB/s) - 'mobilenet_v1_50_160_quantized.tflite' saved [1364512/1364512]

$ ls
mobilenet_v1_50_160_quantized.tflite
```

Although I've used the command line, you can also download the model by going to the model on the website (*https://oreil.ly/NeI87*). Ensure you move the file to the current working directory for the next steps.

We need to get the downloaded model into the container and then copy back the files locally. Docker makes this task somewhat more manageable by using a *bind mount*. This mount operation will link a path from my machine into the container, effectively sharing anything I have into the container. This also works great for files created in the container, and I need them back on the local machine. Those files created in the container will appear automatically in my local environment.

Start the container with the bind mount:

```
$ docker run -it -v ${PWD}:/models tpu-compiler
root@5125dcd1da4b:/# cd models
root@5125dcd1da4b:/models# ls
mobilenet_v1_50_160_quantized.tflite
```

There are a couple of things happening with the previous command. First, I'm using PWD to indicate that the current working directory, where the *mobilenet_v1_50_160_quantized.tflite* file exists, is what I want in the container. The destination path within the container is */models*. And lastly, I'm using the container built with the tag tpu-compiler to specify the container I need. If you used a different tag when building the image, you would need to update that part of the command. After starting the container, I change directories into */models*, list the directory contents, and find the downloaded model in my local machine. The environment is now ready to use the compiler.

Verify the compiler works by calling its help menu:

```
$ edgetpu_compiler --help
Edge TPU Compiler version 15.0.340273435

Usage:
edgetpu_compiler [options] model...
```

Next, run the compiler against the quantized model:

```
$ edgetpu_compiler mobilenet_v1_50_160_quantized.tflite
Edge TPU Compiler version 15.0.340273435

Model compiled successfully in 787 ms.

Input model: mobilenet_v1_50_160_quantized.tflite
Input size: 1.30MiB
Output model: mobilenet_v1_50_160_quantized_edgetpu.tflite
Output size: 1.54MiB
Number of Edge TPU subgraphs: 1
Total number of operations: 31
Operation log: mobilenet_v1_50_160_quantized_edgetpu.log
See the operation log file for individual operation details.
```

The operation took less than a second to run and produced a few files, including the newly compiled model (*mobilenet_v1_50_160_quantized_edgetpu.tflite*) that you can now use with the edge device.

Finally, exit out of the container, go back to the local machine, and list the contents of the directory:

```
$ ls
mobilenet_v1_50_160_quantized.tflite
mobilenet_v1_50_160_quantized_edgetpu.log
mobilenet_v1_50_160_quantized_edgetpu.tflite
```

This is a handy workaround to requiring an operating system for a tool. Now that this container can compile models for the edge device, it can be automated further by porting over models you need with a few lines in a script. Remember that there are a few assumptions made in the process and that you must ensure these assumptions are all accurate at compile time. Otherwise, you will get errors from the compiler. This process is an example of trying to use a nonquantized model with the compiler:

```
$ edgetpu_compiler vision_classifier_fungi_mobile_v1.tflite
Edge TPU Compiler version 15.0.340273435
Invalid model: vision_classifier_fungi_mobile_v1.tflite
Model not quantized
```

Containers for Managed ML Systems

At the heart of advanced next-generation MLOps workflows are managed ML systems like AWS SageMaker, Azure ML Studio, and Google's Vertex AI. All of these systems build on top of containers. Containers are a secret ingredient for MLOps. Without containerization, it is much more challenging to develop and use technologies like AWS SageMaker. In Figure 3-3, notice that the EC2 Container Registry is the location where the inference code image and the training code live.

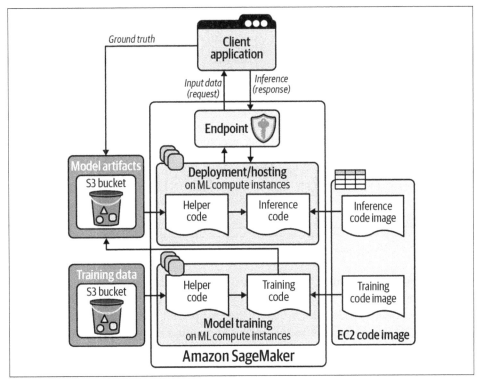

Figure 3-3. SageMaker containers

This process is critically important because it allows DevOps best practices to bake into creating these images—among these most importantly are continuous integrations and continuous delivery. Containers increase the entire ML architecture quality by reducing complexity since the images are already "baked." Intellectual horsepower can shift to other problems like data drift, analyzing the feature store for suitable candidates for a newer model, or evaluating whether the new model solves customer needs.

Containers in Monetizing MLOps

Monetizing MLOps is another crucial problem for both startups and large companies. Containers play a role yet again! In the case of SageMaker, use either an algorithm or a model sold in the AWS Marketplace, as shown in Figure 3-4. They are the mode of delivery for the product sold.

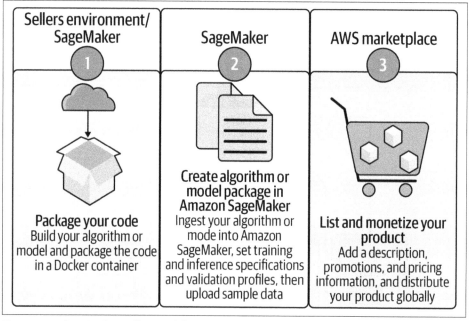

Figure 3-4. SageMaker seller workflow

The advantage of a container as a product is that it is sold much like other products sold in a physical store, such as peanut butter, flour, or milk. In the scenario where a company decides to produce high-quality, organic peanut butter, it may want to focus strictly on making the peanut butter, not building out a network of stores to sell the peanut butter.

Likewise, in companies looking to monetize machine learning, the container is an ideal package for delivering both models and algorithms to customers. Next, let's take a look at how you can build once and run many with containers.

Build Once, Run Many MLOps Workflow

Ultimately a container process for MLOps culminates in many rich options for both product and engineering. In Figure 3-5, you see that a container is an ideal package to monetize intellectual property from a product perspective. Likewise, from an engineering perspective, a container can serve out predictions, do training, or deploy to an edge device like a Coral TPU or Apple iPhone.

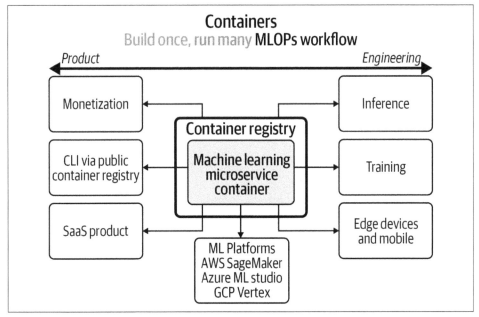

Figure 3-5. Build Once, Run Many MLOps container

MLOps and container technology are complementary in that containers help you deliver business value. MLOps methodologies then build directly on top of this technology to streamline productivity and add value. Next, let's wrap up the chapter and summarize the essential aspects of containers for MLOps.

Conclusion

When operationalizing ML models, you will often encounter many different possibilities for deployment. It is becoming fairly common to see models getting deployed on mobile phones and other (small) devices that you can plug into any computer with a USB port. The problems that edge inferencing provides (like offline, remote, and fast access) can be transformational, specifically for remote regions without access to a reliable source of power and network. Similar to edge devices, containerization enables faster and more reliable reproduction of environments. Reproducible machine environments were a challenging problem to solve just a few years ago. Containerization is exceptionally relevant in that case. Fast scaling of resources and transitioning deployment environments from cloud providers, or even moving workloads from on-premise (local) to the cloud is far easier to accomplish with containers.

With that covered, our next chapter dives into the continuous delivery process for machine learning models.

Exercises

- Recompile a model to work with the Coral Edge TPU from TFHub.
- Use the MobileNet V2 model to perform inference on other objects and get accurate results.
- Create a new container image, based on the Flask example, that serves a model and that provides examples on a `GET` request to interact with the model. Create another endpoint that provides useful metadata about the model.
- Publish the newly created image to a container registry like Docker Hub (*https://hub.docker.com*).

Critical Thinking Discussion Questions

- Would it be possible to use a container to perform online predictions with an edge TPU device like Coral? How? or Why not?
- What is a container runtime, and how does it relate to Docker?
- Name three good practices when creating a Dockerfile.
- What are two critical concepts of DevOps mentioned in this chapter? Why are they useful?
- Create a definition, in your own words, of what the "edge" is. Give some ML examples that can be applied.

## CHAPTER 4

Continuous Delivery for Machine Learning Models

By Alfredo Deza

> Is it really the sad truth that natural philosophy (what we now call science) has so far separated off from its origins that it has left behind only papyrologists—people who take paper in, put paper out, and while reading and writing assiduously, earnestly avoid the tangible? Do they consider direct contact with data to be of negative value? Are they, like some redneck in the novel *Tobacco Road*, actually proud of their ignorance?
>
> —Dr. Joseph Bogen

As a professional athlete, I was often dealing with injuries. Injuries have all kinds of severity levels. Sometimes it would be something minor, like a mild contracture on my left hamstring after intense hurdle workouts. Other times it would be more serious, like insufferable lower back pain. High-performance athletes cannot afford to have days off in the middle of the season. If the plan is to work out seven days a week, it is critical to go through those seven days. Missing out a day has serious repercussions that can diminish (or entirely wipe out) the workouts until that point. Workouts are like pushing a wheelbarrow uphill, and missing a workout means stepping to the side letting the wheelbarrow ride downhill. The repercussion of that action is that you will have to go back and pick up that wheelbarrow to push it up again. You cannot miss out on workouts.

If you are injured and you cannot work out, getting back up in full shape as soon as possible is a priority *as important as finding alternative workouts*. That means that if your hamstring hurts and you can't run, see if you can go to the pool and keep up the cardio plan. Hill repeats are not possible tomorrow because you broke a toe? Then try hopping on the bike to tackle those same hills. Injuries require a war strategy; giving up and quitting is not an option, but if you must retreat, then retreating *the least possible* is considered first. If we cannot fire cannons, let's bring the cavalry. There is always an option, and creativity is as important as trying to recover fully.

Recovery requires strategy as well, but more than strategy, it requires constant evaluation. Since you keep working out as much as possible with an injury, it is essential to evaluate if the injury is getting worse. If you get on the bike to compensate because you can't run, you must be hyper-aware if the bike is making the injury worse. The constant evaluation for injuries is a rather simplistic algorithm:

1. First thing every day, assess if the injury is the same, worse, or better than the day before.

2. If it is worse, then make changes to avoid the previous workouts or alter them. Those may be harming recovery.

3. If it is the same, compare the injury against last week or last month even. Ask the question *"Am I feeling the same, worse, or better than last week?"*

4. Finally, if you feel better, that strongly reinforces that the current strategy is working, and you should continue until fully recovered.

With some injuries, I had to evaluate at a higher frequency (rather than waiting until the next morning). The result of constant evaluation was the key to recovery. In some cases, I had to evaluate if a specific action was hurting me. One time I broke a toe (slammed it into the corner of a bookshelf), and I immediately strategized: can I walk? Do I feel pain if I run? The answer to all of these was a resounding yes. I tried going swimming that afternoon. For the next few weeks, I would constantly check if walking was possible without pain. Pain is not a foe. It is the indicator that helps you decide to keep doing what you are doing or stop and rethink the current strategy.

Constant evaluation, making changes and adapting to the feedback, and applying new strategies to achieve success is exactly what continuous integration (CI) and continuous delivery (CD) are about. Even today, where information about robust deployment strategies is easily available, you often encounter businesses without tests or a poor testing strategy to ensure a product is ready for a new release or even releases that take weeks (and months!). I recall trying to cut a new release of a major open source project, and there were times it would take close to a week. Even worse, the Quality Assurance (QA) lead would send emails to every team lead and ask them if they felt ready for a release or wanted more changes.

Sending emails around and waiting for different replies is not a straightforward way to release software. It is prone to error and highly inconsistent. The feedback loop that CI/CD platforms and steps grant you and your team is invaluable. If you find a problem, you must automate it away and make it not-a-problem for the next release. Constant evaluation, just like injuries with high-performing athletes, is a core pillar of DevOps and absolutely critical for successful machine learning operationalization.

I like the description of continuous as persistence or recurrence of a process. CI/CD are usually mentioned together when talking about the system that builds, verifies, and deploys artifacts. In this chapter, I will detail what a robust process looks like and how you can enable various strategies to implement (or improve) a pipeline to ship models into production.

Packaging for ML Models

It wasn't that long ago I heard about packaging ML models for the first time. If you've never heard about packaging models before, it's OK—this is all fairly recent, and *packaging* here doesn't mean some special type of operating system package like an RPM (Red Hat Package Manager) or DEB (Debian Package) file with special directives for bundling and distribution. This all means getting a model into a container to take advantage of containerized processes to help sharing, distributing, and easy deployment. I've already described containerization in detail in "Containers" on page 68 and why it makes sense to use them for operationalizing machine learning versus using other strategies like virtual machines, but it is worth reiterating that the ability to quickly try out a model from a container regardless of the operating system is a dream scenario come true.

There are three characteristics of packaging ML models into containers that are significant to go over:

- As long as a container runtime is installed, it is effortless to run a container locally.
- There are plenty of options to deploy a container in the cloud, with the ability to scale up or down as needed.
- Others can quickly try it out with ease and interact with the container.

The benefits of these characteristics are that maintainability becomes less complicated, and debugging a nonperformant model locally (or in a cloud offering even) can be as simple as a few commands in a terminal. The more complicated the deployment strategy is, the more difficult it will be to troubleshoot and investigate potential issues.

For this section, I will use an ONNX model and package it within a container that serves a Flask app that performs the prediction. I will use the RoBERTa-SequenceClassification (*https://oreil.ly/DbzOM*) ONNX model, which is very well documented. After creating a new Git repository, the first step is to figure out the dependencies needed. After creating the Git repository, start by adding the following *requirements.txt* file:

```
simpletransformers==0.4.0
tensorboardX==1.9
```

```
transformers==2.1.0
flask==1.1.2
torch==1.7.1
onnxruntime==1.6.0
```

Next, create a Dockerfile that installs everything in the container:

```
FROM python:3.8

COPY ./requirements.txt /webapp/requirements.txt

WORKDIR /webapp

RUN pip install -r requirements.txt

COPY webapp/* /webapp

ENTRYPOINT [ "python" ]

CMD [ "app.py" ]
```

The Dockerfile copies the requirements file, creates a *webapp* directory, and copies the application code into a single *app.py* file. Create the *webapp/app.py* file to perform the sentiment analysis. Start by adding the imports and everything needed to create an ONNX runtime session:

```
from flask import Flask, request, jsonify
import torch
import numpy as np
from transformers import RobertaTokenizer
import onnxruntime


app = Flask(__name__)
tokenizer = RobertaTokenizer.from_pretrained("roberta-base")
session = onnxruntime.InferenceSession(
    "roberta-sequence-classification-9.onnx")
```

This first part of the file creates the Flask application, defines the tokenizer to use with the model, and finally, it initializes an ONNX runtime session that requires passing a path to the model. There are quite a few imports that aren't used yet. You will make use of those next when adding the Flask route to enable the live inferencing:

```
@app.route("/predict", methods=["POST"])
def predict():
    input_ids = torch.tensor(
        tokenizer.encode(request.json[0], add_special_tokens=True)
    ).unsqueeze(0)

    if input_ids.requires_grad:
        numpy_func = input_ids.detach().cpu().numpy()
    else:
        numpy_func = input_ids.cpu().numpy()
```

```
        inputs = {session.get_inputs()[0].name: numpy_func(input_ids)}
        out = session.run(None, inputs)

        result = np.argmax(out)

        return jsonify({"positive": bool(result)})

if __name__ == "__main__":
    app.run(host="0.0.0.0", port=5000, debug=True)
```

The predict() function is a Flask route that enables the */predict* URL when the application is running. The function only allows POST HTTP methods. There is no
description of the sample inputs and outputs yet because one critical part of the application is missing: the ONNX model does not exist yet. Download the RoBERTa-
SequenceClassification (*https://oreil.ly/Pjvit*) ONNX model locally, and place it at the
root of the project. This is how the final project structure should look:

```
.
├── Dockerfile
├── requirements.txt
├── roberta-sequence-classification-9.onnx
└── webapp
    └── app.py
```

```
1 directory, 4 files
```

One last thing missing before building the container is that there is no instruction to
copy the model into the container. The *app.py* file requires the model *roberta-
sequence-classification-9.onnx* to exist in the */webapp* directory. Update the *Dockerfile*
to reflect that:

```
COPY roberta-sequence-classification-9.onnx /webapp
```

Now the project has everything needed so you can build the container and run the
application. Before building the container, let's double-check everything works. Create a new virtual environment, activate it, and install all the dependencies:

```
$ python3 -m venv venv
$ source venv/bin/activate
$ pip install -r requirements.txt
```

The ONNX model exists at the root of the project, but the application wants it in
the */webapp* directory, so move it inside that directory so that the Flask app doesn't
complain (this extra step is not needed when the container runs):

```
$ mv roberta-sequence-classification-9.onnx webapp/
```

Now run the application locally by invoking the *app.py* file with Python:

```
$ cd webapp
$ python app.py
```

```
 * Serving Flask app "app" (lazy loading)
  * Environment: production
    WARNING: This is a development server.
    Use a production WSGI server instead.
  * Debug mode: on
  * Running on http://0.0.0.0:5000/ (Press CTRL+C to quit)
```

Next, the application is ready to consume HTTP requests. So far, I've not shown what the expected inputs are. These are going to be JSON-formatted requests with JSON responses. Use the *curl* program to send a sample payload to detect sentiment:

```
$ curl -X POST  -H "Content-Type: application/JSON" \
  --data '["Containers are more or less interesting"]' \
  http://0.0.0.0:5000/predict

{
  "positive": false
}

$ curl -X POST  -H "Content-Type: application/json" \
  --data '["MLOps is critical for robustness"]' \
  http://0.0.0.0:5000/predict

{
  "positive": true
}
```

The JSON request is an array with a single string, and the response is a JSON object with a "positive" key that indicates the sentiment of the sentence. Now that you've verified that the application runs and that the live prediction is functioning properly, it is time to create the container locally to verify all works there. Create the container, and tag it with something meaningful:

```
$ docker build -t alfredodeza/roberta .
[+] Building 185.3s (11/11) FINISHED
 => [internal] load metadata for docker.io/library/python:3.8
 => CACHED [1/6] FROM docker.io/library/python:3.8
 => [2/6] COPY ./requirements.txt /webapp/requirements.txt
 => [3/6] WORKDIR /webapp
 => [4/6] RUN pip install -r requirements.txt
 => [5/6] COPY webapp/* /webapp
 => [6/6] COPY roberta-sequence-classification-9.onnx /webapp
 => exporting to image
 => => naming to docker.io/alfredodeza/roberta
```

Now run the container locally to interact with it in the same way as when running the application directly with Python. Remember to map the ports of the container to the localhost:

```
$ docker run -it -p 5000:5000 --rm alfredodeza/roberta
 * Serving Flask app "app" (lazy loading)
  * Environment: production
```

```
    WARNING: This is a development server.
    Use a production WSGI server instead.
 * Debug mode: on
 * Running on http://0.0.0.0:5000/ (Press CTRL+C to quit)
```

Send an HTTP request in the same way as before. You can use the *curl* program again:

```
$ curl -X POST  -H "Content-Type: application/json" \
  --data '["espresso is too strong"]' \
  http://0.0.0.0:5000/predict

{
  "positive": false
}
```

We've gone through many steps to package a model and get it inside a container. Some of these steps might seem overwhelming, but challenging processes are a perfect opportunity to automate and leverage continuous delivery patterns. In the next section, I'll automate all of this using continuous delivery and publishing this container to a container registry that anyone can consume.

Infrastructure as Code for Continuous Delivery of ML Models

Recently at work, I saw that a few test container images existed in a public repository, which were widely used by the test infrastructure. Having images hosted in a container registry (like Docker Hub) is already a great step in the right direction for repeatable builds and reliable tests. I encountered a problem with one of the libraries used in a container that needed an update, so I searched for the files used to create these test containers. They were nowhere to be found. At some point, an engineer built these locally and uploaded the images to the registry. This presented a big problem because I couldn't make a simple change to the image since the files needed to build the image were lost.

Experienced container developers can find a way to get most (if not all) files to rebuild the container, but that is beside the point. A step forward in this problematic situation is to create automation that can automatically build these containers from known source files, including the *Dockerfile*. Rebuilding or solving the problem to update the container and re-upload to the registry is like finding candles and flashlights in a blackout, instead of having a generator that starts automatically as soon as the power goes away. Be highly analytical when situations like the one I just described happens. Rather than pointing fingers and blaming others, use these as an opportunity to enhance the process with automation.

The same problem happens in machine learning. We tend to grow easily accustomed to things being manual (and complex!), but there is always an opportunity to automate. This section will not go over all the steps needed in containerization again (already covered in "Containers" on page 68), but I will go into the details needed to automate everything. Let's assume we're in a similar situation to the one I just described and that someone has created a container with a model that lives in Docker Hub. Nobody knows how the trained model got into the container; there are no docs, and updates are needed. Let's add a slight complexity: the model is not in any repository to be found, but it lives in Azure as a registered model. Let's get some automation going to solve this problem.

 It might be tempting to add models into a GitHub repository. Although this is certainly possible, GitHub has (at the time of this writing) a hard file limit of 100 MB. If the model you are trying to package is close to that size, you might not be able to add it to the repository. Further, Git (the version control system) is not meant to handle versioning of binary files and has the side-effect of creating huge repositories because of this.

In the current problem scenario, the model is available on the Azure ML platform and previously registered. I didn't have one already, so I quickly registered RoBERTa-SequenceClassification (*https://oreil.ly/oNgCD*) using Azure ML Studio. Click the Models section and then "Register model" as shown in Figure 4-1.

Figure 4-1. Azure model registering menu

Fill out the form shown in Figure 4-2 with the necessary details. In my case, I downloaded the model locally and need to upload it using the "Upload file" field.

Register a model   ✕

Name *

```
roberta-sequence
```

Description

```
Sentiment prediction using RoBERTa-sequencing ONNX model
```

Model framework *

```
ONNX                                                              ⌄
```

Framework version *

```
1.6
```

Model file or folder *

◉ Upload file   ◯ Upload folder

```
roberta-sequence-classification-9.onnx         |    Browse
```

Add tags

```
Name              | :  | Value                      |   Add tag
```

Add properties

```
Name              | :  | Value                      |   Add property
```

Figure 4-2. Azure model registering form

If you want to know more about registering a model in Azure, I cover how to do that with the Python SDK in "Registering Models" on page 243.

Now that the pretrained model is in Azure let's reuse the same project from "Packaging for ML Models" on page 95. All the heavy lifting to perform the (local) live inferencing is done, so create a new GitHub repository and add the project contents *except* for the ONNX model. Remember, there is a size limit for files in GitHub, so it isn't possible to add the ONNX model into the GitHub repo. Create a *.gitigore* file to ignore the model and prevent adding it by mistake:

```
*onnx
```

After pushing the contents of the Git repository without the ONNX model, we are ready to start automating the model creation and delivery. To do this, we will use GitHub Actions, which allows us to create a continuous delivery workflow in a YAML file that gets triggered when configurable conditions are met. The idea is that whenever the repository has a change in the main branch, the platform will pull the registered model from Azure, create the container, and lastly, it will push it to a container registry. Start by creating a *.github/workflows/* directory at the root of your project, and then add a *main.yml* that looks like this:

```
name: Build and package RoBERTa-sequencing to Dockerhub

on:
  # Triggers the workflow on push or pull request events for the main branch
  push:
    branches: [ main ]

  # Allows you to run this workflow manually from the Actions tab
  workflow_dispatch:
```

The configuration so far doesn't do anything other than defining the action. You can define any number of jobs, and in this case, we define a *build* job that will put everything together. Append the following to the *main.yml* file you previously created:

```
jobs:
  build:
    runs-on: ubuntu-latest
    steps:

      - uses: actions/checkout@v2

      - name: Authenticate with Azure
        uses: azure/login@v1
        with:
          creds: ${{secrets.AZURE_CREDENTIALS}}

      - name: set auto-install of extensions
        run: az config set extension.use_dynamic_install=yes_without_prompt

      - name: attach workspace
        run: az ml folder attach -w "ml-ws" -g "practical-mlops"

      - name: retrieve the model
        run: az ml model download -t "." --model-id "roberta-sequence:1"

      - name: build flask-app container
        uses: docker/build-push-action@v2
        with:
          context: ./
          file: ./Dockerfile
          push: false
          tags: alfredodeza/flask-roberta:latest
```

The build job has many steps. In this case, each step has a distinct task, which is an excellent way to separate failure domains. If everything were in a single script, it would be more difficult to grasp potential issues. The first step is to check out the repository when the action triggers. Next, since the ONNX model doesn't exist locally, we need to retrieve it from Azure, so we must authenticate using the Azure action. After authentication, the *az* tool is made available, and you must attach the folder for your workspace and group. Finally, the job can retrieve the model by its ID.

 Some steps in the YAML file have a uses directive, which identifies what external action (for example actions/checkout) and at what version. Versions can be branches or published tags of a repository. In the case of checkout it is the v2 tag.

Once all those steps complete, the RoBERTa-Sequence model should be at the root of the project, enabling the next steps to build the container properly.

The workflow file is using AZURE_CREDENTIALS. These are used with a special syntax that allows the workflow to retrieve secrets configured for the repository. These credentials are the service principal information. If you aren't familiar with a service principal, this is covered in the "Authentication" on page 238. You will need the service principal's configuration that has access to the resources in the workspace and group where the model lives. Add the secret on your GitHub repository by going to Settings, then Secrets, and finally clicking the "New repository secret" link. Figure 4-3 shows the form you will be presented when adding a new secret.

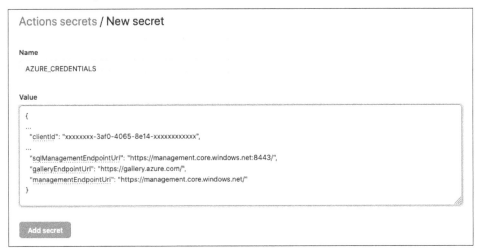

Figure 4-3. Add secret

Commit and push your changes to your repository and then head to the Actions tab. A new run is immediately scheduled and should start running in a few seconds. After a few minutes, everything should've completed. In my case, Figure 4-4 shows it takes close to four minutes.

Figure 4-4. GitHub action success

There are now quite a few moving parts to accomplish a successful job run. When designing a new set of steps (or pipelines, as I'll cover in the next section), a good idea is to enumerate the steps and identify greedy steps. These *greedy steps* are steps that are trying to do too much and have lots of responsibility. At first glance, it is hard to identify any step that might be problematic. The process of maintaining a CI/CD job includes refining responsibilities of steps and adapting them accordingly.

Once the steps are identified, you can break them down into smaller steps, which will help you understand the responsibility of each part faster. A faster understanding means easier debugging, and although it's not immediately apparent, you will benefit from making this a habit.

These are the steps we have for packaging the RoBERTa-Sequence model:

1. Check out the current branch of the repository.

2. Authenticate to Azure Cloud.

3. Configure auto-install of Azure CLI extensions.

4. Attach the folder to interact with the workspace.

5. Download the ONNX model.

6. Build the container for the current repo.

There is one final item missing, though, and that is to publish the container after it builds. Different container registries will require different options here, but most do support GitHub Actions, which is refreshing. Docker Hub is straightforward, and all it requires is to create a token and then save it as a GitHub project secret, along with your Docker Hub username. Once that is in place, adapt the workflow file to include the authentication step before building:

```
- name: Authenticate to Docker hub
  uses: docker/login-action@v1
  with:
    username: ${{ secrets.DOCKER_HUB_USERNAME }}
    password: ${{ secrets.DOCKER_HUB_ACCESS_TOKEN }}
```

Lastly, update the build step to use push: true.

Recently, GitHub has released a container registry offering as well, and its integration with GitHub Actions is straightforward. The same Docker steps can be used with minor changes and creating a PAT (Personal Access Token). Start by creating a PAT by going to your GitHub account settings, clicking Developer Settings, and finally "Personal access" tokens. Once that page loads, click "Generate new token." Give it a meaningful description in the Note section, and ensure that the token has permissions to write packages as I do in Figure 4-5.

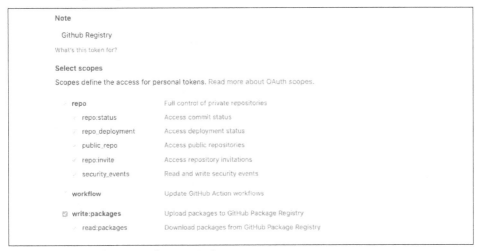

Figure 4-5. GitHub Personal Access Token

Once you are done, a new page is presented with the actual token. This is the only time you will see the token in plain text, so make sure you copy it now. Next, go to the repository where the container code lives, and create a new repository secret, just like you did with the Azure service principal credentials. Name the new secret *GH_REG-ISTRY* and paste the contents of the PAT created in the previous step. Now you are ready to update the Docker steps to publish the package using the new token and GitHub's container registry:

```
- name: Login to GitHub Container Registry
  uses: docker/login-action@v1
  with:
```

```
        registry: ghcr.io
        username: ${{ github.repository_owner }}
        password: ${{ secrets.GH_REGISTRY }}

    - name: build flask-app and push to registry
      uses: docker/build-push-action@v2
      with:
        context: ./
        tags: ghcr.io/alfredodeza/flask-roberta:latest
        push: true
```

In my case, *alfredodeza* is my GitHub account, so I can tag with it along with the
flask-roberta name of the repository. These will need to match according to your
account and repository. After pushing the changes to the main branch (or after merging if you made a pull request), the job will trigger. The model should get pulled in
from Azure, packaged within the container, and finally published as a GitHub Package in its container registry offering, looking similar to Figure 4-6.

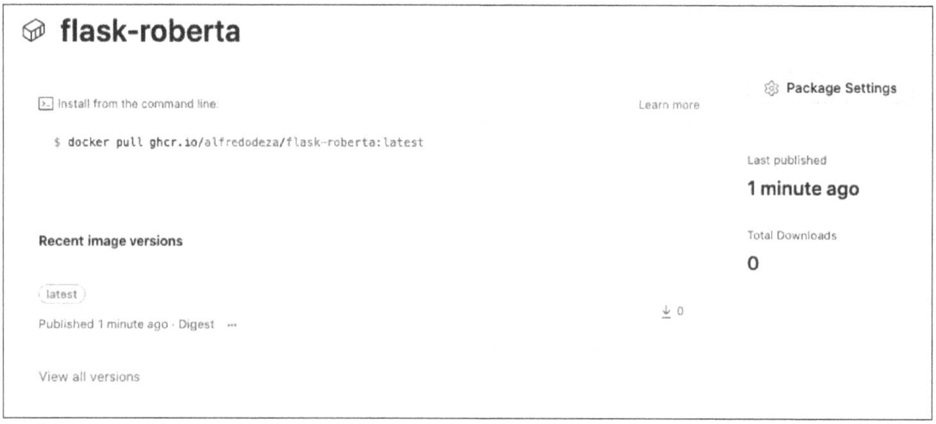

Figure 4-6. GitHub Package container

Now that the container is packaging and distributing the ONNX model in a fully
automated fashion by leveraging GitHub's CI/CD offering and container registry, we
have solved the problematic scenario I assumed at the beginning of the chapter: a
model needs to get packaged in a container, but the container files are not available.
In this way, you are providing clarity to others and to the process itself. It is segmen-
ted into small steps, and it allows any updates to be done to the container. Finally, the
steps publish the container to a selected registry.

You can accomplish quite a few other things with CI/CD environments besides packaging and publishing a container. CI/CD platforms are the foundation for automation
and reliable results. In the next section, I go into other ideas that work well regardless
of the platform. By being aware of general patterns available in other platforms, you
can take advantage of those features without worrying about the implementations.

Using Cloud Pipelines

The first time I heard about pipelines, I thought of them as more advanced than the typical scripting pattern (a procedural set of instructions representing a build). But pipelines aren't advanced concepts at all. If you've dealt with shell scripts in any continuous integration platform, then a pipeline will seem straightforward to use. A pipeline is nothing more than a set of steps (or instructions) that can achieve a specific objective like publishing a model into a production environment when run. For example, a pipeline with three steps to train a model can be as simple as Figure 4-7.

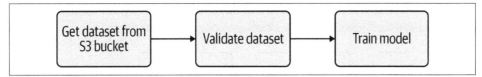

Figure 4-7. Simple pipeline

You could represent the same pipeline as a shell script that does all three things at once. There are multiple benefits with a pipeline that separates concerns. When each step has a specific responsibility (or concern), it is easier to grasp. If a single-step pipeline that retrieves the data, validates it, and trains the model is failing, it isn't immediately clear why that might fail. Indeed you can dive into the details, look at logs, and check the actual error. If you separate the pipeline into three steps and the *train model* step is failing, you can narrow the failure's scope and get to a possible resolution faster.

> One general recommendation that you can apply to the many aspects of operationalizing machine learning is to consider making any operation more straightforward for a future failure situation. Avoid being tempted to go fast and get a pipeline (like in this case) deployed and running in a single step because it is easier. Take the time to reason about what would make it easier for you (and others) to build ML infrastructure. When a failure does happen, and you identify problematic aspects, go back to the implementation and improve it. You can apply the concepts of CI/CD to improvement: continuous evaluation and improvement of processes is a sound strategy for robust environments.

Cloud pipelines are no different from any continuous integration platform out there except that they are hosted or managed by a cloud provider.

Some definitions of CI/CD pipelines you can encounter try to define elements or parts of a pipeline rigidly. In reality, I think that the parts of the pipeline should be loosely defined and not constrained by definitions. RedHat has a nice explanation of pipelines (*https://oreil.ly/rlJUx*) that describes five common elements: build, test, release, deploy, and validate. These elements are mostly for mix-and-match, not to strictly include them in the pipeline. For example, if the model you are building doesn't need to get deployed, then there is no need to pursue a deploy step at all. Similarly, if your workflow requires extracting and preprocessing data, you need to implement it as another step.

Now that you are aware that a pipeline is basically the same as a CI/CD platform with several steps, it should be straightforward to apply machine learning operations to an actionable pipeline. Figure 4-8 shows a rather simplistic assumed pipeline, but this can involve several other steps as well, and like I've mentioned, these elements can be mixed and matched together to any number of operations and steps.

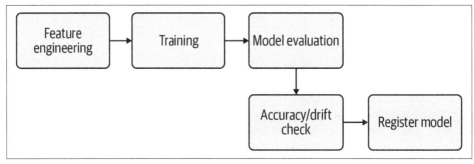

Figure 4-8. Involved pipeline

AWS SageMaker does an outstanding job of providing examples that are ready to use out of the box for crafting involved pipelines that include everything you need to run several steps. SageMaker is a specialized machine learning platform that goes beyond offering steps in a pipeline to accomplish a goal like publishing a model. Since it is specialized for machine learning, you are exposed to features that are particularly important for getting models into production. Those features don't exist in other common platforms like GitHub Actions, or if they do, they aren't as well thought out because the primary goal of platforms like GitHub Actions or Jenkins isn't to train machine learning models but rather be as generic as possible to accommodate for most common use cases.

Another crucial problem that is somewhat hard to solve is that specialized machines for training (for example, GPU-intensive tasks) are just not available or hard to configure in a generic pipeline offering.

Open SageMaker Studio and head over to the Components and Registries section on the left sidebar and select Projects. Several SageMaker project templates show up to choose from, as shown in Figure 4-9.

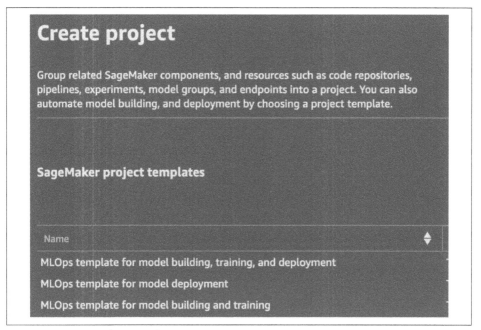

Figure 4-9. SageMaker templates

 Although the examples are meant to get you started, and Jupyter Notebooks are provided, they are great for learning more about the steps involved and how to change and adapt them to your specific needs. After creating a pipeline instance in SageMaker, training, and finally registering the model, you can browse through the parameters for the pipeline, like in Figure 4-10.

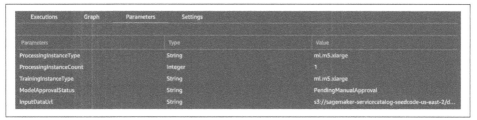

Figure 4-10. Pipeline parameters

Another crucial part of the pipeline that shows all the steps involved is also available, as shown in Figure 4-11.

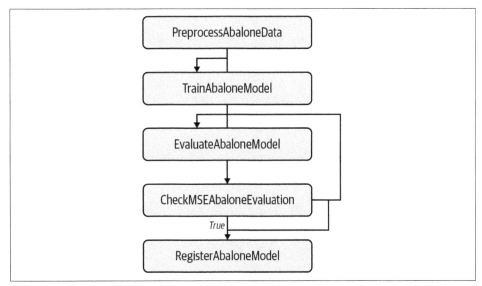

Figure 4-11. SageMaker pipeline

As you can see, preparing data, training, evaluating, and registering a model are all part of the pipeline. The main objective is to register the model to deploy it later for live inferencing after packaging. Not all the steps need to be captured in this particular pipeline, either. You can craft other pipelines that can run whenever there is a newly registered model available. That way, that pipeline is not tied to a particular model, but rather, you can reuse it for any other model that gets trained successfully and registered. Reusability of components and automation is another critical component of DevOps that works well when applied to MLOps.

Now that pipelines are demystified, we can see certain enhancements that can make them more robust by manually controlling rolling out models or even switching inferencing from one model to another.

Controlled Rollout of Models

There are a few concepts from web service deployments that map nicely into strategies for deploying models into production environments, like creating several instances of a live inferencing application for scalability and progressively switching from an older to a newer model. Before going into some of the details that encompass the control part of rolling out models into production, it is worth describing the strategies where these concepts come into play.

I'll discuss two of these strategies in detail in this section. Although these strategies are similar, they have particular behavior that you can take advantage of when deploying:

- Blue-green deployment
- Canary deployment

A blue-green deployment is a strategy that gets a new version into the staging environment identical to production. Sometimes this staging environment is the same as production, but traffic is routed differently (or separately). Without going into details, Kubernetes is a platform that allows for this type of deployment with ease, since you can have the two versions in the same Kubernetes cluster, but routing the traffic to a separate address for the newer ("blue") version while production traffic is still going into the older ("green"). The reason for this separation is that it allows further testing and assurance that the new model is working as expected. Once this verification is complete and certain conditions are satisfactory, you modify the configuration to switch traffic from the current model to the new one.

There are some issues with blue-green deployments, primarily associated with how complicated it can be to replicate production environments. Again, this is one of those situations where Kubernetes is a perfect fit since the cluster can accommodate the same application with different versions with ease.

A canary deployment strategy is a bit more involved and somewhat riskier. Depending on your level of confidence and the ability to progressively change configuration based on constraints, it is a sound way to send models into production. In this case, traffic is routed progressively to the newer model *at the same time the previous model is serving predictions*. So the two versions are live and processing requests simultaneously, but doing them in different ratios. The reason for this percentage-based rollout is that you can enable metrics and other checks to capture problems in real time, allowing you to roll back immediately if conditions are unfavorable.

For example, assume that a new model with better accuracy and no noted drift is ready to get into production. After several instances of this new version are available to start receiving traffic, make a configuration change to send 10% of all traffic to the new version. While traffic starts to get routed, you notice a dismal amount of errors from responses. The HTTP 500 errors indicate that the application has an internal error. After some investigation, it shows that one of the Python dependencies that do the inferencing is trying to import a module that has been moved, causing an exception. If the application receives one hundred requests per minute, only ten of those would've experienced the error condition. After noticing the errors, you quickly change the configuration to send all traffic to the older version currently deployed. This operation is also referred to as a *rollback*.

Most cloud providers have the ability to do a controlled rollout of models for these strategies. Although this is not a fully functional example, the Azure Python SDK can define the percentage of traffic for a newer version when deploying:

```
from azureml.core.webservice import AksEndpoint

endpoint.create_version(version_name = "2",
                        inference_config=inference_config,
                        models=[model],
                        traffic_percentile = 10)
endpoint.wait_for_deployment(True)
```

The tricky part is that a canary deployment's objective is to progressively increase until the `traffic_percentile` is at 100%. The increase has to happen alongside meeting constraints about application healthiness and minimal (or zero) error rates.

Monitoring, logging, and detailed metrics of production models (aside from model performance) are absolutely critical for a robust deployment strategy. I consider them crucial for deployment, but they are a core pillar of the robust DevOps practices covered in Chapter 6. Besides monitoring, logging, and metrics that have their own chapter, there are other interesting things to check for continuous delivery. In the next section, we will see a few that make sense and increase the confidence of deploying a model into production.

Testing Techniques for Model Deployment

So far, the container built in this chapter works great and does exactly what we need: from some HTTP requests with a carefully crafted message in a JSON body, a JSON response predicts the sentiment. A seasoned machine learning engineer might have put accuracy and drift detection (covered in detail in Chapter 6) in place before getting to the model packaging stage. Let's assume that's already the case and concentrate on other helpful tests you can perform before deploying a model into production.

When you send an HTTP request to the container to produce a prediction, several software layers need to go through from start to end. At a high level, these are critical:

1. Client sends an HTTP request, with a JSON body, in the form of an array with a single string.

2. A specific HTTP PORT (*5000*) and endpoint (*predict*) have to exist and get routed to.

3. The Python Flask application has to receive the JSON payload and load it into native Python.

4. The ONNX runtime needs to consume the string and produce a prediction.

5. A JSON response with an HTTP 200 response needs to contain the boolean value of the prediction.

Every single one of these high-level steps can (and should) be tested.

Automated checks

While putting together the container for this chapter, I got into some problems with the *onnxruntime* Python module: the documentation doesn't pin (an exact version number) the version, which caused the latest version to get installed, which needed different arguments as input. The accuracy of the model was good, and I was not able to detect a significant drift. And yet, I deployed the model only to find it fully broken once requests were consumed.

With time, applications become better and more resilient. Another engineer might add error handling to respond with an error message when invalid inputs get detected, and perhaps with an HTTP response with an appropriate HTTP error code along with a nice error message that the client can understand. You must test out these types of additions and behaviors before allowing a model to ship into production.

Sometimes there will be no HTTP error condition and no Python tracebacks either. What would happen if I made a change like the following to the JSON response:

```
{
  "positive": "false"
}
```

Without looking back at the previous sections, can you tell the difference? The change would go unnoticed. The canary deployment strategy would go to 100% without any errors detected. The machine learning engineer would be happy with high accuracy and no drift. And yet, this change has completely broken the effectiveness of the model. If you haven't caught the difference, that is OK. I encounter these types of problems all the time, and they can take me hours sometimes to detect the problem: instead of `false` (a boolean value), it is using `"false"` (a string).

None of these checks should ever be manual; manual verification should be kept to a minimum. Automation should be a high priority, and the suggestions I've so far made can all be added as part of the pipeline. These checks can be generalized to other models for reuse, but at a high level, they can run in parallel as shown in Figure 4-12.

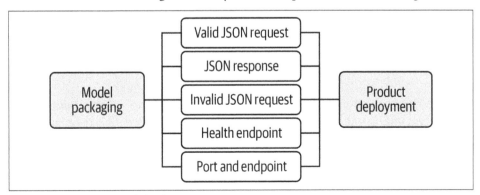

Figure 4-12. Automated checks

Linting

Beyond some of the functional checks I mention, like sending HTTP requests, there are other checks closer to the code in the Flask app that are far simpler to implement, like using a linter (I recommend Flake8 for Python (*https://oreil.ly/MMs0C*)). It would be best to automate all these checks to prevent getting into trouble when the production release needs to happen. Regardless of the development environment you are in, I *strongly* recommend enabling a linter for writing code. While creating the Flask application, I found errors as I adapted the code to work with HTTP requests. Here is a short example of the linter's output:

```
$ flake8 webapp/app.py
webapp/app.py:9:13: F821 undefined name 'RobertaTokenizer'
```

Undefined names break applications. In this case, I forgot to import the `RobertaTo kenizer` from the `transformers` module. As soon as I realized this, I added the import and fixed it. This didn't take me more than a few seconds.

In fact, the earliest you can detect these problems, the better. When talking about security in software, it is typical to hear "software supply chain," where the *chain* is all the steps from development to shipping code into production. And in this chain of events, there is a constant push to *shift left*. If you see these steps as one big chain, the leftmost link is the developer creating and updating the software, and the end of the chain (the farthest to the right) is the released product, where the end-consumer can interact with it.

The earlier you can shift left the error detection, the better. This is because it is cheaper and faster than waiting all the way until it is in production when a rollback needs to happen.

Continuous improvement

A couple of years ago, I was the release manager of a large open source software. The software was so complicated to release that it would take me anywhere from two days up to a whole week. It was tough to make improvements as I was responsible for other systems as well. One time, while trying to get a release out, following the many different steps to publish the packages, a core developer asked me to get in one last change. Instead of saying *"No"* right away, I asked: *"Has this change been tested already?"*

The response was completely unexpected: *"Don't be ridiculous, Alfredo, this is a one-line change, and it is a documentation comment in a function. We really need this change to be part of the release."* The push to get the change in came all the way from the top, and I had to budge. I added the last-minute change and cut the release.

The very first thing the next morning, we came back to users (and most importantly, customers) all complaining that the latest release was completely broken. It would install, but it would not run at all. The culprit was the one-line change that, although it was a comment within a function, was being parsed by other code. There was an unexpected syntax in that comment, so it prevented the application from starting up. The story is not meant to chastise the developer. He didn't know better. The whole process was a learning moment for everyone involved, and it was now clear how expensive this one-line change was.

There was a set of disruptive events that followed. Aside from restarting the release process, the testing phase for the one change took another (extra) day. Lastly, I had to *retire* the released packages and redo the repositories so new users would get the previous version.

It was beyond costly. The number of people involved and the high impact made this an excellent opportunity to assert that this should not be allowed again—even if it is a one-line change. The earlier the detection, the least impact it will have, and the cheaper it is to fix.

Conclusion

Continuous delivery and the practice of constant feedback is crucial for a robust workflow. As this chapter proves, there is a lot of value in automation and continuous improvement of the feedback loop. Packaging containers, along with pipelines and CI/CD platforms in general, are meant to make it easier to add more checks and verifications, which are intended to increase the confidence of shipping models into production.

Shipping models into production is the number one objective, but doing so with very high confidence, in a resilient set of steps, is what you should strive for. Your task does not end once the processes are in place. You must keep finding ways to thank yourself later by asking the question: what can I add today to make my life easier if this process fails? Finally, I would strongly recommend creating these workflows in a way that makes it easy to add more checks and verifications. If it is hard, no one will want to touch it, defeating the purpose of a robust pipeline to ship models into production.

Now that you have a good grasp of delivering models and what the automation looks like, we will dive into AutoML and Kaizen in the next chapter.

Exercises

- Create your own Flask application in a container, publish it to a GitHub repository, document it thoroughly, and add GitHub Actions to ensure it builds correctly.
- Make changes to the ONNX container so that it pushes to Docker Hub instead of GitHub Packages.
- Modify a SageMaker pipeline, so it prompts you before registering the model after training it.
- Using the Azure SDK, create a Jupyter notebook that will increase the percentile of traffic going to a container.

Critical Thinking Discussion Questions

- Name at least four critical checks you can add to verify a packaged model in a container is built correctly.
- What are the differences between canary and blue-green deployments? Which one do you prefer? Why?
- Why are cloud pipelines useful versus using GitHub Actions? Name at least three differences.
- What does *packaging a container* mean? Why is it useful?
- What are three characteristics of package machine learning models?

## CHAPTER 5

AutoML and KaizenML

By Noah Gift

Held down too hard by rules, partial thoughts cannot blossom. Rules without ideas is prison. Ideas without rules is chaos. Bonsai teaches us balance. Balancing rules against innovation is a pervasive problem in all of life. I once saw a play entitled "The Game of Life." The message was that one is often asked to play the game for high stakes before anybody has explained the rules. Moreover, it's not so easy to tell if you are winning. It often seems that beginners (and young people generally) need rules or broad theories for guidance. Then, as experience accumulates, the many exceptions and variations gradually invalidate the rules at the same time that the rules become less needed. A great advantage of bonsai over Life is that one can learn from fatal mistakes.

—Dr. Joseph Bogen

It is an exciting time to be involved in build machine learning systems. Machine learning, i.e., learning from data, has a clear value to humanity in solving problems from autonomous vehicles to more effective cancer screening and treatment. At the same time, automation plays a critical role in enabling this advancement in the automation of model creation, AutoML, and the rest of the tasks surrounding machine learning, something I call KaizenML.

While AutoML is focused strictly on creating a model from clean data, KaizenML is about automating *everything* about the machine learning process and improving it. Let's dive into both topics starting with the reason why AutoML is so essential.

Experts in machine learning, like Andrew Ng, now acknowledge that a data-centric approach has merits over a model-centric process. Another way of stating this is that Kaizen, i.e., continuous improvement of the entire system from the data to the software, to the model, to the feedback loop from the customer, is essential. KaizenML, in my mind, means you are improving all aspects of a machine learning system: data quality, software quality, and model quality.

AutoML

The author Upton Sinclair famously said, "it's difficult to get a man to understand something when his salary depends on his not understanding it." An excellent example of the Upton Sinclair quote in action is the misinformation from social media documented in the Netflix documentary, *The Social Dilemma*. Suppose you work at a company that spreads misinformation at scale and gets paid very well. In that case, it is almost impossible to accept that you are an actor in that process, and your company does, in fact, profit handsomely from misinformation. It contributes to your excellent salary and lifestyle.

Similarly, I have come up with something I call the Automator's law. Once the conversation about automating a task begins, then eventually, the automation occurs. Some examples include replacing data centers with cloud computing and replacing telephone switchboard operators with machines. Many companies have held on to their data centers with "white knuckles," saying the cloud was the root of all evil in the world. Yet, eventually, they either switched to the cloud or are in the process of switching to the cloud.

It took almost 100 years, from around 1880 to 1980, to fully automate switching calls by hand to make a machine do them, but it happened. Machines are great at automating labor-intensive manual tasks. If your job involved switching telephone calls in 1970, you might have scoffed at the idea of automating what you did since you understood how difficult the task was. Today, with data science, it may be that we are switchboard operators furiously pushing hyperparameter values into Python functions and sharing our results on Kaggle, unaware that all of this is in the process of being automated away.

In the book, *How We Know What Isn't So*, Thomas Gilovich points out self-handicapping strategies:

> There really are two classes of self-handicapping strategies, real and feigned. "Real" self-handicapping involves placing visible obstacles to success in one's own path. The obstacles make one less likely to succeed, but they provide a ready excuse for failure. The student who neglects to study before an exam or the aspiring actor who drinks

before an audition are good examples. Sometimes failure is all but guaranteed, but at least one will not be thought to be lacking in the relevant ability (or so it is hoped).

"Feigned" self-handicapping, on the other hand, is in certain respects a less risky strategy, one in which the person merely claims that there were difficult obstacles in the path to success. This kind of self-handicapping consists simply of making excuses for possible bad performance, either before or after the fact.

When data science initiatives fail, it is easy to dive into either of these self-handicapping strategies. An example of this in data science could be by not using AutoML when it could help with certain aspects of a project; this is a "real" handicap to its success. However, one of the golden rules of software engineering is to use the best tools you can for the task at hand. The reason to use the best tools available is they reduce the complexity of the software developed. An excellent example of a "best in class" tool that reduces complexity is GitHub Actions because it is simple to create automated testing. Another example is an editor like Visual Studio Code because of its ability to perform code completion, syntax highlighting, and linting with minimal configuration. Both of these tools dramatically increase developer productivity by simplifying the process of creating software.

With data science, this mantra of "use the best tools available" needs evangelism. Alternatively, if a data science project fails, as they often do, a self-handicapping strategy could be to say the problem was too challenging. In either case, an embrace of automation, when appropriate, is the solution to self-handicapping.

Let's compare food to machine learning in Figure 5-1. Notice that food comes in many forms, from the flour you buy at the store to make your own pizza to the one you have delivered to your house. Just because one is much more complex than another (i.e., making a pizza from scratch versus ordering a ready-made hot pizza) it doesn't mean that the home delivery option isn't also considered food. Difficulty, or lack thereof, does not equate with completeness or realness.

Similarly, not accepting reality doesn't mean that it's not happening. Another way of describing denying reality is to call it "magical thinking." Many magical thinkers said at the start of the COVID-19 pandemic, "This is just like the flu," as a way to reassure themselves (and others) that the danger was not as bad as it appeared to be. The data in 2021 says something entirely different, though. COVID-19 in the USA approached about 75% of the deaths of all combined forms of heart disease, currently the leading cause of death in the USA. Similarly, Justin Fox in a Bloomberg article (*https://oreil.ly/0sXwI*) using the CDC data shows that this pandemic is multiple times more deadly for most age groups than influenza. See Figure 5-2.

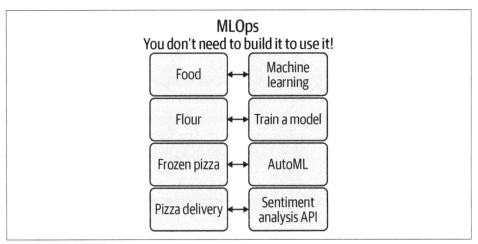

Figure 5-1. Food versus ML

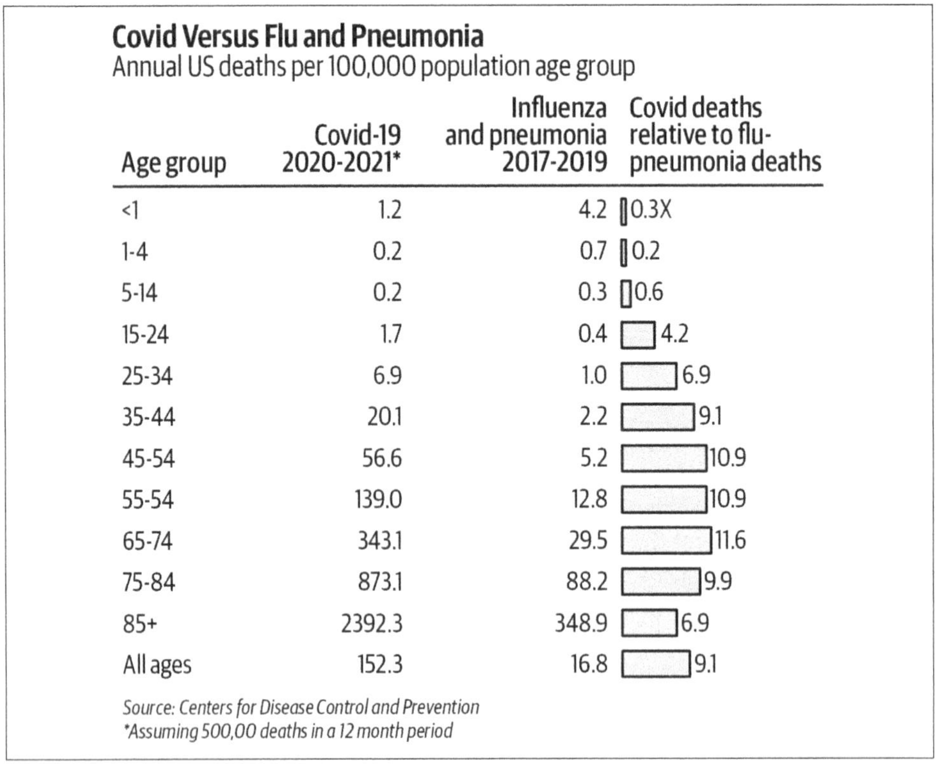

Covid Versus Flu and Pneumonia
Annual US deaths per 100,000 population age group

Age group	Covid-19 2020-2021*	Influenza and pneumonia 2017-2019	Covid deaths relative to flu-pneumonia deaths
<1	1.2	4.2	0.3X
1-4	0.2	0.7	0.2
5-14	0.2	0.3	0.6
15-24	1.7	0.4	4.2
25-34	6.9	1.0	6.9
35-44	20.1	2.2	9.1
45-54	56.6	5.2	10.9
55-54	139.0	12.8	10.9
65-74	343.1	29.5	11.6
75-84	873.1	88.2	9.9
85+	2392.3	348.9	6.9
All ages	152.3	16.8	9.1

Source: Centers for Disease Control and Prevention
*Assuming 500,00 deaths in a 12 month period

Figure 5-2. Covid versus the flu and pneumonia (source: Bloomberg News (https://oreil.ly/pUEFc))

AutoML is an inflection point for data scientists because it shares similarities to other historical trends: automation and magical thinking. Anything that can automate will automate. Accepting this trend instead of fighting it will lead to massively more productive workflows in machine learning. AutoML, in particular, may be one of the most critical technologies to embrace to implement the MLOps philosophy fully.

Before the COVID-19 outbreak, a research scientist from UC Berkeley, Dr. Jennifer Doudna, and collaborator Dr. Emmanuelle Charpentier worked on the difficult task of researching gene editing. When the COVID-19 pandemic began, Dr. Doudna knew she needed to quickly convert this research into a groundbreaking way to accelerate the creation of a vaccine. As a result, she started work to "save the world."

 How is COVID-19 drug discovery related to MLOps? A critical problem in data science is getting a research solution into production. Similarly, a fundamental problem with medical research is getting the discovery into the hands of a patient who benefits from it.

In *The Code Breaker: Jennifer Doudna, Gene Editing, and the Future of the Human Race* (Simon & Schuster Australia), Walter Isaacson describes how Dr. Doudna was "...now a strong believer that basic research should be combined with translational research, moving discoveries from bench to bedside..." The now Nobel Prize–winning scientist Dr. Jennifer Doudna is co-credited, along with Dr. Emmanuelle Charpentier, with creating the research that led to gene editing and commercial application of these CRISPR mechanisms.

One of her rivals, Dr. Feng Zhang, who eventually worked on a competing vaccine, Moderna, mentioned that the UC Berkeley lab wasn't working on applying this in human cells. His critique is that his lab was working on using the CRISPR research by targeting human cells, while Dr. Doudna was focused strictly on the research.

This critique is the heart of a patent dispute about who gets to claim credit for these discoveries, i.e., how much work was research and how much was the application of the research? Doesn't this sound a bit similar to the data science versus software engineering disputes? Ultimately, Dr. Doudna did, in fact, "get it to production" in the form of the Pfizer vaccine. I recently got this vaccine, and like many people, I am thrilled it made it to production.

What else could we collectively accomplish if we had the same sense of urgency as the scientists "operationalizing" the vaccine for COVID-19? When I was an engineering manager at startups, I liked to ask people hypothetical questions. Some variant of "What if you had to save the world on a deadline"? I like this question because it cuts to the heart of things quickly. It cuts to the nature of the problem because if the clock is ticking on saving millions of lives, you work only on the essential components of the problem.

There is an incredible documentary on Netflix entitled *World War II in Colour*. What is impressive about the documentary is that it shows the actual restored and colorized footage of tragic historical events. This really helps you imagine what it might have been like to be present during those events. Along those lines, imagine yourself in a situation where you need to solve a technical problem that would save the world. Of course, if you get it wrong, everyone you know will suffer a horrible fate. However, AutoML or any form of automation coupled with a sense of urgency in solving only the necessary components of a problem can lead to better outcomes globally: i.e., drug discovery and cancer detection.

This form of situational thinking adds a clarifying component to deciding how to solve a problem. Either what you are doing matters, or it doesn't. It is very similar to the way the scientists working on COVID-19 vaccines thought. Either what the scientists did led to a faster COVID-19 vaccine, or it didn't. As a result, every day wasted was a day that more people worldwide succumbed to the virus.

Similarly, I remember going to a fancy startup in the Bay Area around 2016 and remarking on how they received 30M funding from many top-name venture capital firms. The COO then privately told me how he was very concerned that they had no actual product or way to make money. They received even more money many years later, and I am still unsure what their actual product is.

Because this company cannot create revenue, it fundraises. If you cannot fundraise, then you must create revenue. Likewise, if you cannot put your model into production with machine learning, you continue to do "ML research," i.e., working away at tweaking hyperparameters on a Kaggle project. So a good question for Kaggle practitioners to ask is, "Are we sure we aren't just automating our job of tweaking hyperparameters by training Google's AutoML technology?"

We gravitate toward what we excel at doing. There are many beautiful things about focusing on what you do well, such as it leading to a successful career. Still, there are also times to challenge yourself to temporarily think situationally about solving a problem in the most urgent manner possible, much like Drs. Doudna and Zhang did with COVID-19. Does this change the approach you use? For example, if I had four hours to train a model and put it into production to save the world, I would write as little code as possible and use off-the-shelf automation tools like Azure AutoML, Apple Create ML, Google AutoML, H20, or Ludwig. In that case, the follow-up question becomes, why am I writing *any* code, or at least writing the least amount of code possible for all machine learning engineering projects?

The world needs high-quality machine learning models in production, particularly because there are many urgent problems to solve: finding a cure for cancer, optimizing clean energy, improving drug discovery, and creating safer transportation. One way society can collectively do this is to automate what can be automated now and focus on finding ways to automate what cannot be automated today.

AutoML is the automation of the tasks related to training a model on clean data. Not all problems are so simple in the real world, though, and as a result *everything* related to machine learning needs automation. This gap is where KaizenML steps in. Kaizen, in Japanese, means continuous improvement. With KazienML, you continuously improve and automate as the central way you develop machine learning systems. Let's dive into that concept next.

MLOps Industrial Revolution

Many students and practitioners of machine learning find AutoML to be a polarizing topic. Data science is a behavior; AutoML is a technique—they are a small part of building an ML system, and they are complementary. AutoML is polarizing because data scientists assume it will replace their job, when in fact, AutoML is 5% of a gigantic process of automation and continuous improvement, i.e., MLOps/ML engineering/KaizenML, as described in Figure 5-3.

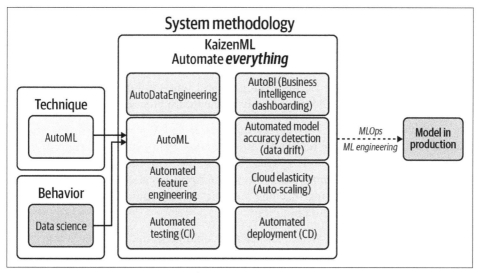

Figure 5-3. AutoML is a tiny part of KaizenML

The industrial revolution from 1760–1840 was a period of dramatic movement of human tasks to automated ones powered by steam and coal machines. This automation led to a rise in population, GDP, and quality of life. Later, around 1870, the second industrial revolution occurred, allowing for mass production and new electrical grid systems.

There is an excellent series on Disney+ called *Made in a Day*. (*https://oreil.ly/nLA7Y*) The first episode shows how Tesla uses robots for car development phases. The robots screw in things, bolt things on, and weld parts together. When looking at this factory, I think about how humans are assisting the robots. Essentially, they feed the robots work that they cannot yet fully automate themselves.

Likewise, when looking at traditional data science workflows full of unique snowflake configurations, with humans "bolting on" hyperparameters, it makes me think of an early Ford assembly plant in the second industrial revolution. Eventually, manual human tasks get automated, and the first thing that is automated is the easiest to automate.

Another question people ask is whether many aspects of machine learning techniques are even necessary, like manually adjusting hyperparameters, i.e., picking the number of clusters. Imagine going to a Tesla factory full of advanced robotics and telling the automation engineers that humans can also weld parts together. This statement would be a non sequitur. Of course, we humans can perform tasks that machines do better than us, but should we? Likewise, with many tedious and manual aspects of machine learning, machines do a better job.

What may occur soon in machine learning and artificial intelligence is that the technique is essentially commoditized. Instead, the automation itself and the ability to execute the automation is the key. The TV show about physical manufacturing has the name "Made in a Day" because cars or guitars manufacture in just one day! Many companies doing machine learning cannot build one software-based model in an entire year, though how could this possibly be the future process?

One possible scenario that I see happening soon is that at least 80% of data science manual training models are replaced with commoditized open source AutoML tools or downloaded pre-built models. This future could happen as both open source projects like Ludwig or commercial projects like Apple CreateML advance in sophistication. Software for training machine learning models could turn into something like the Linux kernel, free and ubiquitous.

If they are in their current form, data science could go bimodal; either you get paid $1M/year, or you're entry-level. Most competitive advantages go into traditional software engineering best practices: data/users, automation, execution, and solid product management and business practices. A data scientist could become a standard skill like accounting, writing, or critical thinking in other cases instead of a job title alone. You could call this the MLOps industrial revolution.

Figure 5-4 is an example of this in practice. Imagine Kaggle as a feedback loop that Google uses to make its AutoML tools much better. Why wouldn't they use the human data scientists' training models to make better AutoML services? In data science 1.0, humans are manually "clicking buttons" just like the switchboard operators of the past. Meanwhile, if they wanted, Google could use these humans to train their AutoML systems to do these manual data science tasks. In data science 2.0, which in many cases is already here, automated tools thoroughly train the previously trained models in Kaggle.

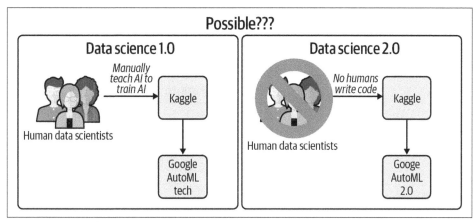

Figure 5-4. Kaggle automation

The MLOps industrial revolution is happening before our eyes as machines play an increasing role in machine learning and data science. What skills do you invest in if these changes are under way? Be world-class at automation and execution both technically and from a business perspective. Also, couple these capabilities with solid domain expertise. In the book *How Innovation Works: And Why It Flourishes in Freedom* (Harper), author Matt Ridley clearly explains how ideas are not the basis of innovation but the combination of the ideas into execution. Essentially, does it work or not, and will someone pay you for it?

Kaizen Versus KaizenML

One problem with talking about data science, AutoML, and MLOps (KaizenML) is that people often misunderstand what each one is. Data science is not a solution any more than statistics is a solution to a problem; it is behavioral. AutoML is just a technique, like continuous integration (CI); it automates trivial tasks. Subsequently, AutoML is not directly competing with data science; cruise control, or semi-autonomous driving for that matter, doesn't compete with a car driver. The driver still must control the vehicle and act as the central arbitrator of what happens. Likewise, even with extensive automation in machine learning, a human must make executive decisions about the bigger picture.

KaizenML/MLOps is a systems methodology that leads to models in production. Machine learning models running in production solving customer problems is the outcome of MLOps. In Figure 5-5, you can see a hypothetical MLOps industrial revolution that could occur in the future. Data and the expertise in handling data effectively becomes a competitive advantage since it is a scarce resource. As AutoML technology progresses, it is possible many things data scientists do today go away. It is uncommon to find modern vehicles without a form of cruise control or with manual transmission. Likewise, it may be infrequent for data scientists to adjust hyperparameters in the future. What could happen then is that current data scientists turn into ML engineers or domain experts who "do data science" as part of their job.

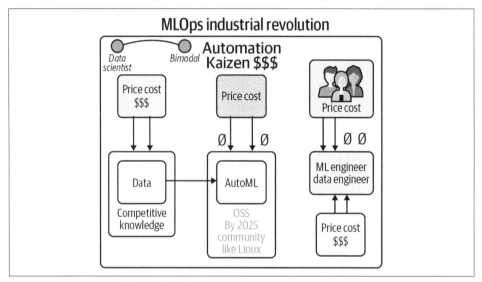

Figure 5-5. MLOps industrial revolution

One issue with talking only about AutoML versus data science is that it trivializes the more significant automation and continuous improvement issues. The automation of machine learning techniques is so polarizing that the core issue disappears: everything should be automated, not just the tedious aspects of ML-like hyperparameter tuning. Automation through continuous improvement allows data scientists, ML engineers, and entire organizations to focus on what matters, i.e., execution. As you can see illustrated in Figure 5-6, Kaizen is a Japanese term for continuous improvement. In post–World War II, Japan builds its automobile industry around this concept. Essentially, if you find something broken or unoptimized, you fix it. Likewise, with KaizenML, every aspect of machine learning, from feature engineering to AutoML, is improved.

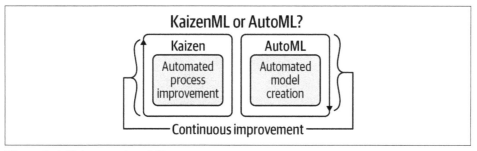

Figure 5-6. Kaizen or AutoML

Every human on earth should do data science and programming because these are forms of critical thinking. The recent pandemic was a big wake-up call about how important to an individual's life understanding data science is. Many people died because they didn't understand the data that showed COVID-19 was not, in fact, just like the flu; it was much, much more deadly. Likewise, stories abound about people refusing to get a vaccine because they incorrectly calculated the risk the vaccine posed to themselves versus the risk COVID-19 posed to themselves or vulnerable members of their community. Understanding data science can save your life, and therefore, anyone should have access to the tools data scientists have.

These tools are "human rights" that don't belong in the hands of an elite priesthood. It is a non sequitur to suggest "elite" people only can write simple programs, understand machine learning, or do data science. Automation will make data science and programming easy enough that every human being will do it, and in many cases, they can do so using even the existing automation available.

KaizenML/MLOps is about a narrow focus on solving problems with machine learning and software engineering (influenced by DevOps) to lead to business value or improvement of the human condition, e.g., cure cancer.

Feature Stores

All complex software systems require automation and simplification of critical components. DevOps is about automating the testing and deployment of software. MLOps is about doing this and also improving the quality of both data and machine learning models. I have previously called these continuous improvements of both data and machine learning models KaizenML. One way to think about this is that DevOps + KaizenML = MLOps. KaizenML includes building Feature Stores, i.e., a registry of high-quality machine learning inputs and the ability to monitor data for drift and register and serve out ML models.

In Figure 5-7, note that in manual data science, everything is bespoke. As a result, the data is low quality, and it is hard to even get to the point where a working model goes into production and solves a problem. However, as more things get automated from data to features, via a Feature Store, to the actual serving out of the model in production, it leads to a better outcome.

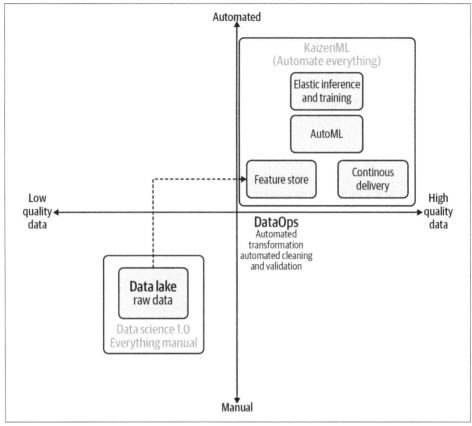

Figure 5-7. Feature Stores as part of KaizenML

Heavily related to KaizenML, i.e., continuously improving machine learning, is the concept of a Feature Store. The Uber Engineering blog has a good breakdown of what problem a Feature Store solves (*https://oreil.ly/ej36j*). According to Uber, it does two things:

- Allows users to add features they built into a shared Feature Store.
- Once features are in the Feature Store, they are easy to use in training and prediction.

In Figure 5-8, you can see that data science is a behavior, but AutoML is a technique. AutoML could be only 5% of the entire problem solved by automation. The data itself needs automation through ETL job management. The Feature Store needs automation to improve the ML inputs. Finally, the deployment requires automation through automated deployment (CD) and the native use of cloud elasticity (autoscaling). Everything requires automation with complex software systems, and Feature Stores are just one of many MLOps components needing continuous improvement, i.e., KaizenML.

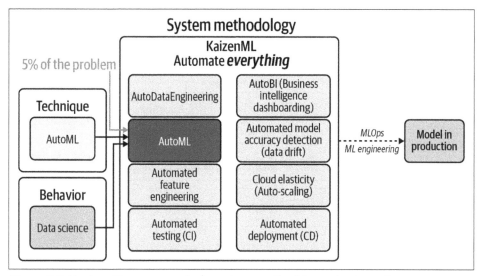

Figure 5-8. Feature Stores are part of a systems methodology of automation

There are many real-world use cases for Feature Stores. For example, Uber explains that it used 10,000 features in the Feature Store (*https://oreil.ly/iuDeG*) to accelerate machine projects and make AutoML solutions on top. In addition, platforms like Databricks (*https://oreil.ly/aqFju*) have Feature Stores built into their big data system. For example, in Figure 5-9, you can see how raw data is the input that gets transformed into a more refined and specialized feature registry that can solve both batch and online problems.

In Figure 5-10, notice that there are both similarities and differences between a traditional data warehouse and an MLOps Feature Store. A data warehouse feeds into business intelligence systems at a high level, and a Feature Store provides inputs into an ML system. Machine learning data processing is repetitive, including normalizing data, cleaning data, and finding appropriate features that improve an ML model. Creating a Feature Store system is yet one more way of fully embracing automation of the entire process of machine learning from ideation to production.

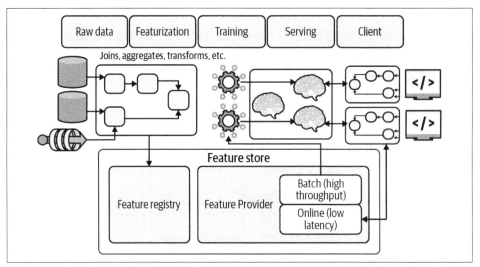

Figure 5-9. Databricks feature store

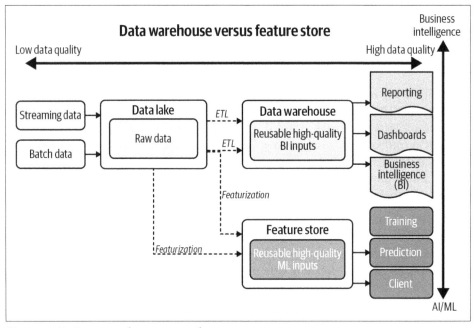

Figure 5-10. Data warehouse versus feature store

Next, let's get out of the theory and practice technique using the Apple ML Ecosystem to build machine learning models. We will do this using its high-level AutoML framework, CreateML.

Apple's Ecosystem

Apple may seem like an unlikely candidate to enter the machine learning tools space until you look a bit deeper. Apple has a rich ecosystem around mobile development. According to Statista (*https://oreil.ly/SEnIY*), the worldwide gross app revenue of the Apple App Store grew from 55.5 billion US Dollars in 2019 to 72.3 billion US Dollars in 2020. Apple benefits from developers creating products that sell in its app store.

I remember talking to a pretty dismissive professor about building "apps for machine learning," presumably because he gravitated toward complexity and discovery in doing research. In a sense, the software industry thinks in an opposite manner of a researcher at a university. Writing academic papers on machine learning is the opposite direction of operationalizing machine learning to "build apps." This ideological difference is the "idea" versus "execution" disconnect discussed earlier.

Apple wants you to build apps in its app store since it takes between 15% and 30% of every transaction. The better Apple makes the developer tools, the more applications live in the app store. There is an expression in business school, "Where do you build a Burger King? Next to McDonald's." This expression is a way of saying that you don't need to spend the money to research where to expand because the top competitor already did the work. You can piggyback on their expertise—likewise, practitioners of machine learning can piggyback on the research Apple has done. They see a future in high-level automated machine learning running on specialized hardware.

Similarly, why do many VC firms fund only companies that top VC firms already funded? Because then they don't need to do any work; they can profit from the expertise of a more knowledgeable firm. Similarly, Apple has tremendous investments from a hardware perspective into on-device machine learning. In particular, Apple develops chips itself, like the A-series: A12-A14, shown in Figure 5-11, including CPUs, GPUs, and dedicated neural network hardware.

Figure 5-11. Apple's A14 chip

Further, newer chips include the Apple M1 architecture, which Apple uses on mobile devices, laptops, and desktop machines, as shown in Figure 5-12.

Figure 5-12. Apple's M1 chip

The development environment makes use of this technology through Apple's model format Core ML (*https://oreil.ly/jyoxD*). There is also a Python package to convert models from third-party training libraries like TensorFlow and Keras.

Core ML is optimized for on-device performance and works in tandem with the Apple hardware. There are several non-obvious workflows to consider:

- Use Apple's Create ML framework to make AutoML solutions.
- Download a pretrained model and optionally convert it to the Core ML format. One location to download models from is tfhub (*https://oreil.ly/ouuNI*).
- Train a model yourself by writing the code in another framework, then converting it to Core ML using coremltools (*https://oreil.ly/vYGcE*).

Let's dig into Apple's AutoML.

Apple's AutoML: Create ML

One of the core innovations with Apple's ML platform is how it exposes power AutoML technology enclosed in an intuitive GUI. Apple Create ML lets you do the following:

- Create Core ML models
- Preview the model performance
- Train models on the Mac (taking advantage of their M1 chip stack)
- Use training control: i.e., pause, save and resume training
- Use eGPU (external GPUs)

Additionally, it tackles various domains from image, video, motion, sound, text, and tabular. Let's dive into AutoML with Apple's CreateML. Notice the entire list of many automated forms of machine learning in Figure 5-13 and how they ultimately converge to the same Core ML model that runs on iOS.

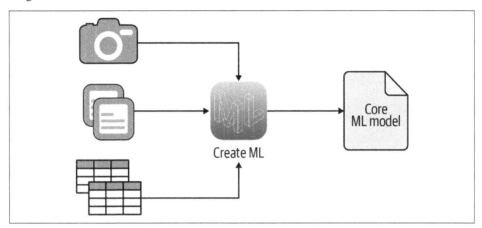

Figure 5-13. Create ML

To get started with Create ML, do the following:

1. Download XCode (*https://oreil.ly/dOCQj*).
2. Open up XCode and right-click the icon to launch Create ML (Figure 5-14).

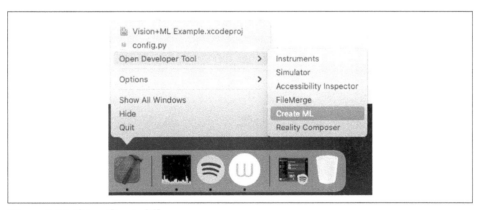

Figure 5-14. Open Create ML

Next, use the Image Classifier template (see Figure 5-15).

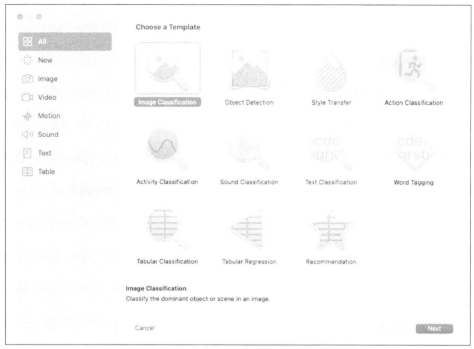

Figure 5-15. Image Classifier Template

You can grab a smaller version of the Kaggle dataset "cats and dogs" in the GitHub repository for the book (*https://oreil.ly/XMB82*). Drop the `cats-dogs-small` dataset onto the UI for Create ML (see Figure 5-16).

Figure 5-16. Upload data

Also, drop the test data (*https://oreil.ly/JRNmt*) onto the test section of the UI for Create ML.

Next, train the model by clicking the train icon. Note that you can train the model multiple times by right-clicking Model Sources. You may want to experiment with this because it allows you to test with "Augmentations" like Noise, Blur, Crop, Expose, Flip, and Rotate (see Figure 5-17). These will enable you to create a more robust model that is more generalizable against real-world data.

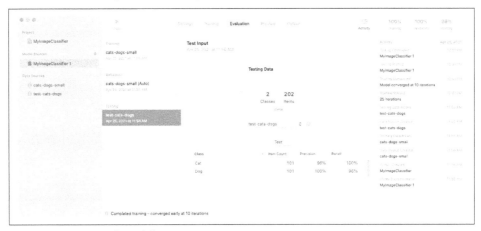

Figure 5-17. Trained model

This small dataset should only take a few seconds to train the model (especially if you have the newer Apple M1 hardware). You can test it out by finding internet pictures of cats and dogs, downloading them, and dragging them into the preview icon (see Figure 5-18).

Figure 5-18. Preview

A final step is to download the model and use it in an iOS application. Note that in Figure 5-19, I use the OS X Finder menu and name the model and save it to my desktop. This final step may be the terminal step for a hobbyist who wants to build a bespoke iOS application that runs just on their phone. Once you save the model, you could optionally convert it to another format like ONNX (*https://onnx.ai*) and then run it on a cloud platform like Microsoft Azure.

Figure 5-19. Create ML model

Great work! You trained your first model that required zero code. The future will be fantastic as more of these tools evolve and get into the hands of consumers.

Optional next steps:

- You can train a more complex model by downloading a larger Kaggle dataset (*https://oreil.ly/uzj4c*)
- You can try other types of AutoML
- You can experiment with augmentation

Now that you know how to train a model using Create ML, let's go a bit deeper into how you further leverage Apple's Core ML tools.

Apple's Core ML Tools

One of the more exciting workflows available for the Apple ecosystem is downloading models and converting them to the Core ML tools via a Python library. There are many locations to grab pretrained models, including TensorFlow Hub.

In this example, let's walk through the code in this Colab notebook (*https://oreil.ly/BBs71*).

First, install the `coremltools` library:

```
!pip install coremltools
import coremltools
```

Next, download the model (based on the official quickstart guide (*https://oreil.ly/Z5vpq*)).

Import tensorflow as tf:

```
# Download MobileNetv2 (using tf.keras)
keras_model = tf.keras.applications.MobileNetV2(
    weights="imagenet",
    input_shape=(224, 224, 3,),
    classes=1000,
)
# Download class labels (from a separate file)
import urllib
label_url = 'https://storage.googleapis.com/download.tensorflow.org/\
    data/ImageNetLabels.txt'
class_labels = urllib.request.urlopen(label_url).read().splitlines()
class_labels = class_labels[1:] # remove the first class which is background
assert len(class_labels) == 1000

# make sure entries of class_labels are strings
for i, label in enumerate(class_labels):
  if isinstance(label, bytes):
    class_labels[i] = label.decode("utf8")
```

Convert the model and set the metadata for the model to the correct parameters:

```
import coremltools as ct

# Define the input type as image,
# set preprocessing parameters to normalize the image
# to have its values in the interval [-1,1]
# as expected by the mobilenet model
image_input = ct.ImageType(shape=(1, 224, 224, 3,),
                           bias=[-1,-1,-1], scale=1/127)

# set class labels
classifier_config = ct.ClassifierConfig(class_labels)

# Convert the model using the Unified Conversion API
model = ct.convert(
    keras_model, inputs=[image_input], classifier_config=classifier_config,
)
```

Now update the metadata of the model:

```
# Set feature descriptions (these show up as comments in XCode)
model.input_description["input_1"] = "Input image to be classified"
model.output_description["classLabel"] = "Most likely image category"
```

```
# Set model author name
model.author = "" # Set the license of the model

# Set the license of the model
model.license = ""# Set a short description for the Xcode UI

# Set a short description for the Xcode UI
model.short_description = "" # Set a version for the model

# Set a version for the model
model.version = "2.0"
```

Finally, save the model, download it from Colab, and open it in XCode to predict (see Figure 5-20).

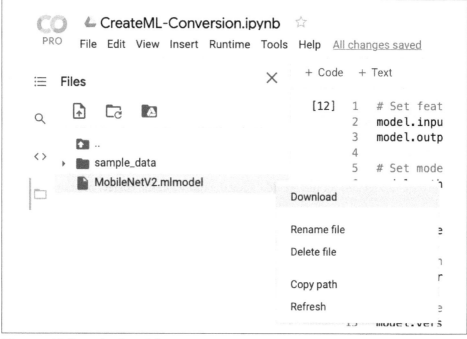

Figure 5-20. Download model

```
# Save model
model.save("MobileNetV2.mlmodel")

# Load a saved model
loaded_model = ct.models.MLModel("MobileNetV2.mlmodel")
```

Figure 5-21 shows an example prediction.

Figure 5-21. Stingray predict

The big takeaway is this process is even easier than using AutoML. Therefore, it may make more sense to download a model created by experts with access to expensive compute clusters than train it yourself in many cases. Apple's Core ML framework allows both the use case of bespoke AutoML as well as using pretrained models.

Google's AutoML and Edge Computer Vision

In the last few years, I have taught hundreds of students in a class called "Applied Computer Vision" at top data science universities. The premise of the course is to build solutions quickly using the most high-level tools available, including Google AutoML and edge hardware like the Coral.AI (*https://coral.ai*) chip that contains a TPU or the Intel Movidius.

Figure 5-22 shows two examples of small form-factor edge machine learning solutions.

Figure 5-22. Edge hardware

One of the surprising things about teaching the class is how quickly students can take "off the shelf" solutions, piece them together, and come up with a solution that solves a problem. I have seen projects including mask detection, license plate detection, and trash sorting applications running on mobile devices with little to no code. We are in a new era, the MLOps era, and it is easier to put code into working applications.

Like Apple and Google, many companies build a vertically integrated stack that provides a machine learning framework, operating systems, and specialized hardware like an ASIC (application-specific integrated circuit) that performs particular machine learning tasks. For example, the TPU, or TensorFlow Processing Unit, is actively developed with regular updates to the chip design. The edge version is a purpose-built ASIC that runs ML models. This tight integration is essential for organizations looking for the rapid creation of real-world machine learning solutions.

There are several critical approaches to computer vision on the GCP platform (similar to other cloud platforms, the service names are different). These options appear in order of difficulty:

- Write machine learning code that trains a model
- Use Google AutoML Vision

- Download a pretrained model from TensorFlow Hub (*https://tfhub.dev*) or another location
- Use the Vision AI API (*https://oreil.ly/7pX3S*)

Let's examine a Google AutoML Vision workflow that ends in a computer vision model deployed to an iOS device. This workflow is essentially the same, whether you use a sample dataset that Google provides or your own:

1. Launch Google Cloud Console and open a cloud shell.

2. Enable the Google AutoML Vision API and give your project permission to it; you would set both the `PROJECT_ID` and `USERNAME`:

   ```
   gcloud projects add-iam-policy-binding $PROJECT_ID \
   --member="user:$USERNAME" \
   --role="roles/automl.admin"
   ```

3. Upload training data and labels via a CSV file to Google Cloud Storage.
   If you set a `${BUCKET}` ` variable `export BUCKET=$FOOBAR`, then three commands are all you need to copy Google sample data. Here is one example for Cloud Classification (cirrus, cumulonimbus, cumulus). You can find a walk-through on Google Qwiklabs under "Classify Images of Clouds in the Cloud with AutoML Vision" (*https://qwiklabs.com*). The `gs://spls/gsp223/images/` location holds the data in this example, and the `sed` command swaps out the specific paths:

   ```
   gsutil -m cp -r gs://spls/gsp223/images/* gs://${BUCKET}
   gsutil cp gs://spls/gsp223/data.csv .
   sed -i -e "s/placeholder/${BUCKET}/g" ./data.csv
   ```

   Additional Datasets Ideal for Google AutoML

   Two other datasets you may also want to try to include are tf_flowers data (*https://oreil.ly/nknp3*) and cats and dogs data (*https://oreil.ly/nEJOd*). Yet another idea is uploading your data.

4. Visually inspect the data.
   One of the valuable aspects of Google's Cloud AutoML systems is using high-level tools to inspect the data, add new labels, or fix data quality control issues. Notice in Figure 5-23 that you have the ability to toggle between the different classification categories, which happen to be flowers.

Figure 5-23. Inspect data

5. Train the model and evaluate.

Training the model is a button click in the console. Google has collected these options into its product Google Vertex AI (*https://oreil.ly/P5m7Y*). Notice in Figure 5-24 that there are a series of actions from Notebooks to Batch Predictions on the left panel. When creating a new training job, AutoML is an option, as well as AutoML Edge.

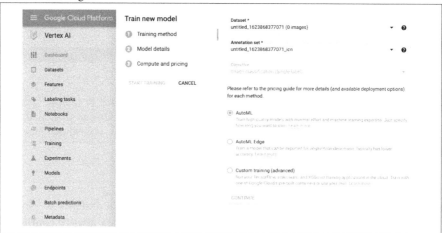

Figure 5-24. Google Vertex AI

6. Afterward, evaluate the trained model using the built-in tools (see Figure 5-25).

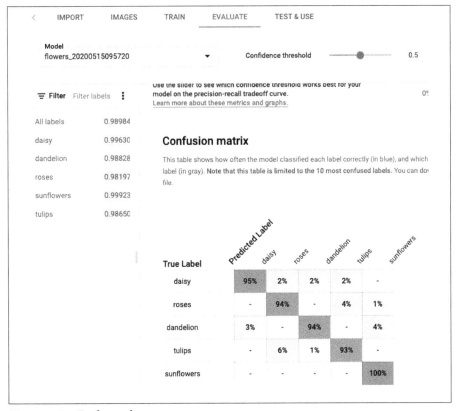

Figure 5-25. Evaluate data

7. Do something with the model: predict online or download.

With Google AutoML vision, there is the ability to create an online hosted end-point or download the model and make predictions on an edge device: iOS, Android, Javascript, Coral Hardware, or a container (see Figure 5-26).

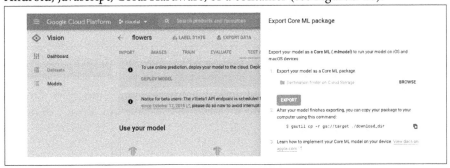

Figure 5-26. Download model

The main takeaway is that Google Cloud offers a well-traveled path from uploading training data to training with minimal or no code required to build machine learning solutions that deploy to edge devices. These options are all integrated as part of Google's managed machine learning platform Vertex AI.

Next, let's dive into Azure's AutoML solutions, which like Google's, have a complete story about managing the lifecycle of MLOps.

Azure's AutoML

There are two primary ways to access the Azure AutoML. One is the console, and the other is programmatic access to the AutoML Python SDK (*https://oreil.ly/EKA0b*). Let's take a look at the console first.

To get started doing AutoML on Azure, you need to launch an instance of Azure ML Studio and select the Automated ML option (see Figure 5-27).

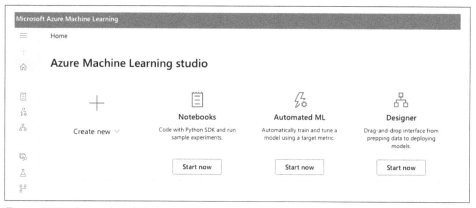

Figure 5-27. Azure AutoML

Next, create a dataset either by uploading it or using an open dataset. In this example, I use the data from the Kaggle Social Power NBA project (*https://oreil.ly/Bsjly*) (see Figure 5-28).

Then, I spin up a classification job to predict which position a player could play based on the features in the dataset. Note that many different types of machine learning predictions are available, including numerical regression and time-series forecasting. You will need to set up storage and a cluster if you have not already done so (see Figure 5-29) .

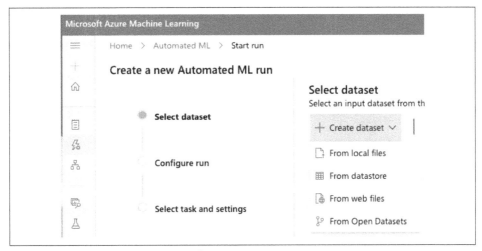

Figure 5-28. Azure AutoML create dataset

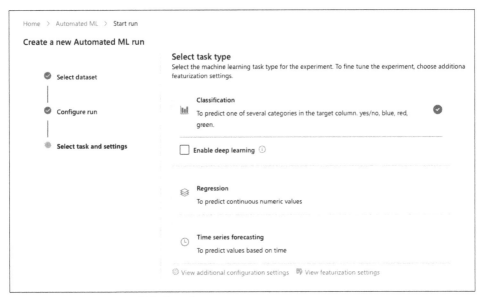

Figure 5-29. Azure AutoML classify

Once jobs complete, you can also ask Azure ML Studio to "explain" how it got to its predictions. A machine learning system explains how a model comes up with forecasts via "explainability," which is a critical upcoming capability of AutoML systems. You can see these explanatory capabilities in Figure 5-30. Notice how deep integration into the ML Studio solution gives this platform technology an extensive feel.

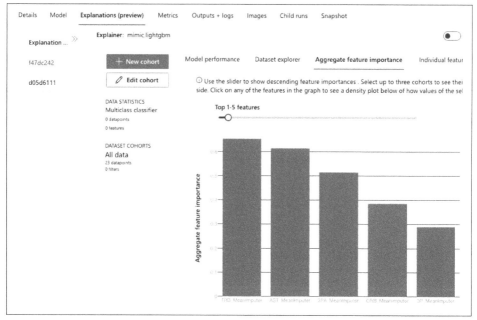

Figure 5-30. Azure AutoML explain

Let's take a look at the other approach. You can use Python to call the same API available from the Azure ML Studio console. This official Microsoft tutorial (*https://oreil.ly/io66Z*) explains it in detail, but the critical section is shown here:

```
from azureml.train.automl import AutoMLConfig

automl_config = AutoMLConfig(task='regression',
                             debug_log='automated_ml_errors.log',
                             training_data=x_train,
                             label_column_name="totalAmount",
                             **automl_settings)
```

AWS AutoML

As the largest cloud provider, AWS also has many AutoML solutions. One of the earliest solutions includes a tool with a bad name, "Machine Learning," that is no longer widely available but was an AutoML solution. Now the recommended solution is SageMaker AutoPilot (Figure 5-31). You can view many examples of SageMaker Autopilot in action from the official documentation (*https://oreil.ly/fDJiE*).

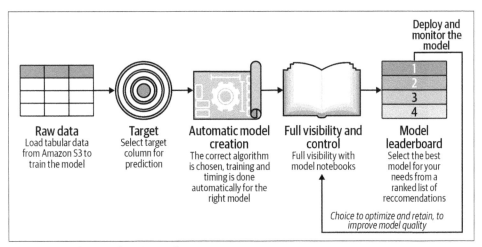

Figure 5-31. SageMaker Autopilot

Let's walk through how to do an Autopilot experiment with AWS SageMaker. First, as shown in Figure 5-32, open SageMaker Autopilot and select a new task.

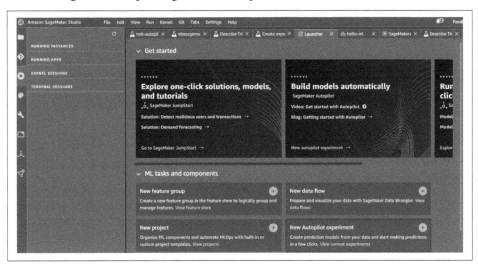

Figure 5-32. SageMaker Autopilot task

Next, I upload the "NBA Players Data Kaggle Project" (*https://oreil.ly/G1TIi*) into Amazon S3. Now that I have data to work with, I create an experiment as shown in Figure 5-33. Notice that I select for a target the draft position. This classification is because I want to create a prediction model that shows what draft position an NBA player deserves based on their performance.

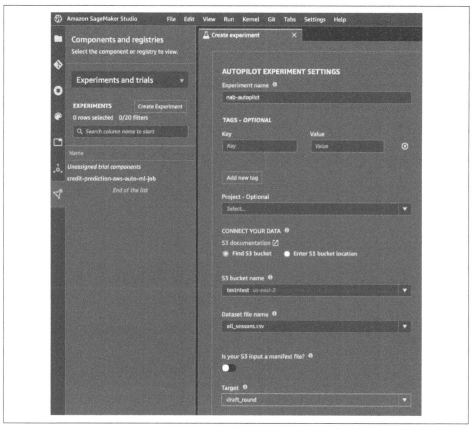

Figure 5-33. Create Autopilot experiment

Once I submit the experiment, SageMaker Autopilot goes through a preprocessing stage through Model Tuning, as Figure 5-34 shows.

Now that the AutoML pipeline is running, you can see the resources it uses in the Resources tab, as shown in Figure 5-35.

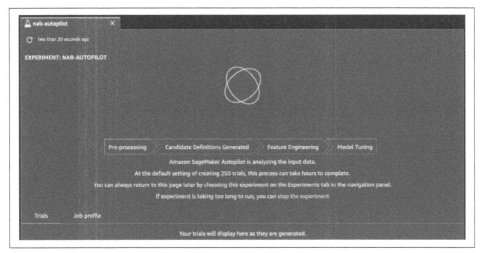

Figure 5-34. Run Autopilot experiment

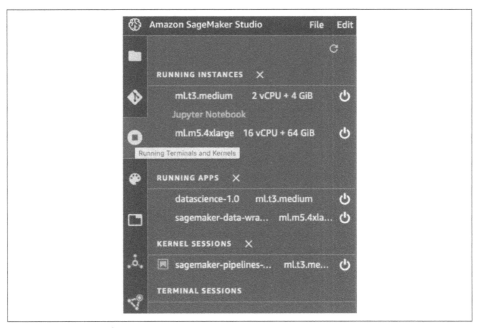

Figure 5-35. Autopilot instances

When the training is complete, you can see a list of models and their accuracy, as shown in Figure 5-36. Note that SageMaker was able to create a highly accurate classification model with an accuracy of .999945.

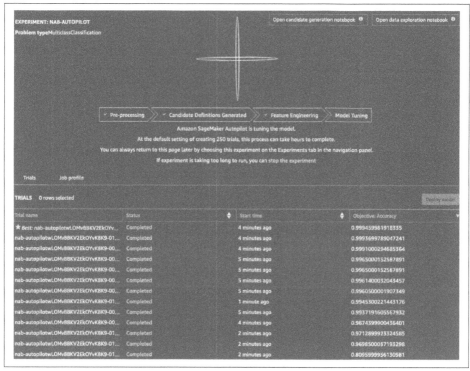

Figure 5-36. Completed Autopilot run

Finally, as shown in Figure 5-37, once the job is complete, you can right-click the model you want to control and either deploy it to production or open it in trail details mode to inspect explainability and/or metrics or charts.

SageMaker Autopilot is a complete solution for AutoML and MLOps, and if your organization is already using AWS, it does seem straightforward to integrate this platform into your existing workflows. It seems especially useful when working with larger datasets and with problems where reproducibility is critically essential.

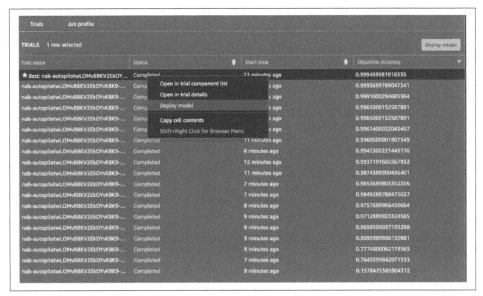

Figure 5-37. Autopilot model

Next, let's discuss some of the open source AutoML solutions that are emerging.

Open Source AutoML Solutions

I still remember fondly my days of working on Unix clusters while working at Caltech in 2000. This particular time was a transitionary time for Unix, though, because even though in many cases Solaris was superior to Linux, it couldn't compete with the price of the Linux operating system, which was free.

I see a similar thing happening with open source AutoML solutions. The ability to train and run models using high-level tools appears to head toward commodification. So let's take a look at some of the options in open source.

Ludwig

One of the more promising approaches to open source AutoML is Ludwig AutoML (*https://oreil.ly/wIFo4*). In Figure 5-38, the output from a Ludwig run shows the metrics useful to evaluate the strength of the model. The advantage to open source is that a corporation does not control it! Here is an example project that shows text classification using Ludwig via Colab notebook (*https://oreil.ly/tb88B*).

First, install Ludwig and set up a download:

```
!pip install -q ludwig
!wget https://raw.githubusercontent.com/paiml/practical-mlops-book/main/chap05/\
    config.yaml
```

```
!wget https://raw.githubusercontent.com/paiml/practical-mlops-book/main/chap05/\
    reuters-allcats.csv
```

Next, the model is just a command line invocation. This step then trains the model:

```
!ludwig experiment \
 --dataset reuters-allcats.csv \
 --config_file config.yaml
```

class	loss	accuracy	hits_at_k
train	0.9258	0.7148	0.9826
vali	0.9134	0.6992	0.9692
test	0.9420	0.7311	0.9781

Figure 5-38. Ludwig

You can find many additional excellent examples of Ludwig in its official documentation (*https://oreil.ly/SMNqY*).

One of the more exciting aspects of Ludwig is that it is under active development. As part of the Linux Foundation, they recently released version 4, which you can see in Figure 5-39. It adds many additional features like working with remote filesystems and distributed out-of-memory tools like Dask and Ray. Finally, Ludwig has a deep integration with MLflow. The Ludwig roadmap shows that it will continue to support and enhance this integration.

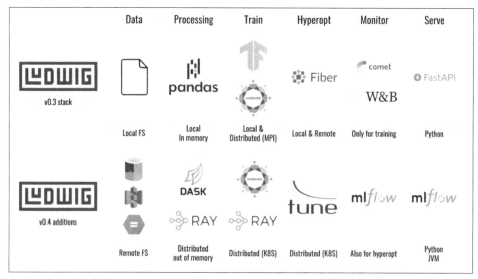

Figure 5-39. Ludwig version 4

FLAML

Another entrant into open source AutoML is FLAML (*https://oreil.ly/TxRe0*). It has a design that accounts for cost-effective hyperparameter optimization. You can see the FLAML logo in Figure 5-40.

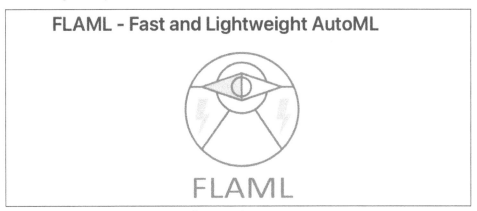

Figure 5-40. FLAML from Microsoft Research

One of the primary use cases for FLAML is to automate an entire modeling process with as little as three lines of code. You can see this in the following example:

```
from flaml import AutoML
automl = AutoML()
automl.fit(X_train, y_train, task="classification")
```

A more comprehensive example shows that in a Jupyter notebook, you first install the library !pip install -q flaml, then configure the AutoML configuration. Then it kicks off a training job to select the optimized classification model:

```
!pip install -q flaml

from flaml import AutoML
from sklearn.datasets import load_iris
# Initialize an AutoML instance
automl = AutoML()
# Specify automl goal and constraint
automl_settings = {
    "time_budget": 10,  # in seconds
    "metric": 'accuracy',
    "task": 'classification',
}
X_train, y_train = load_iris(return_X_y=True)
# Train with labeled input data
automl.fit(X_train=X_train, y_train=y_train,
           **automl_settings)
# Predict
print(automl.predict_proba(X_train))
```

```
# Export the best model
print(automl.model)
```

You can see in Figure 5-41 that, after multiple iterations, it selects an XGBClassifier with a set of optimized hyperparameters.

```
[flaml.automl: 06-16 17:20:13] {1013} INFO - iteration 46, current learner xgboost
[flaml.automl: 06-16 17:20:13] {1165} INFO -  at 10.0s, best xgboost's error=0.0333,    best xgboo
st's error=0.0333
[flaml.automl: 06-16 17:20:13] {1013} INFO - iteration 47, current learner catboost
[flaml.automl: 06-16 17:20:13] {1165} INFO -  at 10.1s, best catboost's error=0.0333,    best xgboo
st's error=0.0333
[flaml.automl: 06-16 17:20:13] {1205} INFO - selected model: XGBClassifier(colsample_bylevel=0.690
2766231016318,
                colsample_bytree=0.7657293008018354, grow_policy='lossguide',
                learning_rate=0.42830712534058824, max_depth=0, max_leaves=5,
                min_child_weight=0.2924296818378054, n_estimators=6, n_jobs=-1,
                objective='multi:softprob', reg_alpha=0.00285817466554831,
                reg_lambda=2.32876649803287, subsample=1.0, tree_method='hist',
                use_label_encoder=False, verbosity=0)
[flaml.automl: 06-16 17:20:13] {963} INFO - fit succeeded
[[0.9206522  0.04071239 0.03863542]
 [0.91942585 0.04199015 0.03858395]]
```

Figure 5-41. FLAML output from model selection

What is exciting about these open source frameworks is their ability to make complicated things possible and easy things automated. Next up, let's take a look at how model explainability works with a project walkthrough.

There is no shortage of open source AutoML frameworks. Here are some additional frameworks to look at for AutoML:

- AutoML

    — H2O AutoML (*https://oreil.ly/OanPd*)

    — Auto-sklearn (*https://oreil.ly/wrchl*)

    — tpot (*https://oreil.ly/lZz6k*)

    — PyCaret (*https://pycaret.org*)

    — AutoKeras (*https://autokeras.com*)

Model Explainability

An important aspect of automation in machine learning is to automate model explainability. MLOps platforms all can use this capability as yet another dashboard for the team to look at during work. For example, an MLOps team starting at work in the morning may look at the CPU and memory usage of servers *and* the explainability report of the model they trained last night.

Cloud-based MLOps frameworks like AWS SageMaker, Azure ML Studio, and Google Vertex AI have built-in model explainability, but you can implement it yourself with open source software as well. Let's walk through an explainability workflow to see how this works using this model explainability GitHub project (*https://oreil.ly/lQpBT*).

Two popular open source Model Explainability frameworks are ELI5 and SHAP. Here is a bit more information about each one.

ELI5

ELI5 (*https://oreil.ly/7yDZb*) stands for "explain like I am five." It allows you to visualize and debug machine learning models and supports several frameworks, including sklearn.

SHAP

SHAP (*https://oreil.ly/LgjDL*) is a "game-theoretic" approach to explain the output of machine learning models. In particular, it has excellent visualizations as well as explanations.

First, using a Jupyter notebook (*https://oreil.ly/Fddra*), let's ingest NBA data from the 2016–2017 season and print out the first few rows using the head command. This data contains AGE, POSITION, FG (Field Goals/Game), and social media data like Twitter retweets:

```
import pandas as pd

player_data = "https://raw.githubusercontent.com/noahgift/socialpowernba/\
master/data/nba_2017_players_with_salary_wiki_twitter.csv"
df = pd.read_csv(player_data)
df.head()
```

Next, let's create a new feature called a winning_season, which allows us to predict whether a player will be part of a team with a winning season. For example, in Figure 5-42, you can see plotting the NBA player's age versus the wins to discover a potential age-based pattern.

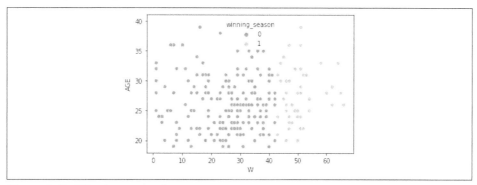

Figure 5-42. Winning season feature

Now, let's move on to modeling and predict wins. But first, let's clean up the data a bit and drop columns that aren't necessary and drop missing values:

```
df2 = df[["AGE", "POINTS", "SALARY_MILLIONS", "PAGEVIEWS",
 "TWITTER_FAVORITE_COUNT","winning_season", "TOV"]]
df = df2.dropna()
target = df["winning_season"]
features = df[["AGE", "POINTS","SALARY_MILLIONS", "PAGEVIEWS",
 "TWITTER_FAVORITE_COUNT", "TOV"]]
classes = ["winning", "losing"]
```

After this cleanup, the shape command prints out the number of rows, 239, and columns, 7:

```
df2.shape
(239, 7)
```

Next up, let's train the model by first splitting the data, then using logistic regression:

```
from sklearn.model_selection import train_test_split
x_train, x_test, y_train, y_test = train_test_split(features, target,
 test_size=0.25,
 random_state=0)
from sklearn.linear_model import LogisticRegression
model = LogisticRegression(solver='lbfgs', max_iter=1000)
model.fit(x_train, y_train)
```

You should see an output similar to the following result that shows the model training is successful:

```
LogisticRegression(C=1.0, class_weight=None, dual=False, fit_intercept=True,
                   intercept_scaling=1, l1_ratio=None, max_iter=1000,
                   multi_class='auto', n_jobs=None, penalty='l2',
                   random_state=None, solver='lbfgs', tol=0.0001, verbose=0,
                   warm_start=False)
```

Now, let's move on to the fun part explaining how the model came up with its SHAP framework predictions. But, first, SHAP needs installation:

```
!pip install -q shap
```

Next, let's use xgboost, another classification algorithm, to explain to the model since SHAP has outstanding support for it:

```
import xgboost
import shap
model_xgboost = xgboost.train({"learning_rate": 0.01},
                              xgboost.DMatrix(x_train, label=y_train), 100)
# load JS visualization code to notebook
shap.initjs()
# explain the model's predictions using SHAP values
# (same syntax works for LightGBM, CatBoost, and scikit-learn models)
explainer = shap.TreeExplainer(model_xgboost)
shap_values = explainer.shap_values(features)
```

```
# visualize the first prediction's explanation
shap.force_plot(explainer.expected_value, shap_values[0,:], features.iloc[0,:])
```

In Figure 5-43, you can see a force plot in SHAP showing the features in red push the
prediction higher, and the features in blue push the prediction lower.

Figure 5-43. SHAP output xgboost

```
shap.summary_plot(shap_values, features, plot_type="bar")
```

In Figure 5-44, a summary plot shows the absolute mean value of what features drive
the model. So, for example, you can see how "off the court" metrics like Twitter and
Salary are essential factors in why the model predicts wins the way it does.

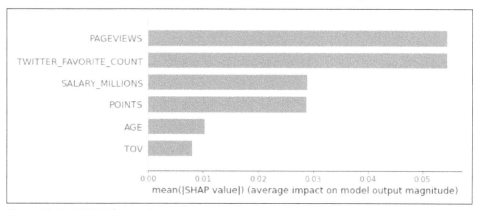

Figure 5-44. SHAP feature importance

Let's see how another open source tool works; this time, let's use ELI5. First, install it
with pip:

```
!pip install -q eli5
```

Next up, permutation importance performs on the original logistic regression model
created earlier. This process works by measuring the amount of accuracy decrease by
removing features:

```
import eli5
from eli5.sklearn import PermutationImportance

perm = PermutationImportance(model, random_state=1).fit(x_train, y_train)
eli5.show_weights(perm, feature_names = features.columns.tolist())
```

You can see in Figure 5-45 that the original logistic regression model has a different feature importance than the XGBoost model. In particular, note that the age of a player has a negative correlation with wins.

Weight	Feature
0.0090 ± 0.0055	TOV
0.0079 ± 0.0136	POINTS
0.0056 ± 0.0000	PAGEVIEWS
0.0056 ± 0.0071	SALARY_MILLIONS
0.0034 ± 0.0055	TWITTER_FAVORITE_COUNT
-0.0079 ± 0.0055	AGE

Figure 5-45. ELI5 permutation importance

Explainability is an essential aspect of MLOps. Just as we have dashboards and metrics for software systems, there should also be explainability for how an AI/ML system came to its prediction. This explainability can lead to healthier outcomes for both stakeholders of the business and the business itself.

Next, let's wrap up everything covered in the chapter.

Conclusion

AutoML is an essential new capability for any team doing MLOps. AutoML improves the ability for a team to push models into production, work on complex problems, and ultimately work on what matters. It is essential to point out that Automated Modeling, i.e., AutoML, is not the only component of KaizenML or continuous improvement. In the oft-cited paper "Hidden Technical Debt in Machine Learning Systems" (*https://oreil.ly/ZZfjY*) the authors mention that modeling is a trivial amount of the work in a real-world ML system. Likewise, it should be no surprise that AutoML, i.e., the automation of modeling, is a small part of what needs to be automated. Everything from data ingestion to feature storage to modeling to training to deployment to an evaluation of the model in production is a candidate for full automation. KaizenML means you are constantly improving every single part of the machine learning system.

Just as automated transmission and cruise-control systems assist an expert driver, automation of the subcomponents of a production machine learning system makes the humans in charge of the ML decisions better. Things can and should be automated, including modeling aspects, software engineering best practices, testing, data engineering, and other essential components. Continuous improvement is a cultural change that doesn't have an end date and fits into any organization wanting to make impactful changes with AI and machine learning.

A final takeaway is that there are many free or nearly free AutoML solutions. Just as developers worldwide use free or roughly free high-level tools like build servers and code editors to improve software, ML practitioners should use automation tools of all types to enhance their productivity.

Next up is the chapter on monitoring and logging. I call this "data science for operations." Before you jump into that topic, take a look at the following exercises and critical thinking questions.

Exercises

- Download XCode and use Apple's Create ML to train a model from a sample dataset you find on Kaggle, or another open dataset location.
- Use Google's AutoML Computer Vision platform to train a model and deploy it to a Coral.AI device (*https://coral.ai*).
- Use Azure ML Studio to train a model and explore the explainability features of Azure ML Studio.
- Use ELI5 (*https://oreil.ly/Nwrck*) to explain a machine learning model.
- Use Ludwig (*https://oreil.ly/GRjgG*) to train a machine learning model.
- Select a SageMaker Automatic Model Tuning example from the official SageMaker examples (*https://oreil.ly/fe71a*) and run through it on your AWS Account.

Critical Thinking Discussion Questions

- Why is AutoML only part of the automation story with modern machine learning?
- How could the NIH (*https://nih.gov*) (National Institutes of Health) use a Feature Store to increase the speed of medical discoveries?
- By 2025, what parts of machine learning will be fully automated and what aspects will not? By 2035, what parts of machine learning will be fully automated and what factors will not?
- How could vertically integrated AI platforms (chips, frameworks, data, and more) give particular companies a competitive advantage?
- How does the chess software industry provide insights into how AI and humans work together for improved outcomes in solving problems for AutoML?
- How does a data-centric approach differ from a model-centric approach to machine learning? How about a KaizenML approach where data, software, and modeling are all treated as equally important?

## CHAPTER 6

Monitoring and Logging

By Alfredo Deza

> Not only is the cerebral anatomy double, and not only is it unarguable that one hemisphere is enough for consciousness; beyond that, two hemispheres following callosotomy have been shown to be conscious simultaneously and independently. As Nagel said of the split-brain, "What the right hemisphere can do on its own is too elaborate, too intentionally directed, and too psychologically intelligible to be regarded merely as a collection of unconscious automatic responses.
>
> —Dr. Joseph Bogen

Both logging and monitoring are core pillars of DevOps principles that are crucial to robust ML practices. Useful logging and monitoring are hard to get right, and although you can leverage cloud services that take care of the heavy lifting, it is up to you to decide and come up with a sound strategy that makes sense. Most software engineers tend to prefer writing code and leave behind other tasks like testing, documentation, and very often logging and monitoring.

Don't be surprised to hear suggestions about automated solutions that can "solve the logging problem." A solid foundation is possible by thinking thoroughly about the problem at hand so that the information produced is usable. The hard work and solid foundation ideals I describe become crystal clear when you face useless information (it doesn't help narrate a story) or cryptic (too hard to understand). A perfect example of this situation is a software issue I opened back in 2014 that captured the following question from an online chat about the product:

"Can anyone help me interpret this line:

```
7fede0763700  0 -- :/1040921 >> 172.16.17.55:6789/0 pipe(0x7feddc022470 \
sd=3 :0 s=1 pgs=0 cs=0 l=1 c=0x7feddc0226e0).fault
```

I'd been working with this software product for almost two years at the time, and I had no idea what that meant. Can you think of a possible answer? A knowledgeable engineer had the perfect translation: "The machine you are on is unable to contact the monitor at 172.16.17.55." I was baffled by what the log statement meant. Why can't we make a change to say that instead? The ticket capturing this issue from 2014, as of this writing, is still open. Even more troubling is that engineering replied in that ticket that "The log message is fine."

Logging and monitoring is hard work because it takes effort to produce meaningful output that helps us understand a program's state.

I've mentioned that it is crucial to have information that helps us narrate a story. This is true of both monitoring and logging. A few years ago, I worked in a large engineering group that delivered one of the world's largest Python-based CMSs (Content Management System). After proposing adding metrics to the application, the general sentiment was that the CMS didn't need it. Monitoring was already in place, and the Ops team had all kinds of utilities tied to thresholds for alerts. The engineering managers rewarded excellence by giving an engineer time to work on any relevant project (not just 20% like some famous tech company). Before working on a relevant project, one had to pitch the whole management team's idea to get buy-in. When my time came, I, of course, chose to add metric facilities to the application.

"Alfredo, we already have metrics, we know the disk usage, and we have memory alerts for every server. We don't get what we gain by this initiative." It is hard to be standing in front of a large senior management group, and trying to convince them of something they don't believe in. My explanation started with the most important button on the website: the subscribe button. That subscribe button was the one in charge of producing paying users and crucial to the business. I explained that, "if we deploy a new version with a JavaScript issue that makes this button unusable, what metric or alert can tell us this is a problem?" Of course, disk usage would be the same, and memory usage would probably not change at all. And yet, the most important button in the application would go unnoticed in an unusable state. In this particular case, metrics can capture the click-through rate of every hour, day, and week for that button. And most importantly, it can help tell a story about how today the website generates more (or perhaps less!) revenue than last year on this same month. Disk usage and memory consumption of servers are worth keeping an eye on, but it isn't the ultimate goal.

These stories aren't explicitly tied to machine learning or delivering trained models to production. Still, as you will see in this chapter, it will help you and your company tell a story and increase confidence in your process by surfacing important issues and pointing at the reason why a model probably needs better data before hitting production. Identifying data drift and accuracy over time is critical in ML operations. Deploying a model into production with a significant change in accuracy should never happen and needs prevention. The earlier these problems are detected, the cheaper it is to fix them. The consequences of having an inaccurate model in production can be catastrophic.

Observability for Cloud MLOps

It is safe to say that most machine learning is taking place in a cloud environment. As such, there are special services from cloud providers that enable observability. For example, on AWS, they have Amazon CloudWatch (*https://oreil.ly/43bvM*), on GCP they have the Google Cloud operations suite (*https://oreil.ly/3YVn1*), and on Azure they have Azure Monitor (*https://oreil.ly/gDIud*).

In Figure 6-1, Amazon CloudWatch is a better example of how these monitoring services work. At a high level, every component of the cloud system sends metrics and logs to CloudWatch. These tasks include the servers, the application logs, the training metadata for machine learning jobs, and the results of production machine learning endpoints.

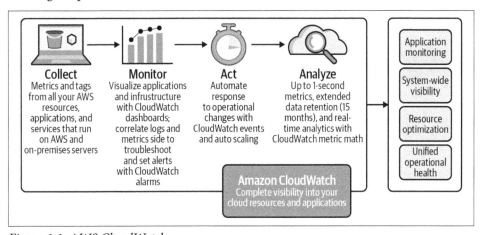

Figure 6-1. AWS CloudWatch

Next, this information becomes part of many different tools, from dashboards to auto-scaling. For example, in AWS SageMaker, this could mean that the production ML service will scale automatically if the individual endpoints exceed more than 75% of their total CPU or memory. Finally, all of this observability allows humans and machines alike to analyze what is going on with a production ML system and act on it.

The experienced cloud software engineer already knows that cloud observability tools are nonoptional components of a cloud software deployment. However, what is unique about MLOps in the cloud is that new components also need granular monitoring. For example, in Figure 6-2, a whole new series of actions take place in an

ML model deployment. Notice, though, that again, CloudWatch collects these new metrics.

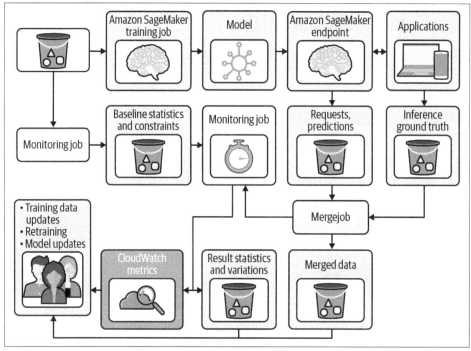

Figure 6-2. AWS SageMaker model monitoring

As the rest of the chapter unfolds, keep in mind that at a high level on a master system like CloudWatch, it collects data, routes alerts, and engages with the dynamic components of cloud computing like elastic scaling. Next, let's get into the details of a finer-grained member of observability: logging.

Introduction to Logging

Most logging facilities have common aspects in how they work. Systems define the log levels they can operate with, and then the user can select at what level those statements should appear. For example, the Nginx web server comes with a default configuration for access logs saved at */var/log/nginx/access.log* and error logs to */var/log/nginx/error.log*. As an Nginx user, the first thing you need to do if you are troubleshooting the web server is to go into those fails and see the output.

I installed Nginx in an Ubuntu server with default configurations and sent some HTTP requests. Right away, the access logs started getting some information:

```
172.17.0.1 [22/Jan/2021:14:53:35 +0000] "GET / HTTP/1.1" \
    "Mozilla/5.0 (Macintosh; Intel Mac OS X 10.15; rv:84.0) Firefox/84.0" "-"
```

```
172.17.0.1 [22/Jan/2021:14:53:38 +0000] "GET / HTTP/1.1" \
    "Mozilla/5.0 (Macintosh; Intel Mac OS X 10.15; rv:84.0) Firefox/84.0" "-"
```

The long log lines pack lots of useful (configurable) information that includes the server's IP address, the time, and type of request alongside the user-agent information. The user-agent in my case is my browser running on a Macintosh computer. These aren't errors, though. These lines show access to the server. To force Nginx to get into an error condition, I changed the permissions on a file to be unreadable by the server. Next, I sent new HTTP requests:

```
2021/01/22 14:59:12 [error] open() "/usr/share/nginx/html/index.html" failed \
    (13: Permission denied), client: 172.17.0.1, server: localhost, \
        request: "GET / HTTP/1.1", host: "192.168.0.200"
```

The log entry explicitly shows that the level of the information is of *"error."* This allows a consumer, like myself, to identify the severity of the information produced by the web server. Back when I was a Systems Administrator and was getting started in necessary tasks like configuration and deployment of production environments, it wasn't clear why these levels were useful. The main point for me was that I could identify an error from the logs' informational content.

Although the idea of making it easier for consumers to identify if an error is valid, it isn't all there is to log levels. If you've tried to debug a program before, you've probably used `print()` statements to help you get useful information about a running program. There are many other ways to debug programs, but using `print()` is still valuable. One drawback is that you have to clean up and remove all those `print()` statements once the problem is solved. The next time you need to debug the same program, you will need to add all those statements back. This is not a good strategy, and it is one of the many situations where logging can help.

Now that some basics on logging are clear, I'll discuss how to configure logging in an application, which tends to be complicated since there are so many different options and decisions to make.

Logging in Python

I'll be working in Python, but most of the concepts in this section should apply cleanly to other languages and frameworks. Log levels, redirection of output, and other facilities are commonly available in other applications. To start applying logging, I will create a short Python script to process a CSV file. No functions or modules; the example script is as close to a Jupyter Notebook cell that you can find.

Create a new file called *describe.py* to see how logging can help in a basic script:

```python
import sys
import pandas as pd

argument = sys.argv[-1]
```

```
df = pd.read_csv(argument)
print(df.describe())
```

The script will take the input from the last argument on the command line and tell the Pandas library to read it and describe it. The idea is to produce a description of a CSV file, but that isn't what happens when you run it with no arguments:

```
$ python derscribe.py
        from os import path
count                  5
unique                 5
top     print(df.describe())
freq                   1
```

What happens here is that the last argument in that example is the script itself, so Pandas is describing the contents of the script. This is not very useful, and to someone that hasn't created the script, the results are shocking, to say the least. Let's take this brittle script a step forward and pass an argument to a path that doesn't exist:

```
$ python describe.py /bogus/path.csv
Traceback (most recent call last):
  File "describe.py", line 7, in <module>
    df = pd.read_csv(argument)
  File "/../site-packages/pandas/io/parsers.py", line 605, in read_csv
    return _read(filepath_or_buffer, kwds)
  ...
  File "/../site-packages/pandas/io/common.py", line 639, in get_handle
    handle = open(
FileNotFoundError: [Errno 2] No such file or directory: '/bogus/path.csv'
```

There is no error checking to tell us if the input is valid and what the script expects. This problem is worse if you are waiting on a pipeline run or some remote data processing job to complete, and you are getting these types of errors. Some developers try to defend against these by catching all exceptions and obscuring the actual error, making it impossible to tell what is going on. This slightly modified version of the script highlights the problem better:

```
import sys
import pandas as pd

argument = sys.argv[-1]

try:
    df = pd.read_csv(argument)
    print(df.describe())
except Exception:
    print("Had a problem trying to read the CSV file")
```

Running it produces an error that would make me very upset to see in production code:

```
$ python describe.py /bogus/path.csv
Had a problem trying to read the CSV file
```

The example is trivial, and because the script is just a few lines long and you know its contents, it isn't that difficult to point at the problem. But if this is running in an automated pipeline remotely, you don't have any context, and it becomes challenging to understand the problem. Let's use the Python logging module to provide more information about what is going on in this data processing script.

The first thing to do is to configure logging. We don't need anything too complicated here, and adding a few lines is more than enough. Modify the *describe.py* file to include these lines, then rerun the script:

```
import logging

logging.basicConfig()
logger = logging.getLogger("describe")
logger.setLevel(logging.DEBUG)

argument = sys.argv[-1]
logger.debug("processing input file: %s", argument)
```

Rerunning it should look similar to this:

```
$ python describe.py /bogus/path.csv
DEBUG:describe:processing input file: /bogus/path.csv
Had a problem trying to read the CSV file
```

Still, not very useful yet, but already informational. This might feel like a lot of boilerplate code for something that a simple `print()` statement could've also accomplished. The logging module is resilient to failures when constructing the message. For example, open a Python interpreter and try using fewer arguments to `print`:

```
>>> print("%s should break because: %s" % "statement")
Traceback (most recent call last):
  File "<stdin>", line 1, in <module>
TypeError: not enough arguments for format string
```

Now let's try the same operation with the logging module:

```
>>> import logging
>>> logging.warning("%s should break because: %s", "statement")
--- Logging error ---
Traceback (most recent call last):
  ...
  File "/.../python3.8/logging/__init__.py", line 369, in getMessage
    msg = msg % self.args
TypeError: not enough arguments for format string
Call stack:
  File "<stdin>", line 1, in <module>
Message: '%s should break because: %s'
Arguments: ('statement',)
```

The last example would not break a production application. Logging should never break any application at runtime. In this case, the logging module is trying to do the variable replacement in the string and failing, but instead of breaking it is advertising the problem and then continuing. A print statement can't do this. In fact, I see using `print()` in Python much like `echo` in shell scripts. There is no control, it is easy to break a production application, and it is hard to control the verbosity.

Verbosity is crucial when logging, and aside from the *error level* in the Nginx example, it has several facilities to empower log consumers to fine-tune the information needed. Before going into log-level granularity and verbosity control, give the script an upgrade in the log formatting to look nicer. The Python logging module is compelling and allows lots of configuration. Update the *describe.py* script where the logging configuration happens:

```
log_format = "[%(name)s][%(levelname)-6s] %(message)s"
logging.basicConfig(format=log_format)
logger = logging.getLogger("describe")
logger.setLevel(logging.DEBUG)
```

The `log_format` is a template with some keywords used when constructing the log line. Note how I didn't have a timestamp before, and although I still don't have it with this update, the configuration does allow me to include it. For now, the logger's name (`describe` in this case), the log level, and the message are all there with some padding and using square brackets to separate the information for better readability. Rerun the script once again to check how the output changes:

```
$ python describe.py
[describe][DEBUG ] processing input file: describe.py
Had a problem trying to read the CSV file
```

Another superpower of logging is to provide the traceback information along with the error. Sometimes it is useful to capture (and show) the traceback without getting into an error condition. To do this, update the *describe.py* script in the except block:

```
try:
    df = pd.read_csv(argument)
    print(df.describe())
except Exception:
    logger.exception("Had a problem trying to read the CSV file")
```

It looks very similar to the `print()` statement from before. Rerun the script and check the results:

```
$ python logging_describe.py
[describe][DEBUG ] processing input file: logging_describe.py
[describe][ERROR ] Had a problem trying to read the CSV file
Traceback (most recent call last):
  File "logging_describe.py", line 15, in <module>
    df = pd.read_csv(argument)
  File "/.../site-packages/pandas/io/parsers.py", line 605, in read_csv
```

```
    return _read(filepath_or_buffer, kwds)
  ...
  File "pandas/_libs/parsers.pyx", line 1951, in pandas._libs.parsers.raise
ParserError: Error tokenizing data. C error: Expected 1 field in line 12, saw 2
```

The traceback is the string representation of the error, not an error itself. To verify this, add another log line right after the except block:

```
try:
    df = pd.read_csv(argument)
    print(df.describe())
except Exception:
    logger.exception("Had a problem trying to read the CSV file")

logger.info("the program continues, without issue")
```

Rerun to verify the outcome:

```
[describe][DEBUG ] processing input file: logging_describe.py
[describe][ERROR ] Had a problem trying to read the CSV file
Traceback (most recent call last):
[...]
ParserError: Error tokenizing data. C error: Expected 1 field in line 12, saw 2

[describe][INFO  ] the program continues, without issue
```

Modifying Log Levels

These types of informational facilities provided by logging are not straightforward with print() statements. If you are writing a shell script, it would be borderline impossible. In the example, we now have three log levels: debug, error, and info. Another thing logging allows is to selectively set the level to what we are interested in. Before changing it, the levels have a *weight* associated with them, and it is essential to grasp them so that changes reflect the priority. From most to least verbose, the order is as follows:

1. debug
2. info
3. warning
4. error
5. critical

Although this is the Python logging module, you should expect a similar weighted priority from other systems. A log level of debug will include every other level, as well as debug. A critical log level will include only critical-level messages. Update the script once again to set the log level to error:

```
log_format = "[%(name)s][%(levelname)-6s] %(message)s"
logging.basicConfig(format=log_format)
logger = logging.getLogger("describe")
logger.setLevel(logging.ERROR)

$ python logging_describe.py
[describe][ERROR ] Had a problem trying to read the CSV file
Traceback (most recent call last):
  File "logging_describe.py", line 15, in <module>
    df = pd.read_csv(argument)
  File "/.../site-packages/pandas/io/parsers.py", line 605, in read_csv
    return _read(filepath_or_buffer, kwds)
  ...
  File "pandas/_libs/parsers.pyx", line 1951, in pandas._libs.parsers.raise
ParserError: Error tokenizing data. C error: Expected 1 field in line 12, saw 2
```

The change causes only the error log message to be displayed. This is useful when trying to reduce the amount of logging to what may be of interest. Debugging encom-
passes most (if not all) messages, while errors and critical situations are much more
sporadic and usually not seen as often. I recommend setting debug log levels for new
production code so that it is easier to catch potential problems. You should expect
problems when producing and deploying new code. Highly verbose output is not that
useful in the long run when an application has proven stable, and there aren't many
surprising issues. Fine-tuning the levels to info or error only is something you can
do progressively.

Logging Different Applications

So far, we've seen log levels of a script trying to load a CSV file. And I haven't gone
into the details of why the logger's name ("*describe*" in the past examples) is significant. In Python, you import modules and packages, and many of these packages
come with their own loggers. The logging facility allows you to set particular options
for these loggers independently from your application. There is also a hierarchy for
loggers, where the "*root*" logger is the parent of all loggers and can modify settings for
all applications and loggers.

Changing the logging level is one of the many things you can configure. In one production application, I created two loggers for the same application: one would emit
messages to the terminal, while the other would write to a logfile. This allowed having
user-friendly messages go to the terminal, omitting large tracebacks and errors pol-
luting the output. At the same time, the internal, developer-oriented logging would
go to a file. This is another example of something that would be very difficult and
complicated to do with a print() statement or an echo directive in a shell script. The
more flexibility you have, the better you can craft applications and services.

Create a new file and save it as *http-app.py* with the following contents:

```
import requests
import logging

logging.basicConfig()

# new logger for this script
logger = logging.getLogger('http-app')

logger.info("About to send a request to example.com")
requests.get('http://example.com')
```

The script configures the logging facility with a basic configuration that emits messages to the terminal by default. It then tries to make a request using the *requests* library. Run it and check the output. It might feel surprising that nothing shows up in the terminal after executing the script. Before explaining exactly why this is happening, update the script:

```
import requests
import logging

logging.basicConfig()
root_logger = logging.getLogger()

# Sets logging level for every single app, the "parent" logger
root_logger.setLevel(logging.DEBUG)

# new logger for this script
logger = logging.getLogger('http-app')

logger.info("About to send a request to example.com")
requests.get('http://example.com')
```

Rerun the script and take note of the output:

```
$ python http-app.py
INFO:http-app:About to send a request to example.com
DEBUG:urllib3.connectionpool:Starting new HTTP connection (1): example.com:80
DEBUG:urllib3.connectionpool:http://example.com:80 "GET / HTTP/1.1" 200 648
```

The Python logging module can set configuration settings globally for every single logger in all packages and modules. This *parent* logger is called the *root* logger. The reason there is output is that the changes set the root logger level to debug. But there is more output than the single line of the *http-app* logger. This happens because the *urllib3* package has its logger as well. Since the root logger changed the global log level to debug, the *urllib3* package is now emitting those messages.

It is possible to configure several different loggers and fine-tune the granularity and verbosity of the levels (as well as any other logging configuration). To demonstrate this, change the *urllib3* package's logging level by adding these lines at the end of the *http-app.py* script:

```
# fine tune the urllib logger:
urllib_logger = logging.getLogger('urllib3')
urllib_logger.setLevel(logging.ERROR)

logger.info("About to send another request to example.com")
requests.get('http://example.com')
```

The updated version retrieves the logger for *urllib3* and changes its log level to error. The script's logger emits a new message before calling `requests.get()`, which in turn uses the *urllib3* package. Rerun the script once more to check the output:

```
INFO:http-app:About to send a request to example.com
DEBUG:urllib3.connectionpool:Starting new HTTP connection (1): example.com:80
DEBUG:urllib3.connectionpool:http://example.com:80 "GET / HTTP/1.1" 200 648
INFO:http-app:About to send another request to example.com
```

Since the log level of *urllib3* got changed before the last request, no more debug messages appear. The info-level message does show up because that logger is still configured at a debug level. These combinations of logging configurations are powerful because it allows you to select what is interesting from other information that can cause *noise* in the output.

Imagine using a library that interacts with a cloud's storage solution. The application you are developing performs thousands of interactions by downloading, listing, and uploading content to the storage server. Suppose the primary concern of the application is to manage datasets and offload them to the cloud provider. Do you think it would be interesting to see an informational message that says a request is about to be made to the cloud provider? In most situations, I would say that is far from useful. Instead, it would be critical to be alerted when the application fails to perform a particular operation with the storage. Further, it may be possible that you are dealing with timeouts when requesting the storage, in which case, changing the log level to indicate when the request happens is crucial to get the time delta.

It is all about flexibility and adapting to your application's lifecycle needs. What is useful today can be information overload tomorrow. Logging goes hand-in-hand with monitoring (covered in the next section), and it is not uncommon to hear about observability in the same conversation. These are foundational to DevOps, and they should be part of the ML lifecycle.

Monitoring and Observability

When I was a professional athlete, my dad, who was also my coach, added a particular chore that I despised: write every day, in a journal, about the workout that I'd just completed. The journal entry needed the following items:

- The planned workout. For example, if it was 10 repetitions of 300 meters at a 42 second pace.

- The results of the workout. For the 300 meters, it would be the actual time performed at each repetition.

- How I felt during and after the session.

- Any other relevant information, like feeling sick or pain from an injury, for example.

I started training professionally at 11 years old. As a teenager, this journaling task felt worse than the worst workouts. I didn't understand the big deal about journaling and why it was vital for me to cover the workout details. I had the guts to tell my dad that this seemed his job, not mine. After all, I was already doing the workouts. That argument didn't go very well for me. The problem is that I didn't understand. It felt like a useless task, without any benefits. I couldn't see or feel the benefits.

It felt more like a disciplinary task at the end of the day instead of a crucial training aspect. A few years after journaling every day (I worked out 14 times a week on average) and having a great season behind me, I sat down with my dad to plan the next season. Instead of a couple of hours of hearing my dad talk to me about what was coming for the next season, he illuminated me by demonstrating how powerful journaling was. *"Alright, Alfredo, let me pull up the last two journals, to check what we did and how you felt, to adapt, increase, and have a great season once again."*

The journals had every piece of information that we needed to plan. He used a phrase that stuck with me for years, and I hope it demonstrates why monitoring and metrics are critical in any situation: *"If we can measure, then we can compare. And if we can compare, only then can we improve."*

Machine learning operations are no different. When a new iteration of a model ships to production, you have to know if it performs better or worse. Not only do you have to know, but the information has to be accessible and straightforward to produce. Processes can create friction and make everything go slower than it should. Automation brings down silly processes and can effortlessly create information availability.

A few years ago, I worked at a startup where the head of sales would send me a CSV file with new accounts to "run some numbers" on it and send him a PDF back with the results. This is horrible; it doesn't scale. And it doesn't survive the bus test.

The bus test is where I can get hit by a bus today, and everything should still work, and everyone that works with me can pick up the slack. All effort in automation and producing metrics is instrumental for shipping robust models to production.

Basics of Model Monitoring

Monitoring in ML operations means everything and anything that has to do with getting a model into production—from capturing information about the systems and services to the performance of the model itself. There is no single silver bullet to implement monitoring that will make everything right. Monitoring and capturing metrics is somewhat similar to knowing the data before figuring out what features and algorithms to use to train a model. The more you know about the data, the better decisions you can make about training the model.

Similarly, the more you know about the steps involved in getting a model to production, the better the choices you make when capturing metrics and setting monitoring alerts. The answer to *"what metric should you capture when training a model?"* is one that I dislike, but is so accurate in this situation: it depends.

Although there are differences between the metrics and types of alerts you can set, there are some useful foundational patterns that you can default to. These patterns will help you clarify what data to collect, how often that collection should occur, and how to best visualize it. Finally, depending on the step in producing a model, the key metrics will be different. For example, when collecting data and cleaning it up, it might be substantial to detect the number of empty values per column and perhaps the time to completion when processing the data.

The past week I was processing system vulnerability data. And I had to make some changes to the application in charge of reading JSON files and save the information in a database. After some changes, the database went from several gigabytes in size to just 100 megabytes. The code change wasn't meant to reduce the size at all, so I immediately knew that I'd made a mistake that needed correction. Encountering these situations are excellent opportunities to determine what metrics (and when) to capture them.

There are a few types of metrics that you can find in most metric-capturing systems:

Counter
As the name implies, this type of metric can be useful when counting any type of item. It is useful when iterating over items. For example, this could be useful for counting empty cell values per column.

Timer
A timer is excellent when trying to determine how long some action will take. This is crucial for performance monitoring, as its core responsibility functionality is to measure time spent during an action. Time spent is commonly seen in monitoring graphs for hosted HTTP APIs. If you have a hosted model, a timer would help capture how long the model took to produce a prediction over HTTP.

Value

> When counters and timers do not fit the metric to capture, values come in handy. I tend to think of values like parts of an algebra equation: even if I don't know what X is, I want to capture its value and persist it. Reusing the example of processing JSON files at work and saving information to a database, a fair use for this metric would be the size (in gigabytes) of the resulting database.

There are two common operations specific to ML that cloud providers need to monitor and capture useful metrics. The first is the target dataset. This can be the same dataset you used to train a model, although special care needs to be put into ensuring that the number (and order) of features doesn't change. The second one is the baseline. The baseline determines what differences may (or may not) be acceptable when a model gets trained. Think about baseline as the acceptable thresholds to determine how fit a model is for production usage.

Now that the basics are clear and that a target dataset with a baseline is understood, let's use them to capture useful metrics when training models.

Monitoring Drift with AWS SageMaker

As I mentioned already, cloud providers will usually need a target dataset and a baseline. This is no different with AWS. In this section, we will produce metrics and capture data violations from an already deployed model. SageMaker is an incredible tool for inspecting datasets, training models, and provisioning models into production environments. Since SageMaker tightly integrates with other AWS offerings like S3 storage, you can leverage saving target information that can quickly be processed elsewhere that has access.

One thing in particular that I like about SageMaker is its Jupyter Notebook offering. The interface is not as polished as Google's Colab, but it packs features like the AWS SDK preinstalled and substantial kernel types to choose from—from (the now deprecated) Python 2.7 to Conda environments running Python 3.6, as shown in Figure 6-3.

 This section doesn't cover the specifics of deploying a model. If you want to dive into model deployment in AWS, see Chapter 7.

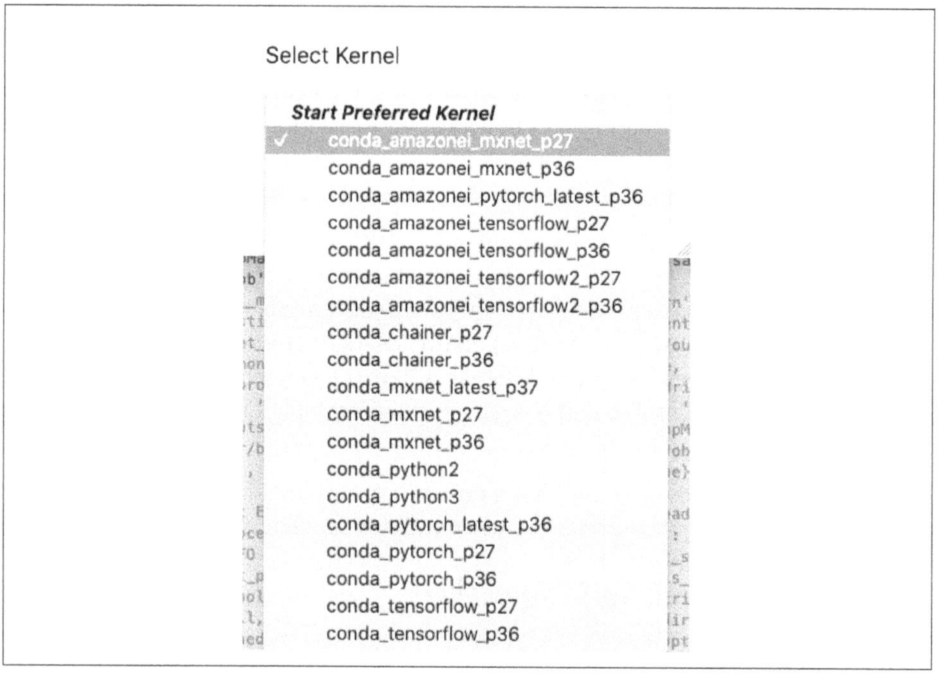

Figure 6-3. SageMaker kernels

Use a SageMaker notebook for this section. Log in to the AWS console, and find the SageMaker service. Once that is loaded, on the left column, find the Notebook Instances link and click it. Create a new instance with a meaningful name. There is no need to change any of the defaults, including the machine type. I've named my notebook *practical-mlops-monitoring* (see Figure 6-4).

When deploying the model, it is important to enable capturing of data. So make sure you use the `DataCaptureConfig` class to do so. This is a quick example that will save it to an S3 bucket:

```
from sagemaker.model_monitor import DataCaptureConfig

s3_capture_path = "s3://monitoring/xgb-churn-data"


data_capture_config = DataCaptureConfig(
    enable_capture=True,
    sampling_percentage=100,
    destination_s3_uri=s3_capture_path
)
```

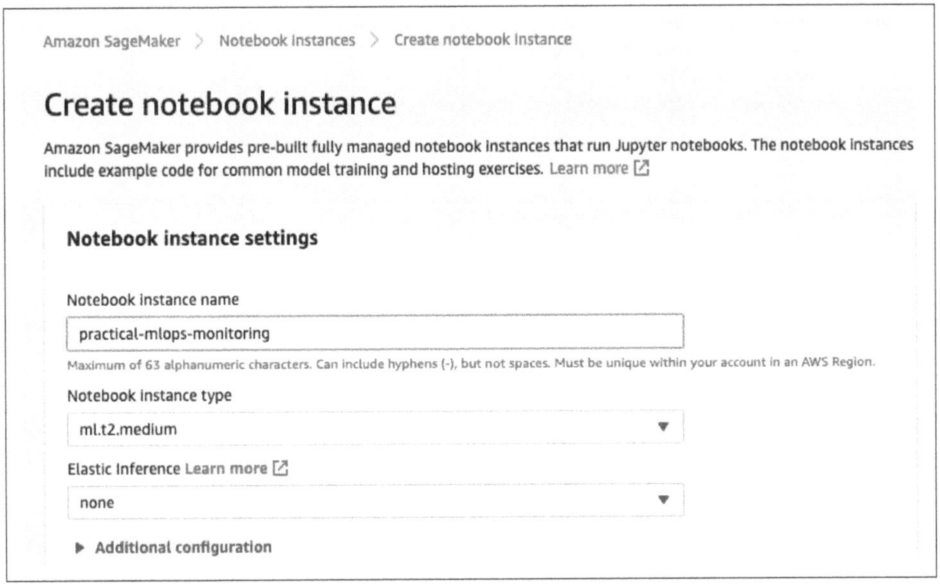
Amazon SageMaker > Notebook instances > Create notebook instance
Create notebook instance
Amazon SageMaker provides pre-built fully managed notebook instances that run Jupyter notebooks. The notebook instances include example code for common model training and hosting exercises. Learn more
Notebook instance settings
Notebook instance name
practical-mlops-monitoring
Maximum of 63 alphanumeric characters. Can include hyphens (-), but not spaces. Must be unique within your account in an AWS Region.
Notebook instance type
ml.t2.medium
Elastic Inference Learn more
none
Additional configuration

Figure 6-4. SageMaker notebook instance

Use the `data_capture_config` when calling `model.deploy()`. In this example, I've previously created a `model` object using the `Model()` class, and assigned the data capture configuration to it, so that when the model gets exercised, the data gets saved to the S3 bucket:

```
from sagemaker.deserializers import CSVDeserializer

predictor = model.deploy(
    initial_instance_count=1,
    instance_type="ml.m4.large",
    endpoint_name="xgb-churn-monitor",
    data_capture_config=data_capture_config,
    deserializer=CSVDeserializer(),
)
```

After the model is deployed and available, send some requests to start making predictions. By sending requests to the model, you are causing the capturing configuration to save critical data needed to create the baseline. You can send prediction requests to the model in any way. In this example, I'm using the SDK to send some requests using sample CSV data from a file. Each row represents data that the model can use to start predicting. Since the input is data, that is the reason I'm using a CSV deserializer, so that the endpoint understands how to consume that input:

```
from sagemaker.predictor import Predictor
from sagemaker.serializers import CSVDeserializer, CSVSerializer
import time
```

```
predictor = Predictor(
    endpoint_name=endpoint_name,
    deserializer=CSVDeserializer(),
    serializer=CSVSerializer(),
)


# About one hundred requests should be enough from test_data.csv
with open("test_data.csv") as f:
    for row in f:
        payload = row.rstrip("\n")
        response = predictor.predict(data=payload)
        time.sleep(0.5)
```

After running, double-check that there is output captured in the S3 bucket. You can list the contents of that bucket to ensure there is actual data. In this case, I'm going to use the AWS command line tool, but you can use the web interface or the SDK (the method doesn't matter in this case):

```
$ aws s3 ls \
  s3://monitoring/xgb-churn-data/datacapture/AllTraffic/2021/02/03/13/
2021-02-03 08:13:33   61355 12-26-957-d5938b7b-fbd8-4e3c-9dbd-741f71b.jsonl
2021-02-03 08:14:33    1566 13-27-365-a59180ea-591d-4562-925b-6472d55.jsonl
2021-02-03 08:33:33   31548 32-24-577-20217dd9-8bfa-4ba2-a7f1-d9717ef.jsonl
2021-02-03 08:34:33   31373 33-25-476-0b843e95-5fe0-4b79-8369-b099d0e.jsonl
[...]
```

The bucket lists about 30 items, confirming that the prediction requests were successful and that data was captured and saved to the S3 bucket. Each file has a JSON entry with some information. The specifics in each entry are hard to grasp. This is what one of the entries looks like:

```
{
  "captureData": {
    "endpointInput": {
      "observedContentType": "text/csv",
      "mode": "INPUT",
      "data": "92,0,176.3,85,93.4,125,207.2,107,9.6,1,2,0,1,00,0,0,1,1,0,1,0",
      "encoding": "CSV"
    },
    [...]
}
```

Once again, the entries reference the CSV content type throughout. This is crucial so other consumers of this data can consume the information correctly. So far, we configured the model to capture data and save it to an S3 bucket. This all happened after generating some predictions with test data. However, there is no baseline yet. The data captured in the previous step is required to create the baseline. The next step requires a target training dataset. As I've mentioned before, the training dataset can be the same one used to train the model. A subset of the dataset might be acceptable if the resulting model doesn't change drastically. This *target dataset* has to have the same features (and in the same order) as the dataset used to train the production model.

 It is common to find online documentation that refers to the *baseline dataset* interchangeably with *target dataset*, since both can initially be the same. This can make it confusing when trying to grasp some of these concepts. It is useful to think about the baseline dataset as the data used to create the gold standard (the baseline) and any newer data as the *target*.

SageMaker makes it easy to save and retrieve data by relying on S3. I've defined locations throughout the SDK examples already, and for the baselining, I will do the same. Start by creating a monitor object; this object is able to produce a baseline and save it to S3:

```
from sagemaker.model_monitor import DefaultModelMonitor

role = get_execution_role()

monitor = DefaultModelMonitor(
    role=role,
    instance_count=1,
    instance_type="ml.m5.xlarge",
    volume_size_in_gb=20,
    max_runtime_in_seconds=3600,
)
```

Now that the monitor is available, use the suggest_baseline() method to produce a default baseline for the model:

```
from sagemaker.model_monitor.dataset_format import DatasetFormat
from sagemaker import get_execution_role

s3_path = "s3://monitoring/xgb-churn-data"

monitor.suggest_baseline(
    baseline_dataset=s3_path + "/training-dataset.csv",
    dataset_format=DatasetFormat.csv(header=True),
    output_s3_uri=s3_path + "/baseline/",
    wait=True,
)
```

When the run completes, a lot of output will get produced. The start of the output should be similar to this:

```
Job Name:  baseline-suggestion-job-2021-02-03-13-26-09-164
Inputs:  [{'InputName': 'baseline_dataset_input', 'AppManaged': False, ...}]
Outputs:  [{'OutputName': 'monitoring_output', 'AppManaged': False, ...}]
```

There should be two files saved in the configured S3 bucket: *constraints.json* and *statistics.json*. You can visualize the constraints with the Pandas library:

```
import pandas as pd

baseline_job = monitor.latest_baselining_job
constraints = pd.json_normalize(
    baseline_job.baseline_statistics().body_dict["features"]
)
schema_df.head(10)
```

This is a short subset of the constraints table that Pandas generates:

```
name            inferred_type   completeness  num_constraints.is_non_negative
Churn             Integral  1.0          True
Account Length  Integral  1.0          True
Day Mins  Fractional  1.0         True
[...]
```

Now that we have a baseline made with a very similar dataset to the one used to train the production model, and we have captured relevant constraints, it is time to analyze it and monitor data drift. There have been several steps involved so far, but most of these steps will not change much from these examples to other more complex ones, which means there are many opportunities here to automate and abstract a lot. The initial collection of data happens once when setting the baseline, and then it shouldn't change unless changes to the baseline are needed. These will probably not happen often, so the heavy lifting of setting the baseline shouldn't feel like a burden.

To analyze the collected data, we need a monitoring schedule. The example schedule will run every hour, using the baseline created in the previous steps to compare against traffic:

```
from sagemaker.model_monitor import CronExpressionGenerator

schedule_name = "xgb-churn-monitor-schedule"
s3_report_path = "s3://monitoring/xgb-churn-data/report"

monitor.create_monitoring_schedule(
    monitor_schedule_name=schedule_name,
    endpoint_input=predictor.endpoint_name,
    output_s3_uri=s3_report_path,
    statistics=monitor.baseline_statistics(),
    constraints=monitor.suggested_constraints(),
    schedule_cron_expression=CronExpressionGenerator.hourly(),
    enable_cloudwatch_metrics=True,
)
```

Once you create the schedule, it will require traffic to generate reports. If the model is already in a production environment, then we can assume (and reuse) existing traffic. If you are testing out the baseline on a test model like I've done in these examples, you will need to generate traffic by invoking a request to the deployed model.

A straightforward way to generate traffic is to reuse the training dataset to invoke the endpoint.

The model I deployed ran for a few hours. I used this script to generate some predictions from the previously deployed model:

```
import boto3
import time

runtime_client = boto3.client("runtime.sagemaker")


with open("training-dataset.csv") as f:
    for row in f:
        payload = row.rstrip("\n")
        response = runtime_client.invoke_endpoint(
            EndpointName=predictor.endpoint_name,
            ContentType="text/csv",
            Body=payload
        )
        time.sleep(0.5)
```

Since I configured the monitoring schedule to capture every hour, SageMaker will not immediately generate reports onto the S3 bucket. After two hours, it is possible to list the S3 bucket and check if reports appear in there.

 Although the model monitor will run hourly, AWS has a 20-minute buffer that may cause a delay of up to 20 minutes after the hour mark. If you've seen other scheduling systems, this buffer might be surprising. This happens because, behind the scenes, AWS is load balancing the resources for scheduling.

The reports consist of three JSON files:

- *contraint_violations.json*
- *contraint.json*
- *statistics.json*

The interesting information related to monitoring and capturing drift is in the *constraint_violations.json* file. In my case, most of the violations look like this entry:

```
feature_name:    State_MI
constraint_check_type:  data_type_check
description:
Data type match requirement is not met. Expected data type: Integral,
Expected match: 100.0%.  Observed: Only 99.71751412429379% of data is Integral.
```

The suggested baseline required 100% of data integrity, and here we are seeing that the model is close enough at 99.7%. Because the constraint is to meet 100%, the violation gets generated and reported. Most of those numbers are similar in my case except for one row:

```
feature_name:    Churn
constraint_check_type:  data_type_check
description:
Data type match requirement is not met. Expected data type: Integral,
Expected match: 100.0%. Observed: Only 0.0% of data is Integral.
```

A 0% is a critical situation here, and this is where all the hard work of setting up the systems to catch and report these changes in predictions is crucial. I want to emphasize that although it took several steps and boilerplate code with the AWS Python SDK, it isn't too complicated to automate and start generating these reports automatically for target datasets. I created the baseline with an automated suggestion, and this will mostly require fine-tuning to define acceptable values to prevent generating violations that are not useful.

Monitoring Drift with Azure ML

MLOps plays a significant role in cloud providers. It isn't surprising that monitoring and alerting (core pillars of DevOps) get offered with well-thought-out services. Azure can analyze data drift and set alerts to capture potential issues before models get into production. It is always useful to see how different cloud providers solve a problem like data drift—perspective is an invaluable asset and will make you a better engineer. The amount of thought, documentation, and examples in the Azure platform makes for a smoother onboarding process. It doesn't take much effort to find learning resources to get up to speed with Azure's offerings.

At the time of this writing, data drift detection on Azure ML is on preview, and some minor issues still need to get worked out that prevent giving solid code examples to try out.

Data drift detection in Azure works similarly to using AWS SageMaker. The objective is to be alerted when drift happens between training and serving datasets. As with most ML operations, it is critical to have a deep understanding of the data (and, therefore, the dataset). An overly simplistic example is a dataset that captures swimsuit sales over a year: if the number of sales per week drops to zero, does that mean the dataset has drifted and should not be used in production? Or that it is probably the middle of winter and no one is buying anything? These open questions are easy to answer when the details of the data are well understood.

There are several causes for data drift, many of which can be wholly unacceptable. Some examples of these causes involve changes in value types (e.g., Fahrenheit to Celsius), empty or null values, or in the example of the swimsuit sale, a *natural drift*, where seasonal changes can affect predictions.

The patterns for setting up and analyzing drift on Azure require a baseline dataset, a target dataset, and a monitor. These three requirements work together to produce metrics and create alerts whenever drift is detected. The monitoring and analysis workflow allows you to detect and alert data drift when there is new data in a dataset while allowing profiling new data over time. You will probably not use historical profiling as much as current drift detection because it is more common to use the most current comparison point than checking against several months ago. It is still useful to have as a comparator where the previous year's performance is more meaningful than comparing against last month. This is particularly true with datasets that are affected by seasonal events. There is not much use in comparing Christmas tree sales against August metrics.

To set up a data drift workflow in Azure, you must start by creating a target dataset. The target dataset requires a *time-series* set on it either using a timestamp column or a *virtual column*. The virtual column is a nice feature because it infers the timestamp from the path where the dataset is stored. This configuration attribute is called the *partition format*. And if you are configuring a dataset to use the virtual column, you will see a partition format referenced in both Azure ML Studio and the Python SDK (see Figure 6-5).

Figure 6-5. Azure partition format

In this case, I'm using a partition format helper so that Azure can use the path to infer the timestamp. This is nice because it instructs Azure that the convention is setting the standard. A path like */2021/10/14/dataset.csv* means that the dataset will end up with a virtual column of October 14th, 2021. Configuration by convention is a golden nugget of automation. Whenever you see an opportunity to abstract (or entirely remove) configuration that can be inferred by a convention (like a path in this case), you should take advantage of it. Less configuration means less overhead, which enables speedy workflows.

Once you have a time-series dataset, you can proceed by creating a dataset monitor. To get everything working, you will need a target dataset (in this case, the time-series dataset), the baseline dataset, and the monitor settings.

The baseline dataset has to have the same features (or as similar as possible) as those of the target dataset. One exciting feature is selecting a time range to slice the dataset with relevant data for the monitoring task. The monitor's configuration is what brings all the datasets together. It allows you to create a schedule to run with a set of exciting features and set the threshold for the data drift percentage tolerable.

The drift results will be available at the Dataset Monitors tab in the Assets section in Azure ML Studio. All the configured monitors are available with highlighted metrics about drift magnitude and a sorted list of the top features with drift. The simplicity of exposing data drift is one thing I like about Azure ML Studio because it can quickly surface the essential pieces of information useful to take corrective decisions.

If there is a need to go deep into the metrics' details, you can use Application Insights to query logs and metrics associated with the monitors. Enabling and setting up Application Insights is covered in "Application Insights" on page 253.

Conclusion

Logging, monitoring, and metrics are so critical that any model getting shipped into production *must implement them* at the risk of hard-to-recover catastrophic failure. High confidence in robust processes for reproducible results requires all of these components. As I've mentioned throughout this chapter, you must make decisions with accurate data that can tell you if accuracy is as high as ever or if the number of errors has increased significantly.

Many examples can be tricky to grasp, but they can all be automated and abstracted away. Throughout this book, you will consistently read about DevOps' core pillars and how they are relevant to operationalizing machine learning. Automation is what binds pillars like logging and monitoring together. Setting up logging and monitoring is usually not exciting work, especially if the idea is to get state-of-the-art prediction models doing exceptional work. But exceptional results cannot happen consistently with a broken foundation.

When I first started training to be a professional athlete, I always doubted my coach, who didn't allow me to do the High Jump every day. *"Before becoming a High Jumper, you must become an athlete."* Strong foundations enable strong results, and in DevOps and MLOps, this is no different.

In the next chapters, you get a chance to dive deeper into each of the three major cloud providers, their concepts, and their machine learning offerings.

Exercises

- Use a different dataset and create a drift report with violations using AWS Sage-Maker.
- Add Python logging to a script that will log errors to STDERR, info statements to STDOUT, and all levels to a file.
- Create a time-series dataset on Azure ML Studio.
- Configure a dataset monitor in Azure ML Studio that will send an email when a drift is detected beyond the acceptable threshold.

Critical Thinking Discussion Questions

- Why might it be desirable to log to multiple sources at the same time?
- Why is it critical to monitor data drift?
- Name three advantages of using logging facilities versus print() or echo statements.
- List the five most common log levels, from least to most verbose.
- What are three common metric types found in metric-capturing systems?

## CHAPTER 7

MLOps for AWS

By Noah Gift

> Everybody was scared of him [Dr. Abbott (because he yelled at everyone)]. When I was attending, there was a new resident named Harris. Harris was still afraid of him [Dr. Abbott] even though he was the chief resident and had been there for 5 years. Later [Dr. Abbott] has a heart attack and then his heart stops. A nurse yells, "Quick, he just had an arrest, come in!" So Harris went in there…leaning on the sternum and breaking ribs and stuff. So Harris starts pumping on Abbott and he woke up. He woke up! And he looked up at Harris and he said, "You! STOP THAT!" So Harris stopped. And that was the last story about Abbott.
>
> —Dr. Joseph Bogen

One of the most common questions I get from students is, "which cloud do I pick?" I tell them the safe choice is Amazon. It has the widest selection of technology and the largest market share. Once you master the AWS cloud, it is easier to master other cloud offerings since they also assume you might know AWS. This chapter covers the foundations of AWS for MLOps and explores practical MLOps patterns.

I have a long, rich history of working with AWS. At a sports social network I ran as the CTO and General Manager, AWS was a secret ingredient that allowed us to scale to millions of users worldwide. I also worked as an SME (subject matter expert) on the AWS Machine Learning Certification from scratch in the last several years. I have been recognized as an AWS ML Hero (*https://oreil.ly/JbWXC*), I am also a part of the AWS Faculty Cloud Ambassador program (*https://oreil.ly/WsPtx*), and have taught thousands of students cloud certifications at UC Davis, Northwestern, Duke, and the University of Tennessee. So you can say I am a fan of AWS!

Due to the sheer size of the AWS platform, it is impossible to cover every single aspect of MLOps. If you want a more exhaustive coverage of all of the available AWS platform options, you can also check out *Data Science on AWS* by Chris Fregly and Antje Barth (O'Reilly), for which I was one of the technical editors.

Instead, this chapter focuses on higher-level services like AWS Lambda and AWS App Runner. More complicated systems like AWS SageMaker are covered in other chapters in this and the previously mentioned book. Next, let's get started building AWS MLOps solutions.

Introduction to AWS

AWS is the leader in cloud computing for several reasons, including its early start and corporate culture. In 2005 and 2006, Amazon launched Amazon Web Services, including MTurk (Mechanical Turk), Amazon S3, Amazon EC2, and Amazon SQS.

To this day, these core offerings are not only still around, but they get better by the quarter and year. The reason AWS continues to improve its offerings is due to its culture. They say it is always "Day 1" at Amazon, meaning the same energy and enthusiasm that happens on Day 1 should happen every day. They also place the customer at the "heart of everything" they do. I have used these building blocks to build systems scaled to thousands of nodes to do machine learning, computer vision, and AI tasks. Figure 7-1 is an actual whiteboard drawing of a working AWS Cloud Technical Architecture shown in a coworking spot in downtown San Francisco.

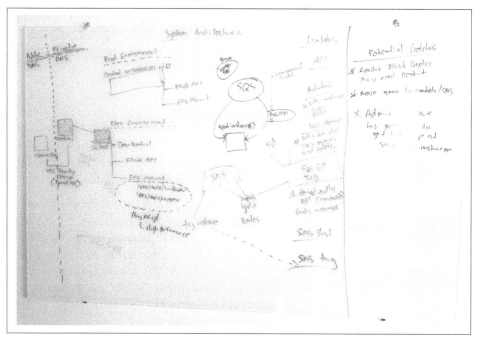

Figure 7-1. AWS Cloud Architecture on whiteboard

This type of culture is very different than Google, which has struggled in cloud computing. The Google culture is research-oriented with heavy academic hiring. The benefits of this culture are open source projects like Kubernetes and TensorFlow. Both are complex engineering marvels. The downside is that the customer is not first in the culture, which has hurt Google in the cloud computing market share. Many organizations balk at not buying professional services and supporting something as critical as cloud computing.

Next, let's take a look at getting started with AWS Services.

Getting Started with AWS Services

To get started with AWS initially requires only a Free Tier account (*https://oreil.ly/ 8hBjG*). If you are at university, you can also use both AWS Academy (*https://oreil.ly/ W079B*) and AWS Educate (*https://oreil.ly/6ZFNh*). AWS Academy provides hands-on certification material and labs. AWS Educate delivers sandboxes for classrooms.

Once you have an account, the next step is to experiment with the various offerings. One way to think about AWS is to compare it to a bulk wholesale store. For example, according to statista (*https://oreil.ly/m6lgS*), Costco has 795 worldwide locations in multiple countries and approximately 1 in 5 Americans shop there. Similarly, according to the 2020 Amazon Web Services whitepaper (*https://oreil.ly/w8Jft*), AWS provides an infrastructure that "powers hundreds of thousands of businesses in 190 countries around the world."

At Costco, there are three approaches considered relevant to an AWS analogy:

- A customer could walk in and order a very inexpensive but reasonable quality pizza in bulk in the first scenario.

- In a second scenario, a customer new to Costco needs to figure out all of the bulk items available to investigate the best way to use Costco. They will need to walk through the store and look at the bulk items like sugar to see what they could build from these raw ingredients.

- In a third scenario, when a customer of Costco knows about the premade meals (such as rotisserie chicken, pizza, and more), and they know about all of the raw ingredients they could buy, they could, in theory, start a catering company, a local deli, or a restaurant utilizing their knowledge of Costco and the services it provides.

A big box retailer the size of Costco charges more money for prepared food, and less money for the raw ingredients. The Costco customer who owns a restaurant may choose a different food preparation level depending on the maturity of their organization and the problem they aim to solve. Figure 7-2 illustrates how these Costco options compare to AWS options.

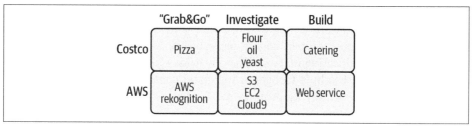

	"Grab&Go"	Investigate	Build
Costco	Pizza	Flour oil yeast	Catering
AWS	AWS rekognition	S3 EC2 Cloud9	Web service

Figure 7-2. Costco versus AWS

Let's take the case of a local Hawaii Poke Bowl stand near a famous Hawaii beach. The owner could buy Costco's premade Poke in bulk and sell it at a price that is approximately twice their cost. But, on the other hand, a more mature BBQ restaurant in Hawaii, with employees who can cook and prepare food, Costco sells this uncooked food at a much lower price than the fully prepared Poke.

Much like Costco, AWS provides different levels of product and it's up to the customer to decide how much they're going to utilize. Let's dig into those options a bit.

Using the "No Code/Low Code" AWS Comprehend solution

The last example showed how using Costco can benefit different restaurant businesses, from one with little to no staff—like a pop-up stand—to a more extensive sit-down facility. The more work Costco does in preparing the food, the higher the benefit to the customer purchasing it, and also the higher the cost for the food. The same concept applies with AWS; the more work AWS does for you, the more you pay and the fewer people you need to maintain the service.

 In economics, the theory of comparative advantage says that you shouldn't compare the cost of something directly. Instead, it would help if you compared the opportunity cost of doing it yourself. All cloud providers have this assumption baked in, since running a data center and building services on top of that data center is their specialization. An organization doing MLOps should focus on creating a product for its customers that generates revenue, not re-creating what cloud providers do poorly.

With AWS, an excellent place to start is to act like the Costco customer who orders Costco pizza in bulk. Likewise, a Fortune 500 company may have essential requirements to add natural language processing (NLP) to its customer service products. It could spend nine months to a year hiring a team and then building out these capabilities, or it could start using valuable high-level services like AWS Comprehend for Natural Language Processing (*https://oreil.ly/z6vIs*). AWS Comprehend also enables users to leverage the Amazon API to perform many NLP operations, including the following:

- Entity detection
- Key phrase detection
- PII
- Language detection
- Sentiment

For example, you can cut and paste text into the Amazon Comprehend Console, and AWS Comprehend will find all of the text's entities. In the example in Figure 7-3, I grabbed the first paragraph of LeBron James's Wikipedia bio, pasted it into the console, clicked Analyze, and it highlighted the entities for me.

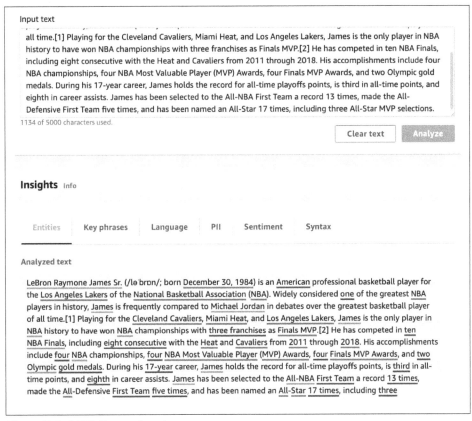

Figure 7-3. AWS Comprehend

Other use cases like reviewing medical records or determining the sentiment of a customer service response are equally straightforward with AWS Comprehend and the boto3 Python SDK. Next, let's cover a "hello world" project for DevOps on AWS, deploying a static website using Amazon S3.

Using Hugo static S3 websites

In the following scenario, an excellent way to explore AWS is to "walk around" the console, just as you would walk around Costco in awe the first time you visit. You do this by first looking at the foundational components of AWS, i.e., IaaS (infrastructure as code). These core services include AWS S3 object storage and AWS EC2 virtual machines.

Here, I'll walk you through deploying a Hugo website (*https://gohugo.io*) on AWS S3 static website hosting (*https://oreil.ly/FyHWG*) using "hello world" as an example. The reason for doing a hello world with Hugo is that it is relatively simple to set up and will give you a good understanding of host services using core infrastructure. These skills will come in handy later when you learn about deploying machine learning applications using continuous delivery.

> It is worth noting that Amazon S3 is low cost yet highly reliable. The pricing of S3 approaches a penny per GB. This low-cost yet highly reliable infrastructure is one of the reasons cloud computing is so compelling.

You can view the whole project in the GitHub repo (*https://oreil.ly/mYjqN*). Notice how GitHub is the source of truth for the website because the entire project consists of text files: markdown files, the Hugo template, and the build commands for the AWS Code build server. Additionally, you can walk through a screencast of the continuous deployment there as well. Figure 7-4 shows the high-level architecture of this project.

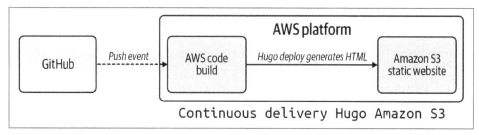

Figure 7-4. Hugo

The short version of how this project works is through the magic of the *buildspec.yml* file. Let's take a look at how this works in the following example. First, note that the hugo binary installs, then the `hugo` command runs to generate HTML files from the checked-out repo. Finally, the `aws` command `aws s3 sync --delete public s3://dukefeb1` is the entire deployment process due to the power of S3 bucket hosting:

```
version: 0.1

environment_variables:
  plaintext:
    HUGO_VERSION: "0.79.1"

phases:
  install:
    commands:
      - cd /tmp
      - wget https://github.com/gohugoio/hugo/releases/download/v0.80.0/\
  hugo_extended_0.80.0_Linux-64bit.tar.gz
      - tar -xzf hugo_extended_0.80.0_Linux-64bit.tar.gz
      - mv hugo /usr/bin/hugo
      - cd
      - rm -rf /tmp/*
  build:
    commands:
      - rm -rf public
      - hugo
  post_build:
    commands:
      - aws s3 sync --delete public s3://dukefeb1
      - echo Build completed on `date`
```

Another way of describing a build system file is that it is a recipe. The information in the build configuration files is a "how-to" to perform the same actions in an AWS Cloud9 development environment.

As discussed in Chapter 2, AWS Cloud9 holds a special place in my heart because it solves a particular problem. Cloud-based development environments let you develop in the exact location where all of the action takes place. The example shows how powerful this concept is. Check out the code, test it in the cloud, and verify the same tool's deployment. In Figure 7-5 the AWS Cloud9 environment invokes a Python microservice.

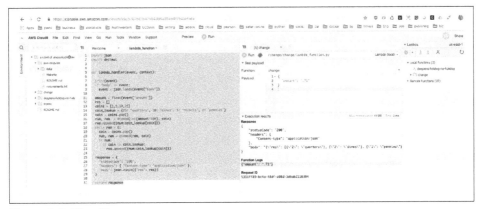

Figure 7-5. Cloud9

You can watch a walkthrough of Hugo deployment on AWS on the O'Reilly platform (*https://oreil.ly/nSiVH*), as well follow an additional, more detailed guide on the Pragmatic AI Labs website (*https://oreil.ly/0AmNU*).

With the foundations of continuous delivery behind us, let's get into serverless on the AWS Platform.

Serverless Cookbook

Serverless is a crucial methodology for MLOps. In Chapter 2, I brought up the importance of Python functions. A Python function is a unit of work that can both take an input and optionally return an output. If a Python function is like a toaster, where you put in some bread, it heats the bread, and ejects toast, then serverless is the source of electricity.

A Python function needs to run somewhere, just like a toaster needs to plug into something to work. This concept is what serverless does; it enables code to run in the cloud. The most generic definition of serverless is code that runs without servers. The servers themselves are abstracted away to allow a developer to focus on writing functions. These functions do specific tasks, and these tasks could be chained together to build more complex systems, like servers that respond to events.

The function is the center of the universe with cloud computing. In practice, this means anything that is a function could map into a technology that solves a problem: containers, Kubernetes, GPUs, or AWS Lambda. As you can see in Figure 7-6, there is a rich ecosystem of solutions in Python that map directly to a function.

The lowest level service that performs serverless on the AWS platform is AWS Lambda. Let's take a look at a few examples from this repo (*https://oreil.ly/TR4E2*).

First, one of the simpler Lambda functions to write on AWS is a Marco Polo function. A Marco Polo function takes in an event with a name in it. So, for example, if the event name is "Marco," it returns "Polo." If the event name is something else, it returns "No!"

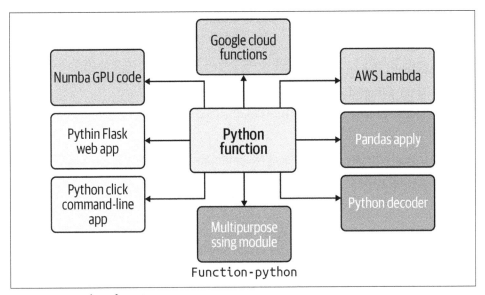

Figure 7-6. Python functions

 Growing up as a teenager in the 1980s and 1990s, Marco Polo was a typical game to play in the summer swimming pool. When I worked as a camp counselor at a pool near my house it was a favorite of the kids I supervised. The game works by everyone getting into a pool and one person closing their eyes and yelling "Marco." Next, the other players in the pool must say, "Polo." The person with their eyes closed uses sound to locate someone to tag. Once someone is tagged, then they are "It."

Here is the AWS Lambda Marco Polo code; note that an `event` passes into the `lambda_handler`:

```
def lambda_handler(event, context):
    print(f"This was the raw event: {event}")
    if event["name"] == "Marco":
        print(f"This event was 'Marco'")
        return "Polo"
    print(f"This event was not 'Marco'")
    return "No!"
```

With serverless cloud computing, think about a lightbulb in your garage. A lightbulb can be turned on many ways, such as manually via the light switch or automatically via the garage door open event. Likewise, an AWS Lambda responds to many signals as well.

Let's enumerate the ways both lightbulbs and lambdas can trigger:

- Lightbulbs
  - Manually flip on the switch
  - Via the garage door opener
  - Nightly security timer that turns on the light at midnight until 6 a.m.
- AWS Lambda
  - Manually invoke via console, AWS command line, or AWS Boto3 SDK
  - Respond to S3 events like uploading a file to a bucket
  - Timer invokes nightly to download data

What about a more complex example? With AWS Lambda, it is straightforward to integrate an S3 Trigger with computer vision labeling on all new images dropped in a folder, with a trivial amount of code:

```
import boto3
from urllib.parse import unquote_plus

def label_function(bucket, name):
    """This takes an S3 bucket and a image name!"""
    print(f"This is the bucketname {bucket} !")
    print(f"This is the imagename {name} !")
    rekognition = boto3.client("rekognition")
    response = rekognition.detect_labels(
        Image={"S3Object": {"Bucket": bucket, "Name": name,}},
    )
    labels = response["Labels"]
    print(f"I found these labels {labels}")
    return labels


def lambda_handler(event, context):
    """This is a computer vision lambda handler"""

    print(f"This is my S3 event {event}")
    for record in event['Records']:
        bucket = record['s3']['bucket']['name']
        print(f"This is my bucket {bucket}")
        key = unquote_plus(record['s3']['object']['key'])
        print(f"This is my key {key}")

    my_labels = label_function(bucket=bucket,
        name=key)
    return my_labels
```

Finally, you can chain multiple AWS Lambda functions together via AWS Step
Functions:

```
{
  "Comment": "This is Marco Polo",
  "StartAt": "Marco",
  "States": {
    "Marco": {
      "Type": "Task",
      "Resource": "arn:aws:lambda:us-east-1:561744971673:function:marco20",
      "Next": "Polo"
    },
    "Polo": {
      "Type": "Task",
      "Resource": "arn:aws:lambda:us-east-1:561744971673:function:polo",
      "Next": "Finish"
    },
    "Finish": {
      "Type": "Pass",
      "Result": "Finished",
      "End": true
    }
  }
}
```

You can see this workflow in action in Figure 7-7.

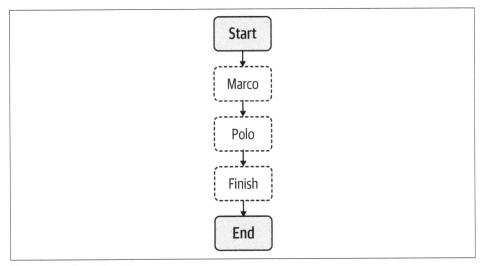

Figure 7-7. Step Functions

Even more fun is the fact that you can call AWS Lambda functions via a CLI. Here is an example:

```
aws lambda invoke \
  --cli-binary-format raw-in-base64-out \
  --function-name marcopython \
  --payload '{"name": "Marco"}' \
  response.json
```

 It is important to always refer to the latest AWS documentation for the CLI as it is an actively moving target. As of the writing of this book, the current CLI version is V2, but you may need to adjust the command line examples as things change in the future. You can find the latest documentation at the AWS CLI Command Reference site (*https://oreil.ly/c7zU5*).

The response of the payload is as follows:

```
{
    "StatusCode": 200,
    "ExecutedVersion": "$LATEST"
}
(.venv) [cloudshell-user@ip-10-1-14-160 ~]$ cat response.json
"Polo"(.venv) [cloudshell-user@ip-10-1-14-160 ~]$
```

 For a more advanced walkthrough of AWS Lambda using Cloud9 and the AWS SAM (Serverless Application Model), you can view a walkthrough of a small Wikipedia microservice on the Pragmatic AI Labs YouTube Channel (*https://oreil.ly/Zy2Ga*) or the O'Reilly Learning Platform (*https://oreil.ly/DsL1k*).

AWS Lambda is perhaps the most valuable and flexible type of computing you can use to serve out predictions for machine learning pipelines or wrangle events in the service of an MLOps process. The reason for this is the speed of development and testing. Next, let's talk about a couple of CaaS, or container as a service, offerings.

AWS CaaS

Fargate is a container as a service offering from AWS that allows developers to focus on building containerized microservices. For example, in Figure 7-8, when this microservice works in the container, the entire runtime, including the packages necessary for deployment, will work in a new environment. The cloud platform handles the rest of the deployment.

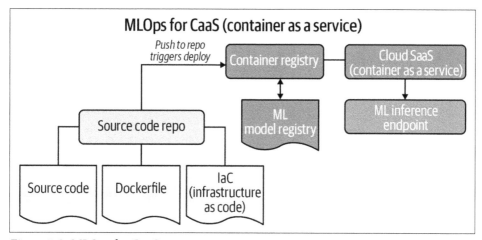

Figure 7-8. MLOps for CaaS

 Containers solve many problems that have plagued the software industry. So as a general rule, it is a good idea to use them for MLOps projects. Here is a partial list of the advantages of containers in projects:

- Allows the developer to mimic the production service locally on their desktop
- Allows easy software runtime distribution to customers through public container registries like Docker Hub, GitHub Container Registry, and Amazon Elastic Container Registry
- Allows for GitHub or a source code repo to be "source of truth" and contain all aspects of microservice: model, code, IaC, and runtime
- Allows for easy production deployment via CaaS services

Let's look at how you can build a microservice that returns the correct change using Flask. Figure 7-9 shows a development workflow on AWS Cloud9. Cloud9 is the development environment; a container gets built and pushed to ECR. Later that container runs in ECS.

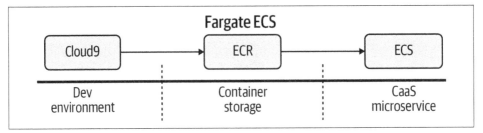

Figure 7-9. ECS workflow

The following is the Python code for *app.py*:

```python
from flask import Flask
from flask import jsonify
app = Flask(__name__)

def change(amount):
    # calculate the resultant change and store the result (res)
    res = []
    coins = [1,5,10,25] # value of pennies, nickels, dimes, quarters
    coin_lookup = {25: "quarters", 10: "dimes", 5: "nickels", 1: "pennies"}

    # divide the amount*100 (the amount in cents) by a coin value
    # record the number of coins that evenly divide and the remainder
    coin = coins.pop()
    num, rem  = divmod(int(amount*100), coin)
    # append the coin type and number of coins that had no remainder
    res.append({num:coin_lookup[coin]})

    # while there is still some remainder, continue adding coins to the result
    while rem > 0:
        coin = coins.pop()
        num, rem = divmod(rem, coin)
        if num:
            if coin in coin_lookup:
                res.append({num:coin_lookup[coin]})
    return res

@app.route('/')
def hello():
    """Return a friendly HTTP greeting."""
    print("I am inside hello world")
    return 'Hello World! I can make change at route: /change'

@app.route('/change/<dollar>/<cents>')
def changeroute(dollar, cents):
    print(f"Make Change for {dollar}.{cents}")
    amount = f"{dollar}.{cents}"
    result = change(float(amount))
    return jsonify(result)
```

```
if __name__ == '__main__':
    app.run(host='0.0.0.0', port=8080, debug=True)
```

Notice that Flask web microservice responds to change requests via web requests to the URL pattern /change/<dollar>/<cents>. You can view the complete source code for this Fargate example in the following GitHub repo (*https://oreil.ly/3qPHM*). The steps are as follows:

1. Setup app: virtualenv + make all

2. Test app local: python app.py

3. Curl it to test: curl localhost:8080/change/1/34

4. Create ECR (Amazon Container Registry)

   In Figure 7-10, an ECR repository enables later Fargate deployment.

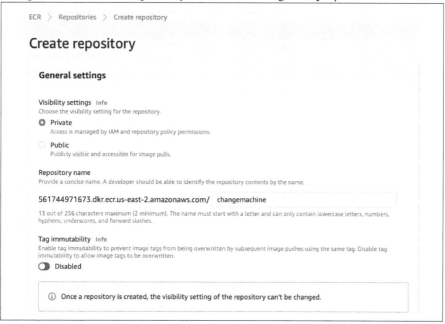

Figure 7-10. ECR

5. Build container

6. Push container

7. Run docker local: docker run -p 8080:8080 changemachine

8. Deploy to Fargate

9. Test the public service

Any cloud service will have rapid, constant changes in functionality, so it is best to read the current documentation. The current Fargate documentation (*https://oreil.ly/G8tPV*) is a great place to read more about the latest ways to deploy to the service.

You can also, optionally, watch a complete walkthrough of a Fargate deployment on the O'Reilly platform (*https://oreil.ly/2IpFs*).

Another option for CaaS is AWS App Runner, which further simplifies things. For example, you can deploy straight from source code or point to a container. In Figure 7-11, AWS App Runner creates a streamlined workflow that connects a source repo, deploy environment, and a resulting secure URL.

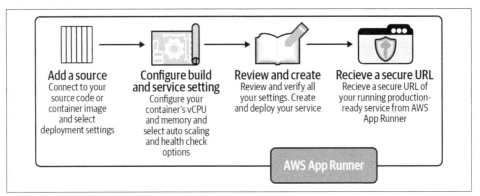

Figure 7-11. AWS App Runner

This repository can easily be converted to an AWS App Runner method in the AWS wizard with the following steps:

1. To build the project, use the command: `pip install -r requirements.txt`.

2. To run the project, use: `python app.py`.

3. Finally, configure the port to use: `8080`.

A key innovation, shown in Figure 7-12, is the ability to connect many different services on AWS, i.e., core infrastructure, like AWS CloudWatch, Load Balancers, Container Services, and API Gateways into one complete offering.

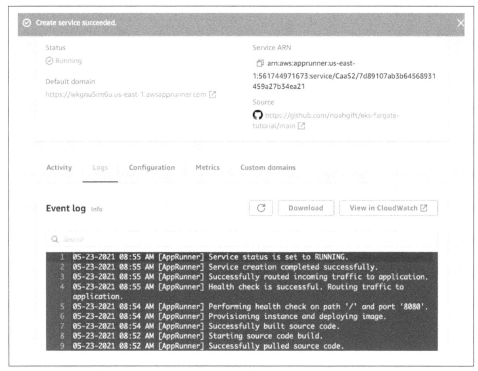

Figure 7-12. AWS App Runner service created

The final deployed service in Figure 7-13 shows a secure URL and the ability to invoke the endpoint and return correct change.

```
[
  {
    "5": "quarters"
  },
  {
    "1": "nickels"
  },
  {
    "4": "pennies"
  }
]
```

Figure 7-13. AWS App Runner deployed

Why is this helpful magic? In a nutshell, all of the logic, including perhaps a machine learning model, are in one repo. Thus, this is a compelling style for building MLOps-friendly products. In addition, one of the more complex aspects of delivering a machine learning application to production is microservice deployment. AWS App Runner makes most of the complexity disappear, capturing time for other parts of the MLOps problem. Next, let's discuss how AWS deals with computer vision.

Computer vision

I teach an applied computer vision course at Northwestern's graduate data science program (*https://oreil.ly/Q6uRI*). This class is delightful to teach because we do the following:

- Weekly video demos
- Focus on problem-solving versus coding or modeling
- Use high-level tools like AWS DeepLens, a deep learning–enabled video camera

In practice, this allows a rapid feedback loop that focuses on the problem versus the technology to solve the problem. One of the technologies in use is the AWS Deep Lens device as shown in Figure 7-14. The device is a complete computer vision hardware developer kit in that it contains a 1080p camera, operating system, and wireless capabilities. In particular, this solves the prototyping problem of computer vision.

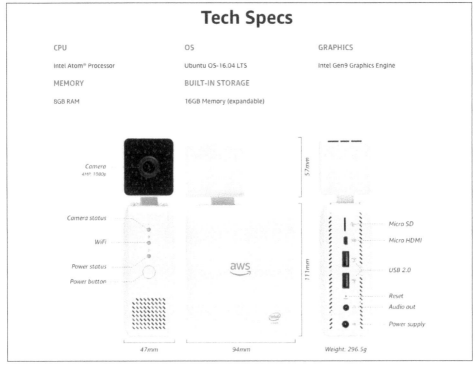

Figure 7-14. DeepLens

Once AWS DeepLens starts capturing video, it splits the video into two streams. The Project Stream shown in Figure 7-15 adds real-time annotation and sends the packets to the MQ Telemetry Transport (MQTT) service, which is a publish-subscribe network protocol.

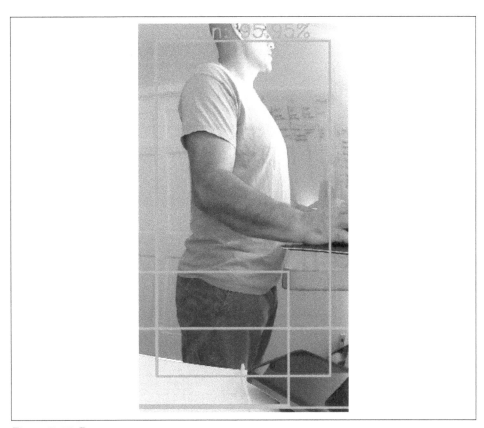

Figure 7-15. Detect

In Figure 7-16, the MQTT packets arrive in real time as the objects get detected in the stream.

The DeepLens is a "plug and play" technology since it tackles perhaps the most challenging part of the problem of building a real-time computer vision prototyping system—capturing the data, and sending it somewhere. The "fun" factor of this is how easy it is to go from zero to one building solutions with AWS DeepLens. Next, let's get more specific and move beyond just building microservices and into building microservices that deploy machine learning code.

Figure 7-16. MQTT

MLOps on AWS

One way to get started with MLOps on AWS is to consider the following question. When given a machine learning problem with three constraints—prediction accuracy, explainability, and operations, which two would you focus on to achieve success, and in what order?

Many academic-focused data scientists immediately jump to prediction accuracy. Building ever-better prediction models is a fun challenge, like playing Tetris. Also, the modeling is glamorous and a coveted aspect of the job. Data scientists like to show how accurate they can train an academic model using increasingly sophisticated techniques.

The entire Kaggle platform works on increasing prediction accuracy, and there are monetary rewards for the precise model. A different approach is to focus on operationalizing the model. This approach's advantage is that later, model accuracy can improve alongside improvements in the software system. Just as the Japanese automobile industry focused on Kaizen or continuous improvement, an ML system can focus on reasonable initial prediction accuracy and improve quickly.

The culture of AWS supports this concept in the leadership principles of "Bias for Action" and "Deliver Results." "Bias for Action" refers to defaulting to speed and delivery results, focusing on the critical inputs to a business, and delivering results quickly. As a result, the AWS products around machine learning, like AWS Sage-Maker, show the spirit of this culture of action and results.

Continuous delivery (CD) is a core component in MLOps. Before you can automate delivery for machine learning, the Microservice itself needs automation. The specifics change depending on the type of AWS service involved. Let's start with an end-to-end example.

In the following example, an Elastic Beanstalk Flask app continuously deploys using all AWS technology from AWS Code Build to AWS Elastic Beanstalk. This "stack" is also ideal for deploying ML models. Elastic Beanstalk is a platform as a service technology offered by AWS that streamlines much of the work of deploying an application.

In Figure 7-17, notice that AWS Cloud9 is a recommended starting point for development. Next, a GitHub repository holds the source code for the project, and as change events occur, it triggers the cloud native build server, AWS CodeBuild. Finally, the AWS Code Build process runs continuous integration, tests for the code, and provides continuous delivery to AWS Elastic Beanstalk.

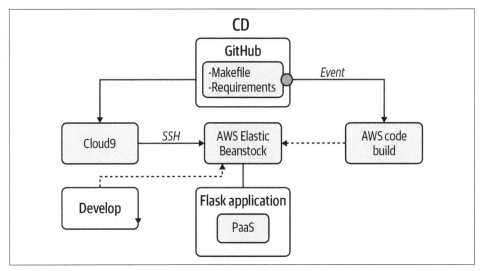

Figure 7-17. Elastic Beanstalk

The source code and a walkthrough of this example are at the following links:

- Source Code (*https://oreil.ly/L8ltB*)
- O'Reilly Platform Video Walkthrough (*https://oreil.ly/JUuLO*)

To replicate this exact project, you can do the following steps:

1. Check out the repository in AWS Cloud9 or AWS CloudShell if you have strong command line skills.

2. Create a Python virtualenv and source it and run `make all`:

```
python3 -m venv ~/.eb
source ~/.eb/bin/activate
make all
```

Note that `awsebcli` installs via requirements, and this tool controls Elastic Beanstalk from the CLI.

3. Initialize new eb app:

```
eb init -p python-3.7 flask-continuous-delivery --region us-east-1
```

Optionally, you use `eb init` to create SSH keys to shell into the running instances.

4. Create remote eb instance:

```
eb create flask-continuous-delivery-env
```

5. Setup AWS Code Build Project. Note your Makefile needs to reflect your project names:

```
version: 0.2

phases:
  install:
    runtime-versions:
      python: 3.7
  pre_build:
    commands:
      - python3.7 -m venv ~/.venv
      - source ~/.venv/bin/activate
      - make install
      - make lint

  build:
    commands:
      - make deploy
```

After you get the project working with continuous deployment, you are ready to move to the next step, deploying an ML model. I highly recommend getting a "hello world" type project working with continuous deployment like this one before you proceed directly into a complex ML project when you are learning new technology. Next, let's look at an intentionally simple MLOps Cookbook that is the foundation for many new AWS Services deployments.

MLOps Cookbook on AWS

With the foundational components out of the way, let's look at a basic machine learning recipe and apply it to several scenarios. Notice that this core recipe is deployable to many services on AWS and many other cloud environments. This following MLOps Cookbook project is intentionally spartan, so the focus is on deploying machine learning. For example, this project predicts height from a weight input for Major League Baseball players.

In Figure 7-18, GitHub is the source of truth and contains the project scaffolding. Next, the build service is GitHub Actions, and the container service is GitHub Container Registry. Both of these services can easily replace any similar offering in the cloud. In particular, on the AWS Cloud, you can use AWS CodeBuild for CI/CD and AWS ECR (Elastic Container Registry). Finally, once a project has been "containerized," it opens up the project to many deployment targets. On AWS, these include AWS Lambda, AWS Elastic Beanstalk, and AWS App Runner.

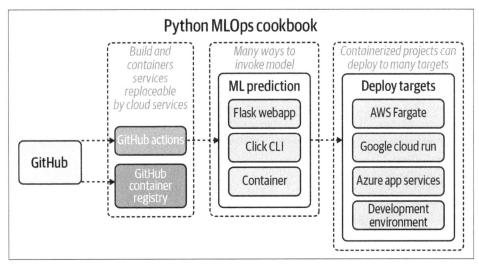

Figure 7-18. MLOps Cookbook

The following files are all useful to build solutions in many different recipes:

Makefile
> The Makefile is both a list of recipes and a way to invoke those recipes. View the Makefile in the example GitHub project (*https://oreil.ly/paYV6*).

requirements.txt
> The requirements file contains the list of Python packages for the project. Typically these packages are "pinned" to a version number, which limits unexpected package dependencies. View the requirements.txt in the example GitHub project (*https://oreil.ly/7p6QH*).

cli.py
> This command line shows how an ML library can also be invoked from the CLI, not just via a web application. View the cli.py in the example GitHub project (*https://oreil.ly/iyI44*).

utilscli.py
> The utilscli.py is a utility that allows the user to invoke different endpoints, i.e., AWS, GCP, Azure, or any production environment. Most machine learning algorithms require data to be scaled. This tool simplifies scaling the input and scaling back out the output. View the utilscli.py in the example GitHub project (*https://oreil.ly/6tjps*).

app.py
> The application file is the Flask web microservice that accepts and returns a JSON prediction result via the /predict URL endpoint. View the app.py in the example GitHub project (*https://oreil.ly/6LTMs*).

mlib.py
> The model handling library does much of the heavy lifting in a centralized location. This library is intentionally very basic and doesn't solve more complicated issues like caching loading of the model or other production issues unique to production deployment. View the mlib.py in the example GitHub project (*https://oreil.ly/wgGPC*).

htwtmlb.csv
> A CSV file is helpful for input scaling. View the htwtmlb.csv in the example GitHub project (*https://oreil.ly/cn8ul*).

model.joblib
> This model is exported from sklearn but could easily be in another format such as ONNX or TensorFlow. Other real-world production considerations could be keeping this model in a different location like Amazon S3, in a container, or even hosted by AWS SageMaker. View the model.joblib in the example GitHub project (*https://oreil.ly/Y4VV9*).

Dockerfile

This file enables project containerization and, as a result, opens up many new deployment options, both on the AWS platform as well as other clouds. View the Dockerfile in the example GitHub project (*https://oreil.ly/QIEAu*).

Baseball_Predictions_Export_Model.ipynb

The Jupyter notebook is a crucial artifact to include in a machine learning project. It shows another developer the thinking behind creating the model and provides valuable context for maintaining the project in production. View the Baseball_Predictions_Export_Model.ipynb in the example GitHub project (*https://oreil.ly/jvs0O*).

These project artifacts are helpful as an educational tool in explaining MLOps but may be different or more complex in a unique production scenario. Next, let's discuss how CLI (command line interface) tools help operationalize a machine learning project.

CLI Tools

In this project, there are two CLI tools. First, the main *cli.py* is the endpoint that serves out predictions. For example, to predict the height of an MLB player, you use the following command to create a forecast: `./cli.py --weight 180`. Notice in Figure 7-19 that the command line option of `--weight` allows the user to test out many new prediction inputs quickly.

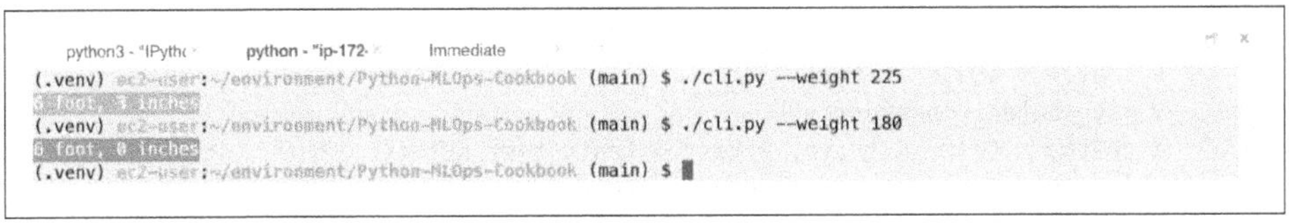

```
python3 - "IPyth      python - "ip-172-      Immediate
(.venv) ec2-user:~/environment/Python-MLOps-Cookbook (main) $ ./cli.py --weight 225
3 foot, 3 inches
(.venv) ec2-user:~/environment/Python-MLOps-Cookbook (main) $ ./cli.py --weight 180
6 foot, 0 inches
(.venv) ec2-user:~/environment/Python-MLOps-Cookbook (main) $
```

Figure 7-19. CLI predict

So how does this work? Most of the "magic" is via a library that does the heavy lifting of scaling the data, making the prediction, then doing an inverse transform back:

```
"""MLOps Library"""

import numpy as np
import pandas as pd
from sklearn.linear_model import Ridge
import joblib
from sklearn.preprocessing import StandardScaler
from sklearn.model_selection import train_test_split
import logging

logging.basicConfig(level=logging.INFO)
```

```python
import warnings

warnings.filterwarnings("ignore", category=UserWarning)


def load_model(model="model.joblib"):
    """Grabs model from disk"""

    clf = joblib.load(model)
    return clf


def data():
    df = pd.read_csv("htwtmlb.csv")
    return df


def retrain(tsize=0.1, model_name="model.joblib"):
    """Retrains the model

    See this notebook: Baseball_Predictions_Export_Model.ipynb
    """
    df = data()
    y = df["Height"].values  # Target
    y = y.reshape(-1, 1)
    X = df["Weight"].values  # Feature(s)
    X = X.reshape(-1, 1)
    scaler = StandardScaler()
    X_scaler = scaler.fit(X)
    X = X_scaler.transform(X)
    y_scaler = scaler.fit(y)
    y = y_scaler.transform(y)
    X_train, X_test, y_train, y_test = train_test_split(
        X, y, test_size=tsize, random_state=3
    )
    clf = Ridge()
    model = clf.fit(X_train, y_train)
    accuracy = model.score(X_test, y_test)
    logging.debug(f"Model Accuracy: {accuracy}")
    joblib.dump(model, model_name)
    return accuracy, model_name


def format_input(x):
    """Takes int and converts to numpy array"""

    val = np.array(x)
    feature = val.reshape(-1, 1)
    return feature


def scale_input(val):
```

```python
    """Scales input to training feature values"""

    df = data()
    features = df["Weight"].values
    features = features.reshape(-1, 1)
    input_scaler = StandardScaler().fit(features)
    scaled_input = input_scaler.transform(val)
    return scaled_input


def scale_target(target):
    """Scales Target 'y' Value"""

    df = data()
    y = df["Height"].values  # Target
    y = y.reshape(-1, 1)  # Reshape
    scaler = StandardScaler()
    y_scaler = scaler.fit(y)
    scaled_target = y_scaler.inverse_transform(target)
    return scaled_target


def height_human(float_inches):
    """Takes float inches and converts to human height in ft/inches"""

    feet = int(round(float_inches / 12, 2))  # round down
    inches_left = round(float_inches - feet * 12)
    result = f"{feet} foot, {inches_left} inches"
    return result


def human_readable_payload(predict_value):
    """Takes numpy array and returns back human readable dictionary"""

    height_inches = float(np.round(predict_value, 2))
    result = {
        "height_inches": height_inches,
        "height_human_readable": height_human(height_inches),
    }
    return result


def predict(weight):
    """Takes weight and predicts height"""

    clf = load_model()  # loadmodel
    np_array_weight = format_input(weight)
    scaled_input_result = scale_input(np_array_weight)
    scaled_height_prediction = clf.predict(scaled_input_result)
    height_predict = scale_target(scaled_height_prediction)
    payload = human_readable_payload(height_predict)
    predict_log_data = {
```

```
        "weight": weight,
        "scaled_input_result": scaled_input_result,
        "scaled_height_prediction": scaled_height_prediction,
        "height_predict": height_predict,
        "human_readable_payload": payload,
    }
    logging.debug(f"Prediction: {predict_log_data}")
    return payload
```

Next, the Click framework wraps the library calls to *mlib.py* and makes a clean interface to serve out predictions. There are many advantages to using command line
tools as the primary interface for interacting with machine learning models. The
speed to develop and deploy a command line machine learning tool is perhaps the
most important:

```
#!/usr/bin/env python
import click
from mlib import predict


@click.command()
@click.option(
    "--weight",
    prompt="MLB Player Weight",
    help="Pass in the weight of a MLB player to predict the height",
)
def predictcli(weight):
    """Predicts Height of an MLB player based on weight"""

    result = predict(weight)
    inches = result["height_inches"]
    human_readable = result["height_human_readable"]
    if int(inches) > 72:
        click.echo(click.style(human_readable, bg="green", fg="white"))
    else:
        click.echo(click.style(human_readable, bg="red", fg="white"))


if __name__ == "__main__":
    # pylint: disable=no-value-for-parameter
    predictcli()
```

The second CLI tool is *utilscli.py*, which performs model retraining and could serve
as the entry point to do more tasks. For example, this version doesn't change the
default model_name, but you could add that as an option by forking this repo (*https://
oreil.ly/dcVf1*):

```
./utilscli.py retrain --tsize 0.4
```

Notice that the *mlib.py* again does the heavy lifting, but the CLI provides a convenient
way to do rapid prototyping of an ML model:

```python
#!/usr/bin/env python
import click
import mlib
import requests

@click.group()
@click.version_option("1.0")
def cli():
    """Machine Learning Utility Belt"""


@cli.command("retrain")
@click.option("--tsize", default=0.1, help="Test Size")
def retrain(tsize):
    """Retrain Model
    You may want to extend this with more options, such as setting model_name
    """

    click.echo(click.style("Retraining Model", bg="green", fg="white"))
    accuracy, model_name = mlib.retrain(tsize=tsize)
    click.echo(
        click.style(f"Retrained Model Accuracy: {accuracy}", bg="blue",
                    fg="white")
    )
    click.echo(click.style(f"Retrained Model Name: {model_name}", bg="red",
                           fg="white"))


@cli.command("predict")
@click.option("--weight", default=225, help="Weight to Pass In")
@click.option("--host", default="http://localhost:8080/predict",
              help="Host to query")
def mkrequest(weight, host):
    """Sends prediction to ML Endpoint"""

    click.echo(click.style(f"Querying host {host} with weight: {weight}",
        bg="green", fg="white"))
    payload = {"Weight":weight}
    result = requests.post(url=host, json=payload)
    click.echo(click.style(f"result: {result.text}", bg="red", fg="white"))


if __name__ == "__main__":
    cli()
```

Figure 7-20 is an example of retraining the model.

```
(.venv) ec2-user:~/environment/Python-MLOps-Cookbook (main) $ ./utilscli.py retrain --tsize 0.1
Retraining Model
Retrained Model Accuracy: 0.18137638458541205
Retrained Model Name: model.joblib
(.venv) ec2-user:~/environment/Python-MLOps-Cookbook (main) $ ./utilscli.py retrain --tsize 0.2
Retraining Model
Retrained Model Accuracy: 0.2802199932746626
Retrained Model Name: model.joblib
(.venv) ec2-user:~/environment/Python-MLOps-Cookbook (main) $ ./utilscli.py retrain --tsize 0.3
Retraining Model
Retrained Model Accuracy: 0.2752994698858813
Retrained Model Name: model.joblib
(.venv) ec2-user:~/environment/Python-MLOps-Cookbook (main) $ ./utilscli.py retrain --tsize 0.4
Retraining Model
Retrained Model Accuracy: 0.24905929566719742
Retrained Model Name: model.joblib
```

Figure 7-20. Model retrain

You can also query a deployed API, which will soon tackle the CLI, allowing you to change both the host and the value passed into the API. This step uses the requests library. It can help build a "pure" Python example of a prediction tool versus only predicting with a curl command. You can see an example of the output in Figure 7-21:

```
./utilscli.py predict --weight 400
```

```
(.venv) ec2-user:~/environment/Python-MLOps-Cookbook (main) $ ./utilscli.py predict
Querying host http://localhost:8080/predict with weight: 225
result: {
  "prediction": {
    "height_human_readable": "6 foot, 3 inches",
    "height_inches": 75.09
  }
}

(.venv) ec2-user:~/environment/Python-MLOps-Cookbook (main) $ ./utilscli.py predict --weight 400
Querying host http://localhost:8080/predict with weight: 400
result: {
  "prediction": {
    "height_human_readable": "7 foot, 1 inches",
    "height_inches": 85.45
  }
}
```

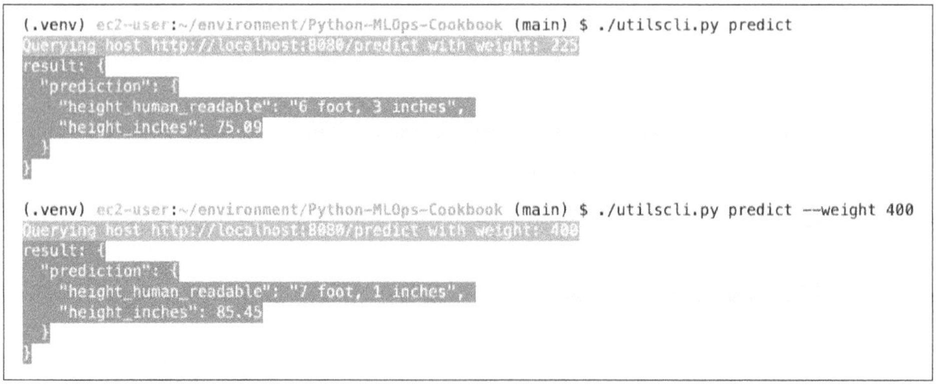

Figure 7-21. Predict requests

Perhaps you are sold on CLI tools as the ideal way to rapidly deploy ML models, thus being a true MLOps-oriented organization. What else could you do? Here are two more ideas.

First, you could build a more sophisticated client that makes async HTTP requests a deployed web service. This functionality is one of the advantages of building utility tools in pure Python. One library to consider for async HTTPS is Fast API (*https://oreil.ly/ohpZg*).

Second, you can continuously deploy the CLI itself. For many SaaS companies, university labs, and many more scenarios, this could be the ideal workflow to adapt speed and agility as a primary goal. In this example GitHub project there is a simple example of how to containerize a command-line tool (*https://oreil.ly/bLC6F*). The three critical files are the Makefile, the *cli.py*, and the Dockerfile.

Notice that the Makefile makes it easy to "lint" the syntax of the Dockerfile using hadolint:

```
install:
  pip install --upgrade pip &&\
    pip install -r requirements.txt

lint:
  docker run --rm -i hadolint/hadolint < Dockerfile
```

The CLI itself is pretty small, one of the valuable aspects of the Click framework:

```
#!/usr/bin/env python
import click

@click.command()
@click.option("--name")
def hello(name):
    click.echo(f'Hello {name}!')

if __name__ == '__main__':
    #pylint: disable=no-value-for-parameter
    hello()
```

Finally, the Dockerfile builds the container:

```
FROM python:3.7.3-stretch

# Working Directory
WORKDIR /app

# Copy source code to working directory
COPY . app.py /app/

# Install packages from requirements.txt
# hadolint ignore=DL3013
RUN pip install --no-cache-dir --upgrade pip &&\
    pip install --no-cache-dir --trusted-host pypi.python.org -r requirements.txt
```

To run this exact container, you can do the following:

```
docker run -it noahgift/cloudapp python app.py --name "Big John"
```

The output is the following:

```
Hello Big John!
```

This workflow is ideal for ML-based CLI tools! For example, to build this container yourself and push it, you could do the following workflow:

```
docker build --tag=<tagname> .
docker push <repo>/<name>:<tagname>
```

This section covered ideas on how to scaffold out Machine Learning projects. In particular, three main ideas are worth considering: using containers, building a web microservice, and using command line tools. Next, let's cover Flask microservices in more detail.

Flask Microservice

When dealing with MLOps workflows, it is essential to note that a Flask ML microservice can operate in many ways. This section covers many of these examples.

Let's first take a look at the core of the Flask machine learning microservice application in the following example. Note, again, that most of the heavy lifting is via the *mlib.py* library. The only "real" code is the Flask route that does the following `@app.route("/predict", methods=['POST'])` post request. It accepts a JSON payload looking similar to `{"Weight": 200}`, then returns a JSON result:

```python
from flask import Flask, request, jsonify
from flask.logging import create_logger
import logging

from flask import Flask, request, jsonify
from flask.logging import create_logger
import logging

import mlib

app = Flask(__name__)
LOG = create_logger(app)
LOG.setLevel(logging.INFO)

@app.route("/")
def home():
    html = f"<h3>Predict the Height From Weight of MLB Players</h3>"
    return html.format(format)

@app.route("/predict", methods=['POST'])
def predict():
    """Predicts the Height of MLB Players"""

    json_payload = request.json
    LOG.info(f"JSON payload: {json_payload}")
    prediction = mlib.predict(json_payload['Weight'])
    return jsonify({'prediction': prediction})
```

```
if __name__ == "__main__":
    app.run(host='0.0.0.0', port=8080, debug=True)
```

This Flask web service runs in a straightforward manner using python app.py. For example, you run the Flask microservice as follows with the command python app.py:

```
(.venv) ec2-user:~/environment/Python-MLOps-Cookbook (main) $ python app.py
* Serving Flask app "app" (lazy loading)
* Environment: production
WARNING: This is a development server. Do not use it in a production...
Use a production WSGI server instead.
* Debug mode: on
INFO:werkzeug: * Running on http://127.0.0.1:8080/ (Press CTRL+C to quit)
INFO:werkzeug: * Restarting with stat
WARNING:werkzeug: * Debugger is active!
INFO:werkzeug: * Debugger PIN: 251-481-511
```

To serve a prediction against the application, run the predict.sh. Notice, a small bash script can help debug your application without having to type out all of the jargon of curl, which can cause you to make syntax mistakes:

```
#!/usr/bin/env bash

PORT=8080
echo "Port: $PORT"

# POST method predict
curl -d '{
   "Weight":200
}'\
    -H "Content-Type: application/json" \
    -X POST http://localhost:$PORT/predict
```

The results of the prediction show that the Flask endpoint returns a JSON payload:

```
(.venv) ec2-user:~/environment/Python-MLOps-Cookbook (main) $ ./predict.sh
Port: 8080
{
  "prediction": {
    "height_human_readable": "6 foot, 2 inches",
    "height_inches": 73.61
  }
}
```

Note that the earlier *utilscli.py* tool could also make web requests to this endpoint. You could also use httpie (*https://httpie.io*) or the postman (*https://postman.com*) tool. Next, let's discuss how a containerization strategy works for this microservice.

Containerized Flask microservice

The following is an example of how to build the container and run it locally. (You can find the contents of *predict.sh* on GitHub (*https://oreil.ly/XhRfL*).)

```
#!/usr/bin/env bash

# Build image
#change tag for new container registery, gcr.io/bob
docker build --tag=noahgift/mlops-cookbook .

# List docker images
docker image ls

# Run flask app
docker run -p 127.0.0.1:8080:8080 noahgift/mlops-cookbook
```

Adding a container workflow is straightforward, and it enables an easier development method since you can share a container with another person on your team. It also opens up the option to deploy your machine learning application to many more platforms. Next, let's talk about how to build and deploy containers automatically.

Automatically build container via GitHub Actions and push to GitHub Container Registry

As covered earlier in the book, the container workflow of GitHub Actions is a valuable ingredient for many recipes. It may make sense to build a container programmatically with GitHub Actions and push it to the GitHub Container Registry. This step could serve both as a test of the container build process and deploy target—say you are deploying the CLI tool discussed earlier. This example is what that code looks like in practice. Note you would need to change the `tags` to your Container Registry (shown in Figure 7-22):

```
build-container:
  runs-on: ubuntu-latest
  steps:
  - uses: actions/checkout@v2
  - name: Loging to GitHub registry
    uses: docker/login-action@v1
    with:
      registry: ghcr.io
      username: ${{ github.repository_owner }}
      password: ${{ secrets.BUILDCONTAINERS }}
  - name: build flask app
    uses: docker/build-push-action@v2
    with:
      context: ./
      #tags: alfredodeza/flask-roberta:latest
      tags: ghcr.io/noahgift/python-mlops-cookbook:latest
      push: true
```

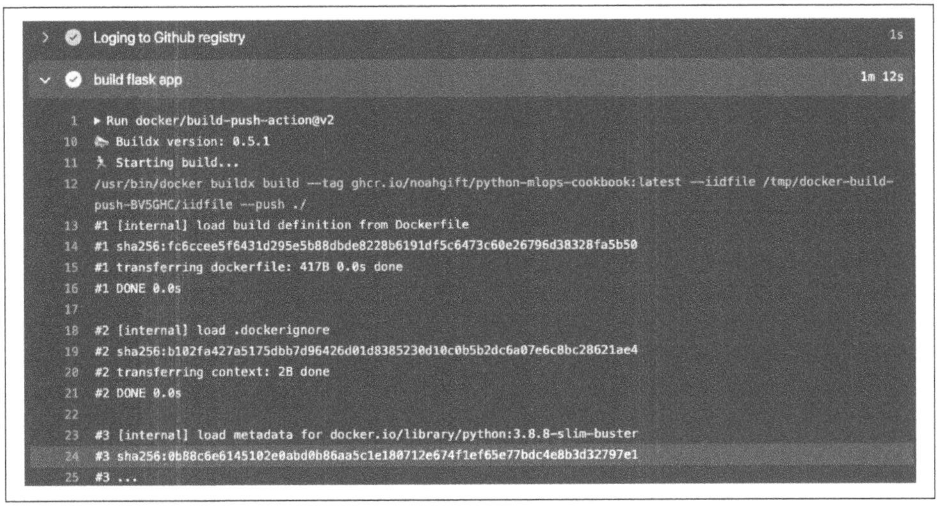

```
>  ✅  Loging to Github registry                                                          1s

✓  ✅  build flask app                                                                 1m 12s

     1  ▶ Run docker/build-push-action@v2
    10  🐳 Buildx version: 0.5.1
    11  ▶ Starting build...
    12  /usr/bin/docker buildx build --tag ghcr.io/noahgift/python-mlops-cookbook:latest --iidfile /tmp/docker-build-
        push-BV5GHC/iidfile --push ./
    13  #1 [internal] load build definition from Dockerfile
    14  #1 sha256:fc6ccee5f6431d295e5b88dbde8228b6191df5c6473c60e26796d38328fa5b50
    15  #1 transferring dockerfile: 417B 0.0s done
    16  #1 DONE 0.0s
    17
    18  #2 [internal] load .dockerignore
    19  #2 sha256:b102fa427a5175dbb7d96426d01d8385230d10c0b5b2dc6a07e6c0bc28621ae4
    20  #2 transferring context: 2B done
    21  #2 DONE 0.0s
    22
    23  #3 [internal] load metadata for docker.io/library/python:3.8.8-slim-buster
    24  #3 sha256:0b88c6e6145102e0abd0b86aa5c1e180712e674f1ef65e77bdc4e8b3d32797e1
    25  #3 ...
```

Figure 7-22. GitHub Container Registry

SaaS (software as a service) build systems and SaaS container registries are helpful outside of just the core cloud environment. They verify to the developers both inside and outside your company that the container workflow is valid. Next, let's tie together many of the concepts in this chapter and use a high-level PaaS offering.

AWS App Runner Flask microservice

AWS App Runner is a high-level service that dramatically simplifies MLOps. For example, the previous Python MLOps cookbook recipes are straightforward to integrate with just a few AWS App Runner service clicks. In addition, as Figure 7-23 shows, AWS App Runner points to a source code repo, and it will auto-deploy on each change to GitHub.

Once it's deployed, you can open up either AWS Cloud9 or AWS CloudShell, clone the Python MLOps Cookbook repo, and then use *utilscli.py* to query the endpoint given to you from the App Runner service. The successful query in AWS CloudShell is displayed in Figure 7-24.

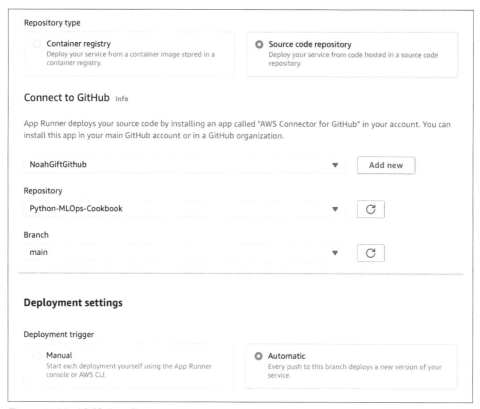

Figure 7-23. AWS App Runner

Figure 7-24. AWS App Runner prediction result

In a nutshell, high-level AWS services allow you to do MLOps more efficiently since less effort goes toward DevOps build processes. So next, let's move onto another computer option for AWS, AWS Lambda.

AWS Lambda Recipes

Install SAM (AWS Serverless Application Model) as AWS documentation instructs (*https://oreil.ly/94HDD*). AWS Cloud9 has it installed already. You can find the recipes on GitHub (*https://oreil.ly/AM38b*). AWS Lambda is essential because of how deeply integral it is to AWS. Let's explore how to use modern best practices to deploy a serverless ML model next.

An efficient and recommended method to deploy software to production is through SAM (*https://oreil.ly/uhBSr*). This approach's innovation combines Lambda functions, event sources, and other resources as a deployment process and development toolkit.

In particular, the key benefits of SAM, according to AWS, include single-deployment configuration, an extension of AWS CloudFormation, built-in best practices, local debugging and testing, and deep integration with development tools, including my favorite, Cloud9.

To get started, first, you should install the AWS SAM CLI (*https://oreil.ly/qPVNh*). After that, you can refer to the official guide for the best results.

AWS Lambda-SAM Local

To get started with SAM Local, you can try the following workflow for a new project:

- Install SAM (as shown previously)
- `sam init`
- `sam local invoke`

> If building on Cloud9, it's probably a good idea to resize using utils/resize.sh (*https://oreil.ly/Tony1*):
>
> ```
> utils/resize.sh 30
> ```
>
> This trick gives you more disk size to build multiple containers with SAM local or any other AWS Container workflow.

Here is a typical SAM init layout, which is only slightly different for an ML project:

```
├── sam-app/
│   ├── README.md
│   ├── app.py
│   ├── requirements.txt
│   ├── template.yaml
│   └── tests
│       └── unit
│           ├── __init__.py
│           └── test_handler.py
│
```

With this foundational knowledge in place, let's move on to doing more with AWS Lambda and SAM.

AWS Lambda-SAM Containerized Deploy

Now let's dive into a containerized workflow for SAM since it supports registering a container that AWS Lambda uses. You can see the containerized SAM-Lambda deploy the project in the following repo (*https://oreil.ly/3ALrA*). First, let's cover the key components. The critical steps to deploy to SAM include the following files:

- *App.py* (the AWS Lambda entry point)
- The Dockerfile (what gets built and sent to Amazon ECR)
- *Template.yaml* (used by SAM to deploy the app)

The lambda handler does very little because the hard work is still happening in the *mlib.py* library. One "gotcha" to be aware of with AWS Lambda is that you need to use different logic handling in lambda functions depending on how they are invoked. For example, if the Lambda invokes via the console or Python, then there is no web request body, but in the case of integration with API Gateway, the payload needs to be extracted from the body of the event:

```
import json
import mlib


def lambda_handler(event, context):
    """Sample pure Lambda function"""

    #Toggle Between Lambda function calls and API Gateway Requests
    print(f"RAW LAMBDA EVENT BODY: {event}")
    if 'body' in event:
        event = json.loads(event["body"])
        print("API Gateway Request event")
    else:
        print("Function Request")

    #If the payload is correct predict it
    if event and "Weight" in event:
        weight = event["Weight"]
        prediction = mlib.predict(weight)
        print(f"Prediction: {prediction}")
        return {
            "statusCode": 200,
            "body": json.dumps(prediction),
        }
    else:
        payload = {"Message": "Incorrect or Empty Payload"}
        return {
```

```
        "statusCode": 200,
        "body": json.dumps(payload),
    }
```

The project contains a Dockerfile that builds the lambda for the ECR location. Notice that it can pack into the Docker container in the case of a smaller ML model and even be programmatically retrained and packed via AWS CodeBuild:

```
FROM public.ecr.aws/lambda/python:3.8

COPY model.joblib mlib.py htwtmlb.csv app.py requirements.txt ./

RUN python3.8 -m pip install -r requirements.txt -t .

# Command can be overwritten by providing a different command
CMD ["app.lambda_handler"]
```

The SAM template controls the IaC (Infrastructure as Code) layer, allowing for an easy deployment process:

```
AWSTemplateFormatVersion: '2010-09-09'
Transform: AWS::Serverless-2016-10-31
Description: >
  python3.8

  Sample SAM Template for sam-ml-predict

Globals:
  Function:
    Timeout: 3

Resources:
  HelloWorldMLFunction:
    Type: AWS::Serverless::Function
    Properties:
      PackageType: Image
      Events:
        HelloWorld:
          Type: Api
          Properties:
            Path: /predict
            Method: post
    Metadata:
      Dockerfile: Dockerfile
      DockerContext: ./ml_hello_world
      DockerTag: python3.8-v1

Outputs:
  HelloWorldMLApi:
    Description: "API Gateway endpoint URL for Prod stage for Hello World ML
    function"
    Value: !Sub "https://${ServerlessRestApi}.execute-api.${AWS::Region}.\
    amazonaws.com/Prod/predict/"
```

```
HelloWorldMLFunction:
    Description: "Hello World ML Predict Lambda Function ARN"
    Value: !GetAtt HelloWorldMLFunction.Arn
HelloWorldMLFunctionIamRole:
    Description: "Implicit IAM Role created for Hello World ML function"
    Value: !GetAtt HelloWorldMLFunctionRole.Arn
```

The only steps left to do are to run two commands: `sam build` and `sam deploy --guided`, which allows you to walk through the deployment process. For example, in Figure 7-25, the `sam build` notice builds the container and then prompts you to either test locally via `sam local invoke` or do the guided deploy.

```
(.venv) ec2-user:~/environment/Python-MLOps-Cookbook/recipes/aws-lambda-sam/sam-ml-predict (main) $ sam build
Building codeuri: . runtime: None metadata: {'Dockerfile': 'Dockerfile', 'DockerContext': './ml_hello_world', 'DockerTag': '
python3.8-v1'} functions: ['HelloWorldMLFunction']
Building image for HelloWorldMLFunction function
Setting DockerBuildArgs: {} for HelloWorldMLFunction function
Step 1/4 : FROM public.ecr.aws/lambda/python:3.8
 ---> cd95409d1c53
Step 2/4 : COPY model.joblib mlib.py htwtmlb.csv app.py requirements.txt ./
 ---> Using cache
 ---> 5529737bad2f
Step 3/4 : RUN python3.8 -m pip install -r requirements.txt -t .
 ---> Using cache
 ---> bd1b0eb99988
Step 4/4 : CMD ["app.lambda_handler"]
 ---> Using cache
 ---> ab29da98e728
Successfully built ab29da98e728
Successfully tagged helloworldmlfunction:python3.8-v1

Build Succeeded
```

Figure 7-25. SAM build

You can invoke a `sam local invoke -e payload.json` with the following body to test locally:

```
{
    "Weight": 200
}
```

Notice that the container spins up, and a payload is sent and returned. This testing process is invaluable before your deploy the application to ECR:

```
(.venv) ec2-user:~/environment/Python-MLOps-Cookbook/recipes/aws-lambda-sam/
sam-ml-predict
Building image..............
Skip pulling image and use local one: helloworldmlfunction:rapid-1.20.0.
START RequestId: d104cf8a-ce6b-4f50-9f2b-c82e99b8016f Version: $LATEST
RAW LAMBDA EVENT BODY: {'Weight': 200}
Function Request
Prediction: {'height_inches': 73.61, 'height_human_readable': '6 foot, 2 inches'}
END RequestId: d104cf8a-ce6b-4f50-9f2b-c82e99b8016f
REPORT RequestId: d104cf8a-ce6b-4f50-9f2b-c82e99b8016f Init
```

```
Duration: 0.08 ms Duration: 2187.82
{"statusCode": 200, "body": "{\"height_inches\": 73.61,\
\"height_human_readable\": \"6 foot, 2 inches\"}"}
```

You can do a guided deployment with testing out of the way, as shown in Figure 7-26. Take special note that the prompts guide each step of the deployment process if you select this option.

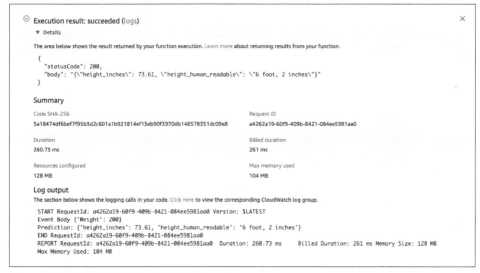

Figure 7-26. SAM guided deploy

Once you have deployed your lambda, there are multiple ways to both use it and test it. Perhaps one of the easiest is to verify the image is via the AWS Lambda Console (see Figure 7-27).

Execution result: succeeded (logs)   ×
  ▼ Details
  The area below shows the result returned by your function execution. Learn more about returning results from your function.

      {
        "statusCode": 200,
        "body": "{\"height_inches\": 73.61, \"height_human_readable\": \"6 foot, 2 inches\"}"
      }

  Summary
  Code SHA-256   Request ID
  5a18474df6bef7f95b3d2c601a1b921814ef13eb90f3970db148578351dc09e8   a4262a19-60f9-409b-8421-084ee5981aa0

  Duration   Billed duration
  260.73 ms   261 ms

  Resources configured   Max memory used
  128 MB   104 MB

  Log output
  The section below shows the logging calls in your code. Click here to view the corresponding CloudWatch log group.
    START RequestId: a4262a19-60f9-409b-8421-084ee5981aa0 Version: $LATEST
    Event Body {'Weight': 200}
    Prediction: {'height_inches': 73.61, 'height_human_readable': '6 foot, 2 inches'}
    END RequestId: a4262a19-60f9-409b-8421-084ee5981aa0
    REPORT RequestId: a4262a19-60f9-409b-8421-084ee5981aa0 Duration: 260.73 ms   Billed Duration: 261 ms Memory Size: 128 MB
    Max Memory Used: 104 MB

Figure 7-27. Test AWS Lambda in Console

Two ways to test the actual API itself include the AWS Cloud9 Console and also the Postman tool. Figures 7-29 and 7-30 show examples of both.

Figure 7-28. Invoke Lambda Cloud9

Figure 7-29. Test AWS Lambda with Postman

Other deployment targets to consider deploying this base machine learning recipe include Flask Elastic Beanstalk and AWS Fargate. Different variations on the recipe include other HTTP services, such as fastapi (*https://oreil.ly/YVz0t*), or the use of a pretrained model available via the AWS Boto3 API versus training your model.

AWS Lambda is one of the most exciting technologies to build distributed systems that incorporate data engineering and machine learning engineering. Let's talk about a real-world case study next.

Applying AWS Machine Learning to the Real World

Let's dive into examples of how to use AWS machine learning resources in the real world. In this section, several MLOps take on what is involved in actual companies doing machine learning.

There are many ways to use AWS for MLOps and an almost infinite number of real-world combinations of services. Here is a partial list of recommended machine learning engineering patterns on AWS:

Container as a service (CaaS)
> For organizations struggling to get something going, CaaS is a great place to start the MLOps journey. A recommended service is AWS App Runner.

SageMaker
> For larger organizations with different teams and big data, SageMaker is an excellent platform to focus on because it allows for fine-grained security and enterprise-level deployment and training.

Serverless with AI APIs
> For small startups that need to move very quickly, an excellent initial approach to doing MLOps is to use pretrained models via an API along with a serverless technology like AWS Lambda.

Case Study: Sports Social Network

This section is a case study on a Sports Social Network built on top of AWS machine learning, with the former Director of Product Management, Rob Loranger. Rob's entry into the world of data and its importance for decision-making began in 2005 when he became a sales engineer specializing in software tools used to design, develop, and manage relational databases, and eventually become a product manager for an enterprise data architecture platform. Since then, Rob has remained a product

---

manager, gaining experience across machine learning–driven software platforms ranging from social networking to data center and telecom network analysis and control.

Rob earned an MBA from the University of California, Davis, where he studied data analytics and machine learning. He gained experience in all ML pipeline activities, from formulating the business problem to choosing, evaluating, and deploying a machine learning model. The tools he has used along the way include Amazon Sage-Maker, Amazon Forecast, Jupyter Notebooks, Minitab, Stata, Weka, Python, and R.

Q: What are 3–5 of the most important things to be aware of deploying and maintaining machine learning systems at scale?

> *A:* Machine learning is not a one-and-done process. You must be committed to continually evaluating the data and the model's accuracy as these change over time. As with all impactful projects, involve the SME (subject matter expert) early and often so that you can build the best understanding of the business problem and the data to be used for testing and validating your machine learning model.
>
> Be sure to make the business problem that you are attempting to solve with machine learning and the impact of solving that problem as straightforward as possible to garner maximum support from critical stakeholders over the project's lifetime.

Q: Explain how a product manager for AI/ML thinks about building ML products.

> *A:* As a product manager for the Sqor Sports social platform, the KPI that mattered most to me, as it was a strong indicator of the platform's stickiness, was monthly active users (MAU). Moreover, to determine that users truly valued the platform, it was essential to see this metric grow significantly over time. Even if the metric maintained a seemingly good steady-state, the platform could still be failing. The steady-state could attribute to situations such as an influx of new users month-over-month that were active only for their first month before leaving or a solid core of niche users who found the platform valuable and continued to use it over time. Either of these would fall well short of the mission of Sqor Sports to be the number one social platform for athletes, teams, and their fans to meaningfully engage with one another.
>
> It was essential to build a rich platform that attracted new users and provide an exciting and unique experience not found anywhere else. Therefore, our strategy improved fan acquisition, fan retention, and viral growth through fans (i.e., fans helping to acquire new fans). Improvements to the platform in these areas would reflect on our core KPI, and MAU would not grow satisfactorily until we got all of these areas right.
>
> By leveraging existing relationships with athletes and teams held by our executive team, board, and business team, we quickly grew the number of athletes and groups on the platform. In turn, by leveraging the athlete and team social content created on Sqor and syndicated across other social networks, we rapidly acquired

fans of these athletes and teams. Moreover, viral growth is a large topic that we will not fully explore here. Still, it was also a core part of our strategy reflected in the product roadmap as features that provided fans with unique content and experiences, and improved fans' ability to create and foster relationships and share content on- and off-platform.

However, early on, fan retention proved challenging as, even though we had a lot of content created by our athletes and teams, fans found it hard to discover and follow new athletes/teams. Therefore, fans typically had a small network of athletes and teams and did not receive enough content from the platform. As a result, the majority of fans became inactive after their first month.

One key aspect of solving this retention problem was rooted in our machine learning–based recommendation engine. Unfortunately, the engine's first several iterations suffered from low data entry leading to poor fan feeds recommendations. However, as we improved the recommendation engine data and algorithm, we began to see the improvements to fan retention we were after, as seen through cohort analysis.

Finally, only with a sizable and growing MAU could we ultimately support our revenue strategy that, early on, consisted solely of a revenue share with athlete merchandise sold on the platform, but with the ultimate goal of providing an enterprise platform to manage social presence (e.g., social media activity, top fans, merchandise sales, etc.).

Q: How can people get ahold of you, and what would you like to share that you are working on with the readers?
    A: You can get ahold of me via email (*rtloranger@gmail.com*) or Linkedin (*https://oreil.ly/GLK60*).

Case Study: Career Advice with Julien Simon, AWS Machine Learning Evangelist

Julien Simon is a prolific content creator and evangelist for the AWS machine learning platform. I was lucky to grab him for some insight into machine learning on the AWS platform.

Q: What is your background, and how did you get involved with operationalizing machine learning?
    A: I'm a software engineer who ended up spending 10 years leading large software and infrastructure teams in several startups. Collecting, storing, and processing data was always a central activity in my teams. Over time, it evolved from relational databases to business intelligence to real-time analytics to machine learning. The latter was actually at the core of one of the companies I worked for. Given our scale at the time (about 500K hits per second), training and deploying

models created all kinds of interesting challenges, from storing data to deploying (and sometimes rolling back) models on hundreds of servers.

Q: *What are 3–5 of the most important things to be aware of deploying and maintaining machine learning systems at scale?*
A: First, can we please agree on the fact that machine learning is software engineering? If we do, then let's also agree that best practices like traceability, versioning, testing, automation, and documentation are not optional. I'm still surprised how deviant machine learning workflows can be, because "things are different." I don't think they are at all. Of course, data science is a very specific discipline, but at the end of the day, it produces code and data artifacts, so let's not reinvent the wheel. A lot of things that have worked well for decades still work with machine learning.

Code and datasets should be versioned and traced. Code and models should be tested. Models should be safely deployed in production, with quality gates and well-understood strategies (canary, blue-green, etc.). Monitoring is also critical, both from an infrastructure perspective (throughput, latency) and from a machine learning perspective (prediction quality, data drift). Finally, your models should also scale up and down according to incoming traffic. And yes, all these processes should be as automated as possible.

Again, nothing really new, but let's start doing it for machine learning too!

Q: *What are you most excited about right now with machine learning and why?*
A: The lazy guy in me loves how we can download and deploy models with just a couple of lines of code. Initiatives like Hugging Face make it extremely easy to add state-of-the-art models to your application, even if you're not a machine learning expert. In general, anything that makes machine learning more accessible is a great step forward: transfer learning, AutoML, and high-level AI services that completely hide all complexity. I often say that we should make machine learning as simple as Amazon S3, so any step in that direction is welcome.

From a technology perspective, I keep a close eye on new hardware that could massively accelerate training and inference. GPUs are nice, yet they feel like a brute force option most of the time. I'm definitely looking forward to more elegant, more cost-effective, and less power-hungry alternatives!

Q: *What are the top 3–5 things a person reading this book can do to succeed in their career doing MLOps?*
A: My number one advice is to learn as much as you can about the business problem that you're trying to solve. Unless you have a deep understanding of it, you won't be able to call the right shots. What do users really care about? What are the key metrics you should be watching? What's the best cost versus performance versus time to market trade-off? All these are critical in achieving success in any machine learning project. Technology is just a tool. Mastering it for its own sake or to beef up your resume is pointless.

In addition, you should also obsess about automation, without which you can't scale your operations. Your data science teams should be able to work completely on their own, training, deploying, and testing their models in their own account. Ops team should only be involved in managing production infrastructure, not dev and test infrastructure. Of course, you need to define the appropriate quality gates to prevent bad models from finding their way into production. If manual approval works best for you, that's fine, but everything else should be automated.

Last but not least, please make sure that you've got your security covered. Here too, best practices should apply (principle of least privilege, encryption, auditing, etc.). AWS has lots of security-related services (IAM, KMS, CloudTrail, S3 bucket policies, etc.), and you should definitely look into them to build a secure data science and machine learning platform.

Q: How can people get ahold of you and what would you like to share that you are working on?

A: I'm always happy to connect on LinkedIn, on Twitter @julsimon (*https://oreil.ly/BN1of*), or YouTube (*https://oreil.ly/cf6pz*), where I build and share as much content as I can, in order to help developers be successful with machine learning on AWS!

Conclusion

This chapter covers both well-traveled roads and unique corners of AWS. A key takeaway is that AWS is the largest cloud platform. There are many different ways to approach a problem using AWS technology, from building an entire company that does machine learning, as the case studies discuss, to using high-level Computer Vision APIs.

In particular, for business and technical leaders, I would recommend the following best practices to bootstrap MLOps capabilities as quickly as possible:

- Engage with AWS Enterprise Support.
- Get your team certified on AWS starting with the AWS Solutions Architect or Cloud Practitioner exam and AWS Certified Machine Learning Specialty.
- Obtain quick wins by using AI APIs like AWS Comprehend, AWS Rekognition, and high-level PaaS offerings like AWS App Runner or AWS Lambda.
- Focus on automation and ensure that you automate everything you can, from the data ingestion and the feature store to the modeling and the deployment of the ML model.
- Start using SageMaker as an MLOps long-term investment and use it for longer term or more complex projects alongside more accessible solutions.

Finally, if you are serious about using AWS as an individual, including starting a career as an AWS machine learning expert, it can be beneficial and lucrative to get certified. Appendix B gives you a quick primer on how to prepare for the AWS Certification exams. A final recommended task would be to go through some exercises and critical thinking questions to practice AWS further.

Our next chapter moves away from AWS and digs into Azure.

Exercises

- Build a machine learning continuous delivery pipeline for a Flask web service using Elastic Beanstalk. You can refer to the GitHub repository (*https://oreil.ly/J5Btz*) as a starting point.
- Start an Amazon SageMaker instance and build and deploy the US census data for the population segmentation example (*https://oreil.ly/yKrhb*).
- Build a CaaS machine learning prediction service using AWS Fargate. You can use this GitHub repo (*https://oreil.ly/opQJh*) as a starting point.
- Build a serverless data engineering prototype using this GitHub repo (*https://oreil.ly/3klFK*) as a starting point.
- Build a computer vision trigger that detects labels; use this GitHub repo (*https://oreil.ly/xKv0p*) as a starting point.
- Use the MLOps Cookbook base project and deploy to as many different targets as you can: Containerized CLI, EKS, Elastic Beanstalk, Spot Instances, and anything else you can think of.

Critical Thinking Discussion Questions

- Why do organizations doing machine learning use a data lake? What is the core problem they solve?
- What is a use case for using prebuilt models like AWS Comprehend versus training your sentiment analysis model?
- Why would an organization use AWS SageMaker versus Pandas, sklearn, Flask, and Elastic Beanstalk? What are the use cases for both?
- What are the advantages of a containerized machine learning model deployment process?
- A colleague says they are confused about where to start with machine learning on AWS due to the variety of offerings. How would you recommend they approach their search?

## CHAPTER 8

MLOps for Azure

By Alfredo Deza

> A third reason for our family to move was that we had never had a proper home since 1933 when, in the midst of the Great Depression, we were dispossessed. It was only years later that I understood how the rural paradise I loved at age 6 disappeared. My parents could not make the payments. My mother abandoned her struggling practice and found a job as receiving physician in a state hospital that provided a few dollars and an apartment too cramped for us all, so my brother and I were sent into what we later called "The Exile."
>
> —Dr. Joseph Bogen

Microsoft's continuous investments in Azure for machine learning are paying off. The number of features offered today makes the platform as a whole a great offering. A few years ago, it wasn't even clear that Azure would get such an influx of top-level engineering and a growing interest in its services.

If you haven't tried Azure at all or haven't seen anything related to machine learning within Microsoft's cloud offering, I highly recommend you give it a chance. Like most cloud providers, a trial period is available with enough credits to try it out and judge for yourself.

One of the examples I usually tend to bring up is that of using Kubernetes. Installing, configuring, and deploying a Kubernetes cluster is not a straightforward task *at all*. It is even more complicated if you factor in associating a machine learning model and scaling its interactions with potential consumers. This is a challenging problem to solve correctly. If you get a chance to go through the deployment settings for a trained model, using a Kubernetes cluster as a target for the model, it boils down to selecting the cluster from a drop-down menu.

Aside from all the features and abstractions of complex problems like deploying models in production, it is *very refreshing* to see an enormous amount of detailed documentation. Although this chapter concentrates on doing operations in machine learning in Azure, it can't possibly capture all of the exciting details. The main documentation resource (*https://oreil.ly/EV9wX*) is an excellent place to bookmark to dive deeper into more information not covered here.

In this chapter, I go through some of the interesting options in Azure, from training a model to deploying it in containers or a Kubernetes cluster. As they are becoming commonplace in machine learning offerings, I will dive into pipelines. Pipelines can enhance the automation further, even when the automation originates outside of the Azure cloud.

There are many ways to perform machine learning tasks within the platform: Azure ML Studio Designer, Jupyter Notebooks, and AutoML, where you can upload a CSV and start training models right away. Finally, most (if not all) features have corresponding support in the SDK (covered in the next section). That flexibility is vital because it allows you to choose the solution that works best for you. So there is no need to follow an opinionated way to operationalize models.

Finally, I will cover practical recommendations on applying some of the core principles of DevOps, such as monitoring and logging using features of Azure Machine Learning.

 Although this chapter is about Azure Machine Learning, it will not cover basics like creating and setting up a new account. If you haven't tried the service yet, you can start here (*https://oreil.ly/LcSb2*).

Azure CLI and Python SDK

The various examples and code snippets in this chapter assume that you have the Azure command line tool and Python SDK (Software Development Kit) installed and available in your environment. Make sure you install the latest version of the CLI (*https://oreil.ly/EPTdV*), and that the machine learning extension is available after installation:

```
$ az extension add -n azure-cli-ml
```

Most of the time, you will need to authenticate from your local system back to Azure. This workflow is similar to other cloud providers. To associate your Azure account with the current environment, run the following command:

```
$ az login
```

Most of the Python examples using Azure's Python SDK will require an account with Azure and the *config.json* file associated with your workspace downloaded locally. This file has all the information necessary to associate the Python code with the workspace. All interactions with the Python SDK should use this to configure the runtime:

```
import azureml.core
from azureml.core import Workspace

ws = Workspace.from_config()
```

To retrieve the *config.json* file, log in to Azure's ML studio (*https://ml.azure.com*) and click the top-right menu (labeled Change Subscription). The submenu will have a link to download the *config.json* file (see Figure 8-1) .

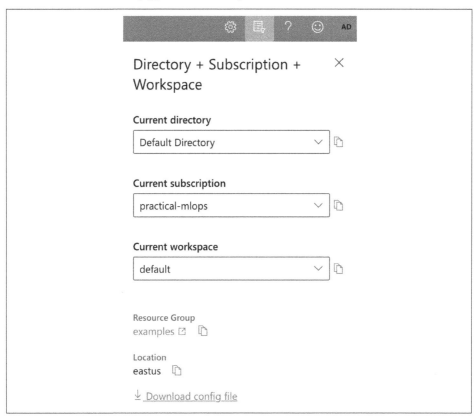

Figure 8-1. Azure JSON config

If *config.json* is not present in the current working directory, using the SDK fails with a traceback:

```
In [2]: ws = Workspace.from_config()
~~~~~~~~~~~~~~~~~~~~~~~~~~~~~~~~~~~~~~~~~~~~~~~~~~~~~~~~~~~~~~~~~~~~
UserErrorException                     Traceback (most recent call last)
<ipython-input-2-e469111f639c> in <module>
----> 1 ws = Workspace.from_config()
```

```
~/.python3.8/site-packages/azureml/core/workspace.py in from_config
    269
    270 if not found_path:
--> 271    raise UserErrorException(
    272      'We could not find config.json in: {} or in its parent directories.'
    273        'Please provide the full path to the config file or ensure that '
```

Now that I've covered some of the basics of using the Azure CLI and the SDK, I will get into more authentication details and some variants you can use in Azure.

Authentication

Authentication should be one of the core pieces of automation when dealing with services. Azure has a *service principal* for access (and access control) to resources. When automating services and workflows, people tend to overlook or even attempt to simplify authenticating in general. It is *very* common to hear recommendations like: *"just use the root user,"* or *"just change file permissions so anyone can write and execute."* A seasoned engineer will know best, but only because they have experienced the pain after accepting these suggestions of lax security and deployment constraints. I very much understand the problem of trying to fix a situation like this one.

When working as a Systems Administrator in a media agency, the Engineering Lead logged directly into the production environment to make a file readable to anyone (needed by the PHP application where it ran). We eventually found out about it. The result of the change meant any HTTP request (and anyone on the internet) had read, write, and execute permissions for that file. Sometimes, a simple fix may be tempting and feel like the best way forward, but this is not always the case. Particularly with security (and authentication in this case), you have to be very skeptical of simple fixes that remove a security constraint.

Always ensure that authentication is done correctly, and do not try to skip or work around these restrictions, even when it is an option.

Service Principal

In Azure, creating a service principal involves several steps. Depending on the constraints you need for the account and resource access, it will vary from one example to another. Adapt the following to fit a specific scenario. First, after logging in with the CLI, run the following command:

```
$ az ad sp create-for-rbac --sdk-auth --name ml-auth
```

That command creates the service principal with the `ml-auth` name. You are free to choose any name you want, but it is always good to have some convention to remember what these names are associated with. Next, take note of the output, and check the `"clientId"` value, which the next steps require:

```
[...]
Changing "ml-auth" to a valid URI of "http://ml-auth", which is the required
format used for service principal names
Creating a role assignment under the scope of:
     "/subscriptions/xxxxxxxx-2cb7-4cc5-90b4-xxxxxxxx24c6"
  Retrying role assignment creation: 1/36
  Retrying role assignment creation: 2/36
{
[...]
  "clientId": "xxxxxxxx-3af0-4065-8e14-xxxxxxxxxxxx",
[...]
  "sqlManagementEndpointUrl": "https://management.core.windows.net:8443/",
  "galleryEndpointUrl": "https://gallery.azure.com/",
  "managementEndpointUrl": "https://management.core.windows.net/"
}
```

Now use the `"clientId"` to retrieve metadata from the newly created service principal:

```
$ az ad sp show --id xxxxxxxx-3af0-4065-8e14-xxxxxxxxxxxx
{
    "accountEnabled": "True",
    "appDisplayName": "ml-auth",
    ...
    ...
    ...
    "objectId": "4386304e-3af1-4066-8e14-475091b01502",
    "objectType": "ServicePrincipal"
}
```

To allow the service principal access to your Azure Machine Learning workspace, you need to associate it with the workspace and resource group:

```
$ az ml workspace share -w example-workspace \
  -g alfredodeza_rg_linux_centralus \
  --user 4386304e-3af1-4066-8e14-475091b01502 --role owner
```

That command is the last one required to complete the process of creating a service principal and associating it with the machine learning account using the `owner` role. The `example-workspace` is the name of the workspace I used in Azure, and `alfredo deza_rg_linux_centralus` is the resource group within that workspace. It is rather unfortunate that there is no output from running that command after a successful call.

Once this account created, you can use it to enable automation with authentication, which prevents prompts and constant authenticating. Make sure to restrict the access and role to the least number of permissions needed.

These examples use the role value of `"owner"` for the service principal, which has widespread permissions. The default value for the `--role` flag is `"contributor,"` which is more restricted. Adapt this value to what suits your environment (and usage) better.

Authenticating API Services

Other environments might not benefit from a service principal account, depending on the workflow at hand. These services can be exposed to the internet, providing interaction with deployed models via HTTP requests. In those cases, you need to decide the type of authentication to be enabled.

Before deploying a model or even configuring any settings for getting a model into production, you need to have a good idea about the different security features available to you.

Azure offers different ways to authenticate, depending on the service you need to interact with. The defaults for these services change, too, depending on the deployment type. Essentially, two types are supported: keys and tokens. Azure Kubernetes Service (AKS) and Azure Container Instances (ACI) have varying support for these authentication types.

Key-based authentication:

- AKS has key-based auth enabled by default.
- ACI has key-based auth disabled by default (but can be enabled). No authentication is enabled by default.

Token-based authentication:

- AKS has token-based auth disabled by default.
- ACI does not support token-based auth.

These types of clusters for deployments are significant enough to grasp before deploying the model to production. Even for test environments, always enable authentication to prevent a mismatch between development and production.

Compute Instances

Azure has a definition for compute instances that describes them as a *managed cloud-based workstation for scientists*. Essentially, it allows you to get started *very quickly* with everything you might need for performing machine learning operations in the cloud. When developing proof of concepts or trying something new from a tutorial, you can leverage the excellent support for Jupyter Notebooks (*https://jupyter.org*) with an enormous amount of dependencies preinstalled and ready to go. Although you can upload your own notebooks, I recommend starting by browsing the thorough samples that exist, as shown in Figure 8-2.

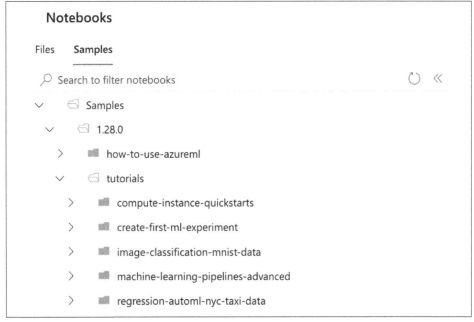

Figure 8-2. Azure notebook samples

One of the most annoying problems to solve when trying to get started running notebooks and tinkering with models is setting up an environment. By offering something ready-to-use and preconfigured specifically for ML, you are enabled to achieve your tasks quickly, moving from ideas in a notebook to production.

Once you are ready to deploy a trained model from a compute instance, you can use the compute instance as a training cluster since it supports a job queue, multiple jobs in parallel, and multi-GPU distributed training. This is a perfect combination for debugging and testing because the environment is reproducible.

Have you ever heard *"But it works on my machine!"* before? I surely have! Even if testing or exploring new ideas, reproducible environments are a great way to normalize development so that there are fewer surprises and collaboration between other engineers is more streamlined. Using reproducible environments is an instrumental part of DevOps that applies to ML. Consistency alongside normalization takes a lot of effort to get right, and whenever you find tools or services that are immediately available, you should take advantage of them right away.

As a Systems Administrator, I've put tremendous effort in normalizing production environments for development, and it is a hard problem to solve. Use Azure compute instances as much as possible!

You can create a compute instance within Azure ML Studio from the various workflows that require one, like when creating a Jupyter Notebook. It is easier to find the Compute link in the Manage section and create one there. Once it loads, multiple choices are presented (see Figure 8-3). A good rule of thumb is to pick a low-cost virtual machine to get started, which avoids higher costs down the road for something that might not be needed just to run a notebook.

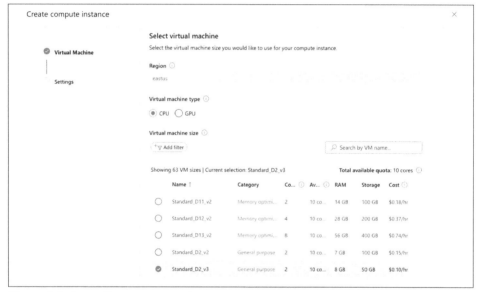

Figure 8-3. Azure Create compute instance

In this example, I'm choosing a `Standard_D2_v3`. Since the names of the various machines offered keep changing, the choices you get might be different.

Deploying

There are several ways of deploying in Azure to interact with a model. If you are dealing with massive amounts of data beyond what is reasonable to deal with in-memory, batch inferencing is a better fit. Azure does provide a lot of useful tooling (general availability for this service was announced in 2020), helping users deal with terabytes of both structured and unstructured data and get inferences from it.

Another way of deploying is for online (sometimes referred to as *instant*) inference. When dealing with smaller datasets (not in the order of terabytes!), it is useful to have a model deployed quickly, accessed over an HTTP API that Azure can create for you programmatically. An HTTP API that gets created for you automatically for a trained model is another one of these features that you should leverage.

Crafting HTTP APIs is not that much work, but offloading that work to a service means you (and your team) have more time to work on more substantial pieces like the quality of your data or the robustness of the deployment process.

Registering Models

The Azure documentation describes registration as something optional. It is indeed optional in that you don't need it to get a model deployed. But as you get used to the process of deploying models and releasing them into production environments, it will become apparent that skimping on features and constraints like authentication (or, in this case, model registration) makes things go easier at first but can create problems later.

I *highly* recommend you register your models and follow a process to do so, even better if this process is fully automated. Granted, you may not need to register every single model you work with, but you most definitely should for select models that get into production. If you are familiar with Git (the version control system) (*https:// oreil.ly/Ttyl0*), then versioning models will feel like a very natural way to reason about changes and modification for production-level models.

These are a few key aspects of model versioning that makes it a compelling feature to use:

- You can identify which model version you are using
- You can quickly select from the various versions, with clarity from descriptions
- You can roll back and select a different model without effort

There are a few ways to register a model. If you are training the model within Azure, then you can use the Python SDK (*https://oreil.ly/6CN0h*) with the result object of a Run class:

```
description = "AutoML trained model"
model = run.register_model(description=description)

# A model ID is now accessible
print(run.model_id)
```

But you aren't required to use Azure to train the model. Perhaps you already have several models trained, and you are considering moving to Azure to get them into production. The Python SDK allows you to register these models as well. Here is an example of how to do this with an ONNX (*https://onnx.ai*) model that is locally available in your system:

```
import os
from azureml.core.model import Model

# assumes `models/` is a relative directory that contains uncompressed
# ONNX models
model = Model.register(
    workspace=ws,
    model_path ="models/world_wines.onnx",
    model_name = "world_wines",
    tags = {"onnx": "world-wines"},
    description = "Image classification of world-wide wine labels"
)
```

One of the refreshing things about Azure is its flexibility. The Python SDK is not the only way to register models. This is how to do it with the Azure CLI:

```
$ az ml model register --name world_wines --model-path mnist/model.onnx
```

You can iterate over several models and get them registered into Azure quickly with some modifications to the previous examples. If you have models available via HTTP, you could potentially download them programmatically and send them over. Use extra metadata to fill out the tags and descriptions; good descriptions make it easier to identify it later. The more automated the process, the better! In Figure 8-4, I'm using the Azure ML Studio to directly upload and register an ONNX model, which is also useful for handling a single model.

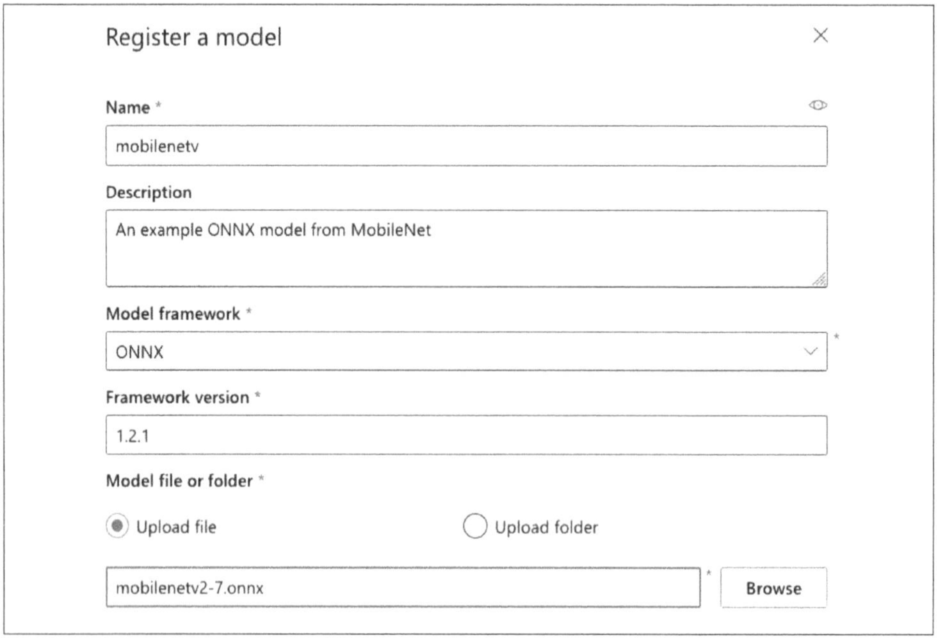

Figure 8-4. Registering a model in Azure

Versioning Datasets

Similar to registering models, the ability to version a dataset solves one of the biggest problems in ML today: enormous datasets that differ slightly are hard (and until recently, impossible) to version nicely. Version control systems like Git are not a good fit for this task, even though version control systems are supposed to help. This mismatch of version control systems that target source code changes and enormous datasets has been a thorn when producing reliable and reproducible production models.

This is another example of how cloud providers like Azure improve workflows with features like dataset versioning. Data is one of the most important pieces when crafting an ML pipeline, and since data can go through many rounds of transformations and cleaning, it is instrumental to version throughout the steps from raw to clean.

Retrieve the dataset first. In this example, the dataset is hosted over HTTP:

```
from azureml.core import Dataset

csv_url = ("https://automlsamplenotebookdata.blob.core.windows.net"
       "/automl-sample-notebook-data/bankmarketing_train.csv")
dataset = Dataset.Tabular.from_delimited_files(path=csv_url)
```

Next, register it using the `dataset` object:

```
dataset = dataset.register(
    workspace=workspace,
    name="bankmarketing_dataset",
    description="Bankmarketing training data",
    create_new_version=True)
```

The `create_new_version` will incrementally set a newer version of the data, even if there is no previous version (versions start at 1). After registering and creating a new version of the dataset, retrieve it by the name and version:

```
from azureml.core import Dataset

# Get a dataset by name and version number
bankmarketing_dataset = Dataset.get_by_name(
    workspace=workspace,
    name="bankmarketing_dataset",
    version=1)
```

> Although it may seem like it, creating a new dataset version *does not mean* Azure makes a copy of the whole dataset with the workspace. Datasets use references to the data in the storage service.

Deploying Models to a Compute Cluster

In this section, you will configure and deploy a model to a compute cluster. Although there are a few steps involved, it is useful to repeat the process a few times to get used to them.

Head over to the Azure ML Studio (*https://ml.azure.com*) and create a new automated ML run by clicking on "New Automated ML run" in the Automated ML section, or directly from the main (home) page by clicking the Create New box with the drop-down. For this part of the process, you will need a dataset available. If you haven't registered a dataset, you can download one and then select From Local File to register it. Follow the steps to upload it and make it available in Azure.

Configuring a Cluster

Back on the "Automated ML run" section, select the available dataset to configure a new run. Part of configuring requires a meaningful name and description. Until this point, all you have configured and made available is the dataset and how it should be used and stored. But one of the critical components of a robust deployment strategy is to ensure that the cluster is solid enough to train the model (see Figure 8-5).

Figure 8-5. Configure an AutoML run

At this point, no cluster should be available in the account. Select "Create a new compute" from the bottom of the form. Creating a new cluster can be done while configuring a run to train a model, or it can be made directly on the Manage section under the Compute link. The end goal is to create a robust cluster to train your model.

It is worth emphasizing to use meaningful names and descriptions whenever possible throughout the many features and products in Azure ML. The addition of these informational pieces is critical to capture (and later identify) what the underlying feature is about. A useful way to solve this is thinking about these as fields, like when writing an email: the *email subject* should capture the general idea about what will be in the body. Descriptions are incredibly powerful when you are dealing with hundreds of models (or more!). Being organized and clear in naming conventions and descriptions goes a long way.

There are two significant cluster types: the *Inference Cluster* and the *Compute Cluster*. It is easy to feel confused until the underlying systems are known: inference clusters use Kubernetes (*https://kubernetes.io*) behind the scenes and Compute Clusters uses virtual machines. Creating both in Azure ML Studio is straightforward. All you need to do is fill out a form, and you get a cluster up and running, ready to train some models. After creation, all of them (regardless of the type) are available as an option to train your model.

Although the Kubernetes cluster (Inference) can be used for testing purposes, I tend to use a Compute Cluster to try different strategies. Regardless of the chosen backend, it is *crucial* to match the workload to the size (and quantity) of machines doing the work. For example, in a Compute Cluster you *must* determine the minimum number of nodes as well as the maximum number of nodes. When parallelizing a model's training, the number of parallel runs cannot be higher than the maximum number of nodes. Correctly determining the number of nodes, how much RAM, and how many CPU cores are adequate is more of a trial-and-error workflow. For the test run, it is best to start with less, and create clusters with more power as needed (see Figure 8-6).

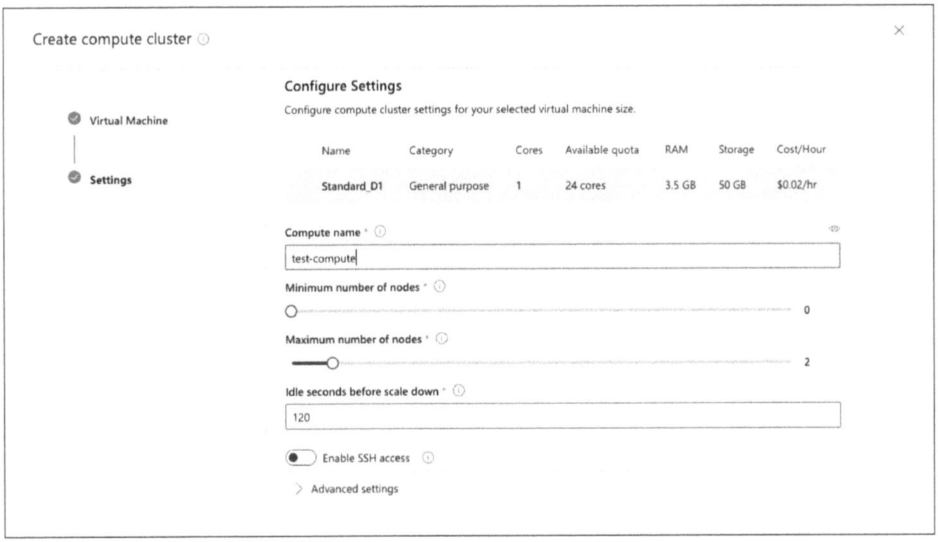

Figure 8-6. Create a Compute Cluster

I choose 0 as the minimum number of nodes in this figure because it prevents getting charged for idle nodes. This will allow the system to scale down to 0 when the cluster is unused. The machine type I've selected is not very performant, but since I'm testing the run, it doesn't matter that much; I can always go back and create a newer cluster.

 The clusters for *training* a model are not the same ones you will use to deploy a model for live (or batch) inferencing. It can be confusing because both strategies (training and inferencing) use the "cluster" term to refer to the group of nodes doing the work.

Deploying a Model

Very much like training a model, when the time comes to deploy a model into production, you have to be aware of the cluster choices available. Although there are a few ways to get this done, there are two key ways to deploy. Depending on the type of deployment use case (production or testing), you have to choose one that fits the best. Following is an excellent way to think about these resources and where they work best:

Azure Container Instance (ACI)
Best for testing and test environments in general, especially if the models are small (under 1 GB in size).

Azure Kubernetes Service (AKS)
All the benefits of Kubernetes (scaling in particular) and for models that are larger than 1 GB in size.

Both of these choices are relatively straightforward to configure for a deployment. In Azure ML Studio, go to Models within the Assets section and select a previously trained model. In Figure 8-7, I chose an ONNX model that I've registered.

There are a couple of essential parts in the form; I chose *ACS* as the compute type, and enabled authentication. This is crucial because once the deployment completes, it will not be possible to interact with the container unless you use keys to authenticate the HTTP request. Enabling authentication is not required but is highly recommended to keep parity between production and testing environments.

After completing the form and submitting it, the process of deploying the model starts. In my example case, I enabled authentication and used ACS. These options don't affect the interaction with the model much, so once the deployment completes, I can start interacting with the model over HTTP, ensuring that requests are using the keys.

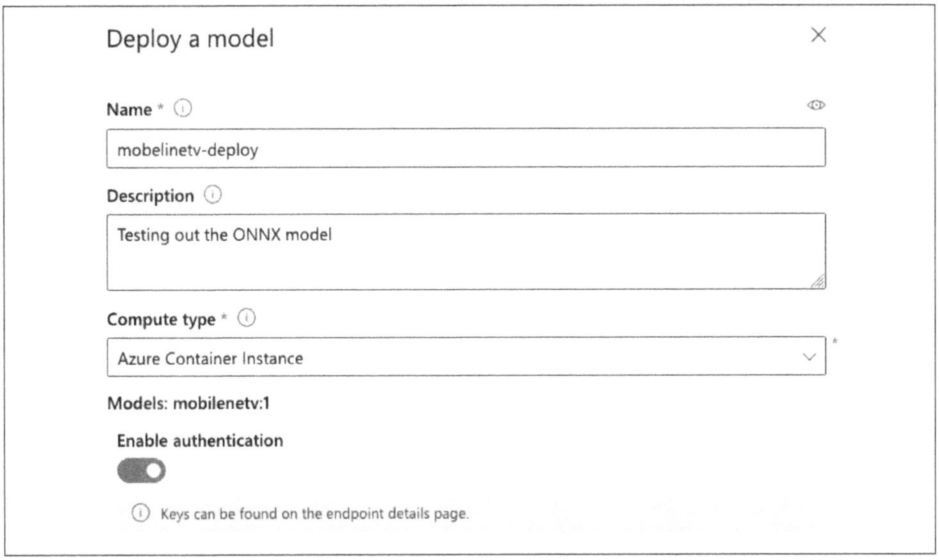

Deploy a model   ✕

Name * ⓘ   👁

mobelinetv-deploy

Description ⓘ

Testing out the ONNX model

Compute type * ⓘ

Azure Container Instance   ⌄   *

Models: mobilenetv:1

Enable authentication

🔘

ⓘ Keys can be found on the endpoint details page.

Figure 8-7. Deploy a model

You can find all the details about the deployed model in the Endpoints section. The name used for the deployment is listed, which links to a dashboard of the deployment details. Three tabs are part of this dashboard: Details, Consume, and Deployment Logs. All of these are full of useful information. If the deployment completes succesfuly, then the logs will probably not be that interesting. In the Details tab, a section will show the HTTP API (displayed as "REST endpoint"). Since I enabled authentication, the page will show the value of "Key-based authentication" as true as shown in Figure 8-8.

REST endpoint
http://48852b98-c98e-420f-98a7-1c9bffa07c64.eastus.azurecontainer.io/score   🗐

Key-based authentication enabled
true

Figure 8-8. REST endpoint

Anything that can talk to an HTTP service with authentication enabled will work. This is an example using Python (no Azure SDK needed for this); the input is using JSON (*https://oreil.ly/Ugp7i*) (JavaScript Object Notation), and the input for this particular model follows a strict schema that will vary depending on the model you are interacting with. This example uses the Requests (*https://oreil.ly/k3YqL*) Python library:

```
import requests
import json

# URL for the web service
scoring_uri = 'http://676fac5d-5232-adc2-3032c3.eastus.azurecontainer.io/score'

# If the service is authenticated, set the key or token
key = 'q8szMDoNlxCpiGI8tnqax1yDiy'

# Sample data to score, strictly tied to the input of the trained model
data = {"data":
    [
      {
        "age": 47,
        "campaign": 3,
        "contact": "home",
        "day_of_week": "fri",
        "default": "yes",
        "duration": 95,
        "education": "high.school",
        "nr.employed": 4.967,
        "poutcome": "failure",
        "previous": 1
      }
    ]
}

# Convert to JSON
input_data = json.dumps(data)

# Set the content type
headers = {'Content-Type': 'application/json'}

# Authentication is enabled, so set the authorization header
headers['Authorization'] = f'Bearer {key}'

# Make the request and display the response
resp = requests.post(scoring_uri, input_data, headers=headers)
print(resp.json())
```

Because the service is exposed with HTTP, it allows me to interact with the API in any way I choose (like using Python in the previous example). Interacting with an HTTP API to interact with the model is compelling because it offers excellent flexibility and gets you immediate results since it is a live inferencing service. In my case, it didn't take long to create the deployment to get responses from the API. This means I'm leveraging the cloud infrastructure and services to quickly try a proof of concept that may end up in production. Trying out models with sample data and interacting with them in environments similar to production is key to paving the way for robust automation later.

When all goes well, a JSON response will get back with useful data from the prediction. But what happens when things break? It is useful to be aware of the different ways this can break and what they mean. In this example, I use input that is unexpected for the ONNX model:

```
{
  "error_code": 500,
  "error_message": "ONNX Runtime Status Code: 6. Non-zero status code returned
  while running Conv node. Name:'mobilenetv20_features_conv0_fwd'
  Missing Input: data\nStacktrace:\n"
}
```

An HTTP status code of 500 indicates that the service had an error caused by invalid input. Make sure that you use the correct keys and authentication methods. Most of the errors from Azure will be easy to grasp and fix; here are a few examples of how those look:

`Missing or unknown Content-Type header field in the request`
Make sure that the right content type (e.g., JSON) is used and declared in the request.

`Method Not Allowed. For HTTP method: GET and request path: /score`
You are trying to make a `GET` request when you probably need a `POST` request that sends data.

`Authorization header is malformed. Header should be in the form: "Authorization: Bearer <token>"`
Ensure that the header is properly constructed and that it has a valid token.

Troubleshooting Deployment Issues

One of the many crucial factors for effective MLOps (of course inherited from DevOps best practices, covered in "DevOps and MLOps" on page 5) is good troubleshooting skills. Debugging or troubleshooting is not a skill that you are born with; it takes practice and perseverance. One way I explain this skill is by comparing it to walking in a new city and finding your way around. Some will say that if I find my bearings with (apparent) ease, then I must have some natural ability. But not really. Pay attention to the details, review those mental details regularly, and question everything. Never assume.

When finding my bearings, I immediately identify the sun's position or the sea (is that East? Or West?), and take mental notes of landmarks or remarkable buildings. Then, I go from beginning to end, reviewing each step mentally: I went left at the hotel until the big church where I turned right, across the beautiful park, and now I'm at the square. Night settles in, and then there isn't a sun position, and I can't remember where to go. Was it left here? Or right? I ask questions, my friends all tell me left, and

I don't assume they are right. Trust but validate. *"If they tell me left, that means I wouldn't have gotten to the park, I'll go their way, wait for a few blocks, and if there is no park, I will backtrack and turn the other way."*

Do not ever assume things. Question everything. Pay attention to details. Trust, but verify. If you practice this advice, your debugging will seem like a natural skill to your peers. In this section, I get into a few details related to containers and containerized deployment in Azure and some of the things you might see come up when they are problems. But you can apply the core concepts anywhere.

Retrieving Logs

Once you deploy a container, you have a few ways of retrieving logs. These are available in Azure ML Studio as well as the command line and the Python SDK. Using the Python SDK means only a few lines after initializing the workspace:

```
from azureml.core import Workspace
from azureml.core.webservice import Webservice

# requires `config.json` in the current directory
ws = Workspace.from_config()

service = Webservice(ws, "mobelinetv-deploy")
logs = service.get_logs()

for line in logs.split('\n'):
    print(line)
```

Run that example code with the name of a service you've previously deployed, and output gets generated with lots of information. Sometimes logs aren't that good and are mostly repetitive. You have to see through the noise and pick up the highlights with useful information. In a successful deployment, most of the output will not mean much.

These are some of the logs from deploying an ONNX model (timestamps removed for brevity):

```
WARNING - Warning: Falling back to use azure cli login credentials.
Version: local_build
Commit ID: default

[info] Model path: /var/azureml-models/mobilenetv/1/mobilenetv2-7.onnx
[info][onnxruntime inference_session.cc:545 Initialize]: Initializing session.
[onnxruntime inference_session Initialize]: Session successfully initialized.
GRPC Listening at: 0.0.0.0:50051
Listening at: http://0.0.0.0:8001
```

Application Insights

Another aspect of retrieving logs and debugging that is valuable to explore is using observability tooling. Observability refers to the means of capturing the state of the system (or systems) at any given point in time. That sounds like a mouthful, but in short, it means that you rely on tooling like dashboards, log aggregation, graphs, and alerting mechanisms to visualize systems as a whole. Because the whole theme of observability is filled with tooling and processes, it is often complicated to get such a thing into production.

Observability is crucial because it isn't about application logs; it is about telling a story about applications when problems arise. Sure, you found a Python traceback in a log, but that doesn't necessarily mean that the Python code needs fixing. What if the input expected was a JSON payload from another system, but instead, the external system sent an empty file? Why would that happen? Observability brings clarity to seemingly chaotic systems. The problems get exponentially more complicated when dealing with distributed systems.

It is not uncommon to define a pipeline system for ingesting data into models that involve several different steps. Source the data, clean it, remove garbage columns, normalize it, and version this new dataset. Suppose all of these are being done with the Python SDK and leveraging triggers from Azure. For example, new data gets into the storage system, which triggers an Azure Function (*https://oreil.ly/zxv74*) that executes some Python. In this chain of events, it is difficult to tell a story without tooling.

Azure offers the right tooling out-of-the-box with the simplest of calls in the SDK. It is called Application Insights (*https://oreil.ly/CnZxv*), and it is packed with all the graphs and dashboards useful right after enabling it. However, it is not only logs or nice graphs that it has to offer. A whole suite of crucial data with a highly visual interface is readily available. Response times, failure rates, and exceptions—they all get aggregated, timestamped, and graphed.

This is how you enable Application Insights in a previously deployed service:

```
from azureml.core.webservice import Webservice

# requires `ws` previously created with `config.json`
service = Webservice(ws, "mobelinetv-deploy")

service.update(enable_app_insights=True)
```

When Application Insights is enabled, the API endpoint section in ML Studio will display it as shown in Figure 8-9.

Figure 8-9. Application Insights enabled

Follow the link provided into the dashboard for the service. A plethora of various charts and informational sources are available. This image captures a small portion of the graphs available for requests made to the deployed model in a container, as shown in Figure 8-10.

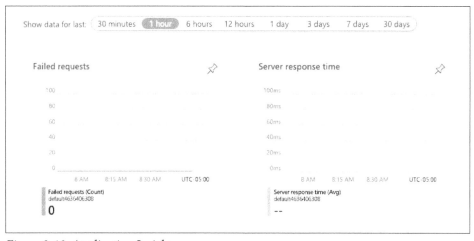

Figure 8-10. Application Insights

Debugging Locally

Following the advice of DevOps principles when debugging, you must question everything and never assume anything. One technique that is useful to debug problems is to run a production service, or in this case, a trained model, in different environments. Containerized deployments and containers in general offer that flexibility, where something that runs in production in Azure can run locally. When running a container locally, which is the same container that runs in production with problems, you can do many more things aside from looking at logs. Debugging locally (potentially on your machine) is a tremendous asset to grasp and take advantage of, while avoiding service disruptions or catastrophic service interruptions. I've been in several situations where the only option was to "log in to the production web server to see what is going on." This is dangerous and highly problematic.

By being skeptical of issues and problems, it is crucial to attempt to replicate the problem. Reproducing the issue is the golden ticket to solving problems. Sometimes, to reproduce customer-facing products, I've reinstalled operating systems from scratch and done deployments in separate environments. Developers jokingly use the phrase *"it works on my machine,"* and I bet you that it almost always holds true—but in reality, it doesn't mean anything. The advice to *"question everything"* can be applied here: deploy multiple times, in different environments, including locally, and try to replicate.

Although it is unreasonable to expect you have to run Azure's Kubernetes offering locally, the Python SDK does offer facilities to expose a (local) web service where you can deploy the same production-grade model, in a container, locally. There are a few advantages to this approach that I've mentioned already. Still, there is another crucial one: most of the Python SDK APIs will work against this local deployment *in addition to* all the container tooling commands you can run to poke the container at runtime. Operations like retrieving the container logs, or getting inside the container to inspect the environment, are all possible and seamless.

 Since these operations are dealing with containerized deployments, it is required to have Docker (*https://docker.com*) installed and running in your environment.

There are a few steps required to run a service locally. First, you must register the model into the current directory:

```
from azureml.core.model import Model

model = Model.register(
  model_path="roberta-base-11.onnx",
  model_name="roberta-base",
  description="Transformer-based language model for text generation.",
  workspace=ws)
```

Next, create an environment, which installs all required dependencies for the model to operate within the container. For example, if the ONNX runtime is required, you must define it:

```
from azureml.core.environment import Environment

environment = Environment("LocalDeploy")
environment.python.conda_dependencies.add_pip_package("onnx")
```

A scoring file (usually named *score.py*) is required to deploy the model. This script is responsible for loading the model, defining the inputs for that model, and scoring data. Scoring scripts are always specific to the model, and there isn't a generic way to write one for any model. The script does require two functions: `init()` and `run()`.

Now, create an *Inference Configuration*, which brings together the scoring script and the environment:

```
from azureml.core.model import InferenceConfig

inference_config = InferenceConfig(
    entry_script="score.py",
  environment=environment)
```

Putting it all together now requires using the `LocalWebservice` class from the Python SDK to launch the model into a local container:

```
from azureml.core.model import InferenceConfig, Model
from azureml.core.webservice import LocalWebservice


# inference with previously created environment
inference_config = InferenceConfig(entry_script="score.py", environment=myenv)

# Create the config, assigning port 9000 for the HTTP API
deployment_config = LocalWebservice.deploy_configuration(port=9000)

# Deploy the service
service = Model.deploy(
  ws, "roberta-base",
  [model], inference_config,
  deployment_config)

service.wait_for_deployment(True)
```

Launching the model will use a container behind the scenes that will run the HTTP API exposed at port 9000. Not only can you send HTTP requests directly to local host:9000, but it is also possible to access the container at runtime. My container runtime didn't have the container ready in my system, but running the code to deploy locally pulled everything from Azure:

```
Downloading model roberta-base:1 to /var/folders/pz/T/azureml5b/roberta-base/1
Generating Docker build context.
[...]
Successfully built 0e8ee154c006
Successfully tagged mymodel:latest
Container (name:determined_ardinghelli,
id:d298d569f2e06d10c7a3df505e5f30afc21710a87b39bdd6f54761) cannot be killed.
Container has been successfully cleaned up.
Image sha256:95682dcea5527a045bb283cf4de9d8b4e64deaf60120 successfully removed.
Starting Docker container...
Docker container running.
Checking container health...
Local webservice is running at http://localhost:9000
9000
```

Now that the deployment finished, I can verify it by running `docker`:

```
$ docker ps
CONTAINER ID      IMAGE          COMMAND
2b2176d66877      mymodel        "runsvdir /var/runit"

PORTS
8888/tcp, 127.0.0.1:9000->5001/tcp, 127.0.0.1:32770->8883/tcp
```

I get in the container and can verify that my *score.py* script is there, alongside the model:

```
root@2b2176d66877:/var/azureml-app# find /var/azureml-app
/var/azureml-app/
/var/azureml-app/score.py
/var/azureml-app/azureml-models
/var/azureml-app/azureml-models/roberta-base
/var/azureml-app/azureml-models/roberta-base/1
/var/azureml-app/azureml-models/roberta-base/1/roberta-base-11.onnx
/var/azureml-app/main.py
/var/azureml-app/model_config_map.json
```

When trying to deploy, I had some issues with the *score.py* script. The deployment process immediately raised errors and had some suggestions:

```
Encountered Exception Traceback (most recent call last):
  File "/var/azureml-server/aml_blueprint.py", line 163, in register
    main.init()
AttributeError: module 'main' has no attribute 'init'

Worker exiting (pid: 41)
Shutting down: Master
Reason: Worker failed to boot.
2020-11-19T23:58:11,811467402+00:00 - gunicorn/finish 3 0
2020-11-19T23:58:11,812968539+00:00 - Exit code 3 is not normal. Killing image.

ERROR - Error: Container has crashed. Did your init method fail?
```

The `init()` function, in this case, needs to accept one argument, and my example was not requiring it. Debugging locally and tinkering with a locally deployed container with a model is very useful and an excellent way to quickly iterate over different settings and changes to the model before trying it out in Azure itself.

Azure ML Pipelines

Pipelines are nothing more than various steps to achieve the desired goal. If you have ever worked with a continuous integration (CI) or continuous delivery (CD) platform like Jenkins (*https://jenkins.io*), then any "pipeline" workflow will feel familiar. Azure describes its ML pipelines as a good fit for three distinct scenarios: machine learning, data preparation, and application orchestration. These have similar setups and configurations while working with different sources of information and targets for their completion.

As with most Azure offerings, you can use the Python SDK or Azure ML Studio to create pipelines. As I've mentioned already, pipelines are *steps* toward achieving an objective, and it is up to you how to order those steps for the end result. For example, a pipeline may have to deal with data; we've covered datasets in this chapter already, so retrieve an existing dataset so that a pipeline step can get created. In this example, the dataset becomes the input of a Python script, forming a distinct *pipeline step*:

```
from azureml.pipeline.steps import PythonScriptStep
from azureml.pipeline.core import PipelineData
from azureml.core import Datastore

# bankmarketing_dataset already retrieved with `get_by_name()`
# make it an input to the script step
dataset_input = bankmarketing_dataset.as_named_input("input")

# set the output for the pipeline
output = PipelineData(
    "output",
    datastore=Datastore(ws, "workspaceblobstore"),
    output_name="output")

prep_step = PythonScriptStep(
    script_name="prep.py",
    source_directory="./src",
    arguments=["--input", dataset_input.as_download(), "--output", output],
    inputs=[dataset_input],
    outputs=[output],
    allow_reuse=True
)
```

 The Azure SDK can change frequently, so be sure to check out the official Microsoft AzureML documentation (*https://oreil.ly/28JXz*).

The example uses the `PythonScriptStep`, one of the many different steps available as a pipeline step. Remember: pipelines are all about steps working toward an objective, and Azure provides different steps for different types of work within the SDK and Azure ML Studio. This step is missing a key part, however: the compute target. But it is already packed with almost everything needed to do data preparation. First, it uses the dataset object and calls `as_named_input`, which the `PythonScriptStep` uses as an argument. The script step is a Python class, but it tries to represent a command line tool, so the arguments use dashes, and the values to those arguments get passed in as items in a list. This is how you retrieve a previously created compute target with the SDK:

```
from azureml.core.compute import ComputeTarget, AmlCompute
from azureml.core import Workspace

ws = Workspace.from_config()

# retrieve the compute target by its name, here a previously created target
# is called "mlops-target"
compute_target = ws.compute_targets["mlops-target"]
```

Aside from the compute target, which we've already covered in this chapter, you can optionally provide a *runtime configuration*, which allows setting environment variables to tell Azure how to manage the environment. For example, if you want to manage your dependencies instead of having Azure handle it for you, then the runtime configuration would be the way to do that. Here is a simplified way to set that particular option:

```
from azureml.core.runconfig import RunConfiguration

run_config = RunConfiguration()

# a compute target should be defined already, set it in the config:
run_config.target = compute_target

# Disable managed dependencies
run_config.environment.python.user_managed_dependencies = False
```

Publishing Pipelines

I've previously made the comparison of continuous integration systems like Jenkins to pipelines: many steps working in a coordinated way to accomplish an objective. But although other CI/CD systems like Jenkins have this capability, one thing that is very tricky to accomplish is to expose these jobs outside of the environment. Azure has a straightforward way to achieve this, both via Azure ML Studio and with the SDK. Essentially, what happens with the pipeline is that it becomes available over HTTP so that any system anywhere in the world can reach the pipeline and trigger it.

The possibilities then are endless. You are no longer tied to using services, pipelines, and triggers from within Azure. Still, your pipeline steps can start elsewhere, perhaps in a closed on-premise environment at your company or a public source code service like GitHub. This is an interesting flexibility because it offers more options, and the constraints of the cloud provider go away. You don't need to create a new pipeline every time you want to publish it. You can encounter this in the documentation while trying to find out how to publish a pipeline. In this example, a previous experiment and run gets retrieved to publish the pipeline:

```
from azureml.core.experiment import Experiment
from azureml.pipeline.core import PipelineRun

experiment = Experiment(ws, "practical-ml-experiment-1")

# run IDs are unique, this one already exists
run_id = "78e729c3-4746-417f-ad9a-abe970f4966f"
pipeline_run = PipelineRun(experiment, run_id)

published_pipeline = pipeline_run.publish_pipeline(
    name="ONNX example Pipeline",
    description="ONNX Public pipeline", version="1.0")
```

Now that you know how to publish it, you can interact with it over HTTP. These API endpoints require authentication, but the SDK has everything you need to get the authentication headers needed to make requests:

```
from azureml.core.authentication import InteractiveLoginAuthentication
import requests

interactive_auth = InteractiveLoginAuthentication()
auth_header = interactive_auth.get_authentication_header()

rest_endpoint = published_pipeline.endpoint
response = requests.post(
    rest_endpoint,
    headers=auth_header,
    json={"ExperimentName": "practical-ml-experiment-1"}
)


run_id = response.json().get('Id')
print(f"Pipeline run submitted with ID: {run_id}")
```

Azure Machine Learning Designer

For the graphically inclined, the Azure Machine Learning designer is a good choice for abstracting away the complexity of building machine learning projects on Azure. The process to train a model is as follows:

1. Sign in to Azure ML Studio.

2. Select the Designer interface as shown in Figure 8-11.

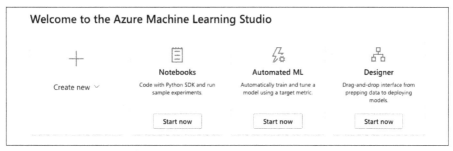

Figure 8-11. Azure ML designer

3. Select a sample project to explore, like the Automobile Regression project in Figure 8-12. Note there are many sample projects to explore, or you can build your ML project from scratch. An excellent resource to investigate ML Designer sample projects is the official Microsoft Azure Machine Learning designer documentation (*https://oreil.ly/NJrfK*).

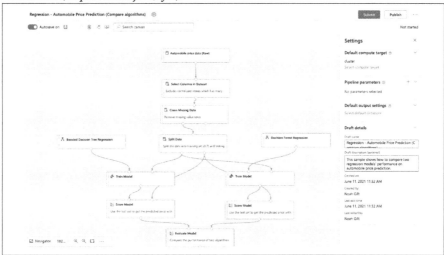

Figure 8-12. Azure ML Designer Automobile Regression project

4. To run the project, submit a pipeline job as shown in Figure 8-13.

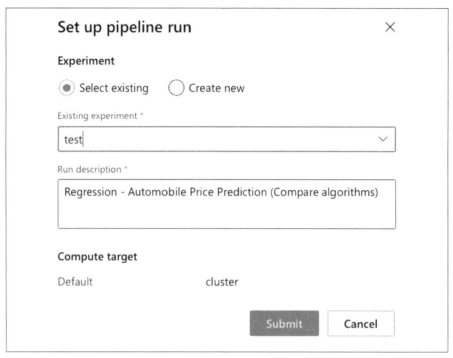

Figure 8-13. Azure ML designer submission

The Azure ML designer may seem a bit fancy, but it can play an essential role in understanding how the Azure ML Studio ecosystem works. By "kicking the tires" on a sample project, you get exposed to all of the essential aspects of Azure ML Studio, including AutoML, storage, compute clusters, and reporting. Next, let's talk about how all of this relates to the ML lifecycle on Azure.

ML Lifecycle

In the end, all tooling and services in Azure are there to help with the model lifecycle. This methodology is not entirely particular to Azure, but it is useful to grasp how these services help you get your models into production. As Figure 8-14 shows, you start with training, which can happen in a Notebook, AutoML, or with the SDK. Then you can move on to validation with Azure Designer or Azure ML Studio itself. Production deployments can then leverage scaling with Kubernetes while keeping attention to problems with Application Insights.

Figure 8-14 tries to make it clear that this is not a linear process, and the constant feedback loop throughout the process of shipping to production can require going back to previous steps to address data issues and other common problems observed in models. However, the feedback loop and constant adjusting is essential for a healthy environment; it is not enough to click a checkbox that enables monitoring or that Kubernetes is handling scaling. Without consistent evaluation, success is impossible, regardless of the cloud provider.

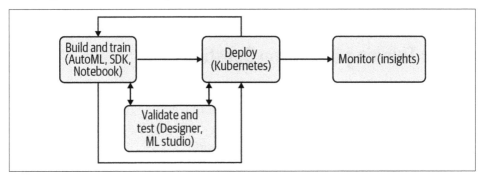

Figure 8-14. ML lifecycle

Conclusion

No doubt Azure is already solving challenging problems related to operationalizing machine learning, from registering and versioning datasets to facilitating monitoring and deploying live inferencing models on scalable clusters. It all feels relatively new, and Azure as a whole is still catching up in functionality to other cloud providers— but this shouldn't matter. The platform of choice (even if it isn't Azure) has to enable workflows with ease; you must leverage what is available. You will see repetition and emphasis on some ideas throughout the book about leveraging technology and avoiding solving challenges with half-baked solutions. Technology reuse will propel any venture. Remember that the most important thing to achieve as an MLOps engineer is to ship models to production, not reinvent cloud features.

The next chapter will dig into the Google Cloud Platform.

Exercises

- Retrieve an ONNX model from a public source and register it in Azure with the Python SDK.
- Deploy a model to ACI and create a Python script that returns the model's response, as it comes back from the HTTP API.
- Deploy a container locally, using Azure's Python SDK, and produce some HTTP requests for live inferencing.

- Publish a new pipeline, and then trigger it. The trigger should show the output of the `run_id` after a successful request.
- Train a model using Azure AutoML from the Python SDK by grabbing a dataset from Kaggle.

Critical Thinking Discussion Questions

- There are many ways to train models on the Azure platform: Azure ML Studio Designer, Azure Python SDK, Azure Notebooks, and Azure AutoML. What are the advantages and disadvantages of each?
- Why is it a good idea to enable authentication?
- How can reproducible environments help deliver models?
- Describe two aspects of good debugging techniques and why they are useful.
- What are some benefits of versioning models?
- Why is versioning datasets important?

## CHAPTER 9

MLOps for GCP

By Noah Gift

> The best bonsai teachers have both a mastery of the reality and an ability not only to explain but to inspire. John once said, "Jin this part and wire it so it will dry with a nice shape." "What shape?" I asked. "You decide," he replied, "it's not for me to sing your song for you!"
>
> —Dr. Joseph Bogen

The Google Cloud Platform (GCP) is unique compared to its competitors. On the one hand, it has been marginally enterprise-focused; on the other, it has world-class research and development that has created category-leading technology, including products like Kubernetes and TensorFlow. Yet one more unique aspect of the Google Cloud is the rich collection of educational resources available to students and working professionals through *https://edu.google.com*.

Let's dive into the Google Cloud with an emphasis on using it to perform MLOps.

Google Cloud Platform Overview

Every cloud platform has pros and cons, so let's start by covering the three main cons of the Google Cloud Platform. First, with Google trailing AWS and Microsoft Azure, one disadvantage of using Google is that it has fewer certified practitioners. In Figure 9-1, you can see that in 2020, AWS and Azure controlled over 50% of the market, and Google Cloud was less than 9%. Hiring talent for the Google Cloud Platform is more challenging as a result.

A second disadvantage is that Google is part of what Harvard Professor Shoshana Zuboff (*https://oreil.ly/le2OC*) calls surveillance capitalism, in which "Silicon Valley and other corporations are mining users' information to predict and shape their behavior." Thus, it is theoretically possible that technology regulation could impact market share in the future.

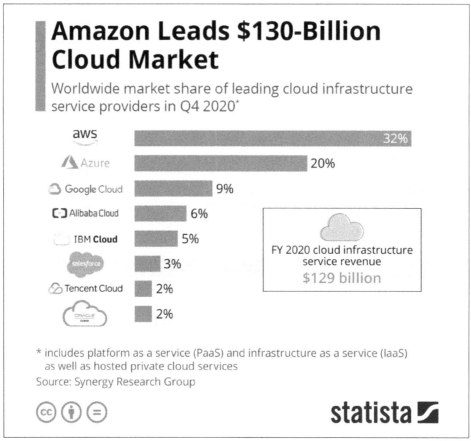

Figure 9-1. GCP Cloud market share

Finally, Google has a reputation for a poor user and customer experience and frequently abandons products like Google Hangouts and the Google Plus social network. Could it then discontinue Google Cloud if it remains the third-best option in the next five years?

While these are substantial challenges, and Google would be wise to address the cultural issues that led to these cons quickly, there are many unique advantages to the Google platform due to its culture. For example, while AWS and Microsoft are customer service-oriented cultures with a rich history of enterprise customer support, Google famously didn't have phone support for most products. Instead, its culture focuses on intense "leet code" style interviews to only "hire the best." Additionally, research and development of mind-numbingly complex solutions that work at "planet-scale" is something it does well. In particular, three of Google's most successful open source projects show this cultural strength: Kubernetes, the Go language, and the deep learning framework TensorFlow.

Ultimately the number one advantage of using the Google Cloud may be that its technology is ideal for a multicloud strategy. Technologies like Kubernetes and Tensor Flow work well on any cloud and are widely adopted. As a result, using Google Cloud could be a hedge for large companies wanting to check the power of their vendor relationship with either AWS or Azure. Additionally, these technologies have wide adoption, so it is relatively straightforward to hire for positions that require expertise in TensorFlow.

Let's take a look at Google Cloud's core offerings. These services divide into four clean categories: Compute, Storage, Big Data, and Machine Learning, as shown in Figure 9-2.

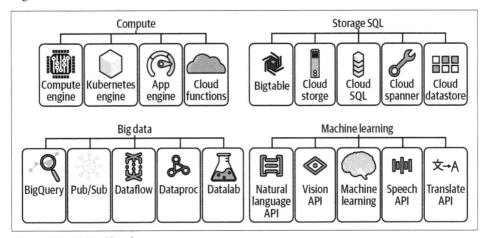

Figure 9-2. GCP Cloud services

Let's define the major components of Google Cloud next, starting with Compute:

Compute Engine
>   Like other cloud vendors (notably AWS and Azure), GCP offers virtual machines as a service. Compute Engine is a service that enables you to create and run virtual machines on Google's infrastructure. Perhaps the most critical takeaway is that there are many different virtual machines, including Compute Intensive, Memory Intensive, Accelerator Optimized, and General Purpose. Additionally, there are preemptible VMs, available for up to 24 hours, suited for batch jobs, and they can save up to 80% on storage costs.

>   As an MLOps practitioner, it is critical to use suitable types of machines for the task at hand. Costs do matter in the actual world, and the ability to accurately

forecast costs could make or break a company doing machine learning. For example, with deep learning, it could be optimal to use Accelerator Optimized instances since they could leverage the additional massively parallel capabilities of NVIDIA GPUs. On the other hand, it would be incredibly wasteful to use these instances for machine learning training that cannot take advantage of GPUs. Similarly, by architecting around preemptible VMs for batch machine learning, an organization could save up to 80% of the cost.

Kubernetes Engine and Cloud Run

Since Google created Kubernetes and maintains it, the support for doing work on Kubernetes is excellent through its GKE (Google Kubernetes Engine). Alternatively, Cloud Run is a high-level service that abstracts away many of the complexities of running containers. Cloud Run is a good starting point for the Google Cloud Platform for organizations wanting a simple way to deploy containerized machine learning applications.

App Engine

Google App Engine is a fully managed PaaS. You can write code in many languages, including Node.js, Java, Ruby, C#, Go, Python, or PHP. MLOps workflows could use App Engine as the API endpoint of a fully automated continuous delivery pipeline using GCP Cloud Build to deploy changes.

Cloud Functions

Google Cloud Functions act as a FaaS (functions as a service). FaaS works well with an event-driven architecture. For example, Cloud Functions could trigger a batch machine learning training job or deliver an ML prediction in response to an event.

Next, let's talk about storage on Google Cloud. Concerning MLOps, the main option to discuss is its Cloud Storage product. It offers unlimited storage, worldwide accessibility, low latency, geo-redundancy, and high durability. These facts mean that for MLOps workflows, the data lake is the location where unstructured and structured data resides for batch processing of machine learning training jobs.

Closely associated with this offering are the big data tools available from GCP. Many offerings assist in moving, querying, and computing big data. One of the most popular offerings is Google BigQuery because it offers a SQL interface, serverless paradigm, and the ability to do machine learning within the platform. Google BigQuery is a great place to start doing machine learning on GCP because you can solve the entire MLOps value chain from this one tool.

Finally, the machine learning and AI capabilities coordinate in a product called Vertex AI. One advantage of Google's approach is that it aims to be an MLOps solution from the beginning. The workflow of Vertex AI allows a structured approach to ML, including the following:

- Dataset creation and storage
- Training an ML model
- Storing the model in Vertex AI
- Deploying the model to an endpoint for prediction
- Testing and creating prediction requests
- Using traffic splitting for endpoints
- Managing the lifecycle of ML models and endpoints

According to Google, these capabilities factor into how Vertex AI enables MLOps, as shown in Figure 9-3. At the center of these seven components is data and model management, the central element of MLOps.

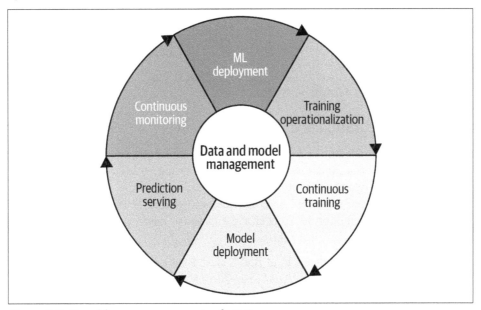

Figure 9-3. Google's seven components of MLOps

This thought process culminates in Google's idea of end-to-end MLOps, as described in Figure 9-4. A comprehensive platform like Vertex AI enables a comprehensive way to manage MLOps.

In a nutshell, MLOps on the Google Cloud Platform is straightforward due to Vertex AI and subcomponents of this system like Google BigQuery. Next, let's get into more detail on CI/CD on GCP, a nonoptional foundational component of MLOps.

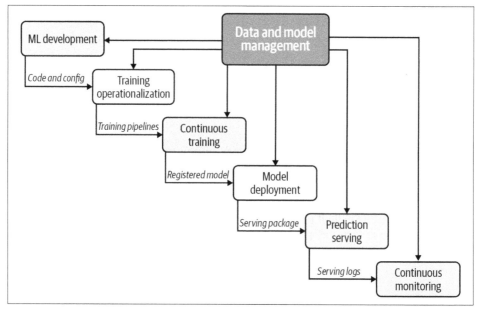

Figure 9-4. End-to-end MLOps on GCP

Continuous Integration and Continuous Delivery

One of the most important and yet neglected areas of a project involves continuous integration. Testing is a fundamental component to doing both DevOps and MLOps. For GCP, there are two main continuous integration options: use a SaaS offering like GitHub Actions or use the cloud native solution Cloud Build (*https://oreil.ly/oTafJ*). Let's take a look at both options. You can view an entire starter project scaffold in this gcp-from-zero GitHub repository (*https://oreil.ly/34TQt*).

First, let's take a look at Google Cloud Build. Here is an example of the configuration file for Google Cloud Build, *cloudbuild.yaml* (*https://oreil.ly/wWbRS*):

```
steps:
- name: python:3.7
  id: INSTALL
  entrypoint: python3
  args:
  - '-m'
  - 'pip'
  - 'install'
  - '-t'
  - '.'
  - '-r'
  - 'requirements.txt'
- name: python:3.7
  entrypoint: ./pylint_runner
  id: LINT
```

```
  waitFor:
  - INSTALL
- name: "gcr.io/cloud-builders/gcloud"
  args: ["app", "deploy"]
timeout: "1600s"
images: ['gcr.io/$PROJECT_ID/pylint']
```

A recommended way to work with Google Cloud is to use the built-in editor along-side the terminal, as shown in Figure 9-5. Note that a Python virtual environment is activated.

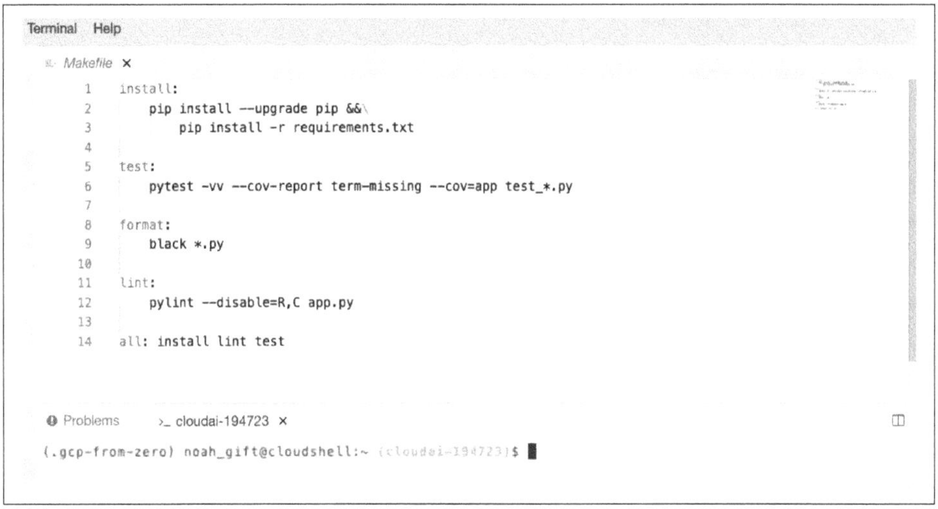

Figure 9-5. GCP editor

One takeaway is that Google Cloud Build is a bit clunky with testing and linting code compared to GitHub Actions, but it does make deploying services like Google App Engine easy.

Now let's look at how GitHub Actions works. You can reference the *python-publish.yml* configuration file (*https://oreil.ly/mJd0T*):

```
name: Python application test with GitHub Actions

on: [push]

jobs:
  build:

    runs-on: ubuntu-latest

    steps:
    - uses: actions/checkout@v2
    - name: Set up Python 3.8
      uses: actions/setup-python@v1
```

```
  with:
    python-version: 3.8
- name: Install dependencies
  run: |
    make install
- name: Lint with pylint
  run: |
    make lint
- name: Test with pytest
  run: |
    make test
- name: Format code
  run: |
    make format
```

A critical difference between the two approaches is that GitHub focuses on delivering an incredible developer experience, while GCP focuses on the cloud experience. One strategy is to use GitHub Actions for developer feedback, i.e., linting and testing code, and to use Google Cloud Build for deployment.

With a handle on CI/CD systems on GCP, let's explore a core Google compute technology, Kubernetes.

Kubernetes Hello World

One way of thinking about Kubernetes is as a "mini-cloud" or a "cloud-in-a-box." Kubernetes allows for the creation of near-infinite application complexity. A few of the capabilities of Kubernetes that make it ideal for MLOps include:

- High-availability architecture
- Autoscaling
- Rich ecosystem
- Service discovery
- Container health management
- Secrets and configuration management
- Kubeflow (end-to-end ML platform for Kubernetes)

Figure 9-6 notes that ML frameworks from TensorFlow to scikit-learn coordinate on top of the core Kubernetes architecture. Finally, Kubernetes, as discussed earlier, can run in many clouds or in your own data center.

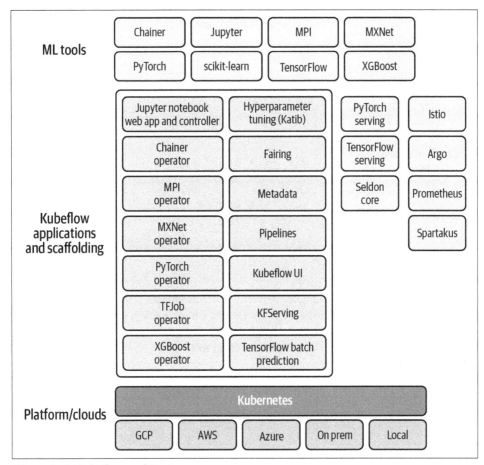

Figure 9-6. Kubeflow architecture

The foundation of the Kubernetes architecture in Figure 9-7 shows the core operations involved in Kubernetes include the following:

- Creating a Kubernetes cluster.
- Deploying an application into the cluster.
- Exposing application ports.
- Scaling an application.
- Updating an application.

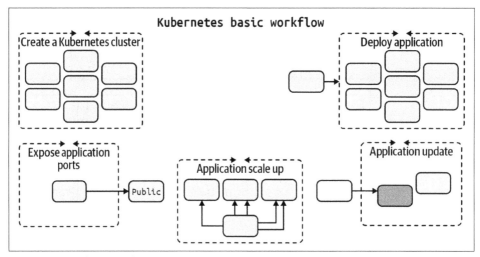

Figure 9-7. Kubernetes basics

The Kubernetes hierarchy in Figure 9-8 shows a Kubernetes control node that manages the other nodes containing one or more containers inside a pod.

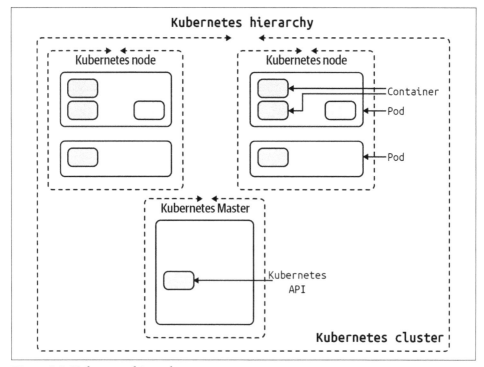

Figure 9-8. Kubernetes hierarchy

There are two main methods: set up a local cluster (preferably with Docker Desktop) or provision a cloud cluster: Amazon through Amazon EKS, Google through Google Kubernetes Engine GKE, and Microsoft through Azure Kubernetes Service (AKS).

One of the "killer" features of Kubernetes is the ability to set up autoscaling via the Horizontal Pod Autoscaler (HPA). The Kubernetes HPA will automatically scale the number of pods (remember they can contain multiple containers) in a replication controller, deployment, or replica set. The scaling uses CPU utilization, memory, or custom metrics defined in the Kubernetes Metrics Server.

In Figure 9-9, Kubernetes is using a control loop to monitor metrics for the cluster and perform actions based on the metrics received.

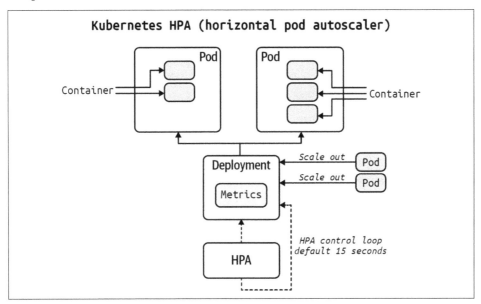

Figure 9-9. Kubernetes autoscaler

Since Kubernetes is a core strength of the Google Platform and how much of MLOps works on the platform, let's dive right into a "hello world" Kubernetes example. This project uses a simple Flask app that returns correct change (*https://oreil.ly/sOcdS*) as the base project and converts it to Kubernetes. You can find the complete source in the repository on GitHub (*https://oreil.ly/ISgrh*).

In Figure 9-10 the Kubernetes nodes attach to the Load Balancer.

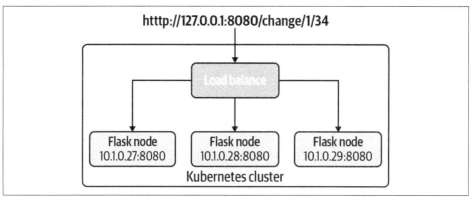

Figure 9-10. Kubernetes hello world

Let's look at the assets in the repository.

- *Makefile (https://oreil.ly/HSX9G)*: Builds project
- *Dockerfile (https://oreil.ly/2Znkk)*: Container configuration
- *app.py (https://oreil.ly/G2Tjt)*: Flask app
- *kube-hello-change.yaml (https://oreil.ly/BCARa)*: Kubernetes YAML Config

To get started, do the following steps:

1. Create Python virtual environment:

    ```
    python3 -m venv ~/.kube-hello && source ~/.kube-hello/bin/activate
    ```

2. Run `make all` to execute multiple build steps, including installing the libraries, linting the project, and running the tests.

Making Use of Certified Containers

One of the Docker workflow advantages for developers is using certified containers from the "official" development teams. In this diagram, a developer uses the official Python base image developed by the core Python developers. This step works using the `FROM` statement, which loads in a previously created container image.

As the developer changes to the Dockerfile, they test locally and then push the changes to a private Docker Hub repo. For example, in Figure 9-11, the changes can become available by a deployment process to a cloud or another developer.

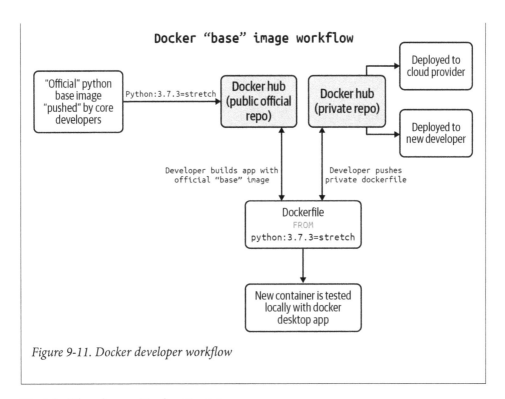

Figure 9-11. Docker developer workflow

Next, build and run a Docker Container:

1. Install Docker Desktop (*https://oreil.ly/oUB0E*)
2. To build the image locally, do the following:

   ```
   docker build -t flask-change:latest .
   ```

   or run `make build`, which has the same command.

3. To verify container run `docker image ls`
4. To run the container do the following:

   ```
   docker run -p 8080:8080 flask-change
   ```

   or run `make run`, which has the same command.

5. In a separate terminal, invoke the web service via `curl`, or run `make invoke` which has the same command:

   ```
   curl http://127.0.0.1:8080/change/1/34
   ```

   Here's the output:

   ```
   $ kubectl get nodes
   [
     {
   ```

```
      "5": "quarters"
    },
    {
      "1": "nickels"
    },
    {
      "4": "pennies"
    }
  ]
```

6. Stop the running Docker container by using Ctrl+C command

Next, run Kubernetes locally:

1. Verify Kubernetes is working via docker-desktop context:

```
(.kube-hello) → kubernetes-hello-world-python-flask git:(main) kubectl \
get nodes

NAME            STATUS    ROLES    AGE    VERSION
docker-desktop  Ready     master   30d    v1.19.3
```

2. Run the application in Kubernetes using the following command, which tells Kubernetes to set up the load-balanced service and run it:

```
kubectl apply -f kube-hello-change.yaml
```

or run make run-kube, which has the same command.

You can see from the config file that a load balancer along with three nodes are the configured application:

```
apiVersion: v1
kind: Service
metadata:
  name: hello-flask-change-service
spec:
  selector:
    app: hello-python
  ports:
  - protocol: "TCP"
    port: 8080
    targetPort: 8080
  type: LoadBalancer

---
apiVersion: apps/v1
kind: Deployment
metadata:
  name: hello-python
spec:
  selector:
```

```
    matchLabels:
      app: hello-python
  replicas: 3
  template:
    metadata:
      labels:
        app: hello-python
    spec:
      containers:
      - name: flask-change
        image: flask-change:latest
        imagePullPolicy: Never
        ports:
        - containerPort: 8080
```

3. Verify the container is running:

```
kubectl get pods
```

Here is the output:

```
NAME                              READY  STATUS   RESTARTS  AGE
flask-change-7b7d7f467b-26htf     1/1    Running  0         8s
flask-change-7b7d7f467b-fh6df     1/1    Running  0         7s
flask-change-7b7d7f467b-fpsxr     1/1    Running  0         6s
```

4. Describe the load balanced service:

```
kubectl describe services hello-python-service
```

You should see output similar to this:

```
Name:                    hello-python-service
Namespace:               default
Labels:                  <none>
Annotations:             <none>
Selector:                app=hello-python
Type:                    LoadBalancer
IP Families:             <none>
IP:                      10.101.140.123
IPs:                     <none>
LoadBalancer Ingress:    localhost
Port:                    <unset>  8080/TCP
TargetPort:              8080/TCP
NodePort:                <unset>  30301/TCP
Endpoints:               10.1.0.27:8080,10.1.0.28:8080,10.1.0.29:8080
Session Affinity:        None
External Traffic Policy: Cluster
Events:                  <none>
```

5. Invoke the endpoint to curl it:

```
make invoke
```

In the next section, run the command `make invoke` to query the microservice. The output of that action is shown here:

```
curl http://127.0.0.1:8080/change/1/34
[
  {
    "5": "quarters"
  },
  {
    "1": "nickels"
  },
  {
    "4": "pennies"
  }
]
```

To clean up the deployment, run `kubectl delete deployment hello-python`.

The next step beyond this basic tutorial is to use either GKE (Google Kubernetes Engine), Google Cloud Run (container as a service), or Vertex AI to deploy a machine learning endpoint. You can use the Python MLOps Cookbook repo (*https://oreil.ly/EYAvj*) as a base to do this. The Kubernetes technology is an excellent foundation for building ML-powered APIs, and with GCP, there are many options available if you use Docker format containers from the start.

With the basics of computing on GCP out of the way, let's discuss how cloud native databases like Google BigQuery go a long way toward adopting MLOps.

Cloud Native Database Choice and Design

One of the crown jewels of the Google Cloud Platform is Google BigQuery, for a few reasons. One of the reasons is how easy it is to get started, and another reason is the widespread publicly available databases. A good list of Google BigQuery open datasets is available on this Reddit page (*https://oreil.ly/2FdDK*). Finally, from an MLOps perspective, one of the killer features of Google BigQuery is the ability to train and host ML models inside the Google BigQuery platform.

In looking at Figure 9-12, notice that Google BigQuery is the center of an MLOps pipeline that can export products to both business intelligence and machine learning engineering, including Vertex AI. This MLOps workflow is made possible because of the DataOps (Operationalization of Data) inputs such as public datasets, streaming API, and the Google Dataflow product. The fact that Google BigQuery performs machine learning inline streamlines the processing of big datasets.

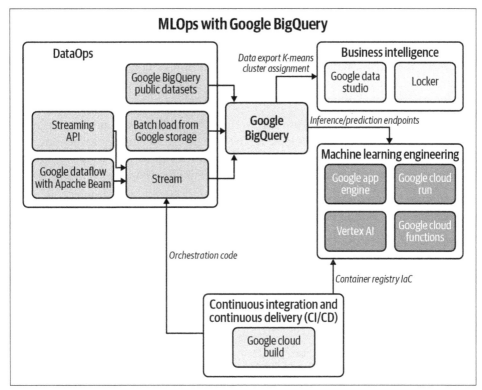

Figure 9-12. Google BigQuery MLOps workflow

An example of this workflow is shown in Figure 9-13, where after the ML modeling occurred in Google BigQuery, the results export to Google Data Studio. The artifact created from BigQuery is K-means clustering analysis shown in this shareable report (*https://oreil.ly/JcpbT*).

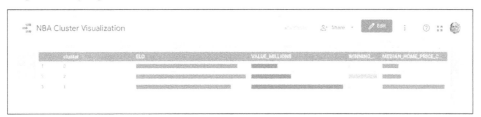

Figure 9-13. Google Data Studio K-means clustering

As a starting point for doing MLOps on the GCP platform, BigQuery is an optimal choice due to the platform's flexibility. Next, let's talk about DataOps and Applied Data Engineering on the GCP platform.

DataOps on GCP: Applied Data Engineering

Data is input necessary for building machine learning at scale, and as such, it is a critical aspect of MLOps. In one sense, the GCP has an almost unlimited amount of ways to automate data flow. This fact is due to the variety of computing and storage options available, including high-level tools like Dataflow.

For the sake of simplicity, let's use a serverless approach to data engineering using Cloud Functions. To do this, let's look at how Google Cloud Functions work and how they can serve double duty as both the ML solution via an AI API call or an MLOps pipeline using Cloud Functions talking to Google Pub/Sub (*https://oreil.ly/DKj58*).

Let's start with an intentionally simple Google Cloud Function that returns the correct change. You can find the complete example here (*https://oreil.ly/MFmyg*).

To get started, open the Google Cloud Console, create a new Cloud Function, and paste the following code inside, as shown in Figure 9-14. You can also "untoggle" the "Require authentication" to "Allow unauthenticated invocations."

```python
import json

def hello_world(request):

    request_json = request.get_json()
    print(f"This is my payload: {request_json}")
    if request_json and "amount" in request_json:
        raw_amount = request_json["amount"]
        print(f"This is my amount: {raw_amount}")
        amount = float(raw_amount)
        print(f"This is my float amount: {amount}")
    res = []
    coins = [1, 5, 10, 25]
    coin_lookup = {25: "quarters", 10: "dimes", 5: "nickels", 1: "pennies"}
    coin = coins.pop()
    num, rem = divmod(int(amount * 100), coin)
    res.append({num: coin_lookup[coin]})
    while rem > 0:
        coin = coins.pop()
        num, rem = divmod(rem, coin)
        if num:
            if coin in coin_lookup:
                res.append({num: coin_lookup[coin]})
    result = f"This is the res: {res}"
    return result
```

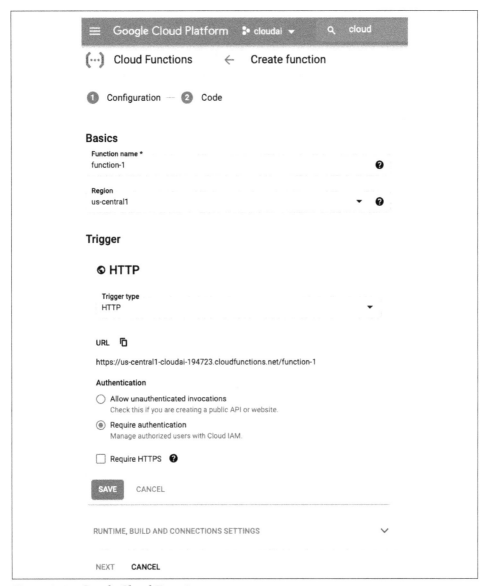

Figure 9-14. Google Cloud Function

To invoke via the `gcloud` command line do the following:

```
gcloud functions call changemachine --data '{"amount":"1.34"}'
```

To invoke via the `curl` command, you can use the following.

```
curl -d '{
    "amount":"1.34"
}'     -H "Content-Type: application/json" -X POST <trigger>/function-3
```

Another approach is to build a command line tool to invoke your endpoint:

```python
#!/usr/bin/env python
import click
import requests


@click.group()
@click.version_option("1.0")
def cli():
    """Invoker"""


@cli.command("http")
@click.option("--amount", default=1.34, help="Change to Make")
@click.option(
    "--host",
    default="https://us-central1-cloudai-194723.cloudfunctions.net/change722",
    help="Host to invoke",
)
def mkrequest(amount, host):
    """Asks a web service to make change"""

    click.echo(
        click.style(
            f"Querying host {host} with amount: {amount}", bg="green", fg="white"
        )
    )
    payload = {"amount": amount}
    result = requests.post(url=host, json=payload)
    click.echo(click.style(f"result: {result.text}", bg="red", fg="white"))


if __name__ == "__main__":
    cli()
```

Finally, one more approach is to either upload your ML model to Vertex AI or call an existing API endpoint that performs computer vision, NLP, or another ML-related task. You can find the complete example on GitHub (*https://oreil.ly/P7JsE*). In the following example, let's use a preexisting NLP API. You will also need to add two third-party libraries by editing the *requirements.txt* file included in the Google Cloud scaffolding (see Figure 9-15).

Figure 9-15. Add requirements

Paste this code into the *main.py* function in the Google Cloud Shell Console:

```python
import wikipedia

from google.cloud import translate


def sample_translate_text(
    text="YOUR_TEXT_TO_TRANSLATE", project_id="YOUR_PROJECT_ID", language="fr"
):
    """Translating Text."""

    client = translate.TranslationServiceClient()

    parent = client.location_path(project_id, "global")

    # Detail on supported types can be found here:
    # https://cloud.google.com/translate/docs/supported-formats
    response = client.translate_text(
        parent=parent,
        contents=[text],
        mime_type="text/plain",  # mime types: text/plain, text/html
        source_language_code="en-US",
        target_language_code=language,
    )
    print(f"You passed in this language {language}")
    # Display the translation for each input text provided
    for translation in response.translations:
        print("Translated text: {}".format(translation.translated_text))
    return "Translated text: {}".format(translation.translated_text)
```

```
def translate_test(request):
    """Takes JSON Payload {"entity": "google"}"""
    request_json = request.get_json()
    print(f"This is my payload: {request_json}")
    if request_json and "entity" in request_json:
        entity = request_json["entity"]
        language = request_json["language"]
        sentences = request_json["sentences"]
        print(entity)
        res = wikipedia.summary(entity, sentences=sentences)
        trans = sample_translate_text(
            text=res, project_id="cloudai-194723", language=language
        )
        return trans
    else:
        return f"No Payload"
```

To invoke the function, you can call it from the Google Cloud Shell:

```
gcloud functions call translate-wikipedia --data\
    '{"entity":"facebook", "sentences": "20", "language":"ru"}'
```

You can see the output of the Russian translation in the Google Cloud Shell terminal in Figure 9-16.

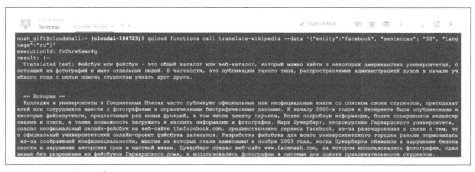

Figure 9-16. Translate

For prototyping data engineering workflows, there is no quicker method than serverless technology like Google Cloud Functions. My recommendation is to solve an initial data engineering workflow using serverless technology and move to more complex tools if necessary.

An important note is that the Vertex AI platform adds many additional data engineering and ML engineering components that enhance larger projects. In particular, the ability to use Explainable AI, track the quality of a model, and use a Feature Store are valuable components of a comprehensive MLOps solution. Let's dive into these options next.

Operationalizing ML Models

Every major cloud platform nows has an MLOps platform. On GCP, the platform is Vertex AI and integrates many individual services it has developed over the years, including AutoML technology. In particular, some of the essential components of MLOps platforms include Feature Stores, Explainable AI, and tracking model quality. If starting an MLOps project at a larger company, the first place to start on GCP would be its Vertex AI platform, just like SageMaker on AWS or Azure ML Studio on Azure.

Another option is to use components as standalone solutions to operationalize ML models on the GCP platform. One service to use is the prediction service (*https://oreil.ly/7cWEV*) to deploy models and then accept requests.

For example, you could test a local sklearn model using a command similar to the following:

```
gcloud ai-platform local predict --model-dir\
  LOCAL_OR_CLOUD_STORAGE_PATH_TO_MODEL_DIRECTORY/ \
--json-instances LOCAL_PATH_TO_PREDICTION_INPUT.JSON \
--framework NAME_OF_FRAMEWORK
```

Later, you could create an endpoint and then call this endpoint from an example shown earlier in the chapter, say Google Cloud Functions, Google Cloud Run, or Google App Engine.

Let's walk through an example of how a Google App Engine project looks on the GCP cloud using this repo as a starting point (*https://oreil.ly/2vC8t*). To start with, notice the core architecture of continuous delivery on GCP. To get started, create a new Google App Engine project as shown in the "light" MLOps workflow in Figure 9-17.

> Notice that this lightweight workflow allows for a transparent and straightforward way to deploy an ML model, but a "heavy" flow could add tremendous value if the features shown, like Explainable AI, are required for a project.

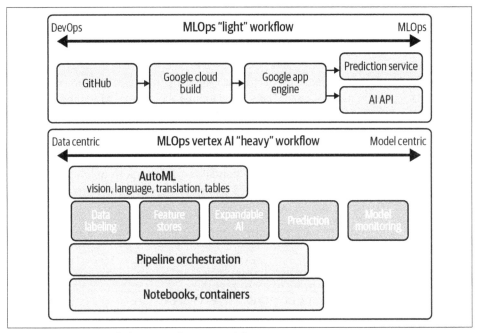

Figure 9-17. MLOps light versus heavy workflows

Next, enable the Cloud Build API as shown in Figure 9-18.

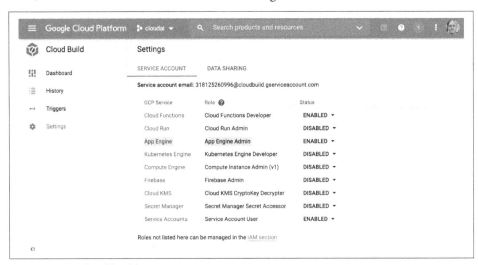

Figure 9-18. Cloud build

The *cloudbuild.yml* file needs only a deploy command:

```
steps:
- name: "gcr.io/cloud-builders/gcloud"
  args: ["app", "deploy"]
timeout: "1600s"
```

The only other requirements are *app.yaml*, *requirements.txt*, and *main.py*, all found in this example repository (*https://oreil.ly/YAy6c*). A final step to make this application do any form of machine learning is to call an ML/AI API or use the AI Platform end-point hosting.

The advantage of the simple approach is that it is easy to set up an entire MLOps pipeline in an hour or two at most. You could also pick and choose from AI APIs, prediction services, and an AutoML endpoint.

There are both "light" and "heavy" approaches to doing MLOps on GCP. This example explored the "light" approach, but there is merit to using the platform technology Vertex AI since it includes advanced features many enterprises desire.

Let's wrap up the chapter and discuss the next steps for using the GCP for MLOps.

Conclusion

One final takeaway on MLOps technologies like Vertex AI is they solve a complicated problem better than most organizations can do themselves. I remember talking to someone at a research lab, and they bragged about how the cloud was overrated since they had a ton of GPUs. A ton of GPUs doesn't give you platform services like these platforms. This statement is a fundamental misunderstanding of how enterprise software and startups work. Comparative advantage is critical for both early-stage startups and Fortune 500 companies. Don't build something worse than what you can buy for a trivial cost.

I recommend taking everything from this chapter and applying it to a final machine learning project that consists of building a cloud native ML application on the GCP. This project should give you the ability to create realistic, working solutions designed with modern techniques.

Before you begin, make sure you read the Sculley et al. (2015) paper to consider technical debt in machine-learning (ML) systems (*https://oreil.ly/d8jrl*). Your project may benefit from using public data from Google BigQuery datasets. Alternately, if using AutoML, data can be tutorial data or custom data.

The main idea is to create a portfolio project demonstrating your ability to do ML engineering on the Google Cloud. Here are the suggested project requirements to think through:

- Source code stored in GitHub
- Continuous deployment from CircleCI
- Data stored in GCP (BigQuery, Google Cloud Storage, etc.)
- ML predictions created and served out (AutoML, BigQuery, AI Platform, etc.)
- Cloud native monitoring
- Google App Engine serves out HTTP requests via REST API with a JSON payload
- Deployed into GCP environment using Google Cloud Build

Here are some items to add to a final project requirements checklist:

- Does the application make ML inference?
- Are there separate environments?
- Is there comprehensive monitoring and alerts?
- Is the correct datastore used?
- Does the principle of least security apply?
- Is data encrypted in transit?

You can see some recent student and top data science projects in the official code repository (*https://oreil.ly/hJkDx*). These projects provide a frame of reference for what you can build, and you are welcome to submit a pull request in the future to get your project added.

- Jason Adams: FastAPI Sentiment Analysis with Kubernetes (*https://oreil.ly/5Omf3*)
- James Salafatinos: Tensorflow.js real-time image classification (*https://oreil.ly/rs4QQ*)
- Nikhil Bhargava: Sneaker Price Predict (*https://oreil.ly/MjU7H*)
- Covid Predictor (*https://oreil.ly/Wm8UF*)
- Absenteeism at Work (*https://oreil.ly/Rrh6S*)

The next chapter discusses machine learning interoperability and how it uniquely solves MLOps problems that crop up from different platforms, technologies, and model formats.

Exercises

- Using Google Cloud Shell Editor, create a new GitHub repository with necessary Python scaffolding using a Makefile, linting, and testing. Add steps such as code formatting in your Makefile.

- Create a "hello world" pipeline to Google Cloud that calls into a Python-based Google App Engine (GAE) project and returns "hello world" as a JavaScript Object Notation (JSON) response.

- Create an ingest to ETL pipeline using CSV files and Google BigQuery. Schedule a reoccurring cron job to batch update the data.

- Train a multiclass classification model on Google AutoML vision and deploy to an edge device.

- Create a production and development environment and deploy a project to both environments using Google Cloud Build.

Critical Thinking Discussion Questions

- What problems does a CI system solve, and why is a CI system an essential part of SaaS software?

- Why are cloud platforms the ideal target for analytics applications, and how does deep learning benefit from the cloud?

- What are the advantages of managed services like Google BigQuery, and how does Google BigQuery differ from a traditional SQL?

- How does ML prediction directly from BigQuery add value to the Google platform, and what advantages could this have for analytics application engineering?

- How does AutoML have a lower total cost of ownership (TCO), and how could it have a higher TCO?

## CHAPTER 10

Machine Learning Interoperability

By Alfredo Deza

> Mammalian brains have considerable power for generalized computation but special functions (e.g., subjectivity) commonly require specialized structures. Such a hypothesized structure has been facetiously termed a "subjectivity pump" by Marcel Kinsbourne. Well, that is exactly what some of us are looking for. And the mechanism for subjectivity is double, as shown by the duality of the anatomy, the success of hemispherectomy, and the split-brain results (in cats and monkeys as well as humans).
>
> —Dr. Joseph Bogen

Peru has *several thousand* potato varieties. As someone who grew up in Peru, I find this surprising to hear. It is easy to assume that most potatoes taste somewhat similar, but this is not the case at all. Different dishes call for different potato varieties. You won't want to argue with a Peruvian cook if the recipe called for *Huayro* potatoes and you want to use the common *baking* potato found in most of the US. If you ever have the chance to be in South America (and certainly in Peru), try the experience of walking around a street market. The number of fresh vegetables, including several dozen potato varieties, can make you dizzy.

I no longer live in Peru, and I miss that variety of potatoes. I can't really cook some dishes and make them taste the same with a common baking potato bought from the local supermarket. It is not the same. I consider that the variety and different tastes provided by such a humble vegetable is critical for Peru's cuisine identity. You still might find it OK to cook with the common baking potato, but at the end of the day it is about choices and selections.

There is empowerment in variety and the ability to pick and choose what fits better. This empowerment is also true in machine learning when dealing with the end product: the trained model.

Trained machine learning models also come with distinct constraints, and most of them aren't going to work in an environment that isn't specifically tailored to support it. The main concept of model interoperability is to be able to *transform* a model from one platform to another, which creates choices. This chapter makes the case that, although there are sound arguments to use out-of-the-box models from a cloud provider and not worry much about vendor lock-in, it is essential to understand how to export models into other formats that can work in other platforms that have different constraints. Much like how containers can work seamlessly in most any system as long as there is an underlying container runtime (as I explain in "Containers" on page 68), model interoperability or having a model exported to different formats is key to flexibility and empowerment. Figure 10-1 demonstrates a rough overview of what this interoperability means by training in any ML framework, transforming the resulting model *once*, to deploy it almost anywhere: from edge devices to mobile phones and other operating systems.

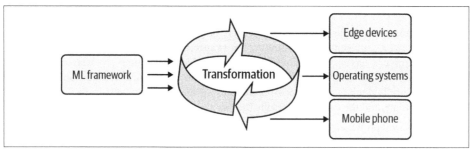

Figure 10-1. Interoperability overview

This situation is like producing screws that can work with any screwdriver, instead of producing screws that can only work with screwdrivers from a single home improvement store. In "Edge Devices" on page 80, we already ran into problems when a model couldn't work with the Edge TPU, and conversion was ultimately necessary. Currently, there are some exciting options, and I'm particularly surprised by ONNX, a community-driven project with open standards that wants to make it easier to interact with models by reducing complexity from toolchains. This chapter will go into some of the details that make ONNX a compelling machine learning choice and how most clouds are already supporting this format.

Why Interoperability Is Critical

Abstracting complex processes and interactions is a typical pattern in software engineering. Sometimes the abstractions can get entirely out of hand, causing the abstraction to be as complex as the underlying software it was trying to abstract. An excellent example of this is Openstack (an open source infrastructure-as-service platform) and its installer. Installing and configuring an infrastructure platform can be very complicated. Different machine types and network topologies create a tricky combination to solve with a one-size-fits-all installer.

A new installer was created to make it easier to install TripleO (Openstack On Openstack). TripleO produced a temporary instance that, in turn, would install Openstack. The project solved many problems associated with installation and configuration, but some thought it was still complicated, and there was a need to abstract further. This is how QuintupleO got created (Openstack On Openstack On Openstack). Without being actively involved in Openstack, I can tell you that it is difficult to deploy and that engineering teams are trying to solve those problems generically. But I'm doubtful that adding another layer is the solution.

It is easy to get persuaded that another layer will make things easier, but in reality, this is very hard to do well while pleasing everyone. I have an open question I often use to design systems: *the system can be very simple and opinionated, or flexible and complex. Which one do you choose?* Nobody likes these options, and everyone pushes for *simple and flexible*. It is possible to create such a system, but it is challenging to attain.

In machine learning, multiple platforms and cloud providers train models in different and particular ways. This doesn't matter much if staying within the platform and how it interacts with the model, but it is a recipe for frustration if you ever need to get that trained model running elsewhere.

While training a dataset with AutoML on Azure recently, I encountered several problems while trying to get local inferencing working. Azure has a "no-code" deployment with AutoML, and several types of trained models support this type of deployment. This means there is no need to write a single line of code to create the inferencing and serve the responses. Azure handles the API documentation that explains what the inputs and expected outputs are. I couldn't find the *scoring script* for the trained model, and I couldn't find any hints about the scoring script that would help me run it locally. There is no obvious way to understand how to load and interact with the model.

The model's suffix implied it is using Python's `pickle` module, so after trying a few different things, I managed to get it loaded but couldn't do any inferencing on it. I had to deal with the dependencies next. AutoML in Azure doesn't advertise the exact versions and libraries used to train a model. I'm currently using Python 3.8 but wasn't able to install the Azure SDK in my system because the SDK only supports 3.7. I had to install Python 3.7, then create a virtual environment and install the SDK there.

One of the libraries (*xgboost*) had a non–backward compatibility for its latest versions (modules were moved or renamed), so I had to guess one that would allow a specific import. That turned out to be 0.90 from 2019. Finally, when training a model with AutoML in Azure, it seems to use the latest version of the Azure SDK *at the time the model gets trained*. But this isn't advertised either. That is, if a model is trained in

January, and you are trying to use it a month later with a few SDK releases in between, you can't use the latest SDK release. You have to go back and find the latest release of the SDK when Azure trained the model.

By no means is this situation meant to be an overly critical description of Azure's AutoML. The platform is excellent to use and could improve by better advertising what versions are used and how to interact with a model locally. The prevalent problem is that you lose control granularity in the process: low code or no code is excellent for speed but can get complicated for portability. I faced all these problems by trying to do local inferencing, but the same could happen if you are leveraging Azure for machine learning in general, but your company is using AWS for hosting.

Another problematic situation that happens often is that scientists that produce a model in one platform have to make assumptions, such as the underlying environment, which includes compute power, storage, and memory. What happens when a model that performs well in AWS needs to deploy in an edge TPU device that is entirely incompatible? Let's assume for a second that your company has this situation covered already and produces the same model targeting different platforms. Still, the resulting model for the edge device is five gigabytes, which is beyond the accelerator's maximum storage capacity.

Model interoperability solves these problems by openly describing the constraints, making it easier to *transform models* from one format to the other while enjoying support from all the prominent cloud providers. In the next section, I'll go into the details of what makes ONNX a solid project for greater interoperability and how you can build automation to transform models effortlessly.

ONNX: Open Neural Network Exchange

As I've mentioned before, ONNX is not only a great choice for model interoperability but also the first initiative toward a system that would allow switching frameworks with ease. The project started in 2017 when both Facebook and Microsoft presented ONNX as an open ecosystem for AI model interoperability and jointly developed the project and tooling to push forward the adoption. Since then, the project has grown and matured as a large open source project with an established structure that includes SIGs (Special Interest Groups) and working groups for different areas like releases and training.

Beyond interoperability, the commonality of the framework allows hardware vendors to target ONNX and impact multiple other frameworks at once. By leveraging the ONNX representation, the optimizations are no longer required to be integrated individually into each framework (a time-consuming process). Although ONNX is relatively recent, it is refreshing to see it well supported across cloud providers. It shouldn't be surprising that Azure even offers native support for ONNX models in its machine learning SDK.

The main idea is to train once in your preferred framework and run anywhere: from the cloud to the edge. Once the model is in the ONNX format, you can deploy it to various devices and platforms. This includes different operating systems as well. The effort to make this happen is substantial. Not many software examples come to mind that can run in several different operating systems, edge devices, and the cloud, all using the same format.

Although there are several machine learning frameworks supported (more being added all the time), Figure 10-2 shows the most common transformation pattern.

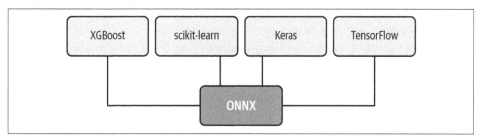

Figure 10-2. Convert into ONNX

You leverage the knowledge and features of the framework you like best and then transform into ONNX. However, as I demonstrate in "Apple Core ML" on page 310, it is also possible (although not that common) to convert an ONNX model into a different runtime as well. These transformations are not "free" either: you can get into problems when new features aren't supported yet (ONNX converters are always catching up), or older models aren't supported with newer versions. I still believe that the idea of commonality and "run anywhere" is a solid one, and it is helpful to take advantage of it when possible.

Next, let's see where you can find pretrained ONNX models, to try some of them out.

ONNX Model Zoo

The *Model Zoo* is often referenced when discussing ONNX models. Although it is usually described as a registry for ready-to-use ONNX models, it is primarily an informational repository in GitHub (*https://oreil.ly/gX2PB*) that has links to several pretrained models contributed by the community and curated in the repository. The models are separated into three categories: vision, language, and everything else. If you are looking to get started with ONNX and do some inferencing, the Model Zoo is the place to go.

In "Packaging for ML Models" on page 95 I used the *RoBERTa-SequenceClassification* model from the Model Zoo. Since I wanted to register in Azure, I was required to add some information like the ONNX runtime version. Figure 10-3 shows how this is all available at the Model Zoo (*https://oreil.ly/ptOGC*) for that particular model.

Model

Model	Download	Download (with sample test data)	ONNX version	Opset version	Accuracy
RoBERTa-BASE	499 MB	295 MB	1.6	11	88.5
RoBERTa-SequenceClassification	499 MB	432 MB	1.6	9	MCC of 0.85

Figure 10-3. Model Zoo

Aside from version and size information, the page will usually have some examples on how to interact with the model, which is crucial if you want to create a proof of concept to try it out quickly. There is one other thing that I believe is worth noting about these documentation pages: getting a *provenance* (a source of truth for the model). In the case of the *RoBERTa-SequenceClassification* model, it originates from *PyTorch RoBERTa*, then to ONNX, and finally made available in the Model Zoo.

It isn't immediately clear why knowing the origin of models and sources of work is essential. Whenever changes are needed or problems are detected that need to be solved, you had better be ready to pinpoint the source of truth so that anything that needs to be modified can be done with confidence. When I was a release manager for a large open source project, I was responsible for building RPM and other package types for different Linux distributions. One day the production repository got corrupted, and I was asked to rebuild these packages. While rebuilding them, I couldn't find what script, pipeline, or CI platform was producing one of these packages included in several dozen of these repositories.

After tracing the various steps involved in finding the origin of that one package, I found that a script was downloading it from a developer's home directory (long gone from the company) in a server that had nothing to do with building packages. A single file sitting in a home directory in a server that had no responsibility for the build system is a ticking bomb. I couldn't tell what the origin of the package was, how to make any updates to it, or the reason it needed to be included in this way. These situations are not uncommon. You must be prepared to have everything in order and have a solid answer when determining the source of truth of all the elements in your production pipeline.

When you are sourcing models from places like the Model Zoo, make sure you capture as much information as possible and include it wherever the destination is for these models. Azure has several fields you can use for this purpose when registering models. As you will see in the following sections, some of the model transformers allow adding metadata. Taking advantage of this seemingly unimportant task can be critical for debugging production problems. Two beneficial practices that have reduced time debugging and accelerated onboarding and maintenance ease is using meaningful names and as much metadata as possible. Using a meaningful name is crucial for identification and providing clarity. A model registered as "production-model-1" does not tell me what it is or what it is about. If you pair this with no additional metadata or information, this will cause frustration and delays when figuring out a production problem.

Convert PyTorch into ONNX

Getting started with a different framework is always daunting, even when the underlying task is to train a model from a dataset. PyTorch does an excellent job at including pretrained models that can quickly help you get started since you can try different aspects of the framework without dealing with curating a dataset and then figuring out how to train it. Many other frameworks (like TensorFlow and scikit-learn) are doing the same, and it is an excellent way to jumpstart learning. In this section, I use a pretrained vision model from PyTorch and then export it to ONNX.

Create a new virtual environment and a *requirements.txt* file that looks like the following:

```
numpy==1.20.1
onnx==1.8.1
Pillow==8.1.2
protobuf==3.15.6
six==1.15.0
torch==1.8.0
torchvision==0.9.0
typing-extensions==3.7.4.3
```

Install the dependencies and then create a *convert.py* file to produce the PyTorch model first:

```python
import torch
import torchvision

dummy_tensor = torch.randn(8, 3, 200, 200)

model = torchvision.models.resnet18(pretrained=True)

input_names = [ "input_%d" % i for i in range(12) ]
output_names = [ "output_1" ]

torch.onnx.export(
    model,
    dummy_tensor,
    "resnet18.onnx",
    input_names=input_names,
    output_names=output_names,
    opset_version=7,
```

```
        verbose=True,
    )
```

Let's go through some of the steps that the Python script goes through to produce an ONNX model. It creates a tensor filled with random numbers using three channels (crucial for the pretrained model). Next, we retrieve the *resnet18* pretrained model available through the *torchvision* library. I define a few inputs and outputs and finally export the model with all that information.

The example is overly simplistic to prove a point. The exported model is not robust at all and full of dummy values that aren't meaningful. The idea is to demonstrate how PyTorch enables you to export the model to ONNX in a straightforward way. The fact that the converter is part of the framework is reassuring because it is responsible for ensuring that this works flawlessly. Although separate converter libraries and projects exist, I prefer frameworks that offer the conversion, like PyTorch.

 The opset_version argument in the export() function is critical. PyTorch's tensor indexing can get you into problems with an unsupported ONNX opset version. Some indexer types do not support anything other than version 12 (the latest version). Always double-check that the versions match the supported features you need.

Run the *convert.py* script, which creates a *resnet18.onnx* file. You should see output similar to this:

```
$ python convert.py
graph(%learned_0 : Float(8, 3, 200, 200, strides=[120000, 40000, 200, 1],
  requires_grad=0, device=cpu),
    %fc.weight : Float(1000, 512, strides=[512, 1], requires_grad=1, device=cpu),
    %fc.bias : Float(1000, strides=[1], requires_grad=1, device=cpu),
    %193 : Float(64, 3, 7, 7, strides=[147, 49, 7, 1], requires_grad=0,
```

Now that the ONNX model is available and produced by the script using PyTorch, let's use the ONNX framework to verify that the model produced is compatible. Create a new script called *check.py*:

```
import onnx

# Load the previously created ONNX model
model = onnx.load("resnet18.onnx")

onnx.checker.check_model(model)

print(onnx.helper.printable_graph(model.graph))
```

Run the *check.py* script from the same directory where *resnet18.onnx* is, and verify that the output is similar to this:

```
$ python check.py
graph torch-jit-export (
  %learned_0[FLOAT, 8x3x200x200]
) optional inputs with matching initializers (
  %fc.weight[FLOAT, 1000x512]
[...]
  %189 = GlobalAveragePool(%188)
  %190 = Flatten[axis = 1](%189)
  %output_1 = Gemm[alpha = 1, beta = 1, transB = 1](%190, %fc.weight, %fc.bias)
  return %output_1
}
```

The verification from the call to the check_model() function should not produce any errors, proving that the conversion has some level of correctness. To fully ensure that the converted model is correct, inferencing needs to be evaluated, capturing any possible drift. If you are unsure about what metrics to use or how to create a solid comparison strategy, check the "Basics of Model Monitoring" on page 174. Next, let's see how we can use the same checking pattern in a command line tool.

Create a Generic ONNX Checker

Now that I've gone through the details of exporting a model from PyTorch to ONNX and having a step to verify, let's create a simple and generic tool that can verify any ONNX model, not just one in particular. Although we dedicate a large section about building powerful command line tools in the next chapter (see "Command Line Tools" on page 321 in particular), we can still try to build something that works well for this use case. Another concept that comes from DevOps and my experience as a Systems Administrator is to attempt automation whenever possible and start with the most straightforward problem first. For this example, I will not use any command line tool framework or any advanced parsing.

First, create a new file called *onnx-checker.py* with a single main() function:

```
def main():
    help_menu = """
    A command line tool to quickly verify ONNX models using
    check_model()
    """
    print(help_menu)


if __name__ == '__main__':
    main()
```

Run the script, and the output should show the help menu:

```
$ python onnx-checker.py

    A command line tool to quickly verify ONNX models using
    check_model()
```

The script is not doing anything special yet. It uses the `main()` function to produce the help menu and a widely used crutch in Python to call a specific function when Python executes the script in the terminal. Next, we need to handle arbitrary input. Command line tool frameworks help with this, no doubt, but we can still have something valuable with minimal effort. To check the script's arguments (we will need those to know what model to check), we need to use the `sys.argv` module. Update the script, so it imports the module and passes it into the function:

```python
import sys

def main(arguments):
    help_menu = """
    A command line tool to quickly verify ONNX models using
    check_model()
    """

    if "--help" in arguments:
        print(help_menu)

if __name__ == '__main__':
    main(sys.argv)
```

The change will cause the script to output the help menu only when using the `--help` flag. The script is still not doing anything useful, so let's update the `main()` function once more to include the ONNX check functionality:

```python
import sys
import onnx

def main(arguments):
    help_menu = """
    A command line tool to quickly verify ONNX models using
    check_model()
    """

    if "--help" in arguments:
        print(help_menu)
        sys.exit(0)

    model = onnx.load(arguments[-1])
    onnx.checker.check_model(model)
    print(onnx.helper.printable_graph(model.graph))
```

There are two crucial changes to the function. First, it is now calling `sys.exit(0)` after the help menu check to prevent the next block of code from executing. Next, if the help condition is not met, it uses the last argument (whatever that is) as the model's path to check. Finally, it uses the same functions from the ONNX framework to the model check. Note that there is no sanitation or verification of inputs at all. This is a very brittle script, but it still proves helpful if you run it:

```
$ python onnx-checker.py ~/Downloads/roberta-base-11.onnx
graph torch-jit-export (
  %input_ids[INT64, batch_sizexseq_len]
) initializers (
  %1621[FLOAT, 768x768]
  %1622[FLOAT, 768x768]
  %1623[FLOAT, 768x768]
[...]
  %output_2 = Tanh(%1619)
  return %output_1, %output_2
}
```

The path I used is to the RoBERTa base model that is in a separate path in my *Downloads* directory. This type of automation is a building brick: the simplest approach possible to do a quick check that can be leveraged later in other automation like a CI/CD system or a pipeline in a cloud provider workflow. Now that we've tried some models, let's see how to convert models created in other popular frameworks into ONNX.

Convert TensorFlow into ONNX

There is a project dedicated to doing model conversions from TensorFlow in the ONNX GitHub repository. It offers a wide range of supported versions from both ONNX and TensorFlow. Again, it is critical to ensure that whatever tooling you choose has the versions your model requires to achieve a successful conversion to ONNX.

Finding the right project, library, or tool for doing conversions can get tricky. For TensorFlow specifically, you can use the onnxmltools (*https://oreil.ly/BvLxv*), which has a `onnxmltools.convert_tensorflow()` function, or the tensorflow-onnx (*https://oreil.ly/E6RDE*) project, which has two ways to do a conversion: with a command line tool, or using the library.

This section uses the *tensorflow-onnx* project with a Python module that you can use as a command line tool. The project allows you to convert models from both TensorFlow major versions (1 and 2) as well as *tflite*, and *tf.keras*. The broad ONNX opset support is excellent (from version 7 to 13) because it allows greater flexibility when planning a conversion strategy.

Before getting into the actual conversion, it is worth exploring how to invoke the converter. The *tf2onnx* project uses a Python shortcut to expose a command line tool from a file instead of packaging a command line tool with the project. This means that the invocation requires you to use the Python executable with a special flag. Start by installing the library in a new virtual environment. Create a *requirements.txt* file to ensure that all the suitable versions for this example will work:

```
certifi==2020.12.5
chardet==4.0.0
```

```
flatbuffers==1.12
idna==2.10
numpy==1.20.1
onnx==1.8.1
protobuf==3.15.6
requests==2.25.1
six==1.15.0
tf2onnx==1.8.4
typing-extensions==3.7.4.3
urllib3==1.26.4
tensorflow==2.4.1
```

Now use `pip` to install all the dependencies at their pinned versions:

```
$ pip install -r requirements.txt
Collecting tf2onnx
[...]
Installing collected packages: six, protobuf, numpy, typing-extensions,
onnx, certifi, chardet, idna, urllib3, requests, flatbuffers, tf2onnx
Successfully installed numpy-1.20.1 onnx-1.8.1 tf2onnx-1.8.4 ...
```

> If you install the *tf2onnx* project without the *requirements.txt* file,
> the tool will not work because it doesn't list `tensorflow` as a
> requirement. For the examples in this section, I'm using `tensor`
> `flow` at version 2.4.1. Make sure you install it to prevent depend-
> ency problems.

Run the help menu to check what is available. Remember, the invocation looks somewhat unconventional because it needs the Python executable to use it:

```
$ python -m tf2onnx.convert --help
usage: convert.py [...]

Convert tensorflow graphs to ONNX.

[...]

Usage Examples:

python -m tf2onnx.convert --saved-model saved_model_dir --output model.onnx
python -m tf2onnx.convert --input frozen_graph.pb  --inputs X:0 \
   --outputs output:0 --output model.onnx
python -m tf2onnx.convert --checkpoint checkpoint.meta  --inputs X:0 \
   --outputs output:0 --output model.onnx
```

I'm omitting a few sections of the help menu for brevity. Calling the help menu is a
reliable way to ensure that the library can load after installation. This wouldn't be
possible if `tensorflow` is not installed, for example. I left the three examples from the
help menu because those are the ones you will need, depending on the type of conversion you are performing. None of these conversions are straightforward unless

you have a good understanding of the internals of the model you are trying to convert. Let's start with a conversion that requires no knowledge of the model, allowing the conversion to work out-of-the-box.

First, download the ssd_mobilenet_v2 (*https://oreil.ly/ytJk8*) model (compressed in a *tar.gz* file) from *tfhub*. Then create a directory and uncompress it there:

```
$ mkdir ssd
$ cd ssd
$ mv ~/Downloads/ssd_mobilenet_v2_2.tar.gz .
$ tar xzvf ssd_mobilenet_v2_2.tar.gz
x ./
x ./saved_model.pb
x ./variables/
x ./variables/variables.data-00000-of-00001
x ./variables/variables.index
```

Now that the decompressed model is in a directory use the *tf2onnx* conversion tool to port *ssd_mobilenet* over to ONNX. Make sure you are using an opset of 13 to prevent incompatible features of the model. This is a shortened exception traceback you can experience when specifying an unsupported opset:

```
File "/.../.../tf2onnx/tfonnx.py", line 294, in tensorflow_onnx_mapping
    func(g, node, **kwargs, initialized_tables=initialized_tables, ...)
File "/.../.../tf2onnx/onnx_opset/tensor.py", line 1130, in version_1
    k = node.inputs[1].get_tensor_value()
File "/.../.../tf2onnx/graph.py", line 317, in get_tensor_value
    raise ValueError("get tensor value: '{}' must be Const".format(self.name))
ValueError: get tensor value:
    'StatefulPartitionedCall/.../SortByField/strided_slice__1738' must be Const
```

Use the --saved-model flag with the path to where the model got extracted to get a conversion working finally. In this case, I'm using opset 13:

```
$ python -m tf2onnx.convert --opset 13 \
  --saved-model /Users/alfredo/models/ssd --output ssd.onnx
2021-03-24 - WARNING - '--tag' not specified for saved_model. Using --tag serve
2021-03-24 - INFO - Signatures found in model: [serving_default].
2021-03-24 - INFO - Using tensorflow=2.4.1, onnx=1.8.1, tf2onnx=1.8.4/cd55bf
2021-03-24 - INFO - Using opset <onnx, 13>
2021-03-24 - INFO - Computed 2 values for constant folding
2021-03-24 - INFO - folding node using tf type=Select,
  name=StatefulPartitionedCall/Postprocessor/.../Select_1
2021-03-24 - INFO - folding node using tf type=Select,
  name=StatefulPartitionedCall/Postprocessor/.../Select_8
2021-03-24 - INFO - Optimizing ONNX model
2021-03-24 - INFO - After optimization: BatchNormalization -53 (60->7), ...
  Successfully converted TensorFlow model /Users/alfredo/models/ssd to ONNX
2021-03-24 - INFO - Model inputs: ['input_tensor:0']
2021-03-24 - INFO - Model outputs: ['detection_anchor_indices', ...]
2021-03-24 - INFO - ONNX model is saved at ssd.onnx
```

These examples might look overly simplistic, but the idea here is that these are building blocks so that you can explore further automation by knowing what is possible in conversions. Now that I have demonstrated what is needed to convert a TensorFlow model, let's see what is required to convert a *tflite* one, another of the supported types from *tf2onnx*.

Download a *tflite* quantized version of the *mobilenet* model from tfhub (*https://oreil.ly/qNqml*). The *tflite* support in *tf2onnx* makes the invocation slightly different. This is one of those cases where a tool gets created following one criterion (convert TensorFlow models to ONNX) and then has to pivot support for something else that doesn't quite fit the same pattern. In this case, you must use the `--tflite` flag, which should point to the downloaded file:

```
$ python -m tf2onnx.convert \
    --tflite ~/Downloads/mobilenet_v2_1.0_224_quant.tflite \
    --output mobilenet_v2_1.0_224_quant.onnx
```

I quickly get into trouble once again when running the command because the supported opset doesn't match the default. Further, this model is quantized, which is another layer that the converter has to resolve. Here is another short traceback excerpt from trying that out:

```
    File "/.../.../tf2onnx/tfonnx.py", line 294, in tensorflow_onnx_mapping
        func(g, node, **kwargs, initialized_tables=initialized_tables, dequantize)
    File "/.../.../tf2onnx/tflite_handlers/tfl_math.py", line 96, in version_1
        raise ValueError
ValueError: \
    Opset 10 is required for quantization.
    Consider using the --dequantize flag or --opset 10.
```

At least this time the error is hinting that the model is quantized and that I should consider using a different opset (versus the default opset, which clearly doesn't work).

 Different TensorFlow ops have varying support for ONNX and can sometimes create problems if the incorrect version is used. The tf2onnx Support Status page (*https://oreil.ly/IJwxB*) can be useful when trying to determine what is the correct version to use.

I'm usually very suspicious when a book or demo shows perfection all the time. There is tremendous value in tracebacks, errors, and getting into trouble—which is happening for me when trying to get *tf2onnx* to work properly. If the examples in this chapter show you how it all "just works," you will undoubtedly think that there is a significant knowledge gap or that the tooling is failing, giving no opportunity to understand why things aren't quite working out. I add these tracebacks and errors because *tf2onnx* has a higher degree of complexity that allows me to get into a broken state without much effort.

Let's fix the invocation and give it an opset of 13 (the highest supported offset at the moment), and try again:

```
$ python -m tf2onnx.convert --opset 13 \
   --tflite ~/Downloads/mobilenet_v2_1.0_224_quant.tflite \
   --output mobilenet_v2_1.0_224_quant.onnx

2021-03-23 INFO - Using tensorflow=2.4.1, onnx=1.8.1, tf2onnx=1.8.4/cd55bf
2021-03-23 INFO - Using opset <onnx, 13>
2021-03-23 INFO - Optimizing ONNX model
2021-03-23 INFO - After optimization: Cast -1 (1->0), Const -307 (596->289)...
2021-03-23 INFO - Successfully converted TensorFlow model \
                   ~/Downloads/mobilenet_v2_1.0_224_quant.tflite to ONNX
2021-03-23 INFO - Model inputs: ['input']
2021-03-23 INFO - Model outputs: ['output']
2021-03-23 INFO - ONNX model is saved at mobilenet_v2_1.0_224_quant.onnx
```

At last, the quantized *tflite* model gets converted to ONNX. There is room for improvement, and like we've seen in the previous steps throughout this section, it is invaluable to have a good grasp of the model inputs and outputs and how the model was created. This know-how is crucial at the time of conversion, where you can provide the tooling as much information as possible to secure a successful outcome. Now that I've converted some models to ONNX, let's see how to deploy them with Azure.

Deploy ONNX to Azure

Azure has very good ONNX integration in its platform with direct support in its Python SDK. You can create an experiment to train a model using PyTorch that can then export to ONNX, and as I'll show you in this section, you can deploy that ONNX model to a cluster for live inferencing. This section will not cover how to perform the actual training of the model; however, I'll explain how straightforward it is to use a trained ONNX model that is registered in Azure and deploy it to a cluster.

In "Packaging for ML Models" on page 95 I covered all the details you need to get a model into Azure and then package it in a container. Let's reuse some of the container code to create the *scoring file*, which Azure needs to deploy it as a web service. In essence, it is the same thing: the script receives a request, which knows how to translate the inputs to make a prediction with the loaded model and then return the values.

These examples uses Azure's *workspace*, defined as a ws object. It is necessary to configure it before starting. This is covered in detail in "Azure CLI and Python SDK" on page 236.

Create the scoring file, call it *score.py*, and add an init() function to load the model:

```
import torch
import os
import numpy as np
from transformers import RobertaTokenizer
import onnxruntime


def init():
    global session
    model = os.path.join(
        os.getenv("AZUREML_MODEL_DIR"), "roberta-sequence-classification-9.onnx"
    )
    session = onnxruntime.InferenceSession(model)
```

Now that the scoring script's basics are out of the way, a run() function is required when running in Azure. Update the *score.py* script by creating the run() function that understands how to interact with the RoBERTa classification model:

```
def run(input_data_json):
    try:
        tokenizer = RobertaTokenizer.from_pretrained("roberta-base")
        input_ids = torch.tensor(
            tokenizer.encode(input_data_json[0], add_special_tokens=True)
        ).unsqueeze(0)

        if input_ids.requires_grad:
            numpy_func = input_ids.detach().cpu().numpy()
        else:
            numpy_func = input_ids.cpu().numpy()

        inputs = {session.get_inputs()[0].name: numpy_func(input_ids)}
        out = session.run(None, inputs)

        return {"result": np.argmax(out)}
    except Exception as err:
        result = str(err)
        return {"error": result}
```

Next, create the configuration to perform the inferencing. Since these examples are using the Python SDK, you can use them in a Jupyter Notebook or using the Python shell directly. Start by creating a YAML file that describes your environment:

```
from azureml.core.conda_dependencies import CondaDependencies

environ = CondaDependencies.create(
  pip_packages=[
    "numpy","onnxruntime","azureml-core", "azureml-defaults",
    "torch", "transformers"]
)
```

```
with open("environ.yml","w") as f:
    f.write(environ.serialize_to_string())
```

Now that the YAML file is done, set up the configuration:

```
from azureml.core.model import InferenceConfig
from azureml.core.environment import Environment


environ = Environment.from_conda_specification(
    name="environ", file_path="environ.yml"
)
inference_config = InferenceConfig(
    entry_script="score.py", environment=environ
)
```

Finally, deploy the model using the SDK. Create the Azure Container Instance (ACI) configuration first:

```
from azureml.core.webservice import AciWebservice

aci_config = AciWebservice.deploy_configuration(
    cpu_cores=1,
    memory_gb=1,
    tags={"model": "onnx", "type": "language"},
    description="Container service for the RoBERTa ONNX model",
)
```

With the `aci_config`, deploy the service:

```
from azureml.core.model import Model

# retrieve the model
model = Model(ws, 'roberta-sequence', version=1)

aci_service_name = "onnx-roberta-demo"
aci_service = Model.deploy(
    ws, aci_service_name,
    [model],
    inference_config,
    aci_config
)

aci_service.wait_for_deployment(True)
```

Several things have happened to get this deployment working. First, you defined the environment with the dependencies required for the inferencing to work. Then you configured an Azure Container Instance, and finally, you retrieved version 1 of the *roberta_sequence* ONNX model and used the `Model.deploy()` method from the SDK to deploy the model. Again, the training specifics of the model aren't covered here. You could very well train any model in Azure, export it to ONNX, register it, and pick up right in this section to continue the deployment process. Few modifications are needed in these examples to make progress. Perhaps different libraries and certainly a different way to interact with the model are required. Still, this workflow empowers you to add another layer of automation to deploy models programmatically from PyTorch to ONNX (or straight from previously registered ONNX models) in a container instance in Azure.

You will want to use ONNX to deploy to other noncloud environments like mobile devices in some other situations. I cover some of the details involved in the next section with Apple's machine learning framework.

Apple Core ML

Apple's machine learning framework is somewhat unique in that there is support to convert Core ML models into ONNX *as well as* convert them from ONNX to Core ML. As I've said already in this chapter, you have to be very careful and ensure that there is support for the model conversion and getting the versions right. Currently, *coremltools* supports ONNX opset versions 10 and newer. It isn't that hard to get into a situation where a model lacks support and breakage occurs. Aside from the ONNX support, you must be aware of the target conversion environment and if that environment supports iOS and macOS releases.

 See the minimum target (*https://oreil.ly/aKJOK*) supported for different environments in the *Core ML* documentation.

Aside from support in a target environment like iOS, there is also a good list of tested models from ONNX known to work well. It is from that list that I'll pick up the MNIST model to try out a conversion. Go to the Model Zoo and find the MNIST section. Download (*https://oreil.ly/Q005Q*) the latest version (1.3 in my case). Now create a new virtual environment and a *requirements.txt* with the following libraries, which include *coremltools*:

```
attr==0.3.1
attrs==20.3.0
coremltools==4.1
mpmath==1.2.1
numpy==1.19.5
onnx==1.8.1
packaging==20.9
protobuf==3.15.6
pyparsing==2.4.7
scipy==1.6.1
six==1.15.0
sympy==1.7.1
```

```
tqdm==4.59.0
typing-extensions==3.7.4.3
```

Install the dependencies so that we can create tooling to do the conversion. Let's create the most straightforward tool possible, just like in "Create a Generic ONNX Checker" on page 301, without argument parsers or any fancy help menus. Start by creating the main() function and the special Python magic needed at the end of the file so that you can call it in the terminal as a script:

```
import sys
from coremltools.converters.onnx import convert

def main(arguments):
    pass

if __name__ == '__main__':
    main(sys.argv)
```

In this case, the script isn't doing anything useful yet, and I'm also skipping implementing a help menu. You should always include a help menu in your scripts so that others can have some idea of the inputs and outputs of the program when they need to interact with it. Update the main() function to try out the conversion. I'll assume that the last argument received will represent a path to the ONNX model that needs converting:

```
def main(arguments):
    model_path = arguments[-1]
    basename = model_path.split('.onnx')[0]
    model = convert(model_path, minimum_ios_deployment_target='13')
    model.short_description = "ONNX Model converted with coremltools"
    model.save(f"{basename}.mlmodel")
```

First, the function captures the last argument as the path to the ONNX model, and then it computes the base name by stripping out the *.onnx* suffix. Finally, it goes through the conversion (using a minimum iOS version target of 13), includes a description, and saves the output. Try the updated script with the previously downloaded MNIST model:

```
$ python converter.py mnist-8.onnx
1/11: Converting Node Type Conv
2/11: Converting Node Type Add
3/11: Converting Node Type Relu
4/11: Converting Node Type MaxPool
5/11: Converting Node Type Conv
6/11: Converting Node Type Add
7/11: Converting Node Type Relu
8/11: Converting Node Type MaxPool
9/11: Converting Node Type Reshape
10/11: Converting Node Type MatMul
11/11: Converting Node Type Add
```

```
Translation to CoreML spec completed. Now compiling the CoreML model.
Model Compilation done.
```

The resulting operation should've produced a *mnist-8.mlmodel* file, which is a Core
ML model that you can now load in a macOS computer that has XCode installed. Use
the Finder in your Apple computer, double-click the newly generated *coreml* model,
and double-click it. The MNIST model should load right away, with the description
included in the converter script as shown in Figure 10-4.

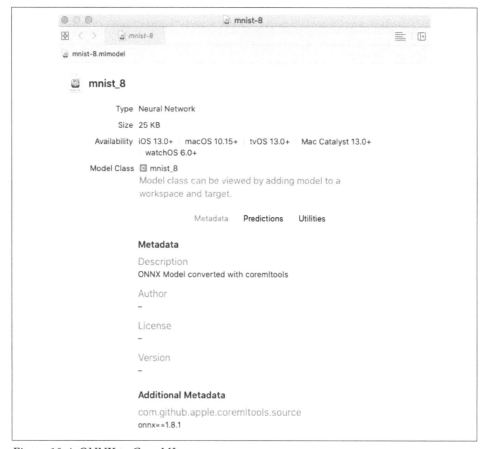

Figure 10-4. ONNX to Core ML

Verify that the Availability section shows the minimum iOS targets of 13, just like the
converter script set them. The Predictions section has useful information about the
inputs and outputs that the model accepts, as shown in Figure 10-5.

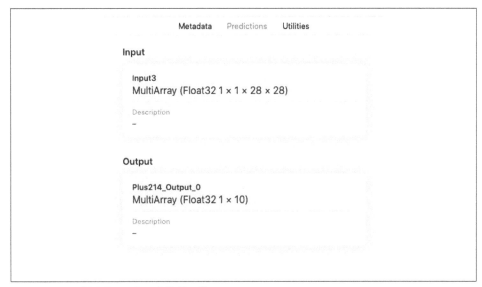

Figure 10-5. ONNX to CoreML Predictions

Finally, the Utilities section provides helpers to deploy that model using a model archive that integrates with CloudKit (Apple's environment for iOS application resources) as shown in Figure 10-6.

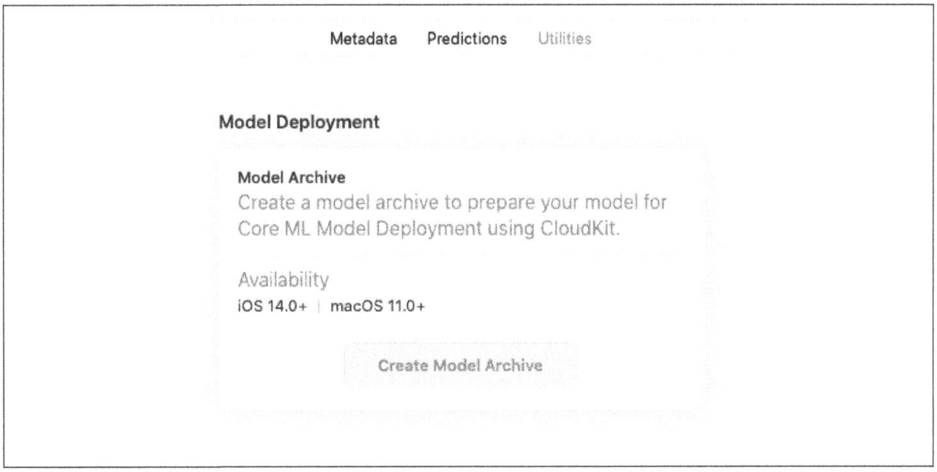

Metadata   Predictions   Utilities

Model Deployment

Model Archive
Create a model archive to prepare your model for
Core ML Model Deployment using CloudKit.

Availability
iOS 14.0+ | macOS 11.0+

Create Model Archive

Figure 10-6. ONNX to Core ML model archive

It is exciting to see broad support for ONNX and growing support in other frameworks and operating systems like OSX in this case. If you are interested in iOS development and deploying models, you can still use the frameworks you are used to. Then, you can do the conversion to the targeted iOS environment for deployment.

This process makes a compelling reason to use ONNX because it allows you to leverage well-established frameworks that you can transform into targeted environments. Next, let's see some other edge integrations that further emphasize the usefulness of the ONNX framework and tooling.

Edge Integration

Recently, ONNX announced a new internal model format known as ORT, which minimizes the build size of the model for optimal deployment on embedded or edge devices. The smaller footprint of a model has several aspects that help on edge devices. Edge devices have limited storage capacity, and most times, the storage isn't fast at all. Reading and writing to small storage devices can quickly become problematic. Further, ONNX, in general, keeps trying to support more and different hardware configurations with varying CPUs and GPUs; not an easy problem to solve, but indeed a welcomed effort. The better and broader the support, the easier it is to get machine learning models deployed to help environments where this was not possible before. As I've covered most of Edge's benefits and crucial aspects in "Edge Devices" on page 80, this section will concentrate on getting a conversion done from an ONNX model down to the ORT format.

Start by creating a new virtual environment, activating it, and then installing the dependencies as shown in this *requirements.txt* file:

```
flatbuffers==1.12
numpy==1.20.1
onnxruntime==1.7.0
protobuf==3.15.6
six==1.15.0
```

There is currently no separate tooling available to install, so you are required to clone the entire *onnxruntime* repository to try a conversion to ORT. After cloning, you will use the *convert_onnx_models_to_ort.py* file in the *tools/python* directory:

```
$ git clone https://github.com/microsoft/onnxruntime.git
$ python onnxruntime/tools/python/convert_onnx_models_to_ort.py --help
usage: convert_onnx_models_to_ort.py [-h]
[...]
Convert the ONNX format model/s in the provided directory to ORT format models.
All files with a `.onnx` extension will be processed. For each one, an ORT
format model will be created in the same directory. A configuration file will
also be created called `required_operators.config`, and will contain the list
of required operators for all converted models. This configuration file should
be used as input to the minimal build via the `--include_ops_by_config`
parameter.
[...]
```

The ORT converter produces a configuration file as well as an ORT model file from the ONNX model. You can deploy the optimized model along with a unique ONNX runtime build. First, try a conversion with an ONNX model. In this example, I downloaded the mobilenet_v2-1.0 (*https://oreil.ly/c7hBm*) ONNX model into the *models/* directory and used it as an argument to the converter script:

```
$ python onnxruntime/tools/python/convert_onnx_models_to_ort.py \
        models/mobilenetv2-7.onnx
Converting optimized ONNX model to ORT format model models/mobilenetv2-7.ort
Processed models/mobilenetv2-7.ort
Created config in models/mobilenetv2-7.required_operators.config
```

The configuration is crucial here because it lists the operators needed by the model. This allows you to create an ONNX runtime with only those operators. For the converted model, that file looks like this:

```
ai.onnx;1;Conv,GlobalAveragePool
ai.onnx;5;Reshape
ai.onnx;7;Add
com.microsoft;1;FusedConv
```

You can accomplish a binary size reduction for the runtime by specifying only the needs of the model. I will not be covering all the specifics on how to build the ONNX runtime from source, but you can use the build guide (*https://oreil.ly/AWP5r*) as a reference for the next steps as we explore what flags and options are helpful in the binary reduction.

First, you must use the `--include_ops_by_config` flag. In this case, the value for this flag is the path to the generated config from the previous step. In my case, that path is *models/mobilenetv2-7.required_operators.config*. I also suggest you try out the `--minimal_build`, which supports loading and executing ORT models only (dropping support for normal ONNX formats). Finally, if you are targeting an Android device, using the `--android_cpp_shared` flag will produce a smaller binary by using the shared *libc++* library instead of the static one that comes by default in the runtime.

Conclusion

The commonality that a framework (and set of tools) like ONNX provides helps the whole machine learning ecosystem. One of the ideals of this book is to provide *practical* examples to get models into production in a reproducible and reliable way. The more comprehensive the support for machine learning models, the easier it will be for engineers to try it out and take advantage of everything machine learning offers. I'm particularly excited about edge applications, especially for remote environments where it is impossible to connect to the internet or have any network connectivity. ONNX is lowering the friction that exists to deploy to those environments. I hope that the effort to continue to make this easier with more tooling and better support will continue to benefit from collective knowledge and contributions. Although we briefly tried command line tools, I go into much more detail on how to make robust command line tools with error handling and well-defined flags in the next chapter. In addition, I cover Python packaging and using microservices, which will give you the flexibility to try different approaches when solving machine learning challenges.

Exercises

- Update all scripts to verify the produced ONNX model with the script from "Create a Generic ONNX Checker" on page 301.
- Modify the Core ML converter script to use the Click framework for better parsing of options and a help menu.
- Group three converters into a single command line tool so that it is easy to make conversions with different inputs.
- Improve the *tf2onnx* converter so that it is wrapped in a new script, which can catch common errors and report them with a more user-friendly message.
- Use a different ONNX model for an Azure deployment.

Critical Thinking Discussion Questions

- Why is ONNX important? Give at least three reasons.
- What is something useful about creating a script without a command line tool framework? What are the advantages of using a framework?
- How is the ORT format useful? In what situations can you use it?
- What are some problems that you may encounter if portability doesn't exist? Give three reasons why improving those problems will improve machine learning in general.

Building MLOps Command Line Tools and Microservices

By Alfredo Deza

The Japanese bombed Pearl Harbor on December 7, 1941 and it at once became impossible to buy tires, clearly needed for the long trip to California. My father scoured the country for old tires for the Ford and for the small house trailer that we had used for several shorter family trips. We left Cincinnati in February 1942 with 22 tires strapped to the roofs of the trailer and the car and before we got to California we used them all.

—Dr. Joseph Bogen

Building command line tools is how I got started with Python years ago, and I believe it is a perfect intersection between software development and machine learning. I remember all those years ago when I struggled to learn new Python concepts that felt very foreign to me as a Systems Administrator: functions, classes, logging, and testing. As a Systems Administrator, I was mostly exposed to shell scripting with Bash writing top-to-bottom instructions to get something done.

There are several difficulties with trying to tackle problems with shell scripting. Handling errors with straightforward reporting, logging, and debugging are all features that don't take much effort in other languages like Python. Several other languages offer similar features like Go and Rust and should hint why using something other than a command language like Bash is a good idea. I tend to recommend using a shell scripting language when a few lines can get the task done. For example, this shell function copies my public SSH key into a remote machine into the authorized keys, allowing my account to access that remote server without requiring a password:

```
ssh-copy-key() {
    if [ $2 ]; then
        key=$2
```

```
    else
        key="$HOME/.ssh/id_rsa.pub"
    fi
    cat "$key" | ssh ${1} \
        'umask 0077; mkdir -p .ssh; cat >> .ssh/authorized_keys'
}
```

The sample Bash function will probably not work well in your enviroment. If you want to try it out, the paths and configuration files will have to match.

Doing the same with a language like Python wouldn't make much sense because it would take many more lines of code and probably a few extra dependencies installed. This function is simple, only does one thing, and is very portable. My recommendation is to look beyond a shell scripting language when the solution is more than a dozen lines or so.

If you find yourself creating small snippets of shell commands often, it is good to create a repository to collect them. The repository (https://oreil.ly/NQTfW) for my aliases, functions, and configurations should show you a good way to start if you need a reference.

The way I learned Python was by automating tedious, repetitive tasks with command line tools, from creating client websites using templates to adding and removing users from the corporate servers. My recommendation to get engaged in learning is to find an interesting problem with a direct benefit for yourself. This way of learning is entirely different from how we were taught in school, and it doesn't necessarily apply to any situation, but it is a good fit for this chapter.

Depending on how you create command line tools, they can be straightforward to install. As the example of a shell command that should work in any Unix environment with ease, there is a similarity with containers and microservices. Because the container bundles the dependencies together, it will work in any system with a proper runtime enabled. We've already gone through some of the components of microservices in "Containers" on page 68, describing some critical differences from monolithic applications.

But there is more to microservices than containers, and almost all cloud providers offer a *serverless* solution. Serverless allows a developer to concentrate on writing small applications without worrying about the underlying operating system, its dependencies, or the runtime. Although the offering may appear overly simplistic, you can leverage the solution to create whole HTTP APIs or a pipeline-like workflow.

You can tie all of these components and technologies back to the command line and some ML features from cloud providers. The mix-and-match aspect of these technologies means that an engineer can craft creative solutions to tricky problems with very little code. Whenever you can automate tasks and enhance productivity, you are applying solid operational skills to help you get models into production robustly.

Python Packaging

Many useful Python command line tools start as a single script file, and then they tend to grow to more complex scenarios with other files and perhaps dependencies. It isn't until the script needs extra libraries that it is no longer feasible to keep the script without packaging. Python packaging is not very good. It pains me to say that after well over a decade of Python experience, but packaging is still an aspect of the language ecosystem full of tricky (unresolved) problems.

If you are tinkering and trying out some automation *with no external dependencies*, then a single Python script is fine without packaging. If, on the other hand, your script requires some other dependencies and perhaps consists of more than one file, then you undoubtedly should consider packaging. Another useful feature of a properly packaged Python application is that it can be published to the Python Package Index (*https://pypi.org*) so that others can install it with tools like *pip* (the Package Installer for Python).

A few years ago, it was problematic to install Python packages on a system: it was impossible to remove them. This sounds unbelievable these days, but it was one of the many reasons why "virtual environments" took off. With virtual environments, fixing dependencies was as easy as removing a directory—while keeping the system packages intact. These days, uninstalling Python packages is easier (and possible!), but dependency resolution is still lacking robustness. Virtual environments are then the suggested way to work on Python projects, so environments are fully isolated, and you can resolve dependency problems by creating a new environment.

It shouldn't be surprising to see recommendations throughout this book (and elsewhere in the Python ecosystem) to use the *virtualenv* module. Since Python 3, the common way to create and activate a virtual environment is with the *Python* executable directly:

```
$ python -m venv venv
$ source venv/bin/activate
```

To verify that the virtual environment is activated, the Python executable should now be different from that of the system Python:

```
$ which python
/tmp/venv/bin/python
```

I recommend using proper Python packaging techniques so that you are well prepared when it is needed. As soon as your command line tool needs a dependency, it will be ready to be declared as a requirement. Your tool's consumers will resolve these dependencies as well, making it easier for others to work with your creation.

The Requirements File

As you will see in the next sections of this chapter, there are two popular ways of defining dependencies. One of them is using a *requirements.txt* file. Installer tools can use this file like *pip* to get dependencies installed from a package index. In this file, the dependencies are declared on a separate line, and optionally, with some versions constraint. In this example, the Click framework doesn't have a constraint, and therefore the installer (pip) will use the latest version. The Pytest framework is *pinned* to a specific version, so pip will always try to find that specific version at install time:

```
# requirements.txt
click
pytest==5.1.0
```

To install dependencies from a *requirements.txt* file, you need to use pip:

```
$ pip install -r requirements.txt
```

Although there is no strict naming rule, you can commonly find dependencies in a plain-text file named *requirements.txt*. Project maintainers can define multiple text files with requirements as well. That is more common when development dependencies are different than when shipping to production, for example. As you will see in the next section, there is also a *setup.py* file that can install dependencies. This is a rather unfortunate side-effect of the state of packaging and dependency management in Python. Both files can achieve the goal of installing dependencies for a Python project, but only *setup.py* can package a Python project for distribution. Because a *setup.py* file is executed at install time by Python, it allows doing anything aside from installation tasks. I don't recommend extending *setup.py* to do anything other than packaging tasks to prevent issues when distributing an application.

Some projects prefer to define their dependencies in a *requirements.txt* file and then reuse that file's contents into the *setup.py* file. You can achieve this by reading the *requirements.txt* and using the dependencies variable:

```
with open("requirements.txt", "r") as _f:
    dependencies = _f.readlines()
```

Distinguishing between these packaging files and knowing their background is useful to prevent confusion and misuse. You should now feel more comfortable discerning if a project is meant for distribution (*setup.py*) or a service or project that doesn't require installation.

Command Line Tools

One of the Python language features is the ability to quickly create applications with almost anything that you can imagine already included, from sending HTTP requests to processing files and text, all the way to ordering streams of data. The ecosystem of libraries available is vast. It doesn't seem surprising that the scientific community has embraced Python as one of the top languages to tackle workloads that include machine learning.

An excellent way of approaching command line tool development is to identify a particular situation that needs solving. Next time you encounter a somewhat repetitive task, try to build a command line tool to automate the steps to produce the result. Automation is another core principle of DevOps that you should apply whenever possible (and as much as it makes sense) to tasks throughout ML. Although you can create a single Python file and use it as a command line tool, the examples in this section will use proper packaging techniques that will allow you to define required dependencies and get the tool installed with Python installers like pip. In the first example tool, I'll show these Python patterns in detail to grasp the ideas behind command line tools that you can apply to the rest of this chapter.

Creating a Dataset Linter

While creating this book, I decided to put together a dataset of wine ratings and descriptions. I couldn't find anything similar, so I started gathering information for the dataset. Once the dataset had a healthy number of entries, the next step was to visualize the information and determine how robust the data was. As usual with the initial data state, this dataset presented several anomalies that took some effort to identify correctly.

One problem was that after loading the data as a Pandas data frame, it was clear that one of the columns was unusable: almost all were NaN (also referred to as null entries). Another issue, which might be the worst of them all, was that I loaded the dataset into Azure ML Studio to perform some AutoML tasks that started yielding some surprising results. Although the dataset had six columns, Azure was reporting about forty.

Lastly, *pandas* added unnamed columns when saving the processed data locally, and I wasn't aware of this. The dataset is available to demonstrate the problems. Load the CSV (comma separated value) file as a *pandas* data frame first:

```
import pandas as pd
csv_url = (
  "https://raw.githubusercontent.com/paiml/wine-ratings/main/wine-ratings.csv"
)
# set index_col to 0 to tell pandas that the first column is the index
df = pd.read_csv(csv_url, index_col=0)
df.head(-10)
```

The table output from pandas looks great but hints that one column may be empty:

```
          name    grape          region     variety  rating  notes
   ...          ...    ...          ...          ...      ...  ...
32765 Lewis Cella...   NaN Napa Valley...  White Wine    92.0 Neil Young'..
32766 Lewis Cella...   NaN Napa Valley...  White Wine    93.0 From the lo..
32767 Lewis Cella...   NaN Napa Valley...  White Wine    93.0 Think of ou..
32768 Lewis Cella...   NaN Napa Valley...    Red Wine    92.0 When asked ..
32769 Lewis Cella...   NaN Napa Valley...  White Wine    90.0 The warm, v..

[32770 rows x 6 columns]
```

When describing the dataset, one of the issues is now clear; the *grape* column doesn't have any items in it:

```
In [13]: df.describe()
Out[13]:
       grape        rating
count    0.0  32780.000000
mean     NaN     91.186608
std      NaN      2.190391
min      NaN     85.000000
25%      NaN     90.000000
50%      NaN     91.000000
75%      NaN     92.000000
max      NaN     99.000000
```

Drop the problematic column, and save the dataset onto a new CSV file, so that you can manipulate the data without having to download the contents every time:

```
df.drop(['grape'], axis=1, inplace=True)
df.to_csv("wine.csv")
```

Rereading the file demonstrates the extra column added by *pandas*. To reproduce the issue, reread the local CSV file, save it as a new file, and look at the first line of the newly created file:

```
df = pd.read_csv('wine.csv')
df.to_csv('wine2.csv')
```

Look at the first line of the *wine2.csv* file to spot the new column:

```
$ head -1 wine2.csv
,Unnamed: 0,name,region,variety,rating,notes
```

The Azure problem was more involved, and it was tough to detect: Azure ML was interpreting new lines and carriage returns in one of the columns as new columns. To find these special characters, I had to configure my editor to show them (usually, they aren't visible). In this example, the carriage return shows as ^M:

```
"Concentrated aromas of dark stone fruits and toast burst^M
from the glass. Classic Cabernet Sauvignon flavors of^M
black cherries with subtle hints of baking spice dance^M
across the palate, bolstered by fine, round tannins. This^M
```

```
medium bodied wine is soft in mouth feel, yet long on^M
fruit character and finish."^M
```

After dropping the column with no items in it, removing the unnamed columns, and getting rid of carriage returns, the data was now in a much healthier state. Now that I've done my due diligence cleaning up, I want to automate catching these problems. I'll probably forget the deal with the extra columns in Azure or a column with useless values in it a year from now. Let's create a command line tool to ingest a CSV file and produce some warnings.

Create a new directory called *csv-linter* and add a *setup.py* file that looks like this:

```python
from setuptools import setup, find_packages

setup(
    name = 'csv-linter',
    description = 'lint csv files',
    packages = find_packages(),
    author = 'Alfredo Deza',
    entry_points="""
    [console_scripts]
    csv-linter=csv_linter:main
    """,
    install_requires = ['click==7.1.2', 'pandas==1.2.0'],
    version = '0.0.1',
    url = 'https://github.com/paiml/practical-mlops-book',
)
```

This file allows Python installers to capture all the details of the Python package like dependencies and, in this case, the availability of a new command line tool called *csv-linter*. Most of the fields in the setup call are straightforward, but it is worth noting the details of the entry_points value. This is a feature of the *setuptools* library, which allows defining a function within a Python file to map back to a command line tool name. In this case, I'm naming the command line tool *csv-linter*, and I'm mapping it to a function (main) that I'll create next inside a file called *csv_linter.py*. Although I've picked *csv-linter* to be the tool's name, it can be named anything at all. Under the hood, the *setuptools* library will create the executable with whatever is declared here. There is no restriction to name it the same as the Python file.

Open a new file named *csv_linter.py* and add a single function that uses the Click framework:

```python
import click


@click.command()
def main():
    return
```

Even when examples don't explicitly mention using Python's virtual environments, it is always a good idea to create one. Having virtual environments is a robust way of isolating dependencies and potential problems with other libraries installed in a system.

These two files are nearly all you need to create a command line tool that (for now) doesn't do anything other than providing an executable available in your shell path. Next, create a virtual environment and activate it to install the newly created tool:

```
$ python3 -m venv venv
$ source venv/bin/activate
$ python setup.py develop
running develop
running egg_info
...
csv-linter 0.0.1 is already the active version in easy-install.pth
...
Using /Users/alfredo/.virtualenvs/practical-mlops/lib/python3.8/site-packages
Finished processing dependencies for csv-linter==0.0.1
```

The *setup.py* script has many different ways to get invoked, but you will primarily be using either the `install` argument or the `develop` one I used in the example. Using `develop` allows you to make changes to the script's source code and get those automatically available in the script, whereas `install` would create a separate (or standalone) script with no ties back to the source code. When developing command line tools, I recommend using `develop` to test changes as you make progress quickly. After calling the *setup.py* script, test out the newly available tool by passing the `--help` flag:

```
$ csv-linter --help
Usage: csv-linter [OPTIONS]

Options:
  --help  Show this message and exit.
```

Getting a help menu without having to write one is great, and it is a feature that a few other command line tool frameworks offer. Now that the tool is available as a script in the terminal, it is time to add useful features. To keep things simple, this script will accept a CSV file as a single argument. The Click framework has a built-in helper to accept files as arguments that ensure that the file exists and produces a helpful error otherwise. Update the *csv_linter.py* file to use the helper:

```
import click


@click.command()
@click.argument('filename', type=click.Path(exists=True))
def main():
    return
```

Although the script isn't doing anything with the file yet, the help menu has been updated to reflect the option:

```
$ csv-linter --help
Usage: csv-linter [OPTIONS] FILENAME
```

Still, not doing something useful. Check what happens if you pass a CSV file that doesn't exist:

```
$ csv-linter bogus-dataset.csv
Usage: csv-linter [OPTIONS] FILENAME
Try 'csv-linter --help' for help.

Error: Invalid value for 'FILENAME': Path 'bogus-dataset.csv' does not exist.
```

Take the tool a step further by using the `filename` argument that is getting passed into the `main()` function with Pandas to describe the dataset:

```
import click
import pandas as pd


@click.command()
@click.argument('filename', type=click.Path(exists=True))
def main(filename):
    df = pd.read_csv(filename)
    click.echo(df.describe())
```

The script uses Pandas, and another Click helper called *echo*, which allows us to print output back to the terminal easily. Use the *wine.csv* file previously saved when processing the dataset as input:

```
$ csv-linter wine.csv
          Unnamed: 0  grape       rating
count   32780.000000    0.0  32780.000000
mean    16389.500000    NaN     91.186608
std      9462.915248    NaN      2.190391
min         0.000000    NaN     85.000000
25%      8194.750000    NaN     90.000000
50%     16389.500000    NaN     91.000000
75%     24584.250000    NaN     92.000000
max     32779.000000    NaN     99.000000
```

Still, this isn't *too helpful*, even though it is now easily describing any CSV file using Pandas. The problem we need to solve here is to alert us about three potential issues:

- Detect zero-count columns

- Warn when Unnamed columns exist

- Check if there are carriage returns in a field

Let's start with detecting zero-count columns. Pandas allows us to iterate over its columns, and has a count() method that we can leverage for this purpose:

```
In [10]: for key in df.keys():
    ...:     print(df[key].count())
    ...:
    ...:
32780
0
32777
32422
32780
32780
```

Adapt the loop into a function separate from main() in the *csv_linter.py* file so that it is isolated and keeps things readable:

```
def zero_count_columns(df):
    bad_columns = []
    for key in df.keys():
        if df[key].count() == 0:
            bad_columns.append(key)
    return bad_columns
```

The zero_count_columns() function takes as input the data frame from Pandas, captures all the columns with a zero-count, and returns them at the end. It is isolated and not coordinating the output with the main() function yet. Since it is returning a list of column names, loop over the contents of the result in the main() function:

```
@click.command()
@click.argument('filename', type=click.Path(exists=True))
def main(filename):
    df = pd.read_csv(filename)
    # check for zero count columns
    for column in zero_count_columns(df):
        click.echo(f"Warning: Column '{column}' has no items in it")
```

Run the script against the same CSV file (note that I removed the .describe() call):

```
$ csv-linter wine-ratings.csv
Warning: Column 'grape' has no items in it
```

At 19 lines, this script would've saved me a lot of time already if I had used it before sending the data into an ML platform. Next, create another function that loops over the columns to check for Unnamed ones:

```
def unnamed_columns(df):
    bad_columns = []
    for key in df.keys():
        if "Unnamed" in key:
            bad_columns.append(key)
    return len(bad_columns)
```

In this case, the function checks if the "Unnamed" string is present in the name but is not returning the names (since we assume they are all similar or even the same), but rather, it returns the total count. With that information, expand the main() function to include the count:

```
@click.command()
@click.argument('filename', type=click.Path(exists=True))
def main(filename):
    df = pd.read_csv(filename)
    # check for zero count columns
    for column in zero_count_columns(df):
        click.echo(f"Warning: Column '{column}' has no items in it")
    unnamed = unnamed_columns(df)
    if unnamed:
        click.echo(f"Warning: found {unnamed} columns that are Unnamed")
```

Run the tool once again against the same CSV file to check the results:

```
$ csv-linter wine.csv
Warning: Column 'grape' has no items in it
Warning: found 1 column that is Unnamed
```

Finally, and perhaps the trickiest one to detect, is finding carriage returns within a large text field. This operation can be expensive, depending on the size of the dataset. Although there are more performant ways to accomplish the iteration, the next example will try to use the most straightforward approach. Create another function that does the work over the Pandas data frame:

```
def carriage_returns(df):
    for index, row in df.iterrows():
        for column, field in row.iteritems():
            try:
                if "\r\n" in field:
                    return index, column, field
            except TypeError:
                continue
```

The loop prevents a TypeError from being raised. If the function does a string check against a different type, like an integer, then a TypeError would get produced. Since the operation can be costly, the function breaks out of the loop at the first sign of a carriage return. Finally, the loop returns the index, column, and the whole field for reporting by the main() function. Now update the script to include the reporting of carriage returns:

```
@click.command()
@click.argument('filename', type=click.Path(exists=True))
def main(filename):
    df = pd.read_csv(filename)
    for column in zero_count_columns(df):
        click.echo(f"Warning: Column '{column}' has no items in it")
    unnamed = unnamed_columns(df)
```

```
if unnamed:
    click.echo(f"Warning: found {unnamed} columns that are Unnamed")

carriage_field = carriage_returns(df)
if carriage_field:
    index, column, field = carriage_field
    click.echo((
        f"Warning: found carriage returns at index {index}"
        f" of column '{column}':")
    )
    click.echo(f"          '{field[:50]}'")
```

Testing this last check is tricky because the dataset doesn't have carriage returns anymore. The repository for this chapter (*https://oreil.ly/aaevY*) includes an example CSV with carriage returns in it. Download that file locally and point the *csv-linter* tool to that file:

```
$ csv-linter carriage.csv
Warning: found carriage returns at index 0 of column 'notes':
        'Aged in French, Hungarian, and American Oak barrel'
```

To prevent having an extremely long field printed in the output, the warning message is only showing the first 50 characters. This command line tool is leveraging the Click framework for the command line tool functionality and Pandas for the CSV inspection. Although it is doing only three checks and is not very performant, it would've been invaluable for me to prevent having issues using the dataset. There are multiple other ways to ensure a dataset is in acceptable shape, but this is an excellent example of how to automate (and prevent) problems that you encounter. Automation is the foundation of DevOps, and command line tools are an excellent way to start the automation path.

Modularizing a Command Line Tool

The previous command line tool showed how to use Python's internal libraries to create a script from a single Python file. But it is entirely possible to use a directory with multiple files that make up a single command line tool. This approach is preferable when the content of a single script starts getting hard to read. There is no hard limit on what should make you split a long file into multiple ones; I recommend grouping code that shares common responsibilities and separating them, especially when there is a need for code reuse. There might not be a use case for code reuse in some situations, but splitting some pieces could still make sense to improve readability and maintenance.

Let's reuse the example of the *csv-linter* tool to adapt the single-file script into multiple files in a directory. The first step is creating a directory with an *__init__.py* file and move the *csv_linter.py* file into it. Using an *__init__.py* file tells Python to treat that directory as a module. The structure should now look like this:

```
$ tree .
.
├── csv_linter
│   ├── __init__.py
│   └── csv_linter.py
├── requirements.txt
└── setup.py

1 directory, 4 files
```

At this point, there is no need to repeat the name of the tool in the Python file, so rename it to something more modular and less tied to the name of the tool. I usually suggest using *main.py*, so rename the file:

```
$ mv csv_linter.py main.py
$ ls
__init__.py main.py
```

Try using the `csv_linter` command once again. The tool should be in a broken state because the files got moved around:

```
$ csv-linter
Traceback (most recent call last):
  File ".../site-packages/pkg_resources/__init__.py", line 2451, in resolve
    return functools.reduce(getattr, self.attrs, module)
AttributeError: module 'csv_linter' has no attribute 'main'
```

This is because the *setup.py* file is pointing to a module that doesn't exist anymore. Update that file so that it finds the `main()` function inside of the *main.py* file:

```
from setuptools import setup, find_packages

setup(
    name = 'csv-linter',
    description = 'lint csv files',
    packages = find_packages(),
    author = 'Alfredo Deza',
    entry_points="""
[console_scripts]
csv-linter=csv_linter.main:main
""",
    install_requires = ['click==7.1.2', 'pandas==1.2.0'],
    version = '0.0.1',
    url = 'https://github.com/paiml/practical-mlops-book',
)
```

The change may be difficult to spot, but the entry point to `csv-linter` is now `csv_linter.main:main`. This change means that *setuptools* should look for a *csv_linter* package with a *main* module with a `main()` function in it. The syntax is a bit tricky to remember (I always have to look it up), but grasping the change details helps visualize how things are tied together. The installation process still has all the old references, so you must run *setup.py* again to make it all work:

```
$ python setup.py develop
running develop
Installing csv-linter script to /Users/alfredo/.virtualenvs/practical-mlops/bin
...
Finished processing dependencies for csv-linter==0.0.1
```

Now that the *csv-linter* tool is in working order again let's split up the *main.py* module into two files, one for the checks and the other one just for the command line tool work. Create a new file called *checks.py* and move the functions that do the checks from *main.py* into this new file:

```python
# in checks.py

def carriage_returns(df):
    for index, row in df.iterrows():
        for column, field in row.iteritems():
            try:
                if "\r\n" in field:
                    return index, column, field
            except TypeError:
                continue


def unnamed_columns(df):
    bad_columns = []
    for key in df.keys():
        if "Unnamed" in key:
            bad_columns.append(key)
    return len(bad_columns)


def zero_count_columns(df):
    bad_columns = []
    for key in df.keys():
        if df[key].count() == 0:
            bad_columns.append(key)
    return bad_columns
```

And now update *main.py* to import the checking functions from the *checks.py* file. The newly updated main module should now look like this:

```python
import click
import pandas as pd
from csv_linter.checks import (
    carriage_returns,
    unnamed_columns,
    zero_count_columns

@click.command()
@click.argument('filename', type=click.Path(exists=True))
def main(filename):
    df = pd.read_csv(filename)
    for column in zero_count_columns(df):
```

```
        click.echo(f"Warning: Column '{column}' has no items in it")
    unnamed = unnamed_columns(df)
    if unnamed:
        click.echo(f"Warning: found {unnamed} columns that are Unnamed")
    carriage_field = carriage_returns(df)
    if carriage_field:
        index, column, field = carriage_field
        click.echo((
            f"Warning: found carriage returns at index {index}"
            f" of column '{column}':")
        )
        click.echo(f"          '{field[:50]}'")
```

Modularizing is a great way to keep things short and readable. When a tool separates concerns in this way, it is easier to maintain and reason about. There have been many times when I've had to work with legacy scripts that were *thousands* of lines long for no good reason. Now that the script is in good shape, we can go into microservices and take some of these concepts further.

Microservices

As I mentioned at the beginning of this chapter, microservices are a new type of application paradigm, entirely opposed to old-style monolithic applications. For ML operations, in particular, it is critical to isolate responsibilities as much as possible from the process of getting models into production. Isolating components can then pave the way for reusability elsewhere, not only tied to a particular process for a single model.

I tend to think about microservices and reusable components as pieces of a Jenga puzzle. A monolithic application would be an extremely tall Jenga tower with many pieces working together to make it stand, but with one major flaw: don't try to touch anything that will bring the whole thing down. On the other hand, if the pieces are put together as robustly as possible (as at the beginning of the puzzle game), then removing pieces and repurposing them to a different spot is straightforward.

It is common for software engineers to quickly create utilities that are tightly coupled to the task at hand. For example, some logic that removes some values from a string, which you can then use to persist it in a database. Once the few lines of code have proven their worth, it is useful to think about reusability for other code base components. I tend to have a utility module in my projects, where common utilities go so that other pieces of the application that need the same facilities can import and reuse them.

Like containerization, microservices allow concentrating more on the solution itself (the code) than the environment (e.g., operating system). One excellent solution for creating microservices is using serverless technologies. Serverless products from cloud providers take many different names (lambda and cloud functions, for example). Still, they all refer to the same thing: create a single file with some code and deploy instantly to the cloud—no need to worry about the underlying operating system or its dependencies. Just select a runtime from a drop-down menu, like Python 3.8, and click a button. Most cloud providers, in fact, allow you to create the function directly in the browser. This type of development and provisioning is fairly revolutionary, and it has been enabling interesting application patterns that were very complicated to achieve before.

Another critical aspect of serverless is that you can access most of the cloud provider's offerings without much effort. For ML, this is crucial: do you need to perform some computer vision operations? A serverless deployment can do this in less than a dozen lines of code. This way of leveraging ML operations in the cloud gets you speed, robustness, and reproducibility: all significant components of DevOps principles. Most companies will not need to create their own model for computer vision from scratch. The phrase "standing on the shoulders of giants" is a perfect fit to grasp the possibilities. Years ago, I worked in a digital media agency with a team of a dozen IT personnel who had decided to run their email servers in-house. Running email servers (correctly) takes a tremendous amount of knowledge and ongoing effort. Email is a *challenging problem to solve*. I can tell you that email would continuously stop working—in fact, it was almost a monthly occurrence.

Finally, let's look at how many options there are to build ML-based microservices on cloud providers. They typically range from more IaaS (infrastructure as a service) to more PaaS (platforms as a service). For example, in Figure 11-1, Kubernetes is a lower-level and complex technology that deploys microservices. In other scenarios, like AWS App Runner, covered earlier in the book, you can point your GitHub repo at the service and click a few buttons to get a fully deployed continuous delivery platform. Somewhere in the middle are cloud functions.

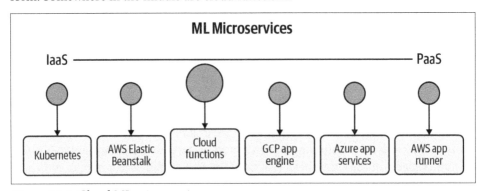

Figure 11-1. Cloud ML microservices

What is your company's core competency? If it isn't state-of-the-art computer vision models, then don't create these yourself. Likewise, work smart, not hard, and build on top of high-level systems like AWS App Runner or Google Cloud Run. Finally, resist the urge to reinvent the wheel and leverage cloud microservices.

Creating a Serverless Function

Most cloud providers expose their ML services in their serverless environments. Computer vision, Natural Language Processing, and recommendation services are just a few. In this section, you will use a translation API to leverage one of the world's most potent language-processing offerings.

> For this serverless application, I will use Google Cloud Platform (*https://oreil.ly/IO8oP*) (GCP). If you haven't signed up for it before, you might get some free credits to try the example in this section, although with the current limits, you should still be able to deploy the cloud function without incurring any costs.

Once logged into GCP, select Cloud Functions from the left sidebar under the Compute section as shown in Figure 11-2.

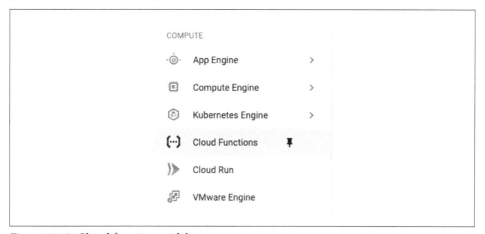

Figure 11-2. Cloud functions sidebar

If you haven't created a function before, a greeting message should show you a link to create one. If you already have deployed a function, a Create Function button should be available otherwise. Creating and deploying a function from the UI involves just a few steps. Figure 11-3 is the form you should expect to fill out.

Figure 11-3. Create a cloud function

The default values for the Basics section are sufficient. In this case, the form comes pre-filled with *function-1* as the name and using *us-central1* as the region. Ensure you set the trigger type to HTTP, and that authentication is required. Click Save and then the Next button at the bottom of the page.

Although unauthenticated invocations to functions are allowed (and as simple as selecting the option in the web form), I strongly suggest you never deploy a cloud function without authentication enabled. Exposed services over HTTP that are not authenticated pose a risk of getting abused. Since a cloud function's usage is tied directly to your account and budget, it can have a substantial financial impact from unauthorized usage.

Once in the Code section, you can select a runtime and an entry point. Select Python 3.8, change the entry point to use *main*, and update the function's name to use main() instead of hello_world() as shown in Figure 11-4.

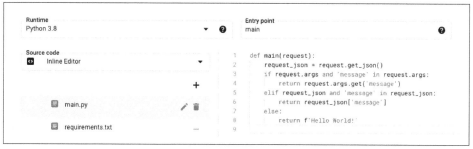

Figure 11-4. Cloud functions code

The ability to choose the entry point for the application opens up the possibilities of creating other functions to assist the main function or determine some other naming convention to interact with the code. Flexibility is great, but having defaults and using conventions is more valuable. Once you've made the necessary changes, click the Deploy button to get this function into a production environment. Once it completes, the function should show in the Cloud Functions dashboard.

Next, after deploying, let's interact with it by sending an HTTP request. There are many ways to accomplish this. To get started, click Actions for the selected function and choose "Test function." A new page loads, and although it may be hard to see it at first, the "Triggering event" section is where you add the body of the request to be sent. Since the function is looking for a "message" key, update the body to include a message like Figure 11-5 shows, then click the Test the function button.

Figure 11-5. Cloud function code—Triggering event

It should only take a few seconds to get the output, which should be the output from the value of the "message" key. Aside from that output, some logs should show up, making this a very straightforward way of interacting with the function. One thing that was not required was doing any authentication steps, although the function was created with authentication enabled. Whenever you are debugging and want to test a deployed function quickly, this is the easiest way by far.

This function accepts JSON (JavaScript Object Notation) as input. Although it isn't clear that the cloud function uses HTTP when testing, it is how the input gets delivered to the function. JSON is sometimes referred to as the *lingua franca* (common language) of web development because programming languages and other services and implementations can consume and produce JSON to native constructs that these languages and services understand.

Although HTTP APIs can restrict what types of requests and what format the body should be, it is relatively common to use JSON to communicate. In Python, you can load JSON into native data structures like lists and dictionaries, which are straightforward to use.

Before exploring other ways to interact with the function (including authentication), let's leverage Google's ML services by using their translation service. By default, all the APIs from Google's Cloud Platform are disabled. If you need to interact with a cloud offering like language translations, you must enable the API before using it. It isn't much of an issue if you create a cloud function (as in this case) and forget to do so. The resulting behavior would be an error captured in the logs, and an HTTP 500 returned as an error response back to the client making the request. This is an excerpt from the logs of a function that tried using the translation API without enabling it first:

```
google.api_core.exceptions.PermissionDenied: 403 Cloud Translation API has not
    been used in project 555212177956 before or it is disabled.
Enable it by visiting:
  https://console.developers.google.com/apis/api/translate.googleapis.com/
then retry. If you enabled this API recently, wait a few minutes for the
action to propagate to our systems and retry."
```

Enable the Cloud Translation API (*https://oreil.ly/6SFRs*) before making any further modifications to the function. Most of the APIs provided by GCP need to be enabled in a similar way, by going to the APIs and Services link (*https://oreil.ly/eV8sr*) and finding the API you need in the Library page.

 If you are not an admin on the GCP account and do not see an API available, you may lack the necessary permissions to enable an API. An account administrator needs to grant you proper permissions.

After enabling the API, head back to the function by clicking its name so its dashboard loads. Once in the dashboard, find the Edit button at the top of the page to make changes to the source code. The Edit section presents you first with options to configure the function itself first and then the code. There is no need to make changes to the deployment configuration, so click Next to finally get to the source. Click the *requirements.txt* link that opens that file to add the API library that is required to interact with the translation service:

```
google-cloud-translate==3.0.2
```

Now click *main.py* to edit the contents. Add the import statement to bring the translate service in, and add a new function that will be in charge of doing the translation:

```
from google.cloud import translate

def translator(text="YOUR_TEXT_TO_TRANSLATE",
    project_id="YOUR_PROJECT_ID", language="fr"):

    client = translate.TranslationServiceClient()
    parent = f"projects/{project_id}/locations/global"

    response = client.translate_text(
        request={
            "parent": parent,
            "contents": [text],
            "mime_type": "text/plain",
            "source_language_code":"en-US",
            "target_language_code":language,
        }
    )
    # Display the translation for each input text provided
    for translation in response.translations:
        print(u"Translated text: {}".format(translation.translated_text))
    return u"Translated text: {}".format(translation.translated_text)
```

This new function takes three arguments to interact with the translation API: the input text, the project ID, and the target language for the translation (defaulting to French). The input text defaults to English, but the function can be adapted to use other languages (e.g., Spanish) as input and English as the output. As long as the language is supported, the function can use the input and output with any combination.

The translation request response is iterable, so a loop is needed after the translation is complete.

Now modify the `main()` function to pass the value from `"message"` into the `translator()` function. I'm using my own project ID (*"gcp-book-1"*) so make sure you update that with your own if trying the next example:

```
def main(request):
    request_json = request.get_json()
    if request_json and 'message' in request_json:
        return translator(
            text=request_json['message'],
            project_id="gcp-book-1"
        )
```

```
    else:
        return f'No message was provided to translate'
```

The `main()` function still requires a `"message"` value assigned in the incoming JSON request but will now do something useful with it. Test it out in the console with a sample JSON input:

```
{"message": "a message that has been translated!"}
```

The output in the test page (shown in Figure 11-6) should be almost immediate.

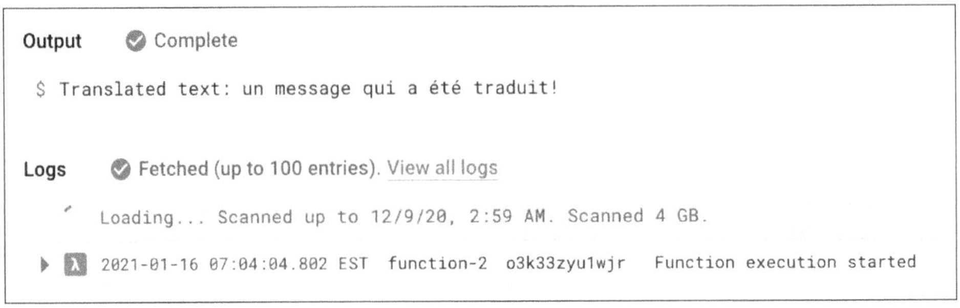

Output   ✅ Complete

```
$ Translated text: un message qui a été traduit!
```

Logs   ✅ Fetched (up to 100 entries). View all logs

```
      Loading... Scanned up to 12/9/20, 2:59 AM. Scanned 4 GB.

▶ λ  2021-01-16 07:04:04.802 EST  function-2  o3k33zyu1wjr   Function execution started
```

Figure 11-6. Translated test

Authenticating to Cloud Functions

I see HTTP access as access democracy: tremendous flexibility for other systems and languages to interact from their implementations into a separate service in a remote location using the HTTP spec. All major programming languages can construct HTTP requests and process responses from servers. Bringing services together with the help of HTTP allows these services to work in new ways, potentially in ways that were not thought of initially. Think of HTTP APIs as extensible functionality that can plug into anything connected to the internet. But connecting over the internet has security implications, like preventing unauthorized access with authenticated requests.

There are a few ways you can interact remotely with a cloud function. I'll start with the command line, using the *curl* program. Although I tend not to use *curl* for interacting with authenticated requests, it does offer a straightforward way of documenting all the pieces that you need to be successful in submitting the request. Install the Google Cloud SDK (*https://oreil.ly/2l7tA*) for your system, and then determine the project ID and the function name you deployed before. The following example uses *curl* with the SDK to authenticate:

```
$ curl -X POST --data '{"message": "from the terminal!"}' \
  -H "Content-Type: application/json" \
  -H "Authorization: bearer $(gcloud auth print-identity-token)" \
  https://us-central1-gcp-book-1.cloudfunctions.net/function-1
```

On my system, using the *function-1* URL, I get the following response:

```
Translated text: du terminal!
```

The command seems very involved, but it presents a better picture of what is needed to make a successful request. First, it declared that the request uses a POST method. This method is commonly used when a payload is associated with a request. In this case, curl is sending JSON from the argument to the --data flag. Next, the command adds two request headers, one to indicate the type of content being sent (JSON) and the other one to indicate that the request is providing a token. The token is where the SDK comes into play because it creates a token for the request, which is required by the cloud function service to verify the request as authenticated. Finally, the URL for the cloud function is used as the target for this authenticated POST request sending JSON.

Try running the SDK command on its own to see what it does:

```
$ gcloud auth print-identity-token
aIWQo6IClq5fNylHWPHJRtoMu4IG0QmP84tnzY5Ats_4XQvClne-A9coqEciMu_WI4Tjnias3fJjali
[...]
```

Now that you understand the required components for the request, try the SDK directly to make the request for you to reach the deployed cloud function:

```
$ gcloud --project=gcp-book-1 functions call function-1 \
    --data '{"message":"I like coffee shops in Paris"}'
executionId: 1jgd75feo29o
result: "Translated text: J'aime les cafés à Paris"
```

I think it is an excellent idea from cloud providers like Google to include other facilities to interact with their services as it happens here with the cloud function. If you only were aware of the SDK command to interact with a cloud function, it would be difficult to use a programming language to construct a request, for example, with Python. These options offer flexibility, and the more flexible an environment is, the better the chances of adapting it in the most reasonable way to fit your environment's needs.

Now let's use Python to interact with the translator function.

The following example will call out directly to the gcloud command using Python, making it easier to quickly demonstrate how to create Python code to interact with the cloud function. However, it isn't a robust way of dealing with authentication. You will need to create a service account (*https://oreil.ly/qNtoc*) and use the *google-api-python-client* to secure the authentication process properly.

Create a Python file called *trigger.py* and add the following code to retrieve the token from the gcloud command:

```
import subprocess


def token():
    proc = subprocess.Popen(
        ["gcloud", "auth", "print-identity-token"],
        stdout=subprocess.PIPE)
    out, err = proc.communicate()
    return out.decode('utf-8').strip('\n')
```

The token() function will call the gcloud command and process the output to make the request. It is worth reiterating that this is a quick way to demonstrate making requests to trigger the function from Python. You should consider creating a Service Account and OAuth2 from the *google-api-python-client* if looking to implement this in a production environment.

Now create the request using that token to communicate with the cloud function:

```
import subprocess
import requests

url = 'https://us-central1-gcp-book-1.cloudfunctions.net/function-1'


def token():
    proc = subprocess.Popen(
        ["gcloud", "auth", "print-identity-token"],
        stdout=subprocess.PIPE)
    out, err = proc.communicate()
    return out.decode('utf-8').strip('\n')


resp = requests.post(
    url,
    json={"message": "hello from a programming language"},
    headers={"Authorization": f"Bearer {token()}"}
)

print(resp.text)
```

Note that I've added the *requests* library (version 2.25.1 in my case) to the script, so you need to install it before continuing. Now run the *trigger.py* file to test it out, ensuring you have updated the script with your project ID:

```
$ python trigger.py
Translated text: bonjour d'un langage de programmation
```

Building a Cloud-Based CLI

Now that you understand the concepts for building a command line tool, packaging it, and distributing it while leveraging the cloud for its ML offerings, it is interesting to see these come together. In this section, I will reuse all the different parts to create one. Create a new directory, and add the following to a *setup.py* file so that packaging is solved right away:

```
from setuptools import setup, find_packages

setup(
    name = 'cloud-translate',
    description = "translate text with Google's cloud",
    packages = find_packages(),
    author = 'Alfredo Deza',
    entry_points="""
    [console_scripts]
    cloud-translate=trigger:main
    """,
    install_requires = ['click==7.1.2', 'requests==2.25.1'],
    version = '0.0.1',
    url = 'https://github.com/paiml/practical-mlops-book',
)
```

The *setup.py* file will create a *cloud-translate* executable mapped to a `main()` function within the *trigger.py* file. We haven't created that function yet, so add the *trigger.py* file that was created in the previous section and add the function:

```
import subprocess
import requests
import click

url = 'https://us-central1-gcp-book-1.cloudfunctions.net/function-2'


def token():
    proc = subprocess.Popen(
        ["gcloud", "auth", "print-identity-token"],
        stdout=subprocess.PIPE)
    out, err = proc.communicate()
    return out.decode('utf-8').strip('\n')


@click.command()
@click.argument('text', type=click.STRING)
def main(text):
    resp = requests.post(
            url,
            json={"message": text},
            headers={"Authorization": f"Bearer {token()}"})

    click.echo(f"{resp.text}")
```

The file isn't that different from the initial *trigger.py* where it runs directly with Python. The Click framework allows us to define a *text* input and then print the output to the terminal when it completes. Run `python setup.py develop` so that everything gets wired together, including the dependencies. As expected, the framework gives us the help menu:

```
$ cloud-translate --help
Usage: cloud-translate [OPTIONS] TEXT

Options:
  --help  Show this message and exit.
$ cloud-translate "today is a wonderful day"
Translated text: aujourd'hui est un jour merveilleux
```

Machine Learning CLI Workflows

The shortest distance between two points is a straight line. Likewise, a command line tool is often the most straightforward approach to using machine learning. In Figure 11-7, you can see that there are many different styles of ML techniques. In the case of unsupervised machine learning, you can train "on the fly"; in other cases, you may want to use a trained nightly model and place it in object storage. Yet, you may wish to use high-level tools like AutoML, AI APIS, or models created by third parties in others.

Notice that there are many different problem domains where adding ML enhances a CLI or is the entire purpose of the CLI. These domains include text, computer vision, behavioral analytics, and customer analysis.

It is essential to point out that there are many targets for deploying command line tools that include machine learning. A filesystem like Amazon EFS, GCP Filestore, or Red Hat Ceph have the advantage of being a centralized Unix mount point for a cluster. The *bin* directory could include ML CLI tools delivered via a Jenkins server that mounts this same volume.

Other delivery targets include the Python Package Repository (PyPI), and public Container Registries like Docker, GitHub, and Amazon. Yet more targets include Linux packages like Debian and RPM. A command line tool that packages machine learning has a much more extensive collection of deployment targets than even a microservice because a command line tool is an entire application.

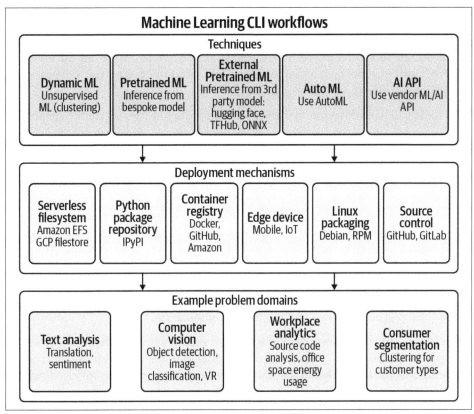

Figure 11-7. Machine learning CLI workflows

A few good examples of projects suitable for doing machine learning with a CLI include the following resources:

DevML

DevML (*https://oreil.ly/pMU53*) is a project that analyzes GitHub organizations and allows ML practitioners to create their own "secret ML" predictions, perhaps by connecting it to streamlit (*https://streamlit.io*) or including developer clustering reports in Amazon QuickSight.

Python MLOps Cookbook

The Python MLOps Cookbook GitHub repo (*https://oreil.ly/4jAUL*) contains a simple ML model as a set of utilities. This project has detailed coverage in Chapter 7.

Spot Price Machine Learning

Yet another ML CLI example is a project on Spot Price Machine Learning Clustering. In this GitHub repository (*https://oreil.ly/OiutZ*), different attributes of AWS spot instances, including memory, CPU, and price, are used to create clusters of machine types that are similar.

With these CLI workflows out of the way, let's move on to wrapping up the chapter.

Conclusion

This chapter has described how to create command line tools from the ground up and use a framework to create tools to perform automation rapidly. Even when examples may look trivial, the details and how things work together are essential aspects. When learning new concepts or subjects that others commonly dread (like packaging in general), it is easy to feel discouraged and try to work around them. Although Python has a long road toward better packaging, getting started is not that hard, and doing the heavy lifting with proper packaging of your tools will make you invaluable in any team. With packaging and command line tools, you are now well-positioned to start bringing different services together for automation.

This chapter did that by leveraging the cloud and its many ML offerings: a powerful translation API from Google. It is critical to remember that there is no need to create all the models from scratch and you should leverage cloud providers' offerings whenever possible, especially when it isn't a core competency of your company.

Finally, I want to emphasize that being able to craft new solutions to tricky problems is an MLOps superpower, based on knowing how to connect services and applications. As you now know, using HTTP, command line tools, and leveraging cloud offerings via their SDKs is a strong foundation to make substantial improvements in almost any production environment.

In the next chapter we go into other details of machine learning engineering, and one of my favorite topics: case studies. Case studies are real-world problems and situations where you can extract useful experiences and apply them today.

Exercises

- Add some more options to the CLI that use cloud functions, like making the URL configurable.
- Find out how the Service Account and OAuth2 work with the Google SDK and integrate it in *trigger.py* to avoid using the *subprocess* module.
- Enhance the cloud function by translating a separate source, like a page from Wikipedia.
- Create a new cloud function that does image recognition and make it work with a command line tool.
- Fork the Python MLOps Cookbook repository (*https://oreil.ly/fX1Uu*) and build a slightly different containerized CLI tool that you publish to a public container registry like DockerHub or GitHub Container Registry.

Critical Thinking Discussion Questions

- Name one possible consequence of unauthenticated cloud functions.
- What are some of the drawbacks of not using a virtual environment?
- Describe two aspects of good debugging techniques and why they are useful.
- Why is knowing packaging useful? What are some critical aspects of packaging?
- Is it a good idea to use an existing model from a cloud provider? Why?
- Explain the trade-offs in deploying an open source CLI tool powered by machine learning using a public container registry versus using the Python Package Repository.

## CHAPTER 12

Machine Learning Engineering and MLOps Case Studies

By Noah Gift

> After accompanying Professor Loewi through his procedure I spent more time in his postop care during which he lectured me further. He signed my copy of his little 62-page book, above his signature in a shaky hand he wrote, "Facts without Theory is chaos, Theory without facts is phantasy.
>
> —Dr. Joseph Bogen

One of the fundamental problems with technology in the real world is that it is tough to know who to listen to for advice. In particular, a multidisciplinary topic like machine learning is a puzzling challenge. How can you find the right mix of real-world experience, current and relevant skills, and the teaching ability to explain it? This "unicorn" teaching ability is what this chapter aims to do. The goal is to distill these relevant aspects into actionable wisdom for your machine learning projects, as shown in Figure 12-1.

Other domains suffer from the curse of the unbounded complexity that comes with a multidisciplinary field. Examples include Nutritional Science, Climate Science, and Mixed Martial Arts. However, a common thread is the concept of an open system versus a closed system. One toy example of a primarily closed system is an insulated cup. In that example, it is easier to model the behavior of a cold liquid since the environment has minimal effect. But if that same cold liquid goes outside in a regular cup, things get murky quickly. The outside air temperature, humidity, wind, and sun exposure alone create cascading complexity in modeling the behavior of that cold liquid.

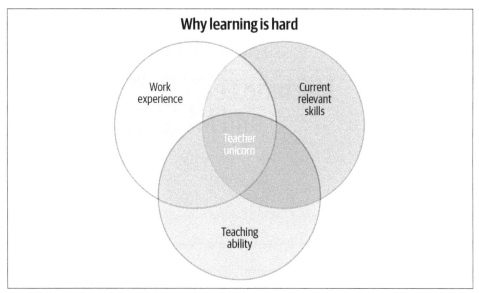

Figure 12-1. Teaching unicorn

This chapter explores how MLOps can leverage learnings from these other domains. It also explores how closed versus open systems influence domain-specific behavior and, ultimately, how to apply this to operationalizing machine learning.

Unlikely Benefits of Ignorance in Building Machine Learning Models

There are many unlikely benefits to ignorance. Ignorance gives you the courage to try something challenging, where if you knew how difficult it was, you would never have done it. Since 2013, ignorance has played a crucial role in two things I have done simultaneously: create a production machine learning model with millions of dollars at stake, including a 100 person company; and learn, train, and compete in Brazilian Jiu-Jitsu with top-ranked professional fighters and Olympians in wrestling and Judo. In some sense, the two things are so intertwined it is hard to separate one from the other in my mind. From 2010–2013 I spent three years taking every statistics, probability, and modeling class I could take at UC Davis in its MBA program while working full-time at startups in San Francisco. Since 2017, I have also taught machine learning and cloud computing at the UC Davis Graduate School of Management. After I graduated, I was ready to take a General Management or Chief Technology Officer position and became one of the first technical employees at a Sports social network as the CTO and General Manager.

Part of the company's culture was that employees would exercise together at a mixed martial arts gym that also did general fitness classes. I accidentally started training in

Brazilian Jiu-Jitsu as I got curious watching the pro fighters grapple. Eventually, before I knew it, I worked alongside professional fighters and learned the basics of submissions. A few times, I even accidentally became choked unconscious in sparring. I remember one time thinking, "I probably should tap to this head and arm choke." Later, I wondered where I was; it looked like a gym, and I didn't know what year it was. Was I in my high school gym in Southern California? How old am I? As blood came back into my brain, I realized that, ah, I got choked out, and I am in the martial arts gym in Santa Rosa, California.

In my first few years of training, I also entered two tournaments, winning the first one, a "novice" category, and then losing an "intermediate" class a couple of years later. In hindsight, I honestly didn't understand what I was doing and faced the real risk of serious injury. I observed many people in the tournaments get severe damage, including head butts, broken shoulders, and ripped knee ligaments. In my second tournament as a 40-year old, I competed against a 20-year-old college football player in the 220-pound weight class. In his last match, he got in a real fight, got headbutted, was bleeding from the nose, and was quite angry. I was apprehensive about his emotional state going into our contest, thinking, "What the hell did I sign up for?"

I also counted my blessings that I was ignorant of the actual danger of competing in martial arts in my thirties and forties. I still enjoy training and learning Brazilian Jiu-Jitsu, but it is likely that if I knew what I knew today, I wouldn't have taken the risks I took with as little skill as I had. Ignorance gave me the courage to, frankly, take dumb risks but also learn more quickly.

Similarly, in 2014, I was just as ignorant as I started the journey of building out a machine learning infrastructure for my company. Today this is known as MLOps. At the time, there wasn't a lot of information about how to operationalize machine learning. As with Brazilian Jiu-Jitsu, I was eager yet ignorant of what really would unfold and the risks at play. Later the terror I felt in Brazilian Jiu-Jitsu was nothing compared to the terror I would experience in building prediction models by myself from scratch with the responsibility for millions of dollars a year.

In the first year, 2013, our company built a sports social network and mobile application. But, as many employees at a startup know, building software is only part of a startup's challenge; two other vital challenges are acquiring users and creating revenue. At the start of 2014, we had a platform, yet no users and no income. So we needed to come up with users quickly, or the startup would go bankrupt.

Building traffic generally occurs in two ways for a software platform. One way is to build organic growth through word of mouth. A second way is to purchase advertising. The problem with buying advertising is that it can quickly become a permanent cost allocation. The dream scenario was for our company to get users to come to our platform without buying ads. We had a relationship with a few sports stars, including former NFL quarterback Brett Favre. This initial "superstar" social media influencer gave us tremendous insight into using organic "growth hacking" to grow our platform.

At one point, this machine learning feedback loop got us into the millions of monthly active users. Then, the Facebook legal team sent us a communication that they would "deplatform us" metaphorically. Our "crime" was creating unique, original sports content that had links to our platform. There is an ongoing question about the potential monopolistic power of Big Tech, and the growth hacking power of our influence algorithm got the attention of Facebook. This was another data point about the real-world success of our prediction system. Let's dive into how we did this next.

MLOps Projects at Sqor Sports Social Network

Building a startup from zero—i.e., zero staff, zero uses, and zero revenue—is a stressful pursuit. From 2013–2016 I spent many hours in the park underneath the Transamerica building in San Francisco, directly under my office, plotting these things. In particular, the epistemic risk, the risk I was unaware of, of betting millions of dollars on machine learning predictions was terrifying. But, in many ways, the technical challenges are much more comfortable than the psychological ones.

Here is an overview of how the system worked. In a nutshell, the user posts original content and then we cross-post the content to other social networks like Twitter and Facebook. We then collected the pageviews generated for our site. The pageviews became the target in our ML prediction system. Figure 12-2 shows the MLOps pipeline for our social media company.

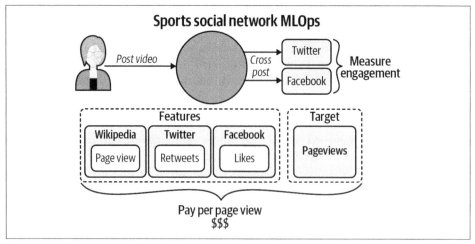

Figure 12-2. MLOps pipeline for sports social network

Later, we collected the social media signals from these users, i.e., their median retweets, median likes, and Wikipedia page views. These became the features and helped us cut through the noise of false data like "fake" followers. We then paid original content creators like Conor McGregor, Brett Favre, Tim McGraw, and Ashlyn Harris by the engagement they generated on our site. It turns out we were way ahead of the game in doing this, and Snapchat pays out millions for users to publish original content on its platform (*https://oreil.ly/mPQq5*).

The most challenging parts of the problem were reliably collecting the data and then deciding to pay millions of dollars based on the predictions. Both were much more complicated than I initially thought. So let's dive into these systems next.

Mechanical Turk Data Labeling

Initially figuring out that social media signals gave us enough predictive power to "growth hack" our platform was a huge breakthrough. But, unfortunately, the most formidable challenge was yet to come.

We needed to collect the social media handles reliably for thousands of "celebrity" social media users. Unfortunately, it didn't go well initially and ended in complete failure. Our first process looked like Figure 12-3.

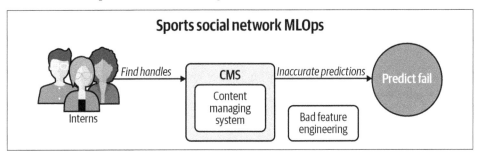

Figure 12-3. Bad feature engineering

Despite some of the interns being future NFL players themselves, the critical problem was that they didn't have the training to input the social media handles reliably. As a result, it was easy to mistake Anthony Davis, the NFL player, with Anthony Davis, the NBA player, and swap Twitter handles. This feature engineering reliability problem would kill the accuracy of our model. We fixed this by adding automation in the form of Amazon Mechanical Turk. We trained a "quorum" of "turkers" to find the social media handles of athletes, and if 7/9 agreed, we found this equated to around 99.9999% accuracy. Figure 12-4 shows Mechanical Turk labeling system for our social media company.

Back in 2014, less was known about data engineering and MLOps. Our labeling system project ran through an incredible athlete, programmer, and former UC Davis graduate Purnell Davis (*https:// oreil.ly/yc14S*). Purnell developed this system from scratch between doing workouts with athletes like NFL player Marshawn Lynch or 300-pound professional MMA fighters, who trained with our company at the same gym during lunch or at the crack of dawn.

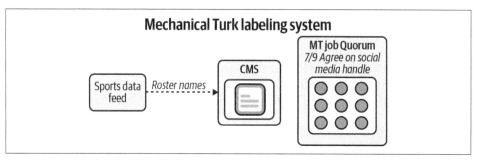

Figure 12-4. Mechanical Turk labeling

Influencer Rank

Once we could get the data labeled, we had to collect data from social media APIs. You can find an excellent example of the type of code necessary to bring this into an ML Engine in this repository (*https://oreil.ly/D6Wqb*).

For example, LeBron James's statistics on Twitter look like the following according to our data collection API:

```
Get status on Twitter

        df = stats_df(user="KingJames")
        In [34]: df.describe()
        Out[34]:
         favorite_count retweet_count
        count 200.000000 200.000000
        mean 11680.670000 4970.585000
        std 20694.982228 9230.301069
        min 0.000000 39.000000
        25% 1589.500000 419.750000
        50% 4659.500000 1157.500000
        75% 13217.750000 4881.000000
        max 128614.000000 70601.000000

        In [35]: df.corr()
        Out[35]:
         favorite_count retweet_count
        favorite_count 1.000000 0.904623
        retweet_count 0.904623 1.000000
```

If you are familiar with the show *The Shop* on HBO, you will know Maverick Carter and LeBron James. We "almost" officially worked with them, but the talks didn't work out. We ultimately developed a relationship with FC Bayern Munchen instead as a critical partner.

This collection data then fed into a prediction model. A talk I gave at the R meetup in the Bay Area in 2014 (*https://oreil.ly/rI0Sw*) shows some of our handiwork. The initial model used the R library Caret (*https://oreil.ly/MtN0Z*) to predict the pageviews. In Figure 12-5 the original prediction algorithms for finding influencers was done in R and this ggplot-based chart shows the accuracy of the prediction.

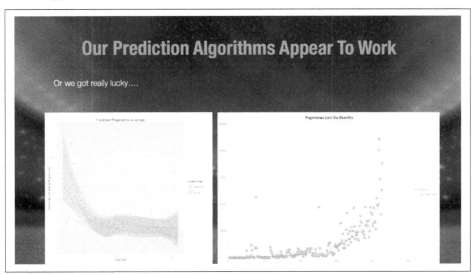

Figure 12-5. Predicted pageviews from social media influencers versus actual pageviews

We then built a payment system model using the pageviews as the target metric. Ultimately, it led to exponential growth that fueled a quick expansion into millions of pageviews a month. But, as I mentioned earlier, the scary part was the sleepless nights wondering if I was bankrupting the company as we spent millions of dollars on the predictions I helped create.

Athlete Intelligence (AI Product)

With a core MLOps pipeline serving out predictions and fueling our growth without purchasing ads, we started to evolve our product into an AI Product called "Athlete Intelligence." We had two AI product managers who managed this full time. The general idea of the core product was for "influencers" to understand what they could expect in payment and brands to use this dashboard to partner directly with athletes.

In Figure 12-6, we used unsupervised machine learning to categorize different aspects of athletes, including their social media influence.

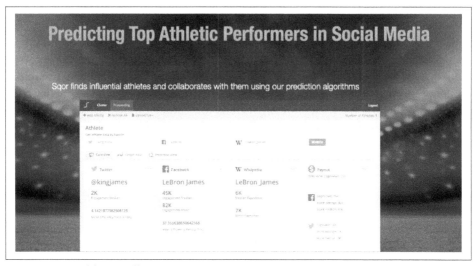

Figure 12-6. Athlete intelligence

Additional features included unsupervised machine learning that "clustered" similar athlete social profiles. This feature allowed us to package different types of athletes into influencer marketing bundles (Figure 12-7).

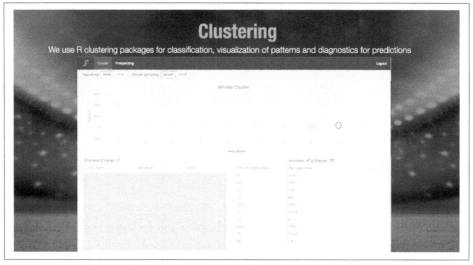

Figure 12-7. Athlete intelligence clustering dashboard

Finally, this growth led to two new revenue products for our company. First was a merchandising platform built on top of Shopify that turned into a 500k/year business, and a second was a multimillion dollar influencer marketing business. We directly contacted brands and connected them with the influencers on our platform. An excellent example of this is the "Game of War" commercial we brokered with Machine Zone and Conor McGregor (*https://oreil.ly/G6JrI*).

In a nutshell, having an effective MLOps pipeline led us to both users and revenue. Without the prediction model, we would have had no users; without the users, we would have had no income; without income, we would have no business. Practical MLOps pay dividends.

Let's talk more about the open versus closed system in the next section. Things seem simple in a controlled environment like academic data science, the martial arts gym in a GI, or theoretical advice on nutrition like calories in versus calories out. Real-world or open systems have many additional influences, though, that are much more challenging to harness.

The Perfect Technique Versus the Real World

Does an armbar (an arm attack that breaks an arm by hyperextending the elbow) by a Brazilian Jiu-Jitsu black belt in the GI (heavy cotton jacket uniform in martial arts) have the same effectiveness against an opponent not wearing a GI? Likewise, in machine learning, what is most important? Is it the accuracy, the technique, or the ability to provide value to a customer or knowledge to a situation?

If you are curious about what it looks like to use an armbar in competition, google "Ronda Rousey armbar," and you will see a master technician at work.

What about a street fight versus a grappling match or a UFC match versus a grappling match? Even nonexperts would agree that the more rules involved in a technique, the less chance it has to succeed in an environment with little or no rules, i.e., the real world.

I learned a lesson by traveling to random gyms to train across the United States when I was on business. On more than one occasion, a brown or black belt expert in doing GI Brazilian Jiu-Jitsu would spar with me in NOGI (no uniform) and instantly try to perform an armbar. I have spent years training with professional fighters who practice NOGI. After getting caught perhaps hundreds of times in the submission, I had learned how to easily escape it by slipping my arm out in a specific way. How did I understand this? I just copied what the pro fighters both did and taught me and practiced it over and over again.

Many experts in GI, from black to brown belts to Olympic medalists, said similar things. "You can't do this in GI," or "I would have had that in GI," or "you shouldn't do this," etc., as they had a horrified or surprised look on their face. Their "perfect model" didn't work and their worldview was shocked. Did this mean I was even close to as good as these experts? No, it meant that they had much better technique than I did in a context that didn't apply to the one we were currently in, grappling without a uniform. Notice in Figure 12-8 how closing the system, or adding rules, to the outside world adds more control yet less realism.

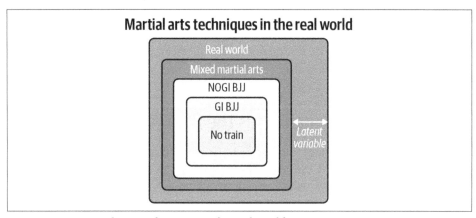

Figure 12-8. Martial arts techniques in the real world

In the book *Critical Thinking* (MIT Press), Jonathan Haber mentions how Ann J. Cahill and Stephan Bloch-Schulman of Elon University make their higher education class like a martial arts studio:

> In such [martial arts] classes, at each successive level of assessment, students are also required to demonstrate that they have maintained the skills they achieved in previous belt levels. Importantly, a decent sensei does not award a belt based on effort: whether a student has tried hard to master a certain action is not relevant. The question is, can the student throw the punch?

When explaining this same MMA (mixed martial arts) and machine learning theory in a class I teach in Northwestern's data science program, I found out one of my students spent 14 years in the NFL. He then pointed out what he admired about MMA because the best athletes don't have technique agendas. Instead, they wait to see what happens and apply the correct technique for the situation at hand.

Interview: Martial Arts and ML Modeling

I interviewed a top black belt and former mixed martial arts fighter to discuss other real-world martial arts and how it relates to ML modeling:

Q: Who are you are and what is your experience in martial arts, sports, and fighting?

> *A:* My name is Jacob Hardgrove. I have been training in Brazilian Jiu-Jitsu for ~20 years. I have competed in both submission grappling and professional MMA events and have an MMA record of 3-0. Besides the BJJ training, to prepare for the MMA events, I have spent a significant amount of time studying and training other forms of martial arts such as western boxing, muay Thai, freestyle, and catch wrestling.

Q: Why do some techniques taught very formally, say GI BJJ, not work as well in a real fight, either on the street or in the cage?

> *A:* My thought process on this question leads me to consider a dichotomy between introducing a concept/technique and the successful implementation of said concept/technique in an uncontrolled environment/situation.
>
> To introduce a technique or concept to a beginner, the instructor strips the technique of as many variables as possible to create an easily repeatable framework. This framework should be as stripped down as much as possible and consist of the primary, essential components required to achieve the desired effect. This framework, according to most traditional martial arts, is referred to as "Kata."
>
> Now, I see people who end up submerging themselves in the world of Jiu-Jitsu lose sight of the fact that they are practicing martial skills against other martial artists and not against untrained but potentially still viable, violent attackers. Unfortunately, this truth can lead to a severe case of "missing the point."

Much like Jacob, the black belt former MMA fighter, I see similar issues in real-world machine learning. As a professor, I teach machine learning at top universities and also am an industry practitioner. The academic tools like sklearn (*https://oreil.ly/sub5D*) and pandas (*https://oreil.ly/uau1J*) and the educational datasets on Kaggle are the "Kata." These datasets and tools are necessary to "strip away" the real-world complexity to teach the material. A critical next step is to make the student aware that machine learning Kata is not real-world. The real world is much more dangerous and complicated.

Critical Challenges in MLOps

Let's discuss some specific challenges in bringing machine learning to production. Three main challenges are ethical and unintended consequences, lack of operational excellence, and focus on prediction accuracy versus the big picture. Operational excellence in implementing machine learning is what matters much more than the technique in the real world. This exact point is clearly articulated in the research paper "Hidden Technical Debt in Machine Learning Systems" (*https://oreil.ly/3RjTA*). The paper's authors found "…it is common to incur massive ongoing maintenance costs in real-world ML systems." Let's discuss some of these issues next.

Ethical and Unintended Consequences

It is easy to get "hand-wavy" or self-righteous about ethics and turn people off. This fact doesn't mean the topic doesn't need discussion. Many companies that deal with social media have created weapons of mass disinformation. According to Tristan Harris (*https://oreil.ly/lIsEw*), "64% of extremist groups that people joined were due to Facebook's own recommendation system" and YouTube "recommended Alex Jones, InfoWars, conspiracy theory videos 15 billion times. So that's more than the combined traffic of the Washington Post, BBC, Guardian, Fox news combined", and 70% of all watch time on YouTube is recommendations.

The consequences are no longer theoretical. Many social networks and big technology companies are actively changing their approach to machine learning–based enabled systems. These updates range from putting facial recognition systems on hold to evaluating the outcomes of recommendation engines more closely. Ethical considerations in the real world also have to be part of an MLOps solution, not just whether the technique has predictive power.

Already some solutions to the problem of echo chambers appear—for example, the *IEEE Spectrum* in the article "Smart Algorithm Bursts Social Networks *Filter Bubbles*" (*https://oreil.ly/HD0w5*). They go on to say, "one team of researchers in Finland and Denmark has a different vision for how social media platforms could work. They developed a new algorithm that increases the diversity of exposure on social networks, while still ensuring that content is widely shared."

This situation is where ethics come into play. If a company or machine learning engineer is 100% focused on increasing engagement and profit, they may not want to lose 10% of their profit to "save the world." This ethical dilemma is a classic case study in externalities. A nuclear power facility might deliver tremendous energy benefits, but if they dump the nuclear waste into the ocean, other innocent victims pay the price yet reap no reward.

Lack of Operational Excellence

Another antipattern of machine learning engineering is the inability to maintain a machine learning model effectively. A good way to reason about this situation is to consider building a wood bookshelf versus growing a fig tree. If you make a bookshelf, you will probably never modify it again; once designed, that is the end of the project. On the other hand, a fig tree is part of an open system. It needs water, sun, soil, nutrients, wind, trimming of branches, and protection from insects and disease. The fig tree adapts to the environment over time but needs oversight from the person who wants to enjoy the figs later. In other words, the fig tree needs maintenance to produce high-quality fruit. A machine learning system, like any software system, is never finished like a bookshelf. Instead, it requires nurturing like a fig tree.

Next, let's imagine a company that predicts credit limits for each new furniture store customer. Let's say an initial model was developed in January 2019. Since then, a lot has changed. There could be substantial data drift (*https://oreil.ly/TvAng*) from the features used to create the model. We know that many retail stores in 2020–2021 went out of business, and the mall business model is under serious threat. COVID-19 accelerated a declining trend for physical retail, among other updates in the underlying data. As a result, the data "drifted," i.e., purchase patterns are widely different post-COVID-19, and the original static machine learning model may not work as intended.

A machine learning engineer would be wise to account for constant retraining of the model (nurturing the fig tree) by setting alerts on the data changes when a data drift threshold occurs. Additionally, business metric monitoring could send an alert if late payments exceed a threshold. For example, let's imagine that typically a company selling furniture has 5% of customers that pay 30 days late on their credit. If suddenly 10% of the customers pay 30 days late, then the underlying ML model may need an update.

The concept of alerts and monitoring for machine learning should not be a surprise to traditional software engineers. For example, we monitor CPU load on individual servers, latency for mobile users, and other key performance indicators. With machine learning operations, the same concept applies.

Focus on Prediction Accuracy Versus the Big Picture

As discussed earlier in the chapter, even world-class practitioners can sometimes focus on the technique at the Big Picture's expense. But, like the "perfect armbar," which doesn't quite work in a different situation, a model can be just as brittle. A great example of the tug of war is the Nate Silver versus Nassim Taleb debate. Issac Faber has an excellent breakdown of the critical points (*https://oreil.ly/0sQhq*) in a Medium article. Isaac points out that not all models are perfect replicas of the real world because they cannot tease out the uncertainty of what we do not know, i.e., immeasurable risk. The debate between Nate Silver versus Nassim Taleb comes down to whether it is possible to model elections or whether it is an illusion to think we can model them. The election events of 2020 do seem to put points in favor of Nassim Taleb.

The black-belt Jacob says the same thing when he points out that a Kata is a simplified version of a practice technique. The complexity of the real world and the training exercise is in inherent conflict. The model or technique may be flawless, but the real world may not care. For example, in the case of the 2020 presidential election, even the best modeler didn't anticipate the probability of an insurrection or state officials pressured to throw out ballots. As Issac describes this problem, it is the difference between aleatory and epistemic uncertainty. The aleatory risk you can measure, say, the probability of heads or tails, but the epistemic risk you cannot, like an insurrection that could overturn a presidential election.

Dr. Steven Koonin, whom I worked for at Caltech for several years, says something similar in his book about climate science. Just like election predictions, nutritional science, and other complex systems, the topic of climate science is instantly polarizing. In the book, *Unsettled* (BenBella Books) Koonin says, "Not only can we be fooled by failing to take a 'big picture view of climate over time, but we can also be fooled by failing to take a big picture view of the planet." Further, he goes on to say, "Projections of future climate and weather events rely on models demonstrably unfit for the purpose." Whether you believe his statement or not, it is worth considering the complexity of real-world modeling of a complex system and what can go wrong.

A good summary of this dilemma is to be cautious about the confidence in a prediction or technique. One of the scariest and most talented grapplers I trained with, Dave Terrell, who fought for the UFC championship, told me, don't ever get in a fight with multiple opponents. The more skill and "skin in the game" a practitioner has, the more they become aware of the epistemic risk. Why risk your life in a street fight with multiple people even if you are a world-class martial artist? Likewise, why be more confident than you should when you predict an election, stock prices, or natural systems?

In practice, the best way to approach this problem in production is to limit the technique's complexity and assume a lower knowledge of epistemic uncertainty. This takeaway could mean a traditional machine learning high explainability is better than a complex deep learning model with marginally better accuracy.

Interview with MLOps Practitioners: Piero Molino

What is your background, and how did you get involved with operationalizing machine learning?

A: I studied computer science at the University of Bari in Italy, where I got a PhD working on open domain question answering (at the intersection of NLP, ML, and information retrieval). Since when I was a student I was trying to use the research systems I was building for creating products that could be used in the real world as opposed to lab prototypes that was never practically used. This led me to work on applied NLP and ML at a few companies (Yahoo!, IBM Watson, Geometric Intelligence, and Uber AI). In most cases I did both research and applications, that's the intersection where I like to work: new ideas that end up being used by people. In Uber AI in particular I touched many ML applications in the company (customer support, expected time of delivery, food and restaurant recommendation, driver dialogue systems), and I developed Ludwig to make my own life easier in jumping from one project to the next, because it allowed me to avoid reinventing the wheel (data preprocessing, a training loop, evaluation functions, etc.) every single time, but made it possible to create prototypes in minutes.

What are 3–5 of the most important things to be aware of deploying and maintaining machine learning systems at scale?

A: My experience has taught me that the model itself is just a relatively small piece inside a broader system when you productionize it, but at the same time it's both one of the most critical (if the model doesn't return satisfactory predictions, all the rest is kinda pointless), and one of the more complex to get right, because data, infrastructure, monitoring (that are very important) have more established standards and are more engineered, so there's less uncertainty on the outcome as opposed to the task of model building. That uncertainty needs to be taken into account in the ML development process.

Another important learning is that the reality of deploying an ML system and observing users behavior often breaks our assumptions, and so the process becomes iterative. For instance, live input data the system receives may end up being very different from training data, the distribution of both inputs and outputs may shift over time, and the fact that the system is being used in many cases will impact the distribution of the data that will be collected (think of a recommender system; the data collected after its first adoption will certainly be biased by the suggestions of the recommender itself). For this reason, monitoring becomes extremely important.

Finally, the data collection process is also extremely important. In my experience I worked on both projects where the training data was obtained through labeling and where data was obtained as a byproduct of a process that happened within the organization. In the former case, defining precisely the data collection process, giving exact instructions to annotators, observing their annotations and their agreement and iterating the process was much more involved than simply submitting data to be annotated and getting it back. In the latter case, deeply understanding the process that generates the data was literally the only way one could make sense of the data, and helps identifying outliers, set model expectations correctly, and understand the uncertainty in model predictions. In my experience, this degree of understanding together with the analysis of model predictions led also to improving the data collection process itself, which in turn led to less noisy data that was used to train better models, so there's a virtuous loop at play here.

What are you most excited about right now with machine learning and why?

A: There are two things that excite me the most. On one hand you have the percolation of ML in other scientific fields, like biology, chemistry, and physics, but also entirely new industries, like graphics and video games (ML for content generation, rendering, and animation, for instance). On the other hand you have what I'm actively working on (I wouldn't work on it if it didn't excite me), which is creating tools and abstractions that make it easier for people without an ML background to use ML for their purposes. The two intersect well; if more people, maybe domain experts in their fields, can access and use ML, the percolation will be faster.

What are the top 3–5 things a person reading this book can do to succeed in their career doing MLOps?

A: Learn to deal with the uncertainty associated with the ML development process, learn to work in cross-functional teams that include people with little to no ML expertise, create repeatable processes, learn to put themselves in the users' shoes, strive to avoid technical debt.

How can people get hold of you and what would you like to share that you are working on?

A: I'm not an avid social media user, but I occasionally post about what I'm working on on Twitter (@w4nderlus7) and on LinkedIn. I'm currently co-running the Stanford MLSys seminar series (*https://oreil.ly/XU1gr*) which I believe most of the readers would be interested in. I also have a personal website (*http://w4nderlu.st*) that I update with my projects, my publications, and some lectures I give. My current main interest is in building tools and abstractions to make ML more accessible to people with less or no ML expertise, so that they can leverage their domain expertise to train and use models achieve their goals.

Interview with MLOps Practitioners: Fancesca Lazzeri

What is your background, and how did you get involved with operationalizing machine learning?

A: I have a background in Economics. Before joining Microsoft, I was Research Fellow in Business Economics at Harvard University, where I was performing statistical and econometric analysis within the Technology and Operations Management Unit. At Harvard, I worked on multiple patent, publication, citations data-driven projects to investigate and measure the impact of external knowledge networks on companies' competitiveness and innovation. This experience gave me the unique opportunity to learn how to extract knowledge from big data, build predictive models from scratch, and how to code in R and Python. This was my first step into the fantastic world of machine learning!

A few years later, I started my career at Microsoft as a data scientist: in my role at Microsoft, I was helping companies transform their operations through machine learning algorithms and AI and, in particular, I was in charge of moving their models from development to a production environment in ways that were robust, fast, and repeatable.

What are 3–5 of the most important things to be aware of deploying and maintaining machine learning systems at scale?

A: Many companies see machine learning deployment as a technical practice. However, it is more of a business-driven initiative that starts within the company; in order to become an AI-driven company, it is important that the people who today successfully operate and understand the business collaborate closely with those teams that are responsible for the machine learning deployment workflow. It is very essential to maintain constant interaction to understand the model experimentation process parallel to the model deployment and consumption steps. Most organizations struggle to unlock machine learning's potential to optimize their operational processes and get data scientists, analysts, and business teams speaking the same language. Moreover, machine learning models must be trained on historical data, which demands the creation of a prediction data pipeline, an activity requiring multiple tasks including data processing, feature engineering, and tuning. Each task, down to versions of libraries and handling of missing values, must be exactly duplicated from the development to the production environment. Sometimes, differences in technology used in development and in production contribute to difficulties in deploying machine learning models. Finally, data science languages can be slow. Python is one of the most popular languages for machine learning applications, but complete production models are rarely deployed in those languages for speed reasons. Porting a Python model into a production language like C++ or Java is challenging, and often results in reduced performance of the original, trained model.

What are you most excited about right now with machine learning and why?

A: I am very excited about the extensive adoption of open source frameworks (such as Fairlearn (*https://oreil.ly/imtPL*) and InterpretML (*https://oreil.ly/1oNYI*)) to support the transparent interpretability and guarantee the fairness of machine learning algorithms. Data scientists know that accuracy is no longer the only concern when developing machine learning models; interpretability and fairness must be considered as well. In order to make sure that machine learning solutions are fair and the value of their predictions easy to understand and explain, it is essential to build open source tools that developers and data scientists can use to assess their machine learning system's fairness and mitigate any observed unfairness issues.

What are the top 3–5 things a person reading this book can do to succeed in their career doing MLOps?

A: They can:

1. Create reproducible ML pipelines.

2. Capture the governance data for the end-to-end ML lifecycle.

3. Monitor ML applications for operational and ML-related issues.

How can people get ahold of you, and what would you like to share that you are working on?

A: You can follow me on Twitter @frlazzeri (*https://oreil.ly/Knbw0*), LinkedIn (*https://oreil.ly/p6L5p*), and Medium (*https://oreil.ly/XhSd2*)). I recently wrote a book, *Machine Learning for Time Series Forecasting with Python* (Wiley, 2020), in which you can find real-world examples, resources, and concrete strategies to explore and transform data and develop usable, practical time series forecasts. At Microsoft I lead an international team (in the USA, Canada, UK, and Russia) of engineers and cloud developer advocates, managing a large portfolio of customers. My team is in charge of building technical content and intelligent automated solutions on Azure, utilizing techniques spanning from IoT, time series forecasting, computer vision, natural language processing, and open source frameworks. Currently I also teach "Introduction to AI with Python" at Columbia University. You can read more about my teaching philosophy and experience in my article, "The Importance of Teaching Machine Learning" (*https://oreil.ly/ELUNv*).

Final Recommendations to Implement MLOps

Before we wrap up, we want to walk you through some tips for implementing MLOps in your organization. First, here are a set of final, global recommendations:

- Start with small wins.

- Use the cloud, don't fight the cloud.

- Get you and your team certified on a cloud platform and an ML specialization.

- Automate from the start of a project. An excellent initial automation step is the continuous integration of your project. Another way of putting this is that "if it isn't automated, it is broken."

- Practice Kaizen, i.e., continuous improvement with your pipeline. This method improves the software quality, the data quality, the model quality, and the customer feedback.

- When dealing with large teams or big data, focus on using platform technology such as AWS SageMaker, Databricks, Amazon EMR, or Azure ML Studio. Let the platform do the heavy lifting for your team.

- Don't focus only on the complexity of techniques, i.e., deep learning versus solving the problem with any tool that works.
- Take data governance and cybersecurity seriously. One way to accomplish this is by using enterprise support for your platform and having regular audits of your architecture and practices.

Finally, there are three laws of automation to consider when thinking about MLOps:

1. Any task that talks about being automated will eventually be automated.
2. If it isn't automated, it's broken.
3. If a human is doing it, a machine eventually will do it better.

Now, let's dig into some tips for dealing with security concerns.

Data Governance and Cybersecurity

There are two seemingly conflicting problems in MLOps: increased cybersecurity concerns and lack of machine learning in production. On the one hand, too many rules, and nothing gets done. On the other hand, ransom attacks on critical infrastructure are increasing, and organizations would be wise to pay attention to how they govern their data resources.

One way to address both issues simultaneously is to have a checklist of best practices. Here is a partial list of best practices for data governance that will improve MLOps productivity and cybersecurity:

- Use PLP (Principle of Least Privilege).
- Encrypt data at rest and in transit.
- Assume systems that are not automated are insecure.
- Use cloud platforms since they have a shared security model.
- Use enterprise support and engage in quarterly architecture and security audits.
- Train staff on platforms used by getting them certified.
- Engage company in quarterly and yearly training on new technology and best practices.
- Create a healthy company culture with standards of excellence, competent employees, and principled leadership.

Next, let's summarize some MLOps Design Patterns that may be useful to you and your organization.

MLOps Design Patterns

The following examples reflect a partial list of recommended MLOps Design Patterns:

CaaS

Container as a service (CaaS) is a helpful pattern for MLOps because it allows developers to work on an ML microservice on their desktop or in a cloud editor and then shares it with other developers or the public via a `docker pull` command. Further, many cloud platforms offer high-level PaaS (platform as a service) solutions to deploy containerized projects.

MLOps Platform

All cloud providers have deeply integrated MLOps platforms. AWS has AWS SageMaker, Azure has Azure ML Studio, and Google has Vertex AI. In cases where a large team, a large project, big data, or all of the above come into play, using the MLOps platform on the cloud you are using will save you a tremendous amount of time in the building, deploying, and maintaining of your ML application.

Serverless

Serverless technology like AWS Lambda is ideal for the rapid development of ML microservices. These microservices can call into cloud AI APIs to do NLP, computer vision, or other tasks or use a pretrained model you developed yourself or one that you downloaded.

Spark-Centric

Many organizations dealing with big data already have experience using Spark. In this situation, it may make sense to use the MLOps capabilities of the managed Spark platform Databricks or managed Spark via the cloud platform, such as AWS EMR.

Kubernetes-Centric

Kubernetes is a "cloud in a box." If your organization is already using it, it may make sense to use the Kubernetes ML-focused technology like mlflow.

In addition to these recommendations, many additional resources in Appendix B discuss topics ranging from data governance to cloud certification.

Conclusion

This book originally came about from a discussion I had with Tim O'Reilly and Mike Loukides at Foo Camp around making ML go 10X faster. The consensus from the group was, yes, it can go 10X faster! Matt Ridley's book *How Innovation Works: And Why It Flourishes in Freedom* (Harper) illustrates that the nonintuitive answer is that innovation is a recombination of ideas with better execution. A current colleague and former professor, Andrew Hargadon, first introduced me to these ideas when I was an MBA student at UC Davis. In his book *How Breakthroughs Happen* (Harvard Business Review Press) Andrew mentions that it is the network effect and the recombination of ideas that matters.

For MLOps, this means that the operational excellence of existing ideas is the secret sauce. Companies that want to solve real problems in machine learning and solve these problems quickly can innovate through execution. The world needs this innovation to help us save more lives through preventive medicine like automated higher accuracy cancer screenings, self-driving cars, and clean energy systems that adapt to the environment.

Nothing should be "off the table" to increase operational excellence. If AutoML speeds up rapid prototyping, then use it. If cloud computing increases the velocity of machine learning model deployment, then implement it. As recent events have shown us, with the COVID-19 pandemic and the resulting breakthrough technology innovations like the CRISPR technology and COVID-19 vaccine, we can do incredible things with the proper sense of urgency. MLOps adds rigor to this urgency and allows us to help save the world, one ML model at a time.

Exercises

- Build a machine learning application as quickly as possible that is both continuously trained and continuously deployed.
- Deploy a machine learning model using the Kubernetes stack.
- Deploy the same machine learning model using continuous delivery with AWS, Azure, and GCP.
- Create an automated security scan of the containers for a machine learning project using a cloud native build system.
- Train a model using a cloud-based AutoML system and using a local AutoML system like Create ML or Ludwig.

Critical Thinking Discussion Questions

- How could you build a recommendation engine that didn't have as many negative externalities as current social media recommendation engines? What would you change, and how?

- What could be done to improve the accuracy and interpretability of modeling complex systems like nutrition, climate, and elections?

- How could operational excellence be the secret ingredient for a company wanting to be a machine learning–related technology leader?

- If operational excellence is a crucial consideration for MLOps, what are your organization's hiring criteria to identify the right talent?

- Explain the role of operational excellence in machine learning concerning enterprise support for cloud computing? Does it matter, and why?

Key Terms

By Noah Gift

This section contains select key terms that crop up often in teaching cloud computing, MLOps, and machine learning engineering:

Alerts
> Alerts are health metrics that have actions associated with them. An example would be an alert that sends a text message to a software engineer when a web service returns multiple error status codes.

Amazon ECR
> Amazon ECR is a container registry that stores Docker format containers.

Amazon EKS
> Amazon EKS is a managed Kubernetes service created by Amazon.

Autoscaling
> Autoscaling is the process of scaling load up or down automatically based on how many resources the nodes are using.

AWS Cloud9
> AWS Cloud9 is a cloud-based development environment running in AWS. It has special hooks for developing serverless applications.

AWS Lambda
> A serverless compute platform by AWS that has FaaS capability.

Azure Container Instances (ACI)
> Azure Container Instances is a managed service from Microsoft that allows you to run container images without managing servers to host them.

Azure Kubernetes Service (AKS)
Azure Kubernetes Service is a managed Kubernetes service created by Microsoft.

`black`
The `black` tool formats the text of Python source code automatically.

Build server
A build server is an application that works in both the testing and deployment of software. Popular build servers can be both SaaS or open source. Here are a few popular options:

- Jenkins (*https://jenkins.io*) is an open source build server that can run anywhere including AWS, GCP, Azure, or a docker container or on your laptop.
- CircleCI (*https://circleci.com*) is a SaaS build service that integrates with a popular Git hosting provider like GitHub.

CircleCI
A popular SaaS (software as a service) build system used in DevOps workflows.

Cloud native applications
Cloud native applications are services that utilize the unique capabilities of the cloud, like serverless.

Container
A container is a set of processes that are isolated from the rest of the operating system. They are often megabytes in size.

Continuous delivery
Continuous delivery is the process of delivering tested software automatically to any environment.

Continuous integration
Continuous integration is the process of automatically testing software upon check-in to the source control system.

Data engineering
Data engineering is the process of automating the flow of data.

Disaster recovery
Disaster recovery is the process of designing a software system to recover despite a disaster. This process could include archiving data to another location.

Docker format container
There are several formats for containers. An emerging form is Docker, which involves the definition of a *Dockerfile*.

Docker

Docker is a company that creates container technology, including an execution engine, collaboration platform via DockerHub, and a container format called *Dockerfile*.

FaaS (function as a service)

A type of cloud computing that facilitates functions that respond to events.

Google GKE

Google GKE is a managed Kubernetes service created by Google.

IPython

The ipython interpreter is an interactive terminal for Python. It is the core of the Jupyter notebook.

JSON

JSON stands for JavaScript Object Notation, and it is a lightweight, human-readable data format used heavily in web services.

Kubernetes clusters

A Kubernetes cluster is a deployment of Kubernetes that contains an entire ecosystem of Kubernetes components, including nodes, pods, the API, and containers.

Kubernetes containers

A Kubernetes container is a Docker image that deploys into a Kubernetes cluster.

Kubernetes pods

A Kubernetes pod is a group of one or more containers.

Kubernetes

Kubernetes is an open source system for automating the operations of containerized applications. Google created it and open-sourced in 2014.

Load testing

Load testing is the process of verifying the scale characteristics of a software system.

Locust

Locust is a load-testing framework that accepts Python-formatted load test scenarios.

Logging

Logging is a process of creating messages about the running state of a software application.

Makefile

A `Makefile` is a file that contains a set of directives used to build software. Most Unix and Linux operating systems have built-in support for this file format.

Metrics

Metrics are the creation of KPIs (Key Performance Indicators) for a software application. An example of a parameter is the percentage of CPU used by a server.

Microservice

A microservice is a lightweight, loosely coupled service. It can be as small as a function.

Migrate

Migrate is the ability to move an application from one environment to another.

Moore's Law

The perception that for some time, the number of transistors on a microchip doubles every two years.

Operationalization

The process of making an application ready for production deployment. These actions could include monitoring, load testing, and setting up alerts.

pip

The `pip` tool installs Python packages.

Ports

A port is a network communication endpoint. An example of a port is a web service running on port 80 via the protocol HTTP.

Prometheus

Prometheus is an open source monitoring system with an efficient time-series database.

pylint

The `pylint` tool checks the Python source code for syntax errors.

PyPI

The Python Package Index, where published packages are available to install with tools like `pip`.

pytest

The `pytest` tool is a framework for running tests on Python source code.

Python virtual environment

A Python virtual environment is created by isolating a Python interpreter to a directory and installing packages in that directory. The Python interpreter can perform this action via `python -m venv yournewenv`.

Serverless

Serverless is a technique of building applications based on functions and events.

SQS queue

A distributed messaging queue built by Amazon with near-infinite reads and writes.

Swagger

A swagger tool is an open source framework that simplifies the creation of API documentation.

Virtual machine

A virtual machine is the emulation of a physical operating system. It can be gigabytes in size.

YAML

YAML is a human-readable serialization format often used in configuration systems. It is easily portable to JSON format.

Technology Certifications

By Noah Gift

The term "MLOps" directly implies a firm connection with IT, Operations, and other traditional technology disciplines via the phrase "Ops." Technology certification has historically played an essential role in validating the skills of industry professionals. The salary for certified professionals is impressive. According to Zip Recruiter (*https://oreil.ly/OuHfS*), in February 2021, an AWS Solutions Architect's average wage was $155k.

One way to think about this topic is to consider the idea of a "Triple Threat." In basketball this means a player that is so well-rounded they have achieved 10+ rebounds, 10+ assists, and 10+ points in a basketball game. You can apply this same approach to an MLOps career. Have a portfolio of examples of your work, get certified, and have either work experience or a relevant degree.

AWS Certifications

Let's cover some AWS certification options.

AWS Cloud Practitioner and AWS Solutions Architect

I recommend certifications for MLOps specialists on the AWS Cloud. The AWS Cloud Practitioner is a more gentle introduction to the AWS certification world, similar to the AWS Solutions Architect certification. I have often taught this certification to students of many different types: Data Science Master's students, nontechnical business professionals, and current IT professionals. Here are some of the more common questions and the answers related to both certifications, with a particular eye toward a person with a machine learning background aiming to pass the exam. Even if you don't get the AWS Certification, these questions are critical for the MLOps practitioner and are worth testing your knowledge level.

Q: I am having trouble connecting RDS (https://oreil.ly/LbcbJ) and sharing connections with a group of people. Is there a more straightforward method?

> A: You may find it more straightforward to use AWS Cloud9 as a development environment to connect to RDS. You can see a walkthrough on Amazon (*https://oreil.ly/lzO0P*).

Q: The cloud services model is confusing. What is PaaS, and how is it different from other models?

> A: One way to think about cloud offerings is to compare them to the food industry. You can purchase food in bulk at a store like Costco (*https://costco.com*). It has a considerable scale, and it can pass the purchase price discounts down to the customer. As a customer, though, you may also need to take that food back to your home, prepare it, and cook it. This situation is similar to IaaS.

> Now let's look at a service like Grubhub (*https://grubhub.com*) or Uber Eats (*https://oreil.ly/zYbpE*). Not only do you not have to drive to the store to pick up the food, but it has been prepared, cooked, and delivered for you. This situation is similar to PaaS. All you have to do is eat the food.

> If you look at PaaS (platform as a service), what it means is as the developer, you can focus on the business logic. As a result, many of the complexities of software engineering go away. An excellent example of two early PaaS services is Heroku (*https://heroku.com*) and Google App Engine (*https://oreil.ly/1MGBA*). A perfect example of a PaaS on AWS is AWS SageMaker (*https://oreil.ly/lCsUY*). It solves many of the infrastructure issues involved with creating and deploying machine learning, including distributed training and serving predictions.

Q: What is the exact definition of an edge location? It isn't apparent.

> A: An AWS edge location (*https://oreil.ly/IjPBi*) is a physical location in the world where a server lives. Edge locations are different from data centers because they serve a more narrow purpose. The closer a user of the content is to the server's physical location, the lower the request's latency. This situation is critical in content delivery like streaming videos and music and also for playing games. The most commonly referred to edge service on AWS is CloudFront. CloudFront is a CDN (Content Delivery Network). Cached or copies of the same movie file live in these locations worldwide via the CDN. This situation allows users to all have a great experience streaming this content.

> Other services that use edge locations include Amazon Route 53 (*https://oreil.ly/0gjiE*), AWS Shield (*https://oreil.ly/FLjh4*), AWS Web Application Firewall (*https://oreil.ly/pcqz9*), and Lambda@Edge (*https://oreil.ly/XGKp9*).

Q: What if one of the data centers in an availability zone (AZ) is affected by fire? How are data centers related to each other in terms of a natural or human-made disaster? How should a system be architected for data replication?

A: As part of the shared security model (*https://oreil.ly/g6Lyp*), Amazon is responsible for the cloud, and the customer is responsible for what is in the cloud. This situation means that data is safe against catastrophic unplanned failures like fires. Additionally, if there is an outage, the data may be unavailable during the outage in that region but restores eventually.

As an architect, it is the customer's responsibility to take advantage of multi-AZ architectures. An excellent example of this is Amazon RDS multi-AZ configuration (*https://oreil.ly/uM7sb*). If an outage occurs in one region, the secondary failover database will already have the data replicated and handle the request.

Q: What is HA?

A: An HA (Highly Available) service builds with availability in mind. This situation means that failure is an expectation, and the design supports redundancy of data and services. An excellent example of an HA service is Amazon RDS (*https://oreil.ly/UYOvl*). In addition, the RDS Multi-AZ design supports minimal interruption in service by allowing multiple versions of the database replication across availability zones.

Q: How do you decide between spot and on-demand?

A: Both spot and on-demand instances are billed a fixed amount for the first minute and then billed by the second. Spot instances are the most cost-effective because they can provide up to 90% savings. Use Spot instances (*https://oreil.ly/OmTPP*) when it doesn't matter when a task runs or is interrupted. In practice, this creates a critical use case for a spot instance. Here are some examples:

- Experimenting with an AWS service
- Training deep learning or machine learning jobs
- Scaling out a web service or other service in combination with on-demand instances

On-demand instances work when a workload runs in a steady state. So, for example, a web service in production wouldn't want only to use spot instances. Instead, it could start with on-demand cases, and when the usage of the service calculates (i.e., 2 c4.large instances), then reserved instances (*https://oreil.ly/tkDVZ*) should be bought.

Q: How does spot hibernation work?

A: There are a few reasons for spot instance interruptions (*https://oreil.ly/w1UJD*), including price (bid higher than maximum price), capacity (there are not enough spot instances unused), and constraints (i.e., the Availability Zone target size is too large). To hibernate, it must have an EBS root volume.

Q: What is a tag for in EC2?

    A: In Figure B-1, an EC2 instance has a tag applied to it. This tag can group types of instances into a logical group like "web servers."

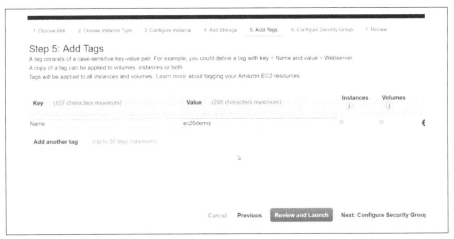

Figure B-1. EC2 tags

The main reason to use a tag for an EC2 resource is to attach metadata to a group of machines. Here is one scenario. Let's say 25 EC2 instances are running a shopping website, and they have no tags. Later a user spins up another 25 EC2 instances to temporarily do a task like training a machine learning model. It may be challenging in the console to determine which machines are temporary (and can be deleted) and the production machines.

Instead of guessing about machines' roles, it is best to assign tags to allow a user to identify a role quickly. This role could be: Key="role", Value="ml" or it could be Key="role", Value="web". In the EC2 console, a user can query by tag. This process then allows for bulk operations like terminating instances. Tags can also play an important role in analyzing cost. If machine roles contain tags, then cost reports could determine if certain machine types are too expensive or using too many resources. You can read the official tag documentation on Amazon (*https:// oreil.ly/cDxyb*).

Q: What is PuTTY?

    A: In Figure B-2, the PuTTY SSH tool allows for remote console access from Windows to a Linux virtual machine.

Figure B-2. PuTTY

PuTTY is a free SSH client used on the Windows operating system. MacOS and Linux have built-in support for SSH. What is SSH? It is a cryptographic network protocol for performing network operations. SSH is for logging in to a remote machine and managing the device via terminal commands.

You can read the official PuTTY documentation here (*https://oreil.ly/zw3fx*).

Q: How is Lightsail different from EC2 or other services?
A: Lightsail is a PaaS or platform as a service. This platform means that a developer solely needs to worry about configuring and developing the WordPress application. EC2 is lower level and is called IaaS (infrastructure as a service). There is a spectrum with cloud computing where lower-level services are provided just like bulk ingredients at Costco. Those bulk ingredients create meals, but it requires skill. Likewise, a person can order meals to get delivered to their house. These meals are more expensive but need little expertise. PaaS is similar; the user pays more for higher-level services.

Other PaaS solutions (outside of AWS) are Heroku (*https://heroku.com*) and Google App Engine (*https://oreil.ly/4v9Qi*). You can read more about cloud services types in the "Cloud Computing" chapter (*https://oreil.ly/F3g78*) of *Python for DevOps* (O'Reilly).

Q: I read about a use case for the AMI that has the following description: "use it to copy that to a fleet of machines (deep learning cluster)." What does a fleet of machine mean?
A: A fleet works the same way a rental car company works. When you ask for a car reservation, they will ask you to pick a group: compact, sedan, luxury, or truck. There is no guarantee of a specific model, only of a particular group. Likewise, because spot instances are an open market, it is possible that a particular machine, say C3.8XLarge is not available, but a similar combination is. You can

request a group of resources identical in CPU, memory, and network capabilities by selecting a fleet. You can read more about EC2 Fleet on Amazon's blog (*https://oreil.ly/EDaGq*).

Q: *What does spikey mean for the sizing of on-demand instances?*

A: A "spikey" workload could be a website that suddenly gets 10X the traffic. Let's say this website sells products. It is usually a flat amount of traffic during the year, but around December, the traffic spikes to 10X the usual traffic. This scenario would be a fair use case for "on-demand" instances to scale out to meet this requirement. The expected traffic pattern should use reserved instances, but for the spike, this should use on-demand. You can read more about spikey traffic (*https://oreil.ly/7JhqV*) and reserved instances on Amazon's blog (*https://oreil.ly/KHKy6*).

Q: *What does the "SUBSECOND" mean for one of AWS Lambda's advantages?*

A: This means that you can design an efficient service and only incur charges for the duration of your request at 100ms intervals. This situation is different from an EC2 instance where you are billed for a continually running instance every second. With a Lambda function, you can design an event-based workflow where a lambda runs only in response to events. A good analogy would be a traditional light that turns off and on. It is easy to use more electricity because the light has a manual switch. A more efficient approach is motion-detection lighting. The lighting will turn off and on according to motion. This approach is similar to AWS Lambda; in response to events, it turns on, performs a task, and then exits. You can read more about Lambda in Amazon's documentation (*https://oreil.ly/y3JoQ*). You also can build a Python AWS Lambda project on GitHub (*https://oreil.ly/ZNmuk*).

Q: *For AWS S3, there are several storage classes. Does the IA (Infrequent Access) tier of storage include both Standard IA and one-zone IA, or are there more types? I see only standard and one-zone in the section of INFREQUENT ACCESS on the AWS website (https://oreil.ly/plbG8).*

A: There are two types of IA (Infrequent Access). Standard IA, which store in three AZ (Availability Zones) and One Zone. A key difference in the One Zone is availability. It has 99.5% availability, less available than both three-zone IA and Standard. The lower cost reflects this diminished availability.

Q: *How does Elastic File System (EFS) work?*

A: EFS conceptually works similar to Google Drive or Dropbox. You can create a Dropbox account and share data with multiple computers or friends. EFS works in a very similar way. The same filesystem is available to machines that mount it. This process is very different than EBS (Elastic Block Storage), which belongs to one instance at a time.

Q: For ELB's use case, I don't understand these two use cases: 1) what's "the single point of access" mean? Is it saying, if you can control your traffic by entering through one port or server, then it's more secure? 2) what does "decoupling application environment" mean?

A: Let's look at a website as an example. The website will be running on port 443, which is the port for HTTPS traffic. This site could be *https://example.com*. The ELB is the only resource exposed to the outside world. When a web browser connects to *https://example.com*, it communicates only to the ELB. At the same time, the ELB will ask the web servers behind it for the information. It then sends that information back to the web browser.

What is an analogy in the real world? It would be like a bank teller in a drive-through. You drive up to the window but connect only to the bank teller. Inside the bank, many people are working, yet you are interacting with only one person. You can read blog posts about ELB on the AWS blog (*https://oreil.ly/nvYV4*).

Q: Why is the use case for ELB the same as the Classic Load Balancer?

A: They share the same traits: access through a single point of entry, decoupled application environment; they provide high availability and fault tolerance, and increase elasticity and scalability.

Elastic Load Balancing refers to a category of load balancers. There is Application Load Balancer, Network Load Balancer, and Classic Load Balancer. At a high level, the Classic Load Balancer is an older load balancer that has fewer features than the Application Load Balancer. It works in situations where older EC2 instances have been in service.

These are called EC2 classic instances. In a new scenario, an Application Load Balancer would be ideal for something like an HTTP service. You can read blog posts about ELB feature comparisons in Amazon's documentation (*https://oreil.ly/ASjxU*).

AWS Certified Machine Learning - Specialty

Business schools and data science schools have completely embraced teaching certifications. At UC Davis, I teach students traditional for-credit material, like machine learning and cloud certifications (*https://oreil.ly/aHoSB*), including both AWS Cloud Practitioner and AWS Certified Machine Learning - Specialty. With AWS, I work closely with many parts of its organization, including AWS Educate, AWS Academy, and AWS ML Hero (*https://oreil.ly/wACTB*).

As you might guess, yes, I recommend getting the AWS Machine Learning certification. Knowing many of the people involved in creating the AWS ML certification, and perhaps some influence on its creation, what I like about it is the heavy focus on MLOps. So let's dive into it in more detail.

The recommended candidate (*https://oreil.ly/B0Np4*) has knowledge and experience of at least 1–2 years developing, architecting, or running ML/deep learning workloads. In practice, this means the ability to express the intuition behind basic ML algorithms, perform basic hyperparameter optimization, experience with ML and deep learning frameworks, follow model-training best practices, and follow deployment and operational best practices. In a nutshell, reading this book is an excellent preparation step for getting certified!

The exam structure divides into several domains: Data Engineering, Exploratory Data Analysis, Modeling, and Machine Learning Implementation and Operations. The last section of the exam, in particular, is on what is essentially MLOps. So let's dive into these sections and see how they apply to concepts covered in this book.

Data Engineering

A central component of data engineering, analytics, and machine learning on AWS is the data lake, which also happens to be Amazon S3. Why use a data lake (Figure B-3)? The core reasons are as follows. First, it provides the ability to handle both structured and unstructured data. A data lake also allows both Analytics and ML workloads. Third, you can work on the data without moving it, which can be critical with big data. And finally, its low cost.

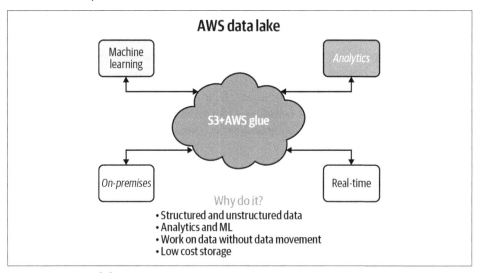

Figure B-3. Data lake

Another important topic on AWS Data Engineering is batch versus streaming data. Let's define streaming data first. Streaming data is typically small data sent from many sources. Examples include log-files, metrics, and time-series data like stock trading information. The leading service on AWS that handles streaming is Kinesis. Here are a few ideal scenarios: time-series analytics problems, real-time dashboards, and real-time metrics.

Batch versus streaming has significant effects on ML pipeline development. There is more control of model training in batch since you can decide when to retrain the ML model. Continuously retraining a model could provide better prediction results but at added complexity. For example, is A/B testing used to test for the accuracy of the new model? Model A/B testing is available in SageMaker endpoints, so this will need to factor into the architecture.

For batch processing, several tools can function as batch processing mechanisms. These include Amazon EMR/Spark, AWS Glue, AWS Athena, AWS SageMaker, and the aptly named AWS Batch service (*https://oreil.ly/tbu9g*). In particular, for machine learning, AWS Batch solves a unique problem. For example, imagine you wanted to scale thousands of simultaneous and individual k-means clustering jobs. One way to do it would be with AWS Batch. Additionally, you can provide a simple interface to the batch processing system by writing a Python command line tool. Here is a snippet of code that shows what that could look like in practice:

```
@cli.group()
def run():
    """AWS Batch CLI"""

@run.command("submit")
@click.option("--queue", default="queue", help="Batch Queue")
@click.option("--jobname", default="1", help="Name of Job")
@click.option("--jobdef", default="test", help="Job Definition")
@click.option("--cmd", default=["whoami"], help="Container Override Commands")
def submit(queue, jobname, jobdef, cmd):
    """Submit a job to AWS Batch SErvice"""

    result = submit_job(
        job_name=jobname,
        job_queue=queue,
        job_definition=jobdef,
        command=cmd
    )
    click.echo(f"CLI:  Run Job Called {jobname}")
    return result
```

Another critical aspect of handling data engineering is using AWS Lambda to process events. It is important to note that AWS Lambda is a glue that integrates deeply into most AWS services. Therefore, doing AWS-based data engineering most likely will encounter AWS Lambda at some point.

The CTO of AWS believes that a "one size database doesn't fit anyone" (*https://oreil.ly/5LEz0*). What he means by this is clearly described in Figure B-4.

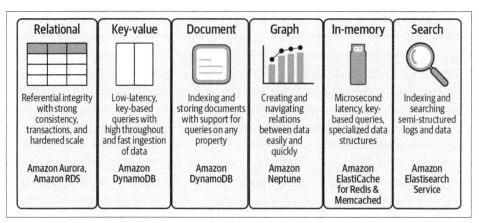

Relational	Key-value	Document	Graph	In-memory	Search
Referential integrity with strong consistency, transactions, and hardened scale	Low-latency, key-based queries with high throughout and fast ingestion of data	Indexing and storing documents with support for queries on any property	Creating and navigating relations between data easily and quickly	Microsecond latency, key-based queries, specialized data structures	Indexing and searching semi-structured logs and data
Amazon Aurora, Amazon RDS	Amazon DynamoDB	Amazon DynamoDB	Amazon Neptune	Amazon ElastiCache for Redis & Memcached	Amazon Elastisearch Service

Figure B-4. One size database

Another way of saying this is to use the best tool for the job. It could be a relational database; in others, it is a key/value database. The following example shows how simple a DynamoDB-based API in Python works. Most of the code is logging.

```python
def query_police_department_record_by_guid(guid):
    """Gets one record in the PD table by guid

    In [5]: rec = query_police_department_record_by_guid(
        "7e607b82-9e18-49dc-a9d7-e9628a9147ad"
        )

    In [7]: rec
    Out[7]:
    {'PoliceDepartmentName': 'Hollister',
     'UpdateTime': 'Fri Mar  2 12:43:43 2018',
     'guid': '7e607b82-9e18-49dc-a9d7-e9628a9147ad'}
    """

    db = dynamodb_resource()
    extra_msg = {"region_name": REGION, "aws_service": "dynamodb",
        "police_department_table":POLICE_DEPARTMENTS_TABLE,
        "guid":guid}
    log.info(f"Get PD record by GUID", extra=extra_msg)
    pd_table = db.Table(POLICE_DEPARTMENTS_TABLE)
    response = pd_table.get_item(
        Key={
            'guid': guid
            }
    )
    return response['Item']
```

Three final items to discuss in data engineering are ETL, Data Security, and Data Backup and Recovery. With ETL, the essential services include AWS Glue, Athena, and AWS DataBrew. AWS DataBrew is the newer service, and it solves a necessary step in building production machine learning models, namely automating the messy steps in cleaning data. For example, in Figure B-5, a dataset, baby names, is profiled without writing a single line of code.

Figure B-5. DataBrew

Later, this same dataset could be a vital part of an MLOps project. One helpful feature is the ability to track the dataset's lineage, where it came from, and what actions involve the dataset. This functionality is available via the "Data lineage" tab (see Figure B-6).

Data governance is a concise way of addressing concerns due to data security and data backup and recovery. AWS, through the KMS (Key Management Service), allows for an integrated encryption strategy. This step is critical because it provides for the implementation of both encryptions at rest and in transit, as well as PLP (Principle of Least Privilege).

Figure B-6. DataBrew lineage

Another aspect of data security is the ability to log and audit access to data. Regular audit of data access is one way to identify risks and mitigate them. For example, you may flag a user regularly looking at an AWS Bucket that has nothing to do with their job and then realize this poses a significant security hole you need to close.

Figure B-7. AWS Cloud-Trail

Finally, data backup and recovery is perhaps one of the most important aspects of data governance. Most AWS services have snapshot capabilities, including RDS, S3, and DynamoDB. Designing a helpful backup, recovery, and lifecyle for data that archives to Amazon Glacier are essential for best practices compliance in data engineering.

Exploratory Data Analysis (EDA)

Before you can do machine learning, first, the data needs exploration. On AWS, several tools can help. These include the DataBrew example from earlier, as well as AWS QuickSight. Let's take a look at what you can accomplish with AWS QuickSight in Figure B-8.

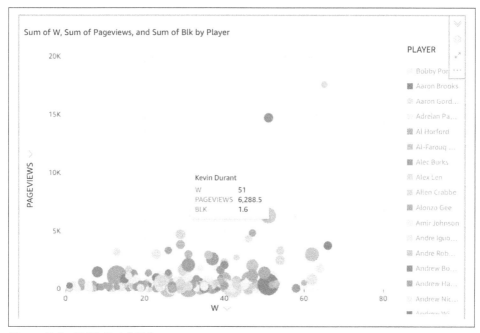

Figure B-8. AWS QuickSight

Notice how this no-code/low-code approach exposes a power-law relationship between wins and popularity on social media, i.e., pageviews from Wikipedia. Fans may gravitate most closely with "winners," take notice of them, and want to read more information about these players. This initial EDA step could immediately lead toward developing a machine learning model that uses fan behavior to predict which teams are more likely to win the NBA season.

Replicating this chart yourself is straightforward: download the CSV file (*https://oreil.ly/czUpe*), tell QuickSight to perform a new analysis, make a new dataset using the CSV file, and then select "create an analysis."

It is essential to understand the role of EDA in MLOps. EDA helps detect outliers, find hidden patterns (via clustering), see data distributions, and create features.

When using clustering, it is essential to remember that data needs to be scaled. Scaling data normalizes the magnitude. For example, if two friends ran "50," importance is vital to consider. One friend could have run 50 miles, and another could have run 50 feet. They are immensely different things. Without scaling, the results of machine learning distort from the magnitude of one variable or column. The following example shows how scaling looks in practice:

```
from sklearn.preprocessing import StandardScaler
from sklearn.preprocessing import MinMaxScaler

scaler = StandardScaler()

print(scaler.fit(numerical_StandardScaler(copy=True,
    with_mean=True, with_std=True)

# output
# [[ 2.15710914 0.13485945 1.6406603 -0.46346815]
```

Another concept in EDA is the idea of preprocessing data. Preprocessing is a broad term that can apply to more than one scenario. For example, machine learning requires data to be numerical, so one form of preprocessing is to encode categorical variables to numerical format.

Encoding categorical data is an essential part of machine learning. There are many different types of categorical variables.

- Categorical (Discreet) Variables

    — Finite set of values: {green, red, blue} or {false, true}
- Categorical Types:

    — Ordinal (ordered): {Large, Medium, Small}
    — Nominal (unordered): {green, red, blue}
- Represented as text

Another form of preprocessing is the creation of new features. Let's take this example of NBA players' ages. A plot shows there is a normal distribution of age with the median around 25 years old (Figure B-9):

```
import pandas as pd
import seaborn as sns
import matplotlib.pyplot as plt

df = pd.read_csv(
    r"https://raw.githubusercontent.com/noahgift/socialpowernba" \
    r"/master/data/nba_2017_players_with_salary_wiki_twitter.csv")
```

```
sns.distplot(df.AGE)
plt.legend()
plt.title("NBA Players Ages")
```

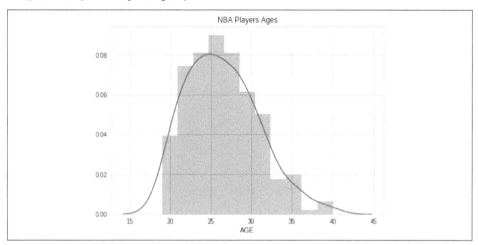

Figure B-9. NBA Players Age

We can take this knowledge to create a new feature. The feature can convert age into several categories: Rookie, Prime, Post Prime, and Pre-Retirement. These categories may lead to future insights:

```
def age_brackets (age):
    if age >17 and age <25:
        return 'Rookie'
    if age >25 and age <30:
        return 'Prime'
    if age >30 and age <35:
        return 'Post Prime'
    if age >35 and age <45:
        return 'Pre-Retirement'
```

We can then use these new categories to group the data and figure out each bracket's median salary:

```
df["age_category"] = df["AGE"].apply(age_brackets)
df.groupby("age_category")["SALARY_MILLIONS"].media
```

Notice, there are dramatic differences in the median salary. When players start, they get paid the least, but their salary roughly triples in their prime. Once they retire, there is a dramatic shift as their pay is half what they were compensated in their peak:

```
age_category
Post-Prime 8.550
Pre-Retirement   5.500
Prime            9.515
```

```
Rookie          2.940
Name: SALARY_MILLIONS, dtype: float64
```

Machine Learning Implementation and Operations (MLOps)

Let's discuss some of the critical components of MLOps in the concept of the AWS ML Certification exam. The following key concepts are essential to consider when building models:

- Monitoring
- Security
- Retraining Models
- A/B Testing
- TCO (Total Cost of Ownership)

What about MLOps itself? The following are critical to consider:

- Are you using a simple enough model?
- Are you using the data lake or wired directly into production SQL DB?
- Do you have alerts set up for prediction threshold failures?
- Do you have development, stage, and production environments?

Finally, two topics are worth discussing: troubleshooting production deployment and efficiency of ML systems. For a production deployment, these concepts include using CloudWatch, searching CloudWatch logs, alerting on critical events, using auto-scale capabilities, and using enterprise support.

For ML systems' cost and efficiency, both on the exam and in the real world, it is essential to understand the following key concepts:

- Spot Instances (show spot code)
- Proper use of CPU versus GPU resources
- Scaling up and scaling down
- Time to market
- AI API versus "Do it Yourself"

Other Cloud Certifications

In addition to AWS, Azure and GCP have notable certifications.

Azure Data Scientist and AI Engineer

Azure has a few certifications (*https://oreil.ly/fLHCh*) that are worth looking at, including the Azure Associate Data Scientist (*https://oreil.ly/SASq0*) and Azure AI Engineer Associate (*https://oreil.ly/T4R8g*). These certifications are broken down into three levels (in order of expertise): fundamentals, associate, and expert. In addition, there are several *learning paths* related to Azure's AI platform that are closely related to MLOps:

- The get-started guide (*https://oreil.ly/dRoNa*)
- Create machine learning models (*https://oreil.ly/wwHTK*)
- Create no-code predictive (*https://oreil.ly/YvywB*) models with Azure Machine Learning
- Build AI solutions with Azure Machine Learning (*https://oreil.ly/xOocn*)

A good starting point is to go through the training guide (*https://oreil.ly/Tpoyk*), which has a compelling list of journeys (for example, Data and AI professionals) and explicit certifications like Azure AI Fundamentals (*https://oreil.ly/atHVw*). These *journeys* allow you to decide the best strategy to pursue the objective that works best.

Additionally, there are free (or mostly free) resources to help you get started on Azure if you are student (*https://oreil.ly/0M5le*) or a faculty member (*https://oreil.ly/9Ca0i*). The offerings tend to change with time, but you can sign up without a credit card and get started right away as of this writing. If you are an educator, there are additional offers and resources (*https://oreil.ly/cEh9m*) available to you that can also be helpful.

GCP

A few notable certifications for MLOps practitioners include the Professional Machine Learning Engineer (*https://oreil.ly/zJ62s*) and Professional Cloud Architect (*https://oreil.ly/wuGi6*). Finally, a very specific MLOps-related certification is the TensorFlow Developer Certificate (*https://oreil.ly/lAtEG*). It allows you to demonstrate your proficiency in using TensorFlow to solve deep learning and ML problems.

SQL-Related Certifications

Minimal knowledge of SQL is necessary to be successful with MLOps. Later though, it is recommended to go deeper on SQL and master it both theoretically and in an applied fashion. Here some recommended resources:

- Databricks Certified Associate Developer for Apache Spark 3.0 (*https://oreil.ly/qI1k7*)
  - Study Material: Databricks website, and O'Reilly Learning Platform
    - O'Reilly Learning Platform: Learning Spark (*https://oreil.ly/MYX1d*)
    - O'Reilly Learning Platform: Spark: The Definitive Guide (*https://oreil.ly/48PNO*)
- Microsoft Certified: Azure Data Fundamentals (*https://oreil.ly/F8SgJ*)
  - Study Material: Coursera, Microsoft Learn and O'Reilly Learning Platform
    - Coursera Course Microsoft Azure DP-900 Data Fundamentals Exam Prep (*https://oreil.ly/WlLuC*)
    - O'Reilly Learning Platform: Exam Ref DP-900 (*https://oreil.ly/vivnp*)
- Oracle Database SQL Certified Associate Certification (*https://oreil.ly/bV6l5*)
  - Study Material: O'Reilly Learning Platform and Oracle
    - O'Reilly Learning Platform: OCA Oracle Database SQL Exam Guide (*https://oreil.ly/HStDe*)
    - Oracle: Oracle Database SQL Certified Associate Certification (*https://oreil.ly/Pfpgh*)
- Google Data Analytics Professional (*https://oreil.ly/YeGPd*)
  - Study Material: Coursera and O'Reilly Learning Platform
    - O'Reilly Learning Platform: Data Governance: The Definitive Guide (*https://oreil.ly/9FLfc*)
    - O'Reilly Learning Platform: Data Science on the Google Cloud Platform (*https://oreil.ly/0qnAW*)
    - O'Reilly Learning Platform: Google BigQuery: The Definitive Guide (*https://oreil.ly/hr9jL*)
    - Coursera: Google Data Analytics Professional (*https://oreil.ly/AtOBK*)

You can find additional references on Coursera (*https://oreil.ly/BZF5P*).

Remote Work

By Noah Gift

In the post COVID-19 world, having a stable home office where you can get work done is critical. Another factor is that remote-first optimizes outcomes. A significant issue with in-person environments is the "appearance" of progress versus actual progress. Getting dragged into meetings for hours that have no result is a good example. Having the "sales" team disrupt the developers writing code in an open office plan is another. When the focus is strictly on outcomes, then remote-first starts to make a lot of sense.

For the last several years, I have been continuously "hacking" my home office to accommodate teaching worldwide and at major top universities, as well as doing remote software engineering and consulting. You can see my setup in Figure C-1. I want to walk you through how to set up your own work space so that you can be productive.

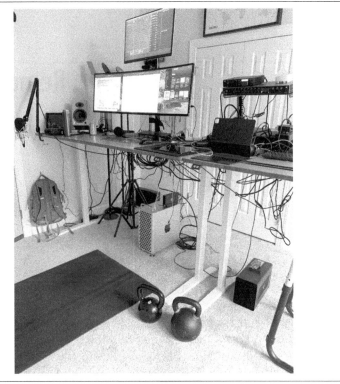

Figure C-1. Working from home

Equipment for Working Remotely

Network

Here is a brief, nonexhaustive list of things to consider if you work remotely. A reliable home network is probably the most critical item on any remote work checklist. Ideally, you can get a low-cost fiber connection for under 100 dollars. Fiber is ideal because you get the same speed both down and up. Note that not only is 1GB fiber standard across many parts of America, 2GB fiber is also becoming widely available.

There are few necessary details to pay attention to in setting up your home network. Let's address these details next.

Physical home network

It is best to plug your workstation into the home fiber or cable network via Ethernet. This step eliminates a whole series of problems that can interfere with remote work, namely wireless issues. An excellent way to accomplish this is to buy an inexpensive network switch that can do 2.5 GB or higher and connect it with Cat6 network cables (which offer speeds up to 10 Gbps). Then if you have a 2GB fiber connection, you can directly take advantage of the full speed.

In addition to the wired network, a mesh network for wireless can pay huge dividends. A recommended wireless setup would be to use a mesh WiFi 6 router. These allow you to blanket your home, even covering areas over 5,000 square feet with wireless speeds that can exceed 1 Gbps. Modern mesh networks also allow for hundreds of simultaneous connections, which should be more than enough for a home network.

Power management and home networking

As your home becomes an actual permanent office, there are two essential things to consider: cost and reliability. For example, if you experience frequent power outages, you could lose significant business income. Likewise, your power bills could increase substantially.

You can help save the environment, lower your home utility costs, and tackle business continuity during power outages. With a solar home setup, you can do the following things. First, use UPS (Uninterruptable Power Supply) for storms and power glitches and plug your important home office and home network equipment into it.

Finally, a Tesla Powerwall battery, or similar batteries, can provide days of backup power as it recharges from solar. This type of setup allows you to work despite any big storms. To further sweeten the deal, there are significant tax savings for a solar design.

Home Work Area

A standing desk, a widescreen monitor, a good microphone, and a good camera go a long way. The general idea is to buy equipment that leads to a more productive, and hopefully, shorter, day. An important thing to consider is to buy the best tools you can afford since they enable you to make money and be productive.

Health and work area

Can you incorporate a standing desk to decrease lower back injuries as well as promote more physical activity? What about doing 100 kettlebell swings via five sets of 20 each day? Can you schedule a daily walk right when your brain starts to feel overloaded? These things seem minor, but small things make for significant changes in enhancing your health, productivity, and happiness.

Finally, can you eliminate most corporate junk food habits and replace them with intermittent fasting coupled with healthy food? Read Appendix F on intermittent fasting to learn about my journey and research into it.

Home workspace virtual studio setup

Having a background that appears behind a camera can add a tremendous level of professionalism. This setup means having great lighting, some "staging," and other items that add to the background. Note that having voice automation could be a huge plus in these setups as the large lights are not needed until you are on camera.

In Figure C-2 my background is setup to look appealing for video conference calls . This is an often forgotten aspect of remote work.

Figure C-2. Studio background

Location, Location, Location

Can you move to a low-cost region where there is access to nature and good schools? In the post-pandemic world, we can expect that a new reality may allow data science–thinking remote workers to optimize health, quality of life, and cost. One driving factor is the cost of homeownership. In certain regions of the United States it doesn't make sense to build a workforce, like the Bay Area. The JCHS (Joint Center for Housing Studies) of Harvard University has many interactive data visualizations that explains this (*https://oreil.ly/a3bK4*). Are you working to live or living to work?

When you optimize your life around work-life balance, family, and health, you may find that an expensive mortgage may be counterproductive to your goals. Working remotely allows you to be thoughtful about your most significant expense: where you live. A good website that helps you decide where to live is Numbeo (*https://oreil.ly/ XCZ3A*); you can factor in weather, cost of living, crime, education, and other factors. In addition, there are many incredible places to live outside traditional tech hubs like New York and San Francisco.

Think Like a VC for Your Career

By Noah Gift

A critical consideration in building a career in machine learning is to think like a VC (venture capitalist). What does a VC do differently than an employee? One thing they do is design for failure by investing in a series of companies. So why not do the same thing for your career? Suppose you think about a multi-company strategy from the beginning. In that case, you can always focus on the long-term process of getting more skills, building side projects and portfolios of work, as well as income outside of just your job.

Further, an understanding of revenue and expenses allows you to build autonomy—autonomy to, let's say, drop what you are doing for the summer and dive deep into the next big MLOps technology. Let's dive into how to think about revenue and expenses.

Pear Revenue Strategy

We live in a new era, where it is possible to start a business with a laptop and an internet connection. As a long-time consultant and entrepreneur, I have developed a framework that works for me. When evaluating who to work with and what project to work on, I think of PPEAR or "pear":

- *P (Passive)*
- *P (Positive)*
- *E (Exponential)*
- *A (Autonomy)*
- *R (Rule of 25%)*

Here is how you can use this framework "side gigs."

Passive

Many people hop from job to job focusing on a higher salary, but salaries are fixed: no matter how great the work you produce is, you still get paid the same. Passive income is a form of investing in exponential results. Every tech worker should have a mixture of salary and some investment in an asset that can deliver exponential results. Ideally this result is directly tied to your work:

- Does this action lead to passive income: books, products, investments?

- Do you own the customer? Ideally, you focus on holding the customer.

- What is the royalty relationship?

Predator (20% or lower)
> There should be a very compelling reason to work with a predator. Perhaps they get you exposure, or they take a chance on you. The downsides of predators are they often have a bureaucratic process. How many layers of people do you have to interact with to get anything done? How long does it take to get something done? It could be 10–100 times longer than working by yourself.

Partner (50% or higher)
> There is a lot to like about an equal partnership. The partner has "skin in the game" in terms of money and their time.

Platform (80% or Higher)
> There are pros and cons to using a platform. The advantages of a platform are that you can retain most of the revenue if you are self-sufficient. The disadvantages are that you may not have a benchmark yet. You may not have a framework for what "good" is. You may want to work with a predator and see how they do things before going right to the platform.

Not everyone wants to be an author or creator, but everyone can be an investor. Maybe this puts 50% of your W2 income into an index fund or renting out a house.

Positive

When working on a project or working with a partner, it must be a positive experience. Even getting paid very well eventually gets old if the environment is toxic. Some questions to ask are:

- Am I happy every day?
- Do I respect the people I work with each day?
- Are the people I am working with high achievers with a track record of success?
- Does my health increase or maintain in sleep, fitness, and nutrition?
- Since you are the average of the five people you spend the most amount of time with, how can you be around positive people?

Exponential

Another important question on a project or working with a partner is exponential potential. Perhaps you have decided to work with a predator partner because of the exponential potential of the project. On the other hand, if you are working with a predator, but the project doesn't have exponential potential, then perhaps it isn't a good project.

Does this project or partnership lead to an exponential reaction in revenue, users, traffic, press, or prestige?

Autonomy

Another important question on a project or working with a partner is autonomy. If you are good at what you do, you need freedom. You know what good is; your partner may not. How much independence do you have? Are you able to ultimately bet on yourself, or is success in the hands of other people?

Some example questions include:

- Does this action increase autonomy or create a dependency?
- Do I learn and grow—a new skill, new prestige, or brand affiliation?
- Is it automatable or manual? Avoid tasks that cannot automate.

Rule of 25%

What color is the money you make? Figure D-1 shows three ways to consider income: employee, consultant, or investor.

Being an employee may be valuable to you because you learn skills and build a network. Keep in mind that this is "red" money, though. This red money can disappear at any time. You are not in control.

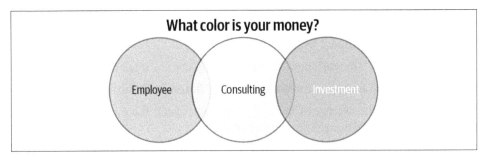

Figure D-1. What color is your money?

Consulting is "yellow" money. It is a massive step in the right direction. You can do some consulting while you work as an employee. This action takes away some of the risks of being an employee. As a consultant, though, you have to be careful never to have one client that is more than 25% of your total income and ideally not more than 25% of your consulting income. Familiarity breeds contempt. The best relationships are when people are on their best behavior and know the link is only there to solve a problem.

Investments like real estate, index funds, and digital products are "green money." This income stream will always pay you. The ideal scenario is to make 80% of your income with green money and limit consulting or employment to 20% of your income.

Notes

The following notes and resources were helpful in building out this appendix:

- Warren Buffet has a famous quote on this subject. He said, "If you don't find a way to make money while you sleep, you will work until you die."
- There was good related advice in the article, "1,000 True Fans? Try 100" (*https://oreil.ly/BL9Hj*).
- Finally, thanks to the feedback and inspirational ideas from Andrew Hargadon (*https://oreil.ly/lys5q*) and Dickson Louie (*https://oreil.ly/pLuPJ*).

Building a Technical Portfolio for MLOps

By Noah Gift

Something I recommend to everybody is to become a "Triple Threat." In basketball, a triple threat position means someone who can score, rebound, or pass. The defender has to guard against all three options. You can also be a triple threat from a career perspective, meaning you can get past the hiring gatekeepers because you have three threats: a technical portfolio, a relevant certification, and either work experience or a relevant degree.

I advise on Cloud Certifications in Appendix B, but here we're going to dive into your technology portfolio. Building a portfolio project builds up your resume, which will have a link to high-quality source code and a demo video, versus another resume that does not. Who would you call in for an interview? I would call in the candidate who already showed me what they could do before we met.

In building a project, pick something you think will "move the needle" in the next two years. Consider the following ideas:

- GitHub project with source code and a *README.md* explaining the project. The *README.md* should be of professional quality and use a business writing style.
- 100% repeatable notebooks or source code.
- Original work (not a copy of a Kaggle project).
- Authentic passion.
- Five-minute final demo video showing how it works.
- The demo needs to be very technical and show precisely how to accomplish a task, i.e., you need to teach someone step by step. (Think about a cooking show where a chef demonstrates how to make chocolate chip cookies. This level of detail needs to be similar.)

- The video should be at least 1080p with a 16:9 aspect ratio.
- Consider recording with a low-cost external mic.

Something to consider in building a Jupyter notebook is to break down the steps in a data science project. Typically the steps are:

- Ingest
- EDA (Exploratory Data Analysis)
- Modeling
- Conclusion

For MLOps portfolio projects, here are a few ideas that have resulted in students getting jobs at major tech companies, i.e., FAANG, and cutting-edge startups as ML engineering, data engineers, and data scientists.

Project: Continuous Delivery of Flask/FastAPI Data Engineering API on a PaaS Platform

An excellent way to test your knowledge of building APIs is the following project:

1. Create a Flask or Fast application on a cloud platform and push source code to GitHub.
2. Configure a cloud native build server (AWS App Runner, AWS Code Build, etc.,) to deploy changes to GitHub.
3. Create a realistic data engineering API.

You can refer to this O'Reilly walkthrough (*https://oreil.ly/29gnT*) of using functions with FastAPI to build Microservices for more ideas, or this sample Github project (*https://oreil.ly/D1eYf*) for a complete working AWS App Runner starter project for FastAPI.

Project: Docker and Kubernetes Container Project

Many cloud solutions involve Docker format containers. Let's leverage Docker format containers in the following project:

1. Create a customized Docker container from the current version of Python that deploys a Python ML application.
2. Push the image to DockerHub, Amazon ECR, Google Container Registry, or some other Cloud Container Registry.

3. Pull the image down and run it on a cloud platform cloud shell: Google Cloud Shell or AWS Cloud9.

4. Deploy an application to a cloud-managed Kubernetes cluster, like GKE (Google Kubernetes Engine), or EKS (Elastic Kubernetes Service), etc.

Project: Serverless AI Data Engineering Pipeline

Reproduce the architecture of the example serverless data engineering project shown in Figure E-1. Then, enhance the project by extending the functionality of the NLP analysis: adding entity extraction, key phrase extraction, or some other NLP feature.

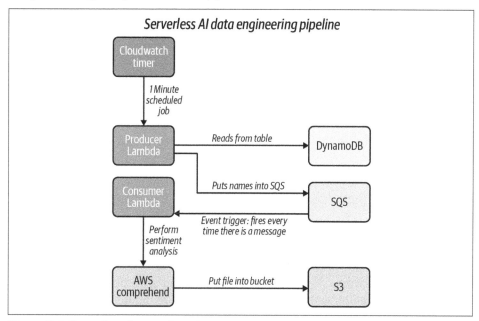

Figure E-1. Serverless data engineering

A good resource for this project is the following repo: *https://github.com/noahgift/awslambda*.

Project: Build Edge ML Solution

Build and deploy an edge-based computer vision solution using one of the technologies covered in the book:

- Intel Movidius Neural Compute Stick 2
- AWS DeepLens
- Coral AI

- SmartPhone (iOS, Android)
- Raspberry Pi

Here are the deliverables for your project:

- Publish your results as a Jupyter notebook, a folder of Colab notebooks, or both in a GitHub repo.
- Write two-page synopsis of a research project in PDF format.
- Include a link to your published works in your two-page synopsis.
- Create a 60-second demo video of your working computer vision project making inference (predictions).
- Submit your project to Intel or AWS Community Projects.

Project: Build Cloud Native ML Application or API

Build a cloud native analytics application hosted on the Google Cloud Platform (GCP), AWS, Azure, or another cloud or technology (i.e., Kubernetes). This project aims to give you the ability to create realistic, working solutions that work with modern techniques.

Before you begin, read "Hidden Technical Debt in Machine Learning Systems" by Sculley et al. (2015) (*https://oreil.ly/keGLy*).

A good idea to limit complexity is to use a public dataset. One example could be a project using public data from a Google BigQuery dataset if using GCP. Alternately, if using AutoML, data can be tutorial data or custom data.

The main idea is for you to think about starting to create a portfolio. Here is a list of suggested project requirements for a GCP project; you can modify the tech stack for a different cloud.

- Source code stored in GitHub
- Continuous deployment from CircleCI
- Data stored in GCP (BigQuery, Google Cloud Storage, etc.)
- ML predictions created and served out (AutoML, BigQuery, etc.)
- Stackdriver installed for monitoring
- Google App Engine serves out HTTP requests via REST API with a JSON payload
- Deployed into GCP environment

- A two-page, single-spaced paper describing the project as a consultant would describe it to a client during the hand-off phase

The following is an example of a final project checklist to consider.

- Does it perform ML prediction/inference?
- Are there separate environments?
- Is there comprehensive monitoring and alerts?
- Is the correct datastore used, i.e., relational, graph, key/value?
- Does the principle of least privilege apply?
- Is the data encrypted in transit and at rest?
- Did you load-test the application to verify performance?

Getting a Job: Don't Storm the Castle, Walk in the Backdoor

The technology industry always has a "dream" job title. These titles come and go. Here are a few: Unix systems administrator, network administrator, webmaster, web developer, mobile developer, data scientist. What happens when these job titles appear is that companies panic about hiring these positions.

Then all progress grinds to a halt, and more and more hoops appear. A classic example is asking someone for ten years of experience on a technology when it has been around for one year. Finally, it becomes impossible to get into "the castle." The front of the castle has guards, hot oil, spears, and a monster waiting in the moat. Instead, think about a backdoor. Often a backdoor is a less prestigious job title.

How to learn

Software-related careers are unique compared to other professions. Software-related jobs have much more in common with professional athletes, martial artists, or musicians. The process of achieving mastery involves an embrace of suffering and a love of making mistakes.

Create your own 20% time

Never trust a company to be the sole source of what you need to learn. You have to carve out your learning pathway. One way to do this is to spend a couple of hours a day learning new technology as a habit. Think about it as an exercise for your career.

Embrace the mistake mindset

It is common to avoid mistakes and want perfection. For example, we try to avoid car accidents, dropped groceries, and other mistakes, and most students want to get a perfect "A" on an exam.

In learning to be a competent software engineer, it is better to flip this on its head. A constant stream of mistakes means you are on the right track. How many mistakes have you made this week? How many have you made today? William Blake said this best in 1790 when he said, "If the fool persisted in his folly, he would become wise."

Finding parallel hobbies to test your learning

If you asked a quorum of successful software engineers with 10+ years of experience, you would hear some version of this: "I am a learning machine." So then, how does a learning machine get better at learning? One method is to pick a sport that takes years to master that you are a complete beginner in and observe yourself.

Two games in particular that are well suited for this activity are rock climbing and Brazilian Jiu-Jitsu. Brazilian Jiu-Jitsu has the added side-effect of teaching you practical self-defense. You will find out that you have blind spots in learning that you can then fix in your "real" job.

Data Science Case Study: Intermittent Fasting

By Noah Gift

Back in the early 1990s I attended Cal Poly San Luis Obispo and majored in nutritional science. I picked this degree because I was obsessed with being a professional athlete. I felt like studying nutritional science could give me an extra edge. I first found research about calorie restriction and aging.

I was also involved in self-experimentation in my nutritional biochemistry class. We centrifuged our blood and calculated LDL, HDL, and total cholesterol levels. In the same course, we supplemented with megadoses of vitamin C and then captured our urine to see what was absorbed. It turned out that nothing was absorbed in a healthy population of college students because the body intelligently responds to the absorption of nutrients by increasing absorption sensitivity when levels are low. Vitamin supplements are often a waste of money.

I took a year of anatomy and physiology and learned how to dissect the human body. I learned about the Krebs cycle and how glycogen storage works.[1] The body produces insulin to increase blood sugar and stores it in the liver and muscle tissues. If those areas are "full," it puts that glycogen into adipose tissue, or "fat." Likewise, when the body is out of glycogen or aerobic activity is underway, fat tissue is the primary fuel. This storage is our "extra" gas tank.

I also spent a year at Cal Poly as a failed Division I Decathlete walk-on. One of the things I learned the hard way was that doing too much weight lifting was actively detrimental to performance in sports like running. I was 6'2", 215 lbs, and could bench

---

1 See the citric acid cycle page on Wikipedia (*https://oreil.ly/BJKbu*).

press 225 around 25 times (similar to an NFL linebacker's bench press performance). I also ran the 1,500m (about a mile) in 4 minutes and 30 seconds and regularly led the pack in three-mile training runs with Division I long-distance runners. I could also dunk a basketball from near the free-throw line and ran the 100m in 10.9.

In a nutshell, I was a good athlete and well-rounded but actively worked for years doing the wrong types of exercises (bodybuilding). My work ethic was off the charts but also wildly ineffective and counterproductive for the sport I chose. I also overestimated my ability to walk on to a Division I sport where I hadn't even done many activities, like pole vault. I almost made the team too—there was one person in front of me. In this part of my life, though, "almost" didn't count. This experience was the first time I had given something my entire focus and effort, yet ultimately failed. It was a humbling experience that was good to get out of the way early in life. I learned about dealing with failure, which has served me well in software engineering and data science.

As a former Silicon Valley software engineer, I later discovered a word for this behavior: YAGNI. YAGNI stands for "You Ain't Gonna Need It." Just like the years I spent putting on 40 pounds of extra muscle that ultimately decreased my sports performance, you can work on the wrong things in software projects. Examples of this include building functionality that you don't use in an application or overly complex abstractions like advanced object-oriented programming. These techniques are literally "dead weight." They are actively harmful because they take time to develop, which could be spent working on valuable things, and permanently slow down the project. Like in my track and field experience, some of the most motivated and talented people can be the worst abusers of adding unneeded complexity to a project.

The field of nutritional science has a YAGNI problem as well, and intermittent fasting is an excellent example of a simplification technique. It works a lot like the way deleting half of a 2,000-word essay can make it better. It turns out the decades of added "complexity" in food can be ignored and deleted: frequent snacks, breakfast, and ultra-processed foods.[2]

You don't need to eat breakfast or snacks. To further simplify, you don't need to eat many times a day. It is a waste of time and money. You also don't need ultra-processed foods: breakfast cereal, protein bars, or any other "man-made" food. It turns out YAGNI strikes again with our diet. You also don't need to buy a unique tool to eat healthy, like books, supplements, or meal plans.

---

2 See "Eating More Ultra-Processed Foods May Shorten Life Span" in Harvard Health Publishing (*https://oreil.ly/5uiEj*).

There is a well-known problem called the traveling salesman problem,[3] which asks the following question: Given a list of cities and the distances between each pair of cities, what is the shortest possible route that visits each city exactly once and returns to the origin city? The problem is essential because there is no perfect solution. In everyday language, this means a solution is too complex to implement in the real world. Moreover, it would take an increasingly long time to create an answer concerning the data. So instead, computer science solves these problems using heuristics. I wrote a heuristic solution in graduate school that isn't particularly innovative, but it comes up with a reasonable answer.[4] The way it works is to pick a city randomly, then you always choose the shortest route when presented with possible routes. At the end solution, the total distance calculates. You then rerun this simulation with however much time you have and then pick the shortest distance.

Intermittent fasting is so effective because it also skips past the unsolvable complexity of counting calories to lose weight. Intermittent fasting is an effective heuristic. Rather than counting calories, instead you don't eat during blocks of the day.[5] These blocks could be as follows:

Daily fasts:

- 8-hour feeding window or 16:8
  — 12p.m.–8p.m.
  — 7a.m.–3p.m.
- 4-hour feeding window or 20:4
  — 6p.m.–10p.m.
  — 7a.m.–11a.m.

Longer fasts with more complex patterns:

- 5:2
  — Five days of normal eating and two days of calorie restriction, typically 500 calories.
- Alternate-day fasting
  — Eat normally one day and restrict calories another, typically 500 calories.

---

3 See the description on Wikipedia (*https://oreil.ly/JUMGQ*).

4 This is available on GitHub (*https://oreil.ly/k4rIk*).

5 See DietDoctor (*https://oreil.ly/qD9on*) and the *New England Journal of Medicine* (*https://oreil.ly/IuoQB*) for more.

I have experimented mainly with daily fasts of 16 hours or 20 hours. As a data scientist, nutritionist, and still competitive athlete, I also come with data. I have data from 2011–2019 of my body weight.[6] From August 2019 to December 2019, I have mostly been on a 12:8 IF routine.

In Figure F-1 I am able to use the data collection from my scale to perform data science on my own body and figure out what works and what doesn't.

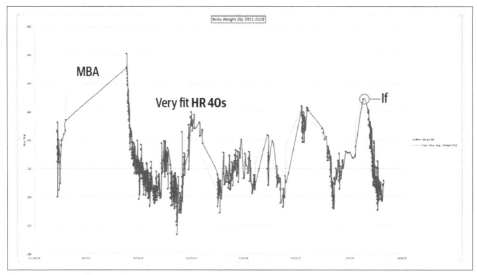

Figure F-1. Body weight

One thing I learned in analyzing body weight and experimenting with data is that a few small things make a big difference:

- Avoiding "human-made" food
- Getting 8 hours of sleep (MBA and startups caused weight gain through sleep loss)
- Daily exercise
- Intermittent fasting
- You cannot exercise your way out of a bad diet (heart rate was in the low 40s)

Figure F-2 shows an example of a meal that is YAGNI-approved.

---

6 This is available on GitHub (*https://oreil.ly/SXM9Y*).

Figure F-2. Healthy food: avocado omelet

Here's the recipe for a mushroom omelet with avocado:

- Eggs
- Shiitake mushrooms
- Cheese
- Avocado
- Salsa

It takes only a few minutes to make, the fats and whole foods make you feel satiated, and it is inexpensive.

When was I "overweight" it was in periods when I didn't follow the previous advice: working crazy hours at startups, eating food that "human" made. Working out in a fasted state takes a bit of getting used to, but I found that it increases performance in many sports I do: bouldering, weight lifting, HIIT training, and Brazilian Jiu-Jitsu. Likewise, I am very productive in writing software, writing books, and doing intellectual work. My main "hack" I add is the regular consumption of plain cold brew coffee and water.

My conclusion is that intermittent fasting is one of the best ways to enhance a person's life dramatically. It costs nothing and is simple to do, primarily if you practice it daily, and is backed by science. Additionally, many people struggle to find data science and machine learning projects to work on that are interesting. Why not use yourself as the test case, as this case study shows?

Notes on Intermittent Fasting, Blood Glucose, and Food

From the *New England Journal of Medicine* (NEJM), "Evidence is accumulating that eating in 6 hours and fasting for 18 hours can trigger a metabolic switch from glucose-based to ketone-based energy, with increased stress resistance, increased longevity, and a decreased incidence of diseases, including cancer and obesity."

From NHS (Nurse's Health Study), "Several lifestyle behaviors may influence whether or not a person can maintain energy balance over the long term. For instance, the consumption of sugar-sweetened beverages, sweets, and processed foods may make it harder to do so, whereas the consumption of whole grains, fruits, and vegetables might make it easier."

This also shows a data science and machine learning approach to solving obesity. Increase the number of servings of nuts, fruits, and yogurt. Decrease or eliminate potato chips, potatoes, and sugar-sweetened beverages (note that there is a link between ultra-processed foods and insulin spikes). These are the top foods that contributed to weight gain:

- Potato chips
- Potatoes
- Sugar-sweetened beverages

These are the top foods that are inversely associated with weight gain (weight loss):

- Nuts
- Fruits
- Yogurt

Lifestyle changes like IF certainly are easier to attempt when you can already see the data behind it!

Additional Educational Resources

By Noah Gift

We all know that one book, one course, or one degree isn't enough—instead, a process of continuous learning is the best method of staying up to date. One way to keep learning is to form a study group at your work, with your friends, or at school to keep growing. The following resources from classes I teach in ML engineering, MLOps, and applied computer vision can help you start.

Additional MLOps Critical Thinking Questions

- A former startup engineering manager mentions that "Agile" project management alone isn't enough to ship a minimum viable product (MVP). Often a 3-month weekly schedule is also needed (i.e., waterfall planning). Discuss your response to this opinion.
- What problems does a continuous integration (CI) system solve?
- Why is a CI system an essential part of SaaS software?
- Why are cloud platforms the ideal target for analytics applications?
- How does deep learning benefit from the cloud?
- What are the advantages of managed services like Google BigQuery?
- How does Google BigQuery differ from a traditional SQL?
- How does machine learning (ML) prediction directly from BigQuery add value to the Google platform?
- What advantages could this have for analytics application engineering?
- How does AutoML have a lower total cost of ownership (TCO)?
- How could it have a higher TCO?

- What problems do different environments solve?

- What problems do a different environment create?

- How can you properly manage unexpected costs in the cloud?

- What are three tools to help you manage costs on the Google Cloud Platform?

- What are three tools to help you manage costs on the AWS Platform?

- What are three tools to help you manage costs on the Azure Platform?

- Why can JavaScript Object Notation (JSON) logging often be better than unstructured logging?

- What are some downsides to alerts that go off too much?

- Create a life-long learning plan by answering the following questions: What skills are you going to learn this quarter, why, and how? What skills are you going to learn by the end of this year, why, and how? What skills are you going to learn by the end of next year, why, and how? What skills are you going to learn by the end of five years, why, and how?

- What problems does a continuous delivery (CD) system solve?

- Why is a continuous delivery system an essential part of data engineering?

- What is the critical difference between continuous integration and continuous delivery?

- Explain how monitoring and logging play a critical role in data engineering.

- Explain what can go wrong with health checks.

- Explain why "data governance" is the "unsung hero" of cybersecurity.

- Explain how testing plays a critical role in data engineering.

- Explain how automation and testing are so closely connected.

- Pick a favorite Python command-line framework and write a hello-world example, and share. Could you explain why you chose it?

- Explain how cloud computing is impacting data engineering.

- Explain how serverless is impacting data engineering.

- Share a simple Python AWS Lambda function and explain what it does.

- Explain what machine learning engineering is.

- Create and share a simple `Dockerfile` that runs a Flask app. Explain how it works.

- Explain what data engineering is.

- Truncate and shuffle a large dataset, load into Pandas, and share your work. Explain the approach you used.

- Explain what DevOps is and how it enhances a data engineering project.
- What problem does the cloud solve when considering real-world computer vision problems?
- How could Colab notebooks and Jupyter Notebooks be used to exchange ideas or build research portfolios?
- What are some critical differences between biological and machine vision?
- What are some real-world use cases of generative modeling?
- Explain how game-playing machines can use computer vision to win.
- What are the pros and cons of using computer vision APIs to solve real-world problems?
- How is AutoML impacting data science now, and how will it impact it in the future?
- What are the real-world use cases of edge-based machine learning?
- What are a few edge-based machine learning platforms?
- How do integrated platforms fit into existing companies' ML strategies?
- How could SageMaker change machine learning model creation in organizations?
- What are the practical use cases of AWS Lambda?
- Explain practical use cases of transfer learning. Please explain how you could use it in a project.
- How could you take an ML model you built to a more advanced phase of functionality?
- What is IAC, and what problem does it solve?
- How should a company decide on what level of cloud abstraction to use for a project: SaaS, PaaS, IaaS, MaaS, serverless?
- What are the different layers of network security on AWS, and what unique problems do each solve?
- What problem do AWS Spot instances solve, and how could you use them in your projects?
- Create a Docker format container and recommend how to use them in a project.
- Evaluate container management services like Kubernetes and hosted Kubernetes and create a solution with them.
- Summarize container registries and how to use them to create custom containers.
- What are containers?
- What problem do containers solve?

- What is the relationship between Kubernetes and containers?
- Accurately evaluate distributed computing challenges and opportunities and apply this knowledge to real-world projects.
- Summarize how eventual consistency plays a role in cloud native applications.
- How does the CAP Theorem play a role in designing for the cloud?
- What are the implications of Amdahl's law for machine learning projects?
- Recommend appropriate use cases for ASICS.
- Consider the implications of the end of Moore's Law.
- What are the problems with a "one size fits all" approach to relational databases?
- How could a service like Google BigQuery change the way you deal with data?
- What problem does a "serverless" database like Athena solve?
- What are the critical differences between block and object storage?
- What are the fundamental problems that a data lake solves?
- What are the trade-offs with a serverless architecture?
- What are the advantages of developing with Cloud9?
- What problems does Google App Engine solve?
- What problems does the Cloud Shell environment solve?

Additional MLOps Educational Materials

Beyond the resources in this book, these are additional resources updated frequently that you can leverage to continue to improve:

- Many other MLOps-related videos are updated weekly on the O'Reilly Platform by Pragmatic AI Solutions (*https://oreil.ly/g8oz3*). You can also review the Katacodas on the O'Reilly Learning Platform.
- Several free books are available on the Pragmatic AI Labs website (*https://paiml.com*).
- Subscribe to the Pragmatic AI Labs YouTube Channel (*https://oreil.ly/4xrBP*).
- Take the Duke and Coursera specialization Building Cloud Computing Solutions at Scale (*https://oreil.ly/8QbE0*).

Education Disruption

A disruption is a break, interruption, or change from the established model or process. This section provides my thoughts on educational disruption and how it affects learning MLOps techniques.

Disruption is always easy to spot in hindsight. Consider the issue with taxi drivers and current services like Lyft and Uber. How did requiring drivers to pay one million dollars for a taxi medallion (*https://oreil.ly/DjMHY*) make sense as a mechanism to facilitate public taxi service (Figure G-1)?

Figure G-1. Taxi medallion[1]

What were the problems that companies like Lyft (*https://lyft.com*) and Uber (*https://uber.com*) solved?

- Lower price
- Push versus Pull (driver comes to you)
- Predictable service
- Habit-building feedback loop
- Async by design
- Digital versus analog
- Nonlinear workflow

Let's consider those same ideas in regard to education.

---

1 Source: CALIFORNIA, SAN FRANCISCO 1996 -TAXI MEDALLION SUPPLEMENTAL LICENSEPLATE - Flickr - woody1778a.jpg.

Current State of Higher Education That Will Be Disrupted

A similar disruption is underway with education. Student debt is at an all-time high with a linear growth rate from 2008, according to Experian (*https://oreil.ly/ugcPX*) as shown in Figure G-2.

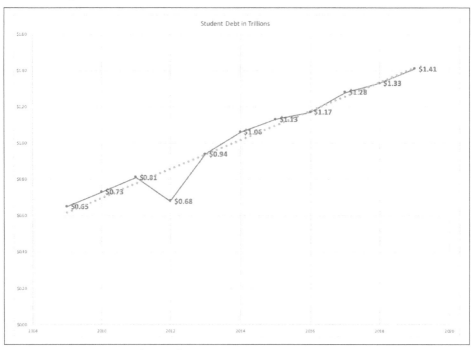

Figure G-2. Experian Student Debt

Simultaneous to that disturbing trend is an equally troubling statistic that 4/10 college grads in 2019 were in a job (*https://oreil.ly/ZfS9y*) that didn't require their degree (Figure G-3).

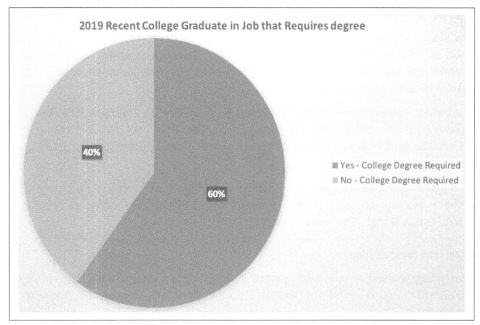

Figure G-3. Jobs requiring degree

This process is not sustainable. Student debt cannot continue to grow every year, and at the same time, produce almost half of the outcomes that do not lead directly to a job. Why shouldn't a student spend four years learning a hobby like personal fitness, sports, music, or culinary arts instead if the outcome is the same? At least in that situation, they would not be in debt and also have a fun hobby they could use for the rest of their life.

In the book *Zero to One* by Peter Thiel (Currency), he mentions the 10X rule. He states that a company will need to be 10X better than its closest competitor to succeed. Could a product or service be 10X better than traditional education? Yes, it could.

10X Better Education

So what would a 10X education system look like in practice?

Built-in apprenticeship

If the focus of an educational program was jobs, then why not train on the job while in school?

Focus on the customer

Much of the current higher-education system's focus is on faculty and faculty research. Who is paying for this? The customer, the student, is paying for this. An essential criterion for educators is publishing content in prestigious journals. There is only an indirect link to the customer.

Meanwhile, companies like Udacity (*https://oreil.ly/EONTI*), Coursera, O'Reilly, and Edx (*https://edx.org*) are directly giving customers these goods. This training is job-specific and continuously updated at a pace much quicker than a traditional university.

It could be that skills taught to a student focus on getting a job outcome only. The majority of students are focused on getting jobs. They are less focused on becoming better human beings. There are other outlets for this goal.

Lower time to completion

Does a degree need to take four years to complete? It may take that long if much of the time of the degree is on nonessential tasks. Why couldn't a degree take one year or two years?

Lower cost

According to USNews (*https://oreil.ly/7uGRp*) the median four-year annual tuition is $10,116 for a Public, In-State University; $22,577 for a Public, Out-of-State University; and $36,801 for a Private university. The total cost of getting a four-year degree (adjusted for inflation) has risen unbounded since 1985 (Figure G-4).

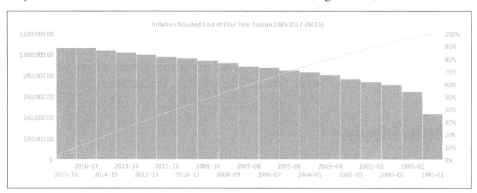

Figure G-4. Tuition inflation adjusted

Could a competitor offer a product that is 10X cheaper? A starting point would be to undo what happened from 1985 to 2019. If the product hasn't improved, but the cost has tripled, this is ripe for disruption.

Async and remote first

Many software engineering companies have decided to become "remote first" (*https://oreil.ly/IpFYA*). In other cases, companies like Twitter are moving to a distributed workforce (*https://oreil.ly/T3j9D*). In building software, the output is a digital product. If the work is digital, the environment can be made entirely async and remote. The advantage of an async and remote first course is distribution at scale.

One of the advantages of a "remote first" environment is an organizational structure focused on the outcomes more than the location. There are tremendous disruptions and waste in many software companies due to unnecessary meetings, noisy working environments, and long commutes. Many students will be heading into "remote first" work environments, and it could be a significant advantage for them to learn the skills to succeed in these environments.

Inclusion first versus exclusion first

Many universities publicly state how many students applied to their program and how few students were accepted. This exclusion-first-based approach is designed to increase demand. If the asset sold is physical, like a Malibu beach house, then yes, the price will adjust higher based on the market. If the product sold is digital and infinitely scalable, then exclusion doesn't make sense.

There is no free lunch, though, and strictly boot camp style programs (*https://oreil.ly/GOrXU*) are not without issues. In particular, curriculum quality and teaching quality shouldn't be an afterthought.

Nonlinear versus serial

Before digital technology, many tasks were continuing operations. A good example is television editing technology. I worked as an editor for ABC Network in the 1990s. You needed physical tapes to edit. Soon the videotapes became data on a hard drive, and that opened up many new editing techniques.

Likewise, with education, there is no reason for an enforced schedule to learn something. Async opens up the possibility of many new ways to learn. Mom could study at night; existing employees could learn on the weekend or during their lunch breaks.

Life-long learning: permanent access to content for alumni with continuous upskill path

Another reason educational institutions should rethink going "remote first" is because it would allow for the creation of courses offered to alumni (for zero cost or a SaaS fee). SaaS could serve as a method of protection against the onslaught of competitors coming. Many industries require constant upskilling. A good example is the technology industry.

It would be safe to say that any technology worker needs to learn a new skill every six months. The current education product doesn't account for this. Why wouldn't alumni be given a chance to learn the material and gain certification on this material? Enhanced alumni could lead to an even better brand.

Regional job market that will be disrupted

As a former Bay Area software engineer and homeowner, I don't see any future advantage to living in the region at the current cost structure (Figure G-5). The high cost of living in hypergrowth regions causes many cascading issues: homelessness, increased commute times, dramatically lowered quality of life, and more.

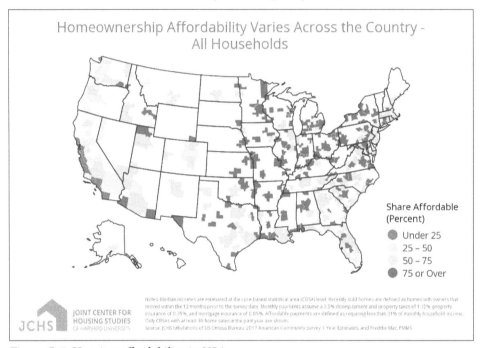

Figure G-5. Housing affordability in USA

Where there is a crisis, there is an opportunity. Many companies realize that whatever benefit lies in an ultra-high cost region, it isn't worth it. Instead, regional centers with excellent infrastructure and low cost of living have a massive opportunity. Some of the characteristics of regions that can act as job growth hubs include access to universities, transportation, low price of housing, and good government policies toward growth.

An excellent example of a region like this is Tennessee. It has free associate degree programs (*https://tnreconnect.gov*) and access to many top universities, low cost of living, and has top research institutes like Oak Ridge National Lab (*https://ornl.gov*).

These regions can dramatically disrupt the status quo, especially if they embrace remote first and asynchronous education and workforces.

Disruption of hiring process

The hiring process in the United States is ready for disruption. It is easily disruptable because of a focus on direct, synchronous actions. Figure G-6 shows how it would be possible to disrupt hiring by eliminating all interviews and replacing them with automatic recruitment of individuals with suitable certifications. This is a classic distributed programming problem that fixes a bottleneck by moving tasks from a serial and "buggy" workflow to a fully distributed workflow. Companies should "pull" from the workers instead of continually pulling on a resource locked up in futile work.

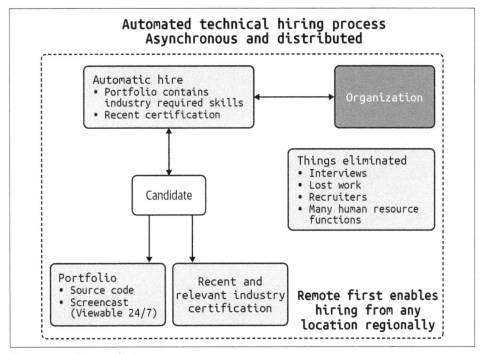

Figure G-6. Disrupt hiring

One reason why cloud computing is such an important skill is that it simplifies many aspects of software engineering. One of the issues it simplifies is building solutions. Many solutions often involve a YAML format file and a little bit of Python code.

Conclusion

Education is no longer static. To be relevant in MLOps requires a growth mindset. This growth mindset means you must learn things on an ongoing basis while producing results. The good news is that the motivated have an increasing chance to succeed if they take advantage of the explosion of technical training opportunities.

Technical Project Management

By Noah Gift

On the first week of the highly technical class on cloud computing, I brought up technical project management and how important it is to do what I describe in this appendix. A student raised their hand in class and asked the following question: "Is this a project management class? I thought this class is about cloud computing?"

Similarly, in the real world, it is easy to think project management doesn't matter. A small amount of technical project management knowledge is critical to MLOps, though. Three essential components of project management are as follows:

- Attempt to plan your project out of the time you have to complete it, i.e., 12 weeks using weekly milestones.

- Do a weekly demo to your team showing the progress.

- Break tasks into 4-hour chunks of time and do them weekly, keeping track of them with a simple task tracking system like Trello or GitHub.

Now, let's cover just enough of the basics to make sure you are successful.

Project Plan

There is nothing unique about MLOps regarding project management. Still, it is worth pointing out a few nonobvious highlights of project management that help build machine learning projects. In particular, one powerful concept in building ML solutions is to think in terms of a 10–12 week schedule and attempt to map out the individual results for each week. In the book's source code repository, there is an example template to follow (*https://oreil.ly/kzPGu*).

A takeaway is that a plan creates the scaffolding necessary to start deploying machine learning code to production, and the weekly demo creates accountability.

In Figure H-1 a week-by-week project plan allows for initial scoping of the complexity of a project.

Week	Milestone: High Level Goal	Weekly Demo Task (30 second video)
1	Kickoff	Kickoff (present plan)
2	Continous Deployment	Continous Deployment
3	Setup GCP	GCP Skeleton Project
4	Big Query Setup	Big Query Integration
5	Big Query Modeling and Prediction	Big Query Prediction
6	AutoML Setup	AutoML Prediction
7	Creation of Multiple Environments	Staging Environment
8	Integrate API	Computer Vision API
9	Stackdriver Setup	Monitoring
10	Finish MVP	MVP

Figure H-1. Project plan

Next, let's discuss the weekly demo.

Weekly Demo

In both real-world scenarios, when I work with a team deploying code to production or in educational systems, the weekly demo and the project plan are essential components that reduce the risk of a project never seeing the light of day. Another hidden fact about doing demos is making the person do the demo understand what they are doing and communicate information.

The Roman proverb "Docendo discimus" states that "by teaching, we learn." This proverb is also related to academic research on learning, and it is one of the more effective teaching approaches I have seen in the industry and the classroom. Video demos are powerful for both the consumer and the creator.

Task Tracking

You can see a basic, public Trello tracking board online (*https://oreil.ly/iJ4iX*). In Figure H-2, notice a simple approach of just three columns: To Do, In Progress, and Done. Each task takes around four hours to complete since this is a good unit of work to break down tasks.

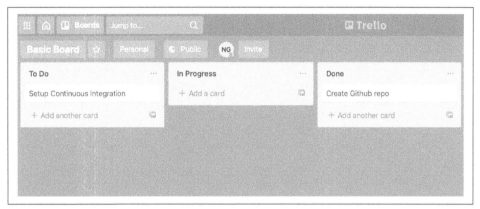

Figure H-2. Ticket tracking with Trello

Finally, each of these tickets typically completes every week. This workflow shows a sense of weekly progress. Note, you can use any board-based tracking system to accomplish the same thing. The main takeaway is to keep it simple! Simple project management systems stick around, but complex ones do not.

Index

A

ACI (Azure Container Instances), 369
AKS (Azure Kubernetes Service), 370
alerts, defined, 369
Amazon ECR, defined, 369
Amazon EKS, defined, 369
Amazon Mechanical Turk, 351
antipatterns, 357-362
API services, authentication, 240
App Engine (see Google App Engine)
App Runner, 202, 221-222
app.py, 210
Apple
    Core ML (see Core ML)
    Create ML, 132-136
    mobile development ecosystem, 131-139
ASICS, 19
authentication
    API services, 240
    authenticating microservices to cloud func-
        tions, 338-340
    Azure, 238-240
    key-based, 240
    service principal, 238-240
automated checks, 113
Automator's law, 30, 118
AutoML, 31, 117-159
    Apple's ecosystem and, 131-139
    AWS, 146-150
    Azure AutoML, 144-146
    basics, 118-129
    Create ML, 132-136
    data science versus, 123
    Feature Stores, 127-129

    FLAML, 153-154
    Google's AutoML and edge computer
        vision, 136-139
    Kaizen versus KaizenML, 125-127
    Ludwig, 151
    MLOps industrial revolution, 123-125
    model explainability, 154-158
    open source solutions, 151-154
autoscaling, defined, 369
AWS, 187-234
    AutoML, 146-150
    AWS Lambda recipes, 223-229
    basics, 188-209
    best practices for bootstrapping MLOps
        capabilities, 233
    CaaS, 198-203
    career advice with AWS ML evangelist
        Julien Simon, 231-233
    certification options, 375-390
    Certified Machine Learning specialist certif-
        ication, 2
    CLI tools for MLOps Cookbook project,
        211-218
    computer vision, 204-205
    DataOps tools, 15
    Flask microservice, 218-222
    getting started with, 189-205
    Hugo static S3 websites, 192-194
    MLOps Cookbook on, 209-222
    MLOps on, 206-209
    no-code/low-code AWS Comprehend solu-
        tion, 190
    real-world ML applications, 229-233
    serverless cookbook, 194-198

Sports Social Network case study, 229-231
AWS App Runner, 202, 221-222
AWS Certified Machine Learning - Specialty certification, 381-390
  data engineering, 382-387
  exploratory data analysis, 387-389
  MLOps, 390
AWS Cloud Practitioner, certification test questions for, 375-381
AWS Cloud9, 25, 193, 369
AWS Cloudshell, 24-25
AWS CloudWatch, 163
AWS Comprehend, 190
AWS DeepLens, 204-205
AWS DeepRacer, 52
AWS Lambda, 33
  defined, 369
  deploying with SAM, 223-229
  recipes, 223-229
  SAM containerized deploy, 224-229
  SAM Local, 223
  serverless applications, 194-198
AWS S3
  Hugo static S3 websites, 192-194
  SageMaker and, 176-181
AWS SageMaker (see SageMaker)
AWS Serverless Application Model (see SAM)
AWS Solutions Architect certification test questions, 375-381
Azure, 235-263
  Application Insights, 253
  authenticating API services, 240
  authentication, 238-240
  Azure CLI and Python SDK, 236-238
  Azure Machine Learning designer, 260-262
  compute instances, 240-242
  debugging locally, 254-257
  deploying, 242-245
  deploying a model, 248-251
  deploying models to a compute cluster, 246-251
  deploying ONNX to, 307-310
  Microsoft Certified: Azure Data Scientist certification, 2
  ML lifecycle, 262
  ML pipelines, 257-262
  MLOps for, 235-263
  publishing pipelines, 259
  registering models, 243-244
  retrieving logs, 252
  service principal, 238-240
  troubleshooting deployment issues, 251-257
  versioning datasets, 245
Azure AI Engineer Associate certification, 391
Azure Associate Data Scientist certification, 391
Azure AutoML, 144-146
Azure Container Instances (ACI), 369
Azure Kubernetes Service (AKS), 370
Azure ML, monitoring drift with, 182-184
Azure Percept, 84
Azure Pipelines, 56-63

B
Baseball_Predictions_Export_Model.ipynb, 211
baseline dataset, target dataset versus, 179
Bash shell, 26-29
  configuration, 28
  files and navigation, 27
  input/output, 27
  list files, 26
  run commands, 26
  writing a script, 28
BigQuery (see Google BigQuery)
bind mount, 87
black tool (Python), 370
Blake, William, 408
blue-green deployment, 111
Bogen, Joseph, xiii, 1, 23, 67, 93, 117, 161, 187, 235, 265, 293, 317, 347
build server, defined, 370

C
CaaS (see container as a service)
canary deployment, 111
career planning
  pear (PPEAR) revenue strategy, 399-402
  thinking like a venture capitalist, 399
case studies, 347-367
  critical challenges in MLOps, 357-362
  ethical/unintended consequences, 358
  Francesca Lazzeri interview, 362
  intermittent fasting, 409-414
  MLOps projects as Sqor sports social network, 350-355
  perfect technique versus the real world, 355-357
  Piero Molino interview, 360-362

unlikely benefits of ignorance in building
    ML models, 348-350
CD (see continuous delivery (CD))
certifications, 375-392
    AWS Certified Machine Learning - Spe-
        cialty, 381-390
    AWS Cloud Practitioner, 375-381
    AWS Solutions Architect, 375-381
    Azure Data Scientist/AI Engineer, 391
    SQL-related, 391
challenges in MLOps
    ethical/unintended consequences, 358
    focus on prediction accuracy versus the big
        picture, 359
    lack of operational excellence, 358
Charpentier, Emmanuelle, 121
CI/CD (continuous integration/continuous
    delivery)
    implementation of, 7
    parallels to recovery from sports injuries, 94
CI/CD pipeline, quality-control checks for, 32
CircleCI, defined, 370
CLI tools (see command line interface tools)
cli.py, 210
cloud computing
    foundations/building blocks, 29-31
    getting started, 31-32
    machine learning and, 3
cloud MLOps, observability for, 163
cloud native applications, defined, 370
cloud pipelines
    continuous delivery, 107-115
    controlled rollout of models, 110
    testing techniques for model deployment,
        112-115
Cloud Run, 268
cloud shell development environments, 24-26
Cloud9 (see AWS Cloud9)
Cloudshell, 24-25
cluster
    configuring, 246-248
    deploying models to a compute cluster,
        246-251
    inference versus compute, 247
command line interface (CLI) tools, 317-344
    basics, 321-331
    building a cloud-based CLI, 341
    creating a dataset linter, 321-328
    machine learning CLI workflows, 342-344

MLOps Cookbook project, 211-218
    modularizing, 328-331
    Python packaging, 319
    requirements file, 320
command line, Linux, 23
Common Vulnerabilities and Exposures
    (CVEs), 75
competitive advantage, 190
compute cluster
    deploying models to, 246-251
    inference cluster versus, 247
Compute Engine, 267
compute instances, Azure, 240-242
computer vision
    AWS, 204-205
    Google's AutoML and edge computer
        vision, 136-139
configuration
    Bash shell, 28
    cluster, 246-248
    configuring continuous integration with
        GitHub Actions, 13-14
    runtime, 259
container as a service (CaaS)
    AWS, 198-203
    MLOps design pattern, 366
containerized workflow, 224-229
containers, 68-80
    best practices, 74-76
    build once, run many MLOps workflow, 91
    creating, 69-72
    defined, 370
    managed ML systems and, 89-91
    monetizing MLOps, 90
    running, 72-74
    runtime, 69
    serving a trained model over HTTP, 76-80
continuous delivery (CD), 6, 93-115
    (see also CI/CD)
    cloud pipelines for, 107-115
    defined, 370
    DevOps best practice, 5
    GCP and, 270-272
    infrastructure as code for continuous deliv-
        ery of ML models, 99-106
    packaging for ML models, 95-99
    testing techniques for model deployment,
        112-115
continuous improvement, 8, 114

continuous integration (CI), 6
    (see also CI/CD)
    configuring with GitHub Actions, 13-14
    defined, 370
    DevOps best practice, 5
    GCP and, 270-272
convergence, 49
Coral Project, 81-84
Core ML, 132, 136-139, 310-314
Create ML, 132-136
customer-focused education, 422
CVEs (Common Vulnerabilities and Expo-
    sures), 75
cybersecurity, 365

D

data drift (see drift)
data engineering
    AWS Certified Machine Learning - Specialty
        certification, 382-387
    defined, 370
    GCP, 282-286
    ML hierarchy of needs and, 15
data governance, 365, 385
data lake, 15, 382
data science
    AutoML versus, 123
    as foundational skill, 54-56
data warehouses, Feature Stores versus, 129
DataOps
    GCP, 282-286
    ML hierarchy of needs and, 15
dataset linter, 321-328
datasets
    baseline versus target, 179
    versioning, 245
Davis, Purnell, 352
debugging (see troubleshooting)
deep learning intuition, 49-49
DeepLens, 204-205
dependencies
    defining in requirements.txt file, 320
    pinning, 74
    Python packaging and, 319
deployment
    Azure, 242-245
    blue-green versus canary, 111
    deploying a model, 248-251
    MLOps, 19

registration, 243-244
    troubleshooting deployment issues, 251-257
descriptive statistics, 37-41, 39
design patterns, 366
development environments, 24-26
DevOps
    best practices, 5
    defined, 5
    implementing, 8-13
    MLOps and, 5-7
    MLOps feedback loop, 18
diet, intermittent fasting and, 409-414
disaster recovery, defined, 370
disruption (see education disruption)
Docker
    containers, 69
    defined, 371
    Dockerfile, 69, 211
    format container, 370
Doudna, Jennifer, 121
drift
    monitoring with AWS SageMaker, 175-182
    monitoring with Azure ML, 182-184

E

EDA (exploratory data analysis), 39, 387-389
edge devices, 80-89
    Apple's ecosystem, 131-139
    ASICS and, 19
    Azure Percept, 84
    Coral, 81-84
    ORT model format and, 314-315
    porting over non-TPU models, 86-89
    TFHub, 85
education disruption, 418-425
    current state of higher education that will be
        disrupted, 420-421
    10X better education, 421-425
educational resources, 415-426
    additional MLOps critical thinking ques-
        tions, 415-418
    additional MLOps educational materials,
        418
    education disruption, 418-425
Elastic Beanstalk Flask app, 207-209
ELI5, 155, 157
engineering, science versus, 2
explainability, 145, 154-158
exploratory data analysis (EDA), 39, 387-389

F

FaaS (see function as a service)
Faber, Issac, 359
Fargate, 198-203
fasting, intermittent, 409-414
Feature Stores, 127-129
feedback loop, 18
FLAML, 153-154
Flask microservice, 218-222
 automatically building container via GitHub
  Actions, 220
 AWS App Runner and, 221-222
 build example, 199-202
 containerized, 220
food, intermittent fasting and, 409-414
foundational skills for MLOps, 23-63
 Bash shell and commands, 26-29
 building an MLOps pipeline from zero,
  56-63
 cloud computing foundations/building
  blocks, 29-31
 cloud shell development environments,
  24-26
 doing data science, 54-56
 getting started with cloud computing, 31-32
 Linux command line, 23
 machine learning key concepts, 50-53
 math for programmers crash course, 37-49
 Python (crash course), 33-35
 Python (tutorial), 36
Fox, Justin, 119
function as a service (FaaS)
 AWS Lambda, 33
 defined, 371

G

GCP (see Google Cloud Platform)
Gilovich, Thomas, 118
GitHub Actions
 automatically building container via, 220
 configuring continuous integration with,
  13-14
 GCP versus, 271
GitHub Container Registry, pushing container
 to, 220
GitHub, file size limitations for, 100
GKE (Google Kubernetes Engine), 268, 371
Google
 AutoML and edge computer vision, 136-139

Professional Machine Learning Engineer
 certification, 2
Google App Engine, 268, 287
Google BigQuery, 268, 280-281
Google Cloud Build, 270
Google Cloud Functions, 282-286
Google Cloud Platform (GCP), 265-290
 advantages of using, 267
 applied data engineering on, 282-286
 certifications, 391
 cloud native database choice/design,
  280-281
 continuous integration/continuous delivery,
  270-272
 disadvantages of using, 265-267
 Kubernetes and, 272-280
 major components, 267
 operationalizing ML models, 287-289
 overview, 265-281
Google Cloud Run, 268
Google Kubernetes Engine (GKE), 268, 371
greedy algorithms, 42-48

H

Haber, Jonathan, 356
Hardgrove, Jacob, 357
Hargadon, Andrew, 367
Harris, Tristan, 358
health issues, in home work area, 395
hierarchy of needs, ML, 7-19
 configuring continuous integration with
  GitHub Actions, 13-14
 DataOps and data engineering, 15
 implementing DevOps, 8-13
 MLOps at top of, 17-19
 platform automation, 16
hiring process, disruption of, 425
hobbies, 408
Horizontal Pod Autoscaler (HPA), 275
housing affordability, 424
HTTP, serving a trained model over, 76-80
htwtmlb.csv, 210
Hugo websites, 192-194

I

IaC (see infrastructure as code)
ignorance, benefits of, 348-350
implementation of MLOps
 data governance and cybersecurity, 365

design patterns, 366
global recommendations, 364
recommendations for, 364-366
inference clusters, 247
infrastructure as code (IaC)
continuous delivery of ML models and, 99-106
DevOps best practice, 6
input/output
Bash shell, 27
instructions (container keywords), 70
instrumentation (DevOps best practice), 6
intermittent fasting, 409-414
interoperability, 293-315
Apple Core ML, 310-314
edge integration, 314-315
importance of, 294-296
ONNX, 296-310
IPython interpreter, defined, 371
Isaacson, Walter, 121

J

James, Lebron, 352
job markets, regional, 424
JSON, defined, 371

K

Kaggle, 206
Kaizen, 4, 125-127
KaizenML, 125-127, 127-129
kernel density plot, 39
key terms, 369-373
key-based authentication, 240
Koonin, Steven, 41, 360
Kubernetes, 272-280
blue-green deployment, 111
defined, 371
Horizontal Pod Autoscaler, 275
Kubernetes clusters, 371
Kubernetes containers, 371
Kubernetes pods, 371
Kubernetes-centric design, 366

L

Lazzeri, Francesca, 362
life-long learning, 423
lifecycle, Azure and, 262
linter

containers and, 74
creating a dataset linter, 321-328
modularizing, 328-331
linting, 32, 114
Linux command line, 23
load testing, defined, 371
Locust, defined, 371
logging, 164
(see also monitoring)
basics, 164
defined, 371
modifying log levels, 169
Python, 165-172
retrieving logs, 252
Loranger, Rob, 229-231
Loukides, Mike, 367
ls command, 26
Ludwig AutoML, 151

M

machine learning (generally)
cloud computing and, 3
interoperability (see interoperability)
key concepts, 50-53
machine learning engineering, tools and processes used in, 3
magical thinking, 119
Makefile, 9, 210
defined, 372
reasons to use, 10
managed ML systems, containers for, 89-91
Maslow's hierarchy of needs, 7
math for programmers
crash course, 37-49
descriptive statistics/normal distributions, 37-41
optimization, 41-49
Mechanical Turk, 351
metrics
defined, 372
for model monitoring, 174
microservices, 331-342
authenticating to cloud functions, 338-340
building a cloud-based CLI, 341
creating a serverless function, 333-338
defined, 69, 372
as DevOps best practice, 5
Microsoft (see Azure entries)
migrate (term), 372

mistake mindset, 408
ML engineering (see hierarchy of needs, ML)
mlib.py, 210
MLOps (generally)
    basics, 1-21
    defined, 4
    deployment possibilities, 19
    DevOps and, 5-7
    feedback loop, 18
    foundational skills for (see foundational
      skills)
    global recommendations, 364
    hierarchy of needs, 7-19
    Kaizen versus KaizenML, 125-127
    recommendations for implementing,
      364-366
    rise of machine learning engineers and
      MLOps, 2
    technical portfolio for, 403-408
    at top of ML hierarchy of needs, 17-19
MLOps Cookbook
    AWS and, 209-222
    CLI tools, 211-218
    Flask microservice, 218-222
MLOps industrial revolution, 123-125
MLOps platform, 366
mobile phones (see edge devices)
model deployment, 248-251
model explainability, 145, 154-158
model lifecycle, 262
Model Zoo, 297-299
model.joblib, 210
Molino, Piero, 360-362
monitoring, 6, 161-185
    (see also logging)
    basics, 161
    basics of model monitoring, 174-175
    as DevOps best practice, 6
    metrics for, 174
    monitoring drift with AWS SageMaker,
      175-182
    monitoring drift with Azure ML, 182-184
    observability and, 172-184
    observability for cloud MLOps, 163
Moore's Law, defined, 372

N

natural language processing (NLP), 190
network

physical home network, 394
    power management for home networking,
      395
    for working remotely, 394
NLP (natural language processing), 190
normal distributions, 37-41

O

O'Reilly, Tim, 367
observability
    Application Insights, 253
    monitoring and, 172-184
ONNX (Open Neural Network Exchange),
    296-310
    converting Core ML models into, 310-314
    converting PyTorch into, 299-301
    converting TensorFlow into, 303-307
    creating a generic ONNX checker, 301-303
    deploying to Azure, 307-310
    edge integration with ORT, 314-315
    Model Zoo, 297-299
    packaging for ML models, 95-99
open source AutoML solutions, 151-154
    FLAML, 153-154
    Ludwig, 151
operationalization, defined, 372
optimization, 41-49

P

packaging, 95-99
Pandas, 39
pear (PPEAR) revenue strategy, 399-402
    autonomy, 401
    exponential potential of projects, 401
    passive income, 400
    rule of 25%, 401
    work as positive experience, 400
pip, defined, 372
pipelines, 259
    (see also cloud pipelines)
    Azure ML pipelines, 257-262
    building an MLOps pipeline from zero,
      56-63
    publishing, 259
platform automation, 16
ports, defined, 372
PPEAR (see pear revenue strategy)
Professional Cloud Architect (GCP certifica-
    tion), 391

Professional Machine Learning Engineer (GCP certification), 391
project management (see technical project management)
project plan (in technical project management), 427
Prometheus, defined, 372
pylint, defined, 372
PyPI, defined, 372
pytest, defined, 372
Python
    Azure CLI and Python SDK, 236-238
    command line tools, 321-331
    crash course, 33-35
    energy inefficiency of, 34
    logging different applications, 170-172
    logging in, 165-172
    machine learning project structure, 8-13
    minimalistic tutorial, 36
    MLOps Cookbook, 209-222
    modifying log levels, 169
    project scaffold, 8
    requirements file, 320
    slowness of, 33
    testing/linting code, 32
Python functions, 36, 194
Python SDK, 236-238
Python virtual environment, defined, 373
PyTorch, converting into ONNX, 299-301

R
Red Hat, 69
regional job markets, 424
registration, Azure, 243-244
registries, 68
reinforcement learning, 52
"remote first" education, 423
remote work, 393-397
    equipment for, 394-396
    health issues, 395
    home work area, 395
    home workspace virtual studio setup, 396
    location, 396
    network, 394
requirements.txt, 210, 320
requirements.txt file, 10, 320
Ridley, Matt, 125, 367
rule of 25% (income), 401
rule of 25% (MLOps), 20

run commands, 26
runtime configuration, 259

S
S3 (see AWS S3)
SageMaker, 16
    model monitoring, 163
    monetizing MLOps, 90
    monitoring drift with, 175-182
    pipeline creation, 108-110
SageMaker AutoPilot, 146-150
SAM (AWS Serverless Application Model)
    AWS Lambda recipes, 223-229
    AWS Lambda-SAM containerized deploy, 224-229
SAM Local, 223
science, engineering versus, 2
script, writing a, 28
self-handicapping, 118
serverless (term), 373
Serverless Application Model (see SAM)
serverless methodology
    AWS, 194-198
    creating a serverless function, 333-338
    as recommended MLOps design pattern, 366
service principal, 238-240
SHAP, 155, 156
shell
    Bash shell and commands, 26-29
    cloud shell development environments, 24-26
    defined, 26
shell script, writing a, 28
Silver, Nate, 359
Simon, Julien, 231-233
Sinclair, Upton, 118
Spark-centric design, 366
SQL-related certifications, 391
Sqor sports social network case study, 350-355
    Athlete Intelligence (AI product), 353-355
    influencer rank, 352
    Mechanical Turk data labeling, 351
SQS queue, defined, 373
SSH access, 72
statistics, descriptive, 37-41
supervised machine learning, 50
swagger, defined, 373

T

Taleb, Nassim, 359
target dataset, baseline dataset versus, 179
task tracking (in technical project management), 429
technical communication (DevOps best practice), 6
technical portfolio, building a, 403-408
    project example: cloud native ML application or API, 406
    project example: Docker and Kubernetes container project, 404
    project example: edge ML solution, 405
    project example: serverless AI data engineering pipeline, 405
    strategies for getting a job, 407
technical project management, 427-429
    as DevOps best practice, 6
    project plan, 427
    task tracking, 429
    weekly demo, 428
technology certifications (see certifications)
TensorFlow
    converting into ONNX, 303-307
    TFHub, 85
TensorFlow Developer Certificate, 391
TensorFlow Playground, 49
TensorFlow Processing Unit (see TPU)
"10X better" education system, 421-425
Terrell, Dave, 360
testing
    automated checks, 113
    continuous improvement and, 114
    linting, 114
    model deployment, 112-115

    Python code, 32
TFHub (TensorFlow Hub), 85
theory of competitive advantage, 190
Thiel, Peter, 421
token-based authentication, 240
TPU (TensorFlow Processing Unit)
    Coral Project and, 81-84
    porting over non-TPU models, 86-89
troubleshooting
    Application Insights, 253
    debugging locally, 254-257
    deployment issues, 251-257
    retrieving logs, 252

U

unsupervised machine learning, 50-52
USB Accelerator, 81
utilscli.py, 210

V

versioning, of datasets, 245
Vertex AI, 268
virtual environment, Python, 11
virtual machines
    containers versus, 68
    defined, 373
vision (see computer vision)

Y

YAML, defined, 373

Z

Zhang, Feng, 121
ZSH, 26, 28

About the Authors

Noah Gift is the founder of Pragmatic A.I. Labs. He lectures at MSDS, at Northwestern, Duke MIDS Graduate Data Science Program, the Graduate Data Science program at UC Berkeley, the UC Davis Graduate School of Management MSBA program, UNC Charlotte Data Science Initiative, and University of Tennessee (as part of the Tennessee Digital Jobs Factory). He teaches and designs graduate machine learning, MLOps, AI, and data science courses, and consults on machine learning and cloud architecture for students and faculty. As a former CTO, individual contributor, and consultant he has over 20 years' experience shipping revenue-generating products in many industries including film, games, and SaaS.

Alfredo Deza is a passionate software engineer, speaker, author, and former Olympic athlete with almost two decades of DevOps and software engineering experience. He currently teaches machine learning engineering and gives worldwide lectures about software development, personal development, and professional sports. Alfredo has written several books about DevOps and Python, and continues to share his knowledge about resilient infrastructure, testing, and robust development practices in courses, books, and presentations.

Colophon

The animal on the cover of *Practical MLOps* is a Dalmatian (*Canis lupus familiaris*). Though now found around the globe, this breed of dog can be traced back to present-day Croatia in the historical Dalmatia region.

The Dalmatian is a medium-sized muscular dog that stands between 19 to 23 inches (or 48 to 58 cm) and has a distinctive white coat with black spots. A highly cultivated breed, these dogs are popular family pets as well as entrants in kennel club competitions. They display propensities for health problems related to their breeding (including deafness, allergies, and urinary stones) and typically have a lifespan between 11 and 13 years. The Dalmatian was bred as a hunting dog, but then were often used as carriage dogs, trotting alongside horse-drawn carriages of the wealthy to protect the carriages and their inhabitants, and were considered status symbols during the Regency period in England. They would also commonly protect the horses and carriages of brewers, Romani caravans, and firefighters.

Many of the animals on O'Reilly covers are endangered; all of them are important to the world.

The cover illustration is by Karen Montgomery, based on a black and white engraving from Wood's *Animate Creation*. The cover fonts are Gilroy Semibold and Guardian Sans. The text font is Adobe Minion Pro; the heading font is Adobe Myriad Condensed; and the code font is Dalton Maag's Ubuntu Mono.

Milton Keynes UK
Ingram Content Group UK Ltd.
UKHW030923251123
433249UK00005B/9